EFFECTIVE BUSINESS REPORT WRITING

THIRD EDITION

Leland Brown

Professor of Business Communications
Eastern Michigan University

PRENTICE-HALL, INC., ENGLEWOOD CLIFFS, NEW JERSEY

Library of Congress Cataloging in Publication Data

Brown, Leland.
   Effective business report writing.

   Bibliography: p.
   1. Business report writing.   I. Title.
HF5719.B76 1973   651.7'8   73-934
ISBN 0-13-241653-0

10 9 8 7 6 5 4 3

PRINTED IN THE UNITED STATES OF AMERICA

Prentice-Hall International, Inc., *London*
Prentice-Hall of Australia, Pty., Ltd., *Sydney*
Prentice-Hall of Canada, Ltd., *Toronto*
Prentice-Hall of India Private Ltd., *New Delhi*
Prentice-Hall of Japan, Inc., *Tokyo*

To My Wife

Hilda Lee Heatwole Brown

CONTENTS

Chapter 3

APPLYING PRINCIPLES FOR UNDERSTANDING AND PERSUADING   65

Chapter 6

RESEARCHING DATA, FACTS, AND IDEAS   181

Chapter 7

REASONING WITH DATA

Chapter 8

WRITING, REVISING, AND EDITING

Chapter 9

WRITING PRELIMINARY AND SUPPLEMENTARY SECTIONS

PREFACE

BECAUSE IT IS IMPOSSIBLE for executives to have personal contact with everyone in their company and to receive firsthand the vast amount of information needed for decision making and problem solving, communication through reports continues to be very important to all concerned. As in the two earlier editions, the primary purpose of this book is to discuss the principles and practices of business report writing required of men and women in their professional careers in business, industry, and government so they may be stimulated into thinking and presenting reports creatively and functionally and thus be more effective communicators in the decision-making and problem-solving processes. The book should prove helpful both to the businessman who presents or uses reports and to the student or reader who seeks to develop his communicative abilities.

In the 3rd Edition, there has been a complete restructuring of materials rather than a drastic change in the scope of the book. It retains the clear presentation of basic steps in the report writing process. Shorter report forms formerly found in several chapters have been brought together in Chapter 2, focusing on reports that get the job done from day to day. Chapter 3 provides a primer or review of basic logic and writing skills and techniques applied to report writing. Chapter 6 combines bibliographical, primary, and business research formerly in separate chapters into one unified whole. Chapters dealing with visual aids and oral reports have been brought forward to chapters 4 and 5, placed in a broader perspective, and expanded to meet today's demands in report presentation (other than written reports). The other chapters dealing with report stages of preparation have been streamlined, making the units more usable. New illustrations, cases, and problems have been added, the better ones in the former edition updated and retained.

Reorganization makes the text material more unified and usable for students and instructors. By having short reports early, the student can handle assignments more meaningfully without having to check bits from various chapters. Further discussion of principles can then be backed up by writing experiences. Bibliographical sources, reference data, and documentation relegated to the appendices are available for handy reference as needed. Sufficient communication theory approach has been given for a basis of reporting experiences and usage.

It is impossible to acknowledge all the help and assistance I have had. I am grateful for all the students I have taught, for I have learned much from them; and former students both at Tulane University and Eastern Michigan University have contributed illustrative and problem material from their companies. I am also grateful for my longtime association with members of the American Business Communication Association and other organizations in which I have been active, with other authors and publishers of communication texts. To colleagues for an exchange of ideas and materials and to Professors Margaret Zaug, University of Toledo, and David B. Still, Cape Cod Community College who reviewed the manuscript, I am appreciative of their time, effort, and worthwhile suggestions. Thanks also go to girls in the office for their secretarial and typing assistance, to my wife for her help in proofreading, and to my family for their interest. To numerous businessmen and companies throughout the United States, I am thankful for all their help and cooperation.

Leland Brown

ABOUT REPORTS
AND
REPORT WRITING

1

THERE HAS NEVER BEEN a greater need than today for effective communicators. People in all social and business strata need to communicate among themselves and with other groups. People in business constantly reach out to other people to persuade them. They must constantly be able to create and unify responsible voices that can fulfill wants and needs of individuals, that will get the job done in the business organization, and that will influence political, industrial, and social leaders.

Ask any businessman or make a survey of management personnel to determine what is the most important ability that they use constantly or look for in selecting and placing personnel. The answer in nearly every instance will be the ability to communicate well. Look at the employment advertisements in the *Wall Street Journal,* your nearest metropolitan newspaper, or some professional magazine.

**MANAGER
GENERAL ACCOUNTING**

FOR RETAIL FIRM

Responsible for all financial reporting and managing of a staff of forty people. Must have ability to develop meaningful financial reports. CPA required.

**PUBLIC RELATIONS
AND ADVERTISING**

Financially oriented growth company . . . requires a Director of Business Development to handle communications with shareholders and the financial community; public relations, production of annual and quarterly reports, brochures, and limited amount of advertising. . . .

**EXCELLENT OPPORTUNITY FOR MANAGER
OF PATENT LIAISON**

Nationally known corporation has an immediate need for a scientifically trained person with patent experience to:

Collaborate with our Research-Development-Engineering in the preparation of patent memoranda

Write and edit domestic and foreign patent applications in cooperating with our New York patent department

Evaluate existing patents

Be involved in our domestic and foreign activities

EMPLOYEE RELATIONS SUPERVISOR

. . . has an opening for a personnel representative to handle personnel grievances and to assist in arbitrations and negotiations in a medium-sized plant. . . .

EXECUTIVE SALES

. . . . optimum background will include a history of successful selling at a five-figure income. . . . The man who has managed a business also has the qualifications we are seeking. Position requires outstanding verbal facility combined with sufficient depth to dominate interviews with men at all levels. . . .

ARE YOU READY TO MAKE YOUR MARK?

DIRECTOR BIO-CHEMICAL RESEARCH

IF YOU ARE:

- Growing impatient to move ahead and itching to put into motion your ideas in directing people in projects in a profit motivated environment.

- Growth oriented, a motivator of people and a good communicator.

- Energetic and unyielding in your demands for a high standard of excellence.

- One who shows a sense of urgency in his efforts and yet is realistic in his planning.

- A Ph.D. in chemical or biological science with about 10 years' experience in drug product development.

YOU WILL BE:

- Reporting to a vice president.

- Maintaining close contact with top-level marketing and medical executives in our business.

- Seeking new product opportunities in the medical community and creating new areas of research activity to serve clinical needs.

- A key member of our management team helping us to expand our drug and chemical product lines.

FINANCIAL ANALYST

FINANCIAL SYSTEMS ASSOCIATE

We have an excellent new position opening for an MBA graduate which will provide the maximum of overall exposure along with heavy individual responsibility while working with a small financial staff.

Major responsibility will include new product evaluation from a statistical and qualitative standpoint; acquisition studies, analysis of operations and forecasting.

. . . .

Requirements are a degree in accounting, preferably two years' diversified accounting experience, the ability to express yourself clearly in oral and written presentations, the capability to work effectively with line personnel to insure development in meaningful information. Duties include . . . and in development of procedures to meet financial information requirements and assistance in the design and implementation of divisional procedures. . . .

MANAGER
OF
COMMUNICATIONS

. . . .
You will provide expertise to all levels of management which will establish and maintain effective channels of communication between management and employees in order to improve understanding among employees and to improve morale productivity and stability.

. . . .

All these excerpts from job advertisements have several things in common. Communication effectiveness is either sought or is implied as a required skill. The ability to analyze, to think critically, to make decisions, to persuade, and to lead and direct others is inherent in almost every position—whether it be in accounting and finance, sales, advertising, public relations, industrial relations, research and development, communications, supervisory positions, or other areas of management.

There has been such a tremendous volume of activity within each operational area of business enterprises that effective and regular communication with behind-the-scenes developments by presenting business information and data through business reports is necessary for all concerned. Decisions are made and influenced at many different levels in the management structure. The larger the business, the greater the need for reports, for its efficiency depends on the quality and quantity of information flowing through all personnel.

With division of labor and delegation of authority among a large number of employees, reports can be a unifying force that helps build cooperation and knits together the activities of each department. Only if an executive receives information from below can he weigh results, make decisions, and initiate appropriate action. Reports are also helpful in understanding a particular problem and finding its solution, in measuring performance and cost, in checking conformance with policy, and in both long-term and current planning. Business report writing is one vital means of communication in a business enterprise, and without reports it would be difficult to operate a business.

The purpose of this book is to discuss the principles and practices of business report writing required of men and women in their professional careers in business, industry, and government. Its emphasis is on concepts and their illustrations and applications. Attention is given to understanding the report problem and situation, planning the investigation and research, and organizing data to reach conclusions and to presenting facts, ideas, and courses of action in reports. It seeks to help the reader to develop his analytical and persuasive abilities, and it should stimulate him into thinking and writing business reports creatively and functionally, for the very nature of the communication process itself and the implications it has for report writers are creative and functional.

THE COMMUNICATION PROCESS AND THE NATURE OF BUSINESS REPORTS

Communication is the transmission and interchange of facts, ideas, feelings, or courses of action. In a broad sense, communication encompasses all the processes by which one person's mind might affect another's. The other person is influenced in some way. Once he perceives the message— whether it has been transmitted orally, in writing, or visually—the perception changes the information he possesses and therefore influences him in some way. In the case of reports, he has received data that enable him to draw conclusions, make decisions, or solve problems. He then either is persuaded to accept the recommended course of action and takes steps for its implementation or decides on an alternative. Should the message get no response or a rejection, then effective communication has not taken place.

The simple diagram that follows indicates the elements that make up the communication process and its cyclical nature:

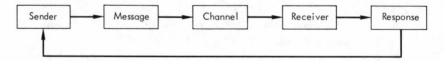

The response of the receiver serves as feedback to the sender and makes the process circular rather than straight-lined. Communication begins when something stimulates the communicator through his sensory organs. The latter send impulses to his brain and from there to his muscles and glands, which in turn produce feelings and preverbal tensions. He translates these into words according to his customary verbal patterns; these words provide "meaning" for him. Out of this development he recognizes the need or has the desire to transmit his feelings and ideas to someone. Once the communicator has a purpose, he can decide what to say and how to say it to gain a favorable response from the receiver. He then selects, adapts, and transmits his message through some written, audio, or visual channel. The recipient is stimulated, and the resulting nervous impulses travel to his brain. They are translated into meaning according to his customary verbal patterns, and he responds by communicating to Mr. A or to Mr. C or by doing or not doing what Mr. A asked him to do. Thus communication is a two-way process, for there is always a communicator and a receiver. It is a continuing process, for each time a person communicates, another person responds by further communicating facts, ideas, feelings, or attitudes. It is a creative process, for new ideas and emotions are generated, and new ones or new combinations of old ones are transmitted. It is highly functional because it always begins with a need or a desire—a purpose to be fulfilled. When the purpose has been accomplished, effective communication has taken place.

Let us look at how business report writing fits into the communication process: A report writer has been investigating a particular problem whose solution he wants to present to the management group in his company for its decision. He has gathered all the necessary facts and interpreted them; he has arrived at a solution.

The writer will need to use the tools of communication—words and visual aids—to frame his message into a report for transmission to the reader. To the writer this has meaning; he has a grasp of the facts; he has an insight into the problem. The reader who receives the report, however, will comprehend the message only if the words used have meaning to him. The report's message will succeed when the reader responds. Whether that response is favorable or unfavorable will depend on how well the reader understands the message and is motivated to the desired action.

A business report, then, is a factual presentation of data or information directed to a particular reader or audience for a specific business purpose. In essence a good report is a collection and organization of facts to be communicated to someone who will make use of them. It is a highly specialized type of communication, flexible in subject content, organization, form, and use.

The facts contained in a business report may be a record of past transactions or accomplishments, a release of information, an account of conditions past and present, an analysis of conditions for determining future policies, or a recommendation of a course of action to be followed. These facts must be accurate, complete, and arranged for easy comprehension, reading, and action.

The reporter either has first-hand information that he presents from his experience and knowledge or gathers information from an investigation, using one or several methods of research. He may use bibliographical sources, interviews, questionnaires, observation, letters of inquiry, or experiments. Data may consist of notes, statistics, tables, charts, figures, quoted material, and other information (all the result of research), plus his own ideas and conclusions—the result of his logical reasoning and creative thinking.

The word *report* itself is derived from the Latin, *reporto,* meaning carry or bring back, for the report brings back facts from research. Before it is written, the facts must be classified, examined, evaluated, arranged, interpreted, and recorded. They are finally outlined in the report.

In oral reporting as well as in writing, emphasis is on presenting the facts to accomplish a specific purpose. They must, therefore, be clearly stated and practical. Visual aids help, as does the division of material into sections and the use of subject headings. Because the report is directed to the reader and his use, the language for conveying the message and everything about the report must be marshaled to meet his needs. Reports should always be creative. Every report is different. It varies according to the reader, the nature of the material presented, its purpose, and the writer.

IMPLICATIONS FOR THE REPORT WRITER

For the report writer, an understanding of the communication process and of the nature of business reports has important implications.

Reports are purposeful. They all start with a need, desire, or purpose either to inform or to analyze. The accomplishment of the purpose depends on the reporter's understanding of people and their feelings, his interpretations of the facts, his recognition of the purpose the report is to fulfill, and his ability to motivate action.

The report's message must be in the realm of the reader's experience and knowledge. To have meaning, words must refer to something comprehensible to the reader. The writer must predict the reader's frame of reference and direct his message within it. The writer should always have a specific reader in mind and assume that he is intelligent. Language used should always be simple, concrete, and familiar for ready comprehension.

A report should be adapted to the reader's needs and the use he will make of it. From the information available about him, the writer adapts the message to the reader's interests, knowledge, peculiarities, desires, and needs.

A report requires a great deal of intellectual activity of the writer. The writer must have ideas and be able to express them. He must be able to think of different combinations of ideas and to reason through facts to valid conclusions. The creative elements of report writing are used to help make the report functional, for in accomplishing its purpose the report is used as an instrument of action in carrying out a functional operation within a business enterprise. As such it must be persuasive and motivational.

REQUIREMENTS FOR AN EFFECTIVE REPORT

The best practical test for the effectiveness of a business report is to check how well it accomplished its purpose. Did management make the vacation policy changes that the personnel director recommended? Did the company purchase the $150,000 of new equipment needed in an expansion program? What were the results of the employee survey on fringe benefits? Were changes in the present program made? This type of testing demands a measuring of the end result. A helpful test for the writer is to use a checklist for improving the report by careful revision before final preparation and distribution. This is an aid for ensuring a report's motivating action. Simply ask,

1. Does it meet the needs of the situation, purpose, message, and reader?
2. Is it well planned and organized?
3. Does it adapt format and presentation to purpose, message, and reader?
4. Does it reflect good, clear thinking?
5. Does it present material for easy and quick comprehension?
6. Does it interest the reader?
7. Does it make appropriate use of visual aids?
8. Does it motivate action?
9. Does it solve the problem in the best possible way?

The degree to which a report does things asked in this checklist largely determines its degree of effectiveness. Poor reports are a waste of time for both reader and writer and become costly when undesired responses occur.

Report writing is both an art and a science. It is an art because it requires a certain amount of inherent creative ability on the part of the writer. Nevertheless, abilities that are helpful, if not already present, can be developed, and the necessary techniques, procedures, and skills can be acquired. To make his report creative and functional, the writer must use all his knowledge, experience, abilities, and understanding of human nature to direct his report to a particular reader for a specific purpose and to develop his material accordingly.

RELATION OF WRITER, MESSAGE, AND READER

When the report is clearly understood the reader should be interested and receptive. Interest and acceptance, however, depend in part on the relationship between the writer and the reader.

The writer should accept the reader as his equal in the total communication process. He must also recognize the reader as an individual, since his wants and needs must be met in the report. Often the reader of a business report is an executive who receives reports from the men responsible to him and in turn reports to other executives on his own level or above him. The advertising director, the personnel manager, the public relations director, the accountant—all receive reports from their assistants and report to executives of equal or higher rank in other departments.

There are of course all kinds of readers. Not all reports are distributed within the company, nor are all reports solutions to problems. The annual report, for example, goes to the general public and must capture the attention and interest of its readers. Each report should be tailored for a particular reader or group of readers according to the information that is available about them. The writer should consider the reader's position in relation to his own. Where is he in the organization's chain of command? Near the top or the bottom? What is his job? What function does he perform in the company? Is he a single reader or a member of a group of readers? How will he use the report?

The answers to these questions will decide the form used, the routing of the report, and the manner in which it is transmitted. They will also be helpful in determining what to say and in suggesting what is to be done. The more the writer knows about the reader's age, sex, educational level, occupation, position, interests, feelings, and attitudes, the better the rapport he will be able to establish. Individual differences in experience and personality makeup vitally affect the process of assimilating the message.

For a reader who is familiar with the report's subject matter it is not always necessary to begin with explanatory details. The writer can plunge immediately into the results of his investigation and the solution to the problem at hand. The reader who is unacquainted with the situation, on the other hand, has to be given background details at the beginning of the report so he can more easily understand what follows. Emphasis must be given to making the report usable in accomplishing a definite purpose.

In the fast-moving pace of today's business a report must be planned to conserve the reader's time. It should give him exactly what he wants and needs, no more and no less. The use of subject headings guides his reading. Using tables and charts and following the principles of good business writing—conciseness, clearness, and correctness—save space and time.

Every consideration is given the reader because the report's message must reach *him* and must serve *his* purpose. Otherwise the communication process has not been completed nor has the report been effective.

By showing him consideration, the writer is adapting the report to the reader. From the information available about him, the writer adapts the report's message to the reader's interests, knowledge, peculiarities, desires, and needs. The subject matter is related to the reader. It is interpreted for his understanding and use. Figures are presented in the easiest and most logical way. Special terms and expressions are made clear. Significant facts of interest and use to the reader are emphasized. The writer must know his subject and how the report is to be used. He must use this knowledge in adapting his material to the reader, whose major interest lies in the facts and their interpretation, for to be effective the report must stimulate the reader to action.

Reports must be adapted to the reader's point of view as well as to his knowledge and experience, his method of thinking, and the nature of the subject matter. Adapting to the reader's point of view merely means fulfilling his needs. Because the reader's method of thinking may also determine the report's organization, let him draw his own conclusions when he wants to. If he prefers to be told conclusions, tell him. If he thinks data through logically, organize and present them so he can.

The nature of the subject matter and its use determine the form and type of the report, but form is used as the means to an end and not as an end in itself.

Language and style must also be adapted to the reader, the material, and its intended use. Material of popular interest directed to the public must be presented in an appealing manner to capture general interest. On the other hand, since a report offering an executive the solution to a problem in the company already has his interest, the language and style should effect clear, quick comprehension on his part to facilitate immediate action.

Distinctions in style and language are also made in adapting the report to readers with technical, semitechnical, or nontechnical backgrounds. A report intended for an executive will probably be understood with little difficulty, for he has a college level of comprehension derived from either his experience or formal education. The language and style must still be adapted, however, to saving his time. On the other hand, a report that will be distributed to the firm's semiskilled labor force must be written on a tenth-grade level of understanding, and its language adapted accordingly.

Adaptation of reports provides flexibility in report writing. Because of inherent differences in situations and individuals, the report writer has a tremendous responsibility in meeting this demand placed upon him. It means that each report is different from all other reports. The subject matter of a report is developed according to the reader's needs and the particular purpose the report is to accomplish. Only in this way can adaptation fully be made and the report accomplish its purpose.

KINDS AND FUNCTIONS OF REPORTS

Reports function in the four general areas of communication carried on by a business enterprise [1]:

EMPLOYEE REPORTS: booklets, pamphlets, memorandums, newsletters—reports to inform, to build favorable attitudes and loyalties, to create good employee relations.

OPERATIONAL AND TECHNICAL REPORTS: manuals, procedural statements, orders, records, facts for decision-making—reports to give and receive information vital to operating and carrying on the business of the firm.

MANAGEMENT REPORTS: solutions to problems, decisions made, policies formulated—reports to aid management in its function of planning, decision- and policy-making, and solving problems.

CUSTOMER AND PUBLIC REPORTS: sales promotional materials, pamphlets, annual reports, news reports—reports to advertise and sell the company name and products, to create goodwill, to build good relations.

Reports within a company pass between those who supervise and those who carry on the work, those who are the policy makers and those who carry out policies, employees and employers, subordinates and superiors, management and labor. External reports are sent to stockholders, customers, the general public, and interested individuals.

---

[1] L. Brown, *Communicating Facts and Ideas in Business*, 2nd ed. (Englewood Cliffs, N.J.: Prentice-Hall, Inc., 1970), pp. 248–49.

Internal reports move *vertically* through the organizational channels, *horizontally* between departments or individuals on the same level, and *radially* inside and outside the company. Many reports in the downward flow of communication are informational, for they increase their readers' general knowledge about the organization and work of the company. They may give opinions on various subjects, information about the company's employee benefits, or notices about Red Cross and United Fund drives. Of course, much instructional reporting of this nature is of transitory value.

Reports moving downward also transmit policies, procedures, and orders. A policy statement furnishes a guiding principle for a specific action to be taken. A statement of procedures represents in detail the steps to be followed in carrying out a policy. One cannot always differentiate, however, between a policy statement and a statement of procedures, because a specific policy statement may at times include the detailed steps for its execution.

Many reports in the upward flow of communication contain financial statements or statistics to show the present condition of the business and to be made a part of its permanent records. Reports explaining work done, anticipated problems, progress, increases and decreases, and periods or distances over which they operated all fall into this same informational category.

The interchange of reports between departments or among men on the same level represents a horizontal flow of communication, aimed to coordinate the work of the various departments or divisions. Such reports are especially vital to large companies in which the work is decentralized.

Radially, reports are distributed throughout the company to reach everyone and frequently are also sent outside the company. A good example of this type of report is the annual report, which is of interest not only to all employees but also to stockholders, the general public, and other groups. These reports differ greatly from internal reports sent vertically and horizontally. With most internal reports the reader is already interested in the contents because they affect his work and are of practical value to him in his job, but the writer of a radially transmitted report must present his material to obtain the attention and interest of as many readers as possible.

It is highly important that the flow of communication through business reports be kept open in a company. The informed employee is a happy and productive worker. Facts and their analysis are necessary for all decisions requiring appropriate action. *Effective communication through reports is an integral part of operating any business successfully.*

Although reports are used to achieve a large number of different purposes, ranging from a simple one such as a statement of personnel policy concerning vacation pay to a recommendation for purchasing $250,000 worth of electronic equipment, basically they are used either to inform or to analyze. Thus, on the basis of function, there are two kinds of reports—*informational* and *analytical reports*.

Informative reports serve as a record of data. Facts are organized and presented to the reader to use as he sees fit or to retain as a part of his knowledge on the subject. The report keeps the reader informed, and as a result of being informed, he is better able to perform his work, or the information affects his attitudes toward his work and relations with the people with whom he works. The results of an investigation may also be given for the reader himself to interpret and analyze. Some of the reports that inform are periodic reports, progress reports, policy statements, employee booklets, readership surveys, reports on sales, credit reports, committee minutes, reports on single interviews, some production reports, and some public relations reports. Their information may be presented in any of the informal, short report forms or in a formal, long report.

In addition to presenting data, a report may also include an interpretation and analysis of facts or results and recommendations. It then becomes an *analytical report*. Some specific types of analytical reports are advertising reports, examination reports, accounting reports, statistical analyses, analyses of present business conditions, product analyses, market surveys, employee-attitude surveys, some production reports, and some personnel reports. *Analytical reports* carry the process of report presentation a step further than the informational report. The reader has his data interpreted for him; it is analyzed in relation to his problem, and his task is to decide on the action to be taken. Analytical reports are used often as a basis for a decision.

Analytical reports may also contain conclusions and recommend desired changes. They would then perform three functions—presenting facts, analyzing facts, and recommending action. Used in this way, they often present a solution to a problem. Although the reader may accept or reject the recommended action, the report itself results in action one way or another and is of greatest use in dealing with business operations, construction, or production. Some sales reports, personnel reports, surveys, improvement reports, and justification reports fall into this category because of the special function each performs in recommending action.

A few reports cannot be classified according to the general functions mentioned, because they may perform any or several of them and still perform additional special functions of their own. The corporation's annual report and reports written for employee publications and trade journals are examples of this type. So much emphasis has been placed on annual reports in today's business world that they warrant special treatment in Chapter 11. Another special type of report, the research report, which is the result of pure research done in the scientific laboratory, is beyond the scope of this book. Such a report is used by business firms, especially in the development of new products and processes, and the presentation of its data involves the same techniques and procedures discussed here. The chief difference is in the method of research used to obtain the data—laboratory research.

REQUIREMENTS FOR REPORT WRITERS

All the communication skills—reading, writing, speaking, and listening—are used in the investigation and presentation of material in business reports. It would be difficult indeed to gather data, whether from bibliographical sources, interviews, questionnaires, or observation, without using any or all of the four skills. Likewise one can hardly interpret, outline, organize, or present any information without relying on one or all of them.

Ineffective communication is often caused by false observation or inaccurate interpretation and analysis of what is read, seen, or heard. An understanding of human behavior is of paramount importance in preparing and writing reports, for human relations are the core of all communication. There must be a response from the receiver before the total communication process can take place.

So few reports are made up from information the writer has at hand that he needs to understand the procedures and techniques of various research methods. He must know what to look for, where to look, and how to use the information he finds. He should develop the ability to understand a problem, see it in relationship to other problems, recognize what is needed, evaluate possible courses of action, and decide on the best solution.

The reporter needs to be able to plan the investigation and complete his report presentation within a particular time limit. A report that must be completed in an hour will be different from one written in a day, a week, or a month. But in the business world, if an hour is all the time there is, the efficient worker will come up with an effective answer to get the job done.

The ability to organize data and to reach logical conclusions is necessary. Outlining material is another requisite, as also is the ability to use statistics, tables, and charts. Being able to achieve exactness and directness in communicating facts and ideas completely, clearly, concisely, and persuasively completes the list of skills necessary to prepare and present a report.

These requirements assume a mastery of grammar, spelling, and punctuation and proficiency in the use of the English language. Knowledge of business principles and operations is necessary to be able to adapt data for a particular reader and purpose. Familiarity with business situations that give rise to the need for reports and their function will also aid in adjusting to the report's use and reader.

The writer must also develop personal attributes that he will call on for his investigation and presentation. Intellectual honesty—giving recognition to every source, acknowledging quoted material, presenting both sides of an issue, showing all the facts and their implications without disguising or coloring them, distinguishing between fact and opinion—simply means being honest in the treatment of the subject and toward the reader. Lead the reader to the truth. Initiative, resourcefulness, persistency, good work habits, and dependability are admirable qualities to possess. Patience, persuasiveness, and imaginative ingenuity should also be added to the list.

To meet these requirements and to develop the personal qualities necessary for the report writer should be your goal in your study of this book. You will be developing your ability to think creatively and logically and to communicate effectively through business reports. This should prove to be challenging and a great asset in your professional career whether it be in business, industry, government, or education. It will be up to you to use all your knowledge, experience, abilities, and understanding of human nature to direct your reports to the specific reader for a particular purpose and to develop your material accordingly.

FOR DISCUSSION AND WRITING

1. Why is there so great a need for effective communicators in business today? For effective reports in every functional area and position in business?

2. Look up several bibliographical sources on the communication process to find several definitions, models of communication, and theories of communication; then analyze them for common elements and evaluation.

3. Bring to class a business report from a company, industry, or the government. Be prepared to discuss how the relationship of its reader, message, and writer affected its content and organization.

4. What is the common basis for all reports, and how does each report differ from all other reports? Why?

5. What effect does conserving the reader's time have upon the report's message and presentation?

6. Discuss the following principle: Effective communication through reports depends on an understanding of people and their feelings, on facts and their interpretations, and on recognition of the report's purpose and use.

7. What would be the result if the flow of communication through reports in a business enterprise were stopped?

8. Evaluate a report you have written by using the questions on page 9 as a checklist of requirements.

9. What can you do to develop your abilities to write creative and functional reports?

10. How will becoming proficient in writing business reports help you in your chosen career?

11. Why is it important that business reports motivate action?

12. Read some supplementary references on each of the four general areas of communication in which reports function, and report orally to the class on how reports play a vital role.

13. Your younger brother, who is a high school senior, has written and asked you why you are taking a course in business report writing. Answer him, explaining some of the things you will be studying and doing and what you hope to accomplish.

14. As a member of the management team in your company, you are initiating a series of bulletins to be issued to members of top and middle management for the purpose of improving their communication effectiveness in general and specifically their written and oral reports. Write the first one of the series. It will introduce the idea for the bulletin series, your purpose, and the need for improving communication and reports. It could define and explain the communication process on the assumption that an understanding of it is necessary for any communication to be effective.

15. A family business friend who is to be giving a speech at the national meeting of the American Business Communication Association has asked you for ideas and suggestions. He is to speak on the role of business communication in the business school curriculum. Answer him with your ideas on how a course in business report writing fits in.

16. Begin making a classified and an annotated bibliography of books on the subject of business reports and related areas. This should be done on file cards for later reference use.

17. Write a brief report for the director of training in Ark Chemical Corporation in which you show the need for training in report writing. Working in the research and development departments are about sixty-five chemical and laboratory technicians who would be eligible for such training. In your report, you will want to stress the need for the training. Would you want to include suggestions as to when, where, and how the training should be conducted? Would you want to recommend who should do it? And even the nature of it?

WRITING REPORTS
TO GET THE JOB DONE
FROM DAY TO DAY

2

IN EVERYDAY BUSINESS OPERATIONS, decisions are made; problems arise and are solved; facts, figures, and ideas are called for and used. Let us take a look at some of the events and action taking place in a representative company to understand the use of reports in getting the job done from day to day.

THE CASE OF BROWN'S VELVET CO., INC.[1]

In 1905, a young man, Benjamin C. Brown (the company's founder), had been fascinated by the number of merchants and the variety of products sold daily on the streets of New Orleans. He reasoned that should he find the right items and sell and service them better than his competitors, there would be a place for him among the city's growing list of merchants. He secured a two-story frame house and, with the help of some associates, made and sold coffee, chocolate, biscuits, doughnuts, rolls, and other items. A brisk business thrived.

Not content with his products, however, Benjamin constantly strived for improvement. He had been intrigued from his boyhood with the taste of "handmade" ice cream. With this item plus the advantage of New Orleans' semitropical climate, he recognized the opportunities that ice cream would offer as a "big seller," and so a new product was launched. In the early days ice cream was turned by hand.

From these early beginnings Brown's Velvet Co., Inc. was spawned. As a consequence, the company's entry into the processing and sale of milk and ice cream began in earnest. Today the company serves the Louisiana, Mississippi, Alabama, and Florida areas; in fact, it is one of the largest dairy products industries in the entire Gulf-South. The principal plant locations are in New Orleans and Baton Rouge, Louisiana, where milk and ice-cream products are manufactured, processed, and delivered to thousands of customers.

Some 550 loyal and dedicated employees comprise the Brown's Velvet family. Many are members of third-generation personnel who are

[1] Illustrations used in this case courtesy of Brown's Velvet Co., Inc., New Orleans, Louisiana, Mr. Alfred W. Brown, Jr.

largely responsible for the reputation and extremely high standards maintained. Several problem situations calling for reports follow.

Flavors for Brown's Velvet Ice Cream come from all around the world, for example,

Vanilla—Madagascar	Pineapples—Hawaii
Cocoa—Dutch East Indies	Cherries—Michigan
Bananas—Honduras	Black walnuts—Tennessee

It is vitally important that only the best flavors obtainable worldwide are added to the ice-cream mix in exactly the right proportions for uniformly fine flavors. Thus there is a constant problem in quality control of the manufacturing process and in getting the right supply of all flavors to meet customer demand. Data and records are kept on the supply, distribution, and sale. Should one flavor not sell as well as another or should it not sell as well in one size of container as another, changes must be made in the kinds and quantities manufactured. Such was the situation as taken up in the memo (See Memo 1) to the ice-cream sales department from the vice president of production.

The problem arose out of a need for decreasing manufacturing costs and distributing in quantities and containers to meet consumer use. Decisions were made after consulting both sales and production departments and analyzing sales and production data. Once the decisions were made, they needed to be disseminated for action—hence the purpose of this memorandum report. It follows a good organizational pattern, meeting the needs of the reader and moving him to action. Its effectiveness is also dependent somewhat on the decisiveness and finality of its statements and on the authority of its writer and his position. (See Memo 1)

Size	Flavors Available at All Times		Special Promotions
	Regular Ice Cream		
Half gallons	Vanilla	Tutti Frutti	Cherry Vanilla
	3 Flavors	Black Walnut	Pecan Krunch
	Chocolate	Cream Cheese	Strawberry
	Cherry Vanilla	Blackberry Royale	Peach
	Pecan Krunch	Banana	Rum Raisin
	Strawberry	Chocolate Chip	Royal Hawaiian Pineapple
	Strawberry Ripple	Lemon Custard	
	Fudge Ripple	Peppermint Stick	
Pints	Vanilla	Chocolate	
	3 Flavors	Fudge Ripple	
	Strawberry	Pecan Krunch	
3 gallons	Vanilla	Fudge Ripple	Rum Raisin
	Chocolate	Black Walnut	Royal Hawaiian Pineapple
	Strawberry	Lemon Custard	Strawberry
	Pecan Krunch	Peppermint Stick	Pecan Krunch
	Cherry Vanilla	Banana	Cherry Vanilla
			Peach

Size	Flavors Available at All Times		Special Promotions
2-gallon molds	NONE		
Cut 8 quarts	Vanilla	Strawberry	
	3 Flavors	Chocolate	

	Plantation Ice Cream		
Half gallons	Vanilla	Fudge Ripple	
	Chocolate	3 Flavors	
	Strawberry		
3 gallons	Vanilla	Strawberry	
	Chocolate	Fudge Ripple	
2-gallon molds	NONE		
Cut 8 quarts	NONE		

	Ice Milk		
Half gallons	Chocolate	3 Flavors	
	Fudge Ripple	Vanilla	

	Delmonico Ice Cream		
Half gallons	Vanilla	Strawberry	
	Chocolate		
Quarts	Vanilla	Cherry Vanilla	
	Chocolate	Pecan Krunch	
	Strawberry		
Pints	Vanilla	Chocolate	
3 gallons	Vanilla	Cherry Vanilla	
	Chocolate	Pecan Krunch	
	Strawberry		
2-gallon molds	NONE		
Cut 8 quarts	NONE		

	Sherbet		
Half gallons	Pineapple	Lime	
	Orange		
Pints	Pineapple	Lime	
	Orange		
3 gallons	Pineapple	Lime	
	Orange		
2-gallon molds	NONE		
Cut 8 quarts	NONE		

Although tornados and hurricanes are not restricted to the southern United States, each year major hurricanes take their toll of damage in the South. The following memorandum to all employees shows the company's concern and helpful attitude toward its employees, especially in time of need. (See Memo 2)

Another memo to employees is concerned with problems in operating the employee lounge. Although it does speak with the voice of authority and is demanding in tone, which puts teeth into its statements,

Memo 1

December 19, 197–

MEMO TO ICE CREAM SALES DEPARTMENT:

The management of this company has been greatly bothered by in-
creasing costs over the past few years. Reviewing this situation,   ← Statement of
we find that one of the primary reasons for higher costs is the   problem and cause
large and varied number of items that this company produces.

I believe each of you can understand that it costs more to make
ten half gallons of Honeydew than five thousand half gallons of
Vanilla--a normal run. Accordingly, after consultation with the   ← Decision made
Sales Department and Production Department, we have modified our
197- production schedule and are dropping certain flavors and
items from our list.

On the attached pages you will find those items and flavors which
will be available at all times. At present, this list is not
complete and additional pages will be forwarded to you as they are   ← Decision explained
made up. For the present, we are only tackling the worst offenders.

We do not wish to work a hardship on any one territory or individual, nor do we wish to lose a good account because of a special
flavor that we do not produce. However, there must be a stopping
point, if we are to reduce our costs. Also, there must be very
few individuals who can approve of any special item being made.
Accordingly, any deviation from the attached list must be approved
by either Alfred W. Brown, Sr., Alfred W. Brown, Jr., and
B. Temple Brown, Jr.
                                                                            Action and ex-
By copy of this letter, the Shipping Office is instructed to take   ception stated
the order. It will be up to the local salesman to contact the cus-
tomer and explain our company's position. Should the local salesman be unable to convince the customer than an item cannot be made,
he must submit, to one of the above named men, a request in
writing that that item be manufactured.

The Ice Cream Production Department will be instructed not to
manufacture special items unless written approval is given by one
of the above named men.

I hope I have made myself clear in this matter, and I expect the
full cooperation of each and every one of you. If you have any   ← Cooperation
questions or problems, I will be very happy to talk them over   expected
with you at any time.

Very sincerely yours,

Alfred W. Brown, Jr.

AWBJr/era

Enclosures
Alfred W. Brown, Jr.
Vice President

Memo 2

Memo to: All Employees

From: The Management

When Camille struck the Coast, she damaged the homes of some of
our employees along with thousands of others. The one hit the
hardest, by far, was Cliff Vogt, the company's Gulf Coast refri-   Direct statement of
geration mechanic, who has been with the company for 15 years.   what happened

Cliff's home was a total loss from both wind and water. His un-
insured loss was over $5,000. He and his family are presently
living in a trailer in Waveland, Mississippi.

As if this wasn't enough, Cliff, in his efforts to help others,   Need for assistance
was assisting the City of Waveland to replace their shortwave   stressed
antenna at town hall when the ladder he was standing on came in
contact with a high tension wire. Luckily Cliff is alive but he
was badly burned and the consequent fall broke his back. He will
be bedridden for at least six to eight months.

As we did after hurrican Betsy, we are again asking you to help
your fellow employee. Whatever you give, the company will match   Request for help,
dollar for dollar. Whatever you give is tax-deductible.   Company's share

If you wish, whatever you give will be deducted from your salary
over a two-pay period at the latter part of January, 197-   Easy action
        provided
Below is provided a space for your gift and how you want it handled.

PLEASE BE GENEROUS.

I wish to contribute $_____ to the Brown's Velvet Family

Camille Fund. The above amount is to be deducted from my salary
in

        One Pay

        Two pays, beginning January 24, 197_

it also points out benefits to the employee and that it is, after all, his lounge and accordingly his responsibility. (See Memo 3)

February 21, 197–

To Employees Using the Lounge:

This lounge is furnished by the Company for your convenience. It is, in effect, your lounge. In return the Company expects you to help keep it clean. We assume your home is kept clean and therefore, using this same assumption, we expect the lounge to be kept clean. In fact, we insist upon it, for we have visitors whom at times we bring into the lounge.   ← Appeal for cooperation

The Company also furnishes the ice cream and deep freeze for your pleasure. BUT the materials on the bottom shelf are for experimental and research purposes and are not to be touched. This has been repeatedly violated and is now endangering the ice-cream privileges. Also, the coffee urn and Coke machines are placed here for your convenience but we expect you to pay for your drinks.   ← Requests and reasons

There is no trouble with the Coke machine, but whenever the coffee box runs out of money, then we will discontinue buying coffee and that will be the end of that. If you have been guilty of this in the past, I shouldn't have to say any more. It is your privilege, and whether you keep it or not is entirely up to you.   ← Motivated action

A. M. Herald

AMH/dh

Memo 3

Trouble in the maintenance department necessitated the next memorandum to department heads. Maintenance men had been doing work unauthorized and work requested without the required work order. This resulted in delay work, work stoppage, and upsetting priority of work. No wonder the vice president took a firm stand that the policy be strictly adhered to, although he allows an exception for emergency work. (See Memo 4)

MEMORANDUM

TO: All Department Heads   July 16, 197–

SUBJECT: MAINTENANCE WORK ORDERS

From this date forward, all work to be done by the
Maintenance Department shall be accomplished via the ◄— Action
Maintenance Work Order.

Maintenance personnel will be instructed to work on a
project only as directed by a Work Order. The only
exception to this rule will be those items of an   ◄— Implementation
emergency nature which affect production. Then a Work
Order must be created after the work is completed.

All Department Heads should inform their employees of
the procedure. Your cooperation is appreciated.

              Alfred W. Brown, Jr.

Memo 4

Form reports come into use in Brown's Velvet Co., Inc. as they do in other companies where routine data are called for and used for analysis and decisions. A common one is the Salesmen's Daily Report. The report (page 28) calls for basic information for sales, promotion, and distribution usage. Note that it emphasizes new accounts and handling complaints.

The form report (page 29), likewise for salesmen to complete, is useful as a check and control device on salesmen as well as a follow-up on their remarks whenever executive decision or action is warranted.

By showing concern for employees and helping them in difficult situations, management maintains good employee relations, the result of the following memorandum:

May 18, 197–

TO ALL BROWN'S VELVET EMPLOYEES:

RE: CASHING PAYROLL CHECKS:

The following applies to employees who do not have an account with the National American Bank, Lee Circle Branch.

In recent months, a number of stolen and forged checks have been cashed at our local banks. As a result of this, the National American Bank, Lee Circle Branch, has been requiring employees cashing payroll checks, at the bank, to have their checks approved by an Officer of the Bank. The Cashiers

---

BROWN'S VELVET
SALESMEN'S DAILY REPORT

SALESMAN'S NAME_____   DATE_____

SALES CALLS

SALES CALLS MADE_____

NEW CUSTOMERS_____

NEW ACCOUNTS CALLED ON	ADDRESS	COMMENT	ROUTE

NEW ACCOUNTS

ROUTE	CUSTOMER NAME	ADDRESS

CUSTOMER COMPLAINTS

ROUTE	CUSTOMER NAME	ADDRESS

GENERAL COMMENTS AND CUSTOMERS LOST

will not cash the checks without this approval. Because of the delay and inconvenience this causes, the Bank has printed Identification Cards for the use of our employees who are cashing their *payroll checks* at the National American Bank, Lee Circle Branch. These Identification Cards shall be issued to those employees who request one. The employee will then be able to go to the cashier's window, *SIGN HIS OR HER CHECK AT THE WINDOW IN THE PRESENCE OF THE CASHIER,* show the Identification Card, and have his check cashed.

This is for cashing *BROWN'S VELVET PAYROLL CHECKS ONLY.* Employees who wish to have a card should contact one of the following:

R. E. Hood   Nolan Burris

SALESMEN'S DAILY REPORT

SALESMAN_____ DATE_____

_____ REMARKS_____

CUSTOMER_____

ADDRESS_____

TOWN_____

CUSTOMER_____

ADDRESS_____

TOWN_____

CUSTOMER_____

ADDRESS_____

TOWN_____

CUSTOMER_____

ADDRESS_____

TOWN_____

CUSTOMER_____

ADDRESS_____

TOWN_____

CUSTOMER_____

ADDRESS_____

TOWN_____

The company had been receiving milk at the plant for its manufacturing processes on Sundays. This necessitated a crew of workmen to
work on Sunday to handle it. Suppliers also found it hard to deliver on
weekends. The following announcement sent to the involved personnel
indicates the decision made in solving this problem. The decision based
on past knowledge and experience pointed to the need for change. The
announcement mentions advantages that made the action acceptable.

July 5, 197–

To:

Mr. Hugh E. Morris	Mrs. Edith Atwell
Dr. H. G. Nelson	Mr. Frank McManus
Mr. Glen Griffin	Mr. Walsdorf Gibson
Mr. George Jenkins	Mr. John Porter

Mr. Rudolph Schmidt

Starting July 10, 197–, all milk will be received on Friday instead of
Sunday. This move is being made to aid our supplier in making deliveries.
At the same time, we will be able to close our Milk Plant and give all
employees Saturdays and Sundays to be with their families.

For this new plan to work, it will be necessary for all personnel to
give their complete cooperation. I know I can count on you for it.

Sincerely,

Alfred W. Brown, Jr.
Vice President

AWB,JR/dmj

The flow of reports in the company was endless. Brown's Velvet
planned to do its own tire repairs on company trucks and other vehicles.
Formerly Hubes Tire Company was used. Therefore appropriate announcements and arrangements were made. In another instance, they
formulated and distributed a policy statement dealing with unauthorized
credit. Automobile Accident and Report of Injury forms needed to be
made available and instructions for their use given. All sorts of things
happen in the company and reports are written.

There are several conclusions that we can make from analyzing the
situations and reports at Brown's Velvet:

1. Most reports in a company are memorandums used to handle whatever situation comes up in getting the job done from day to day.

2. Once a decision is made, a course of action planned, or a problem

solved, it must be disseminated to the management and employees involved for their action and implementation.

3. Most reports add a bit of information to the recipient's storehouse of knowledge and experience. This he uses now or later as needed.

4. The writer considers the effect of the report's message on the reader. A report must not only get its message accepted and acted upon but also maintains harmonious relationships and favorable attitudes toward the job, people, and company.

CLASSIFICATION OF REPORTS

Because business reports cover a wide variety of subjects, dealing with all phases of business activity, there are many ways of classifying them. Reports are used for a multitude of purposes and present their messages in a variety of forms. If you were to jot down all the kinds of reports used by any one company, you might have a list running something like this:

Policy statements	Advertising reports
Periodic reports	Employee bulletins
Progress reports	Accounting reports
Credit reports	Market surveys
Sales reports	Personnel reports
Committee minutes	Statistical analyses
Public relations reports	Product analyses
Annual reports	Readership studies
Attitude surveys	Research reports

Although the list is not exhaustive, it is representative. It also indicates the functioning of reports in different situations with different readers, internally and externally. And classification is not so important as understanding the report-writing situation and being able to adapt report material to the reader's purpose.

Here we have considered the nature of reports according to their informative or analytical purpose and their functioning in a company in relation to employees, management, and the public. For the rest of this chapter let us consider the various forms of short, informal reports. On the basis of form there are two major divisions of reports: informal, short reports and formal, long reports. The type used depends on several factors, such as

1. Complexity and treatment of the material.
2. Length of the report.
3. Interest to the reader.
4. Purpose and objectives to be accomplished.
5. Time for preparation.

    6. Permanent or temporary value of the report.

    7. Formality of relationship of reader and writer in the situation.

    8. Intended use of the report.

Informal, short reports, as their name implies, are written for informal situations, vary in length from one to ten pages, and deal with subjects or problems of temporary or current interest to speed up the process of keeping someone informed and getting action accomplished. They generally have neither a table of contents nor a cover because there is no need for them. The pages are usually paper-clipped or stapled.

They take on a variety of forms (although memorandums and letter reports predominate) and speed up the recording and flow of information. Yet form is a means to an end and not an end in itself. The form depends on the reader, the problem, the purpose, and the use of the report. Forms also vary from one business firm to other business firms. At one time or another, however, most companies use the following short report forms:

Memorandum	Form report
Letter	Committee minutes
Bulletin	Short formal or technical report
Booklet	

All these are treated in this chapter.

MEMORANDUM REPORTS

The memorandum report is an internal communication, usually handling routine business, but sometimes it is mailed outside the firm. Often it presents data related to a special problem. In organization, in the use it makes of subject headings, and in the purpose it may accomplish, it is very similar to the bulletin and letter reports. It differs chiefly in its form and tone. Although both types of reports are informal and short, the memorandum report is less personal, less formal, shorter, and at times more matter-of-fact than the letter report.

It is most often used to speed up the flow of current information from one department or office to another within the same company. It often provides figures used in compiling statistics, records what is going on in a firm, or coordinates the work of various men. Unless it degenerates into mere paper work and many unnecessary records, it will save the time of a busy executive by providing him with a record of information on the operations of each department and thus enable him to coordinate the work of the entire firm. It gives him the information and analysis needed for the basis of sound decisions on his part.

Details of form should be observed from the specimen memorandum report that follows. There is no inside address or salutation such as a business letter would have. Instead are simple "To," "From," "Subject," and "Date" lines that convey the needed information. Memorandums are usually referred to by numbers or subject matter rather than by dates. Sometimes the printed letterhead is omitted at the top of the page, and sometimes there is an identification line or label indicating the department originating the report. Subject headings may or may not be used. Although there is no complimentary close or signature, sometimes memorandums are signed or initialed at the end. At other times they may be initialed beside the name on the "From" line. In general the headings are printed like letterheads and filled in as the paper is used. If printed paper is not available, the headings are typed at the top of the page.

SMITH MANUFACTURING COMPANY
1617 South Rendon Street
Philadelphia, Pennsylvania

Date: January 3, 197–

To: Mr. Henry Smith, General Manager

From: John M. Jones, Sales Manager

Subject: Sales by Districts for the Month Ending December 31

Here are the figures of sales reported by districts for the month of December, 197–, which you requested in our telephone conversation yesterday.

District	December Sales	December Sales a Year Ago
Bookington	$10,465	$12,472
Cooder	15,298	30,364
Northington	25,783	25,750
Misserd	18,590	18,473

Sales dropped about 50 percent in the Cooder area and about 20 percent in Bookington. The other two districts held their own. This may be partly explained, in my opinion, by the fact that there is a new sales supervisor in the Cooder area, and half of his salesforce are inexperienced men. This does not mean they are to blame for the decrease in sales, but they should be given a chance to prove their worth. I shall see what I can do to help them.

The major purpose of this report is to inform. Sales figures are given with a possible explanation of the decrease in the one instance. There is no need for subject headings because the report is short and contains only a few facts.

Sometimes a memorandum form is used as a cover to route a longer or more formal report through specific channels. It may then contain a request for each reader to comment, initial, or send the report on its way to the next person.

Date:

To:

From:

Subject:

Remarks: Please initial after reading and pass report on to the next person.
John Adams
Henry Brown
James Joneson
Alfred Smith

Little investigation is needed for most memorandum reports. There are times, however, when they are used to present an analysis and recommendation in addition to information. The following specimen report indicates this use. Its organizational pattern, as well as its purpose and form, should be examined.

October 17, 197–

TO: Mr. John Jenks, 2nd Vice-President

FROM: Lee M. Krackson, Trust Officer

SUBJECT: Recommending foreclosure of Riverdale First Mortgage Bonds

Defaulted Interest Payments

In the Jones Custodian account #4000, we are holding some par value, $8\frac{1}{2}$ percent Riverdale First Mortgage bonds, secured by property located at the Northeast corner of Sixth and Western Avenues, Bridgeport, Connecticut. The past two semiannual interest payments are overdue along with general real estate taxes for the years 1967, 1968, and 1969.

Mr. Dickins' Proposal

To assist Mr. Dickins, the mortgagor, we previously offered to reduce interest payments to $7\frac{1}{2}$ percent, provided Mr. Dickins would pay up the back taxes. He agreed to this offer, but did not fulfill his promise. Foreclosure proceedings began, and in answer Mr. Dickins has offered this proposal:

1. That we drop foreclosure suit immediately.
2. That we assume court costs and attorney fees encountered in foreclosure suit.
3. That we reduce interest payments to 6¾ percent.
4. That we waive past-due interest payments.
5. That we deliver canceled interest notes to him.

Bank's Investment

Our total investment is approximately $42,850.00. The mortgaged property was appraised on January 17, 1969 at $53,000.00.

Recommending Foreclosure

Because Mr. Dickins refused our plan and because he made no cash deposit ensuring good faith in his proposal, it is my recommendation that his offer be rejected and foreclosure continued. Please sign and return enclosed carbon of this memorandum if this recommendation meets with your approval.

LMK:bc

Enclosure

BULLETINS

Bulletins are used for both internal and external communication. They are brief and to the point. They nearly always include information of more permanent value than memorandums and are distributed to a sufficient number of readers to warrant their reproduction in quantity. For this reason they are not addressed to any particular person. Nor is any special form necessarily used. Sometimes they are not even labeled as a bulletin. When they are labeled, however, they have a top form heading similar to that of the memorandum report. Usually they consist of one to three pages, but sometimes they are longer and fastened together as small booklets, having a combination cover and title page on the outside.

Bulletins are used much the same way as memorandum reports—to inform their readers. Most companies issue policy bulletins to supervisors to keep them informed of personnel changes and policies. The supervisors in turn file the bulletins in policy manuals for reference and inform the employees under them of the policy or revision. In the following sample policy bulletin, numbered paragraphs have been used for convenient reference.

Personnel Policy Bulletin Number 57
Date of Issue: May 16, 197–

Distribution: Subject:

Division Managers   Expenses Incidental to
Branch Managers   Transferring Personnel
Office Managers

To treat all employees uniformly, it is advisable to outline a general
policy for handling expenses for transfer of employees:

1.   The Company will pay all necessary moving expenses covering
household goods. Arrangements for moving should be cleared with our
local traffic manager.

2.   The transportation for the employee as well as his family will be
paid to the new location. If the transportation is by car, the regular mile-
age allowance will be paid.

3.   Storage charges will be paid for a period not in excess of thirty days
if storage is necessary pending the arrival of the employee and his family
or if the new home is not available.

4.   If it is impossible for an employee to make permanent living arrangements immediately, the Company will pay up to thirty days for living
expenses prior to the arrival of his family. When an employee has located, no further living expenses will be allowed. If a single employee
cannot make suitable living arrangements, the Company will pay expenses up to a period of one week, or until he is located, whichever is
sooner.

5.   Traveling expenses to and from an employee's former home for
one trip will be paid after he has been transferred.

6.   The Company will not reimburse an employee for any penalty
suffered under a lease for an apartment, home, or other living quarters.
The Company will not reimburse an employee for loss suffered incidental
to the sale of real estate.

7.   The foregoing does not apply to a new employee. It is the general
practice for a new employee to report to the location where he is assigned
without any reimbursement for traveling or other expenses.

Careful consideration should be given to all factors before an employee
is transferred. The employee should clearly understand *in advance* what
expenses will be assumed by the Company. The importance of arranging
these details *prior* to the transfer cannot be overemphasized. There may
be unusual conditions which will require special handling. Any exceptions to this general policy as outlined must be approved by the vice-
president in charge of the Division and confirmed by him in writing.
In the case of the executives reporting to the president, such authorization will be made by Robert J. Mikovich in the same way.

The heading of the policy bulletin is very similar to the heading of
a memorandum report. Its purpose is identification. There is no consistency among companies as to the form used for a bulletin or even its
use. It is important, as in letter and memorandum reports, to present

The following bulletin distributed to insurance agents is not only an illustration of bulletin form and use but also contains practical suggestions for improving one's dictation skills. Dictating routine reports such as memorandums, letters, bulletins, and the like saves the time and effort of the reporter.

G | **FIELD UNDERWRITING EDUCATION BULLETIN**

BULLETIN NO. 5   March 1970

Are you suffering from "Dictaphonitis"?

Before answering that question let's take a look at some of the symptoms:

1. Multi-syllable words appear in place of simple ones.
2. Two paragraphs appear when one would do the job.
3. Paragraphs are 15 lines or longer in length.
4. Required action is vague -- sometimes hidden in the memo.

If your memos have any of these symptoms, you have got "it" and should take immediate steps to "take the cure."

In order to prescribe the proper treatment it is necessary to know the cause. In most cases, "dictaphonitis" is caused by the dictator not knowing what he wants to accomplish before he starts dictating. Also, many people feel that talking to a machine involves a different vocabulary then when talking to an individual.

Fortunately, "dictaphonitis" can be cured very easily -- just follow these few basic rules:

1. Have a good idea what you want to accomplish before you start to dictate. We are not recommending that you write out a memo or letter before dictating it but definitely recommend that you know what you want to say before you start dictating.

2. Reverse the symptoms -- for example, if you use multi-syllable words, try using simple ones.

3. "Write it as you would say it" is over-simplification but it still is a good technique to follow.

4. Use "dated action memos". For example, if you want a reply by a certain date, ask for it by that date. Don't write: "Will you take care of this matter" -- write: "Will you take care of this matter by January 15."

5. Make it easy for the Agent to act. This can be done in several ways. If you have a series of questions leave space after each question for the Agent to write the answer. If you want an "OK" just ask him to write "OK" at the bottom of the memo and return it to you. Whenever possible, try to leave enough space on your memo that the Agent can give you his answers on it. It will save him time and he will be more likely to answer your memo.

Make your memos effective -- get rid of "dictaphonitis" and follow the basic principles of good letter writing.

its contents in a clear, readable manner, to adhere to only one major subject in any one bulletin, to be accurate, and to consider the reader and purpose.

LETTER REPORTS

Because letter reports are letters that present business information or deal with a business problem, they contain the parts of a business letter, and their general form and layout are the same. They differ, however, from business letters in style of writing and in organization of content by being less personal and less psychological in nature. The letter report format, below, shows the use of the parts of a business letter and a typical outline of its contents. Note the organizational pattern followed here, the emphasis on directness in presenting factual information rather than personalization, and consideration for conserving the reader's time and effort.

NAME AND ADDRESS OF FIRM

Date

Name and Inside Address

Subject or Reference Line

Salutation:

Introduction: This may be a brief statement of the problem situation giving rise to the report, reasons for the report, or questions defined. It should establish contact with the reader and orient him to the problem and the report.

Summary: This may be a summary of findings, conclusions, or recommendations, whichever is of the most value or importance.

Development of the report: This will include description or explanation of method of obtaining data, the facts, theories, and reasoning that led to the conclusions.

Concluding statements: This may be a suggestion, a request, proposal, or implementation for action.

Complimentary close,

Signature

Typed name
Position

Initials

List of enclosures or attachments

Enclosures may consist of tables, charts, or some graphic or pictorial presentation that will support the conclusions in the body of the report or add data to the written presentation which analyzes and interprets the figures or statistics given in an attachment to the report.

A distributor of grocery and drug products to supermarkets was confronted with the problem of having supermarkets keep fully stocked shelves at all times. In this connection he made a study of several supermarkets to determine the effect on sales of fully stocked shelves. Sales of several brands in each of ten commodity products were checked for a two-week period under normal shelf-stock conditions and then again for two weeks under fully stocked shelf conditions. The results of the survey were of interest to dealers and managers of supermarkets. The distributor accordingly presented the results in a letter report, "Advantages of Fully Stocked Shelves," in which he recommended maintaining fully stocked shelves at all times. The first paragraph served an introductory function, mentioning the purpose of the survey and orienting the reader. It caught the reader's attention because he was affected by the problem. The next two sections presented the survey's results and analysis under the following subject headings: Effect of Diversification, Sales in Relation to Number of Items Stocked, and Margin and Turnover. Emphasis was placed on effects on the reader and led to the conclusion that it is profitable to maintain fully stocked shelves. A table was included which compared the items sold under normal conditions and under full-stocked conditions and which proved an increase in sales. Another table, showing the specific items checked under both sets of conditions and the percent of change, was attached to the letter report. It likewise substantiated the suggestion to maintain fully stocked shelves.

In addition to accomplishing its mission of fully stocking shelves, it built favorable relations between the distributor and his supermarkets, for it indicated his concern for passing on information that would help them increase sales.

BOOKLETS

As a report form, booklets are very much like bulletins; in fact, some firms use them interchangeably, for they serve the same informative function and are used for both internal and external communication. Since booklets, however, generally contain subject matter of more than temporary value, they are reproduced in quantity. Booklets also differ from bulletins in length. They are often longer than three pages and, in some instances, are practically book length. Instead of having the top-heading identification of a memorandum report or bulletin, they resemble books. In this respect they are similar in form to short formal reports because they have covers, title pages, sometimes tables of contents, and sometimes covering letters or letters of transmittal depending on their purpose, readers, and length.

Booklets run the gamut from formal to informal treatment in their style and general makeup. They should be made so attractive and interesting that they will be sure to be read. When a new employee joins a firm, common practice is to give him several informative booklets: One might be on the history of the company, another on employee benefits, and another on the company retirement plan. The following selected pages from two booklets used by R. J. Reynolds Tobacco Co. indicate differences between formal and informal booklets. The first examples are from the booklet given to all new employees on the company's retirement plan. Notice the plain formal cover.

The following is taken from the first two pages of the same booklet:

EMPLOYEES' RETIREMENT PLAN

OF

R. J. REYNOLDS TOBACCO
COMPANY

———

BOOKLET OF INFORMATION

———

INTRODUCTION

The purpose of this booklet is to inform employees in nontechnical language as to the benefits provided for them under the Employees' Retirement Plan of the Company. However, this booklet is not a substitute for the Plan and the statements here made are subject to the detailed provisions of the Plan. A copy of the Plan and the Agreement of Trust under the Plan is available to each employee.

The plan provides for payment of retirement allowances to employees who are covered by the Plan and who retire because of age or disability. These retirement allowances are in addition to any old-age benefits to which employees are entitled under the Revised Federal Social Security Law.

In order to provide for payment of the retirement allowances, a Trust Fund has been established which is administered by a Trustee. Each year the Company makes a contribution to this Trust Fund. It is estimated that the

Employees' Retirement Plan

of

R. J. REYNOLDS TOBACCO CO.

Booklet of Information

Simple, formal booklet cover.

Courtesy R. J. Reynolds Tobacco Co.

contributions made and to be made to the Fund by the Company, together with income on investments held in the Fund, will be sufficient to pay the retirement allowances provided by the Plan.

GENERAL

Employees Covered

Every regular, full-time employee of the Company is covered by the Plan. However, a person who became an employee after 1966 is not eligible for the benefits of the Plan unless he was less than 50 years of age at the time of his employment.

Retirement Allowance

Retirement allowances are paid monthly. The amount of the allowance depends upon the employee's wage or salary (not including any profit participations or amounts paid by the Company for insurance or retirement benefits) and years of credited service completed before retirement.

Credited Service

Credited service means continuous service and is limited to maximum of 40 years, except that service rendered prior to 1946 by an employee while under age 25 is not included as credited service.

. . . .

The next excerpts are from Reynolds' booklet, "Facts about *Your Job and Company*," which is also given to all new employees. This booklet is informally done with a number of illustrative drawings on nearly every page. Inside an attractive cover, which shows a picture of the main office building at Winston-Salem, North Carolina, is a letter from the president:

R. J. REYNOLDS TOBACCO COMPANY
Winston-Salem, N.C.

Dear

The purpose of this little booklet is to serve as a handy source of information for you about your Company. It tells about its early history and progress, the quality tobacco products upon which our business is based, the benefits each of us as an employee enjoys, and the responsibilities we share together in our work.

Your job is a big part of your life. It affects your future and the future of your family. By working together to make better quality products, we improve our Company and ourselves.

I wish you much happiness and contentment in your part of this job.

Sincerely,

President

On the back of the president's letter in a frame of two shades of blue are these two sentences:

We believe in

Ourselves and in

our Fellow Workers.

We believe in Our

Company and

its Products;

their Good Name

is our Good Name.

The table of contents presented next has an interesting title, "What's Inside."

A representative page from the booklet indicates its informal style which is sure to capture the employee's interest.

SHORT REPORTS

By resembling the long formal report [2] in both style of presentation and parts used as prefatory and supplementary elements, short reports take on more formal aspects than memorandum reports, bulletins, letters, and the like. In fact the major difference between long and short formal reports concerns the scope, the purpose, the length, and the inclusion or exclusion of elements such as title page, letter of transmittal, table of contents, appendix, and so forth. Although informal short reports run from one to three pages, the formal short report may run up to ten pages, and anything beyond that is considered long. Short reports are made formal by dressing them up with additional parts and by using

[2] See Chapter 9.

3

Interesting table of contents attracts employees' attention.

Courtesy R. J. Reynolds Tobacco Co.

Benefits and Services to YOU

Your job as a regular employee of this Company brings you more than just the wages you receive. You become eligible for a number of benefits and services which contribute to your well-being, your health and your security.

It is to your interest to know just what these programs are and how they benefit you personally. The several Benefit Plans and Services are referred to below, together with sources of detailed information.

EMPLOYEES' RETIREMENT PLAN

As a contribution to the continued security of regular employees, your Company maintains a Retirement Plan. The plan is supported entirely by the Company at no cost to the employees.

The funds which have already been contributed by your Company to establish this Plan and the additional sums it sets aside each year to maintain the Plan are all placed in trust for the purposes of the Plan and cannot be used for any other purpose.

10

Inside the employees' booklet.

Courtesy R. J. Reynolds Tobacco Co.

a formal writing style. Companies frequently get the job done through short formal reports.

To facilitate the writing of effective reports, most companies devise report-writing manuals. Although details of form and of developing the text differ among business firms, there are certain elements commonly agreed upon. Technical and research departments are very conscious of the use of manuals and set forth definite guidelines for their technical men to follow in presenting research results. Caterpillar Tractor Company, Chrysler Corporation Engineering Office, and Standard Oil of California, for instance, follow a recommended format of the following divisions:

1. *Title.* This should state clearly, concisely, and specifically the overall scope of the project. It identifies the report by subject, number, department or person responsible for it, and date. This first part prepares the reader for transferring his attention from other things to the report. This may be done by filling out the printed form provided at the top of page 1 of the report or by composing a title page with appropriate information and arrangement. (Note the illustrations on pages 46 and 47.) The printed form is devised to fit most situations in which it is used. The title page contains basic information for the particular report, but its arrangement varies according to the formality of the situation.

2. *Introductory sections.* The function of introductory sections is to give the reader background information, to let him know what the report is about. The writer should keep in mind that many of the readers have had no contact with the work prior to reading the report. He should state the objectives and reasons for the investigation, its relation to other work in the laboratory or area, the expected use of the results, and any background information that will help the reader to view the report in its true perspective. These things may be accomplished by adding a Letter of Transmittal, Table of Contents, Preface, or Introduction to precede the body of the report (sometimes referred to as the report text).[3] In any of these parts divisional headings such as *object, purpose, method, previous research,* and the like may be used as guides for the reader.

3. *Summation.* Emphasis is placed in the summation section on what was found out and what should be done about it. It is desirable that the reader have the recommendations and conclusions early in the report to facilitate both understanding and action. A conclusion should be brief and to the point. It is based on sound reasoning and interpretation of data. It is the basis for the recommendation. Tell the reader in a summary statement what you found out. Conclusions are your judgments and are not meant to be a listing of what happened or the results, both of which come later in the discussion sections of the report.

Recommendations are statements of what you think should be done about the conclusions reached. They represent your thinking about the direct application of findings to the solution of problems. They might also include implementation suggestions.

In some cases the nature of the material in the report or the investigation has been such that a conclusion cannot be drawn. Then the summation becomes

3 For illustrative examples and treatment of these parts, see pages 307-312 .

Chemical Research Staff	Report Subject:			
	Project No.	Date	Department	Report No.
Technical Corporation	Author	Department Head		Supervisor
	Abstract:			
Conclusions:				

First page—technical report.

a summary of the results or main points discussed. In other instances conclusions and recommendations may be preceded by a summary of the entire report or of any one section needing to be highlighted for special attention, interest, or use.

4. *Technical and discussion sections.* The technical and discussion sections fill in the details that led to the conclusions and recommendations. When you write under these sectional headings, you support and explain your conclusions and recommendations. You might well begin by amplifying subjects touched upon in the introduction, especially when these topics need further description and explanation. Give details about what you tested, equipment used, how you did the work—your research methodology—and what happened. Follow with significant, pertinent observations, results, and interpretations. When the

```
                        S U B J E C T



                        Sub Title



                           by



                           for



                          Date
                         Company
```

Title page—short report.

discussion includes figures from tables, charts, graphs, or some form of visual aid, the visual presentation should be a part of the text.

Visual forms appear in a report where they function best. The more significant ones appear in the discussion or technical section as an integral part of the report text. Those "just for the record" belong at the back of the report in a special graphic aids section, following and supporting the discussion section, or in the appendix, or simply attached to the report's text in case of shorter, more informal reports, such as memorandums and letters.

5. *Supplementary sections.* Graphic aids too bulky and cumbersome to be in the discussion section or complete tables from which lesser ones and charts have been made to be placed in the report text may be in a special graphic aids section as a supplementary part of the short formal or technical report. References, list of symbols, glossary, sample calculations, bibliography, sample questionnaire, correspondence—in fact, any useful relevant information and evidence that is not an integral part of the report text—becomes a supplement. In long formal reports they are grouped together in an appendix and there may or not be an index for further reference use. In short reports they are simply labeled as exhibits and attached to the back of the report text. Including a bibliography as a supplementary part is dependent on the writer's having used it as a part of his research methodology.

This general organization covered in the five-point outline is recommended for short and long reports of varying lengths and degrees of formality. The length and complexity of the report will determine the use of subject headings and subheads. The order of the general headings in the outline just presented may be followed or adjusted in order to present your information most efficiently.

Your goal is communicating to the reader, for you want him to have the information you have developed. Take a look again at a diagram of the communication process. You as the writer can arrange the material and sections in the sequence best for presenting the material to the reader to get the job done efficiently.

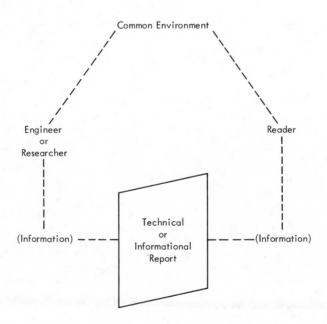

FORM REPORTS

Form reports are used to help reduce the work of reporting routine information, to keep records, to provide data for computer programming, and to make decisions. How many times have you heard the following statements: "There is simply too much reporting and paper work done around here. It is just so much extra work and should be eliminated." Although some are written unnecessarily, many reports that may seem useless to people who resent having to do them and who do not fully understand their use are really time-savers and provide needed information. Forms should be devised to function, and when they no longer serve their purpose, discarded. People filling out forms should be made aware of the data's use so they can understand their role on the job. Printed forms containing appropriate headings calling for blanks to be filled in provide uniform information and data that can be quickly reported, spotted, and used. Such reports may be daily, weekly, or monthly sales figures, accounting ratios, production costs or what have you. They often have little permanent value unless they become part of a total picture, but they do provide current data.

In reporting monthly status of group life insurance, for example, the insurance agent has a record of his own efforts, and the company has a basis for comparing the work of all their agents in this area. Personnel departments make wide use of form reports for recording facts about employees—not only for the record but also as aids in adjusting employees to their jobs and in giving salary increases and promotions. A university might use a faculty evaluation or profile sheet for similar purposes. Students, likewise, might use a survey form for evaluating their instructors. Progress reports on projects or people become useful.

It is important that form reports be carefully planned in order to secure only the needed information. They must be carefully worded so the person filling them out can do so quickly and accurately. Whenever the data are to be tabulated and compiled into a larger report, the forms should be planned to make tabulation of figures possible. The same applies to data and information for computer storage and retrieval.

COMMITTEE MINUTES AND REPORTS

In today's business world, management operates under varying theories and styles of management—management by objectives, participatory management, management by concepts and ideas, and even authoritative management. All these have two things in common: management through people in committees and small groups, and management through communication. Although committee minutes are not usually thought of as reports, they have enough characteristics of informative reports to warrant brief treatment here, and certainly a report presented as a result of a committee's investigation and solution to a problem is important to the everyday operations in a business enterprise. They may be used in carrying out suggestions passed on by a group, or in informing others of the group's activities, or in serving the committee as a change agent by presenting a solution or implementation for action. If the committee meets regularly at a specified time, the minutes become a periodic progress report of what took place at each meeting.

Writing minutes can be routine, particularly if the meeting agenda followed Robert's Rules of Order and a standardized pattern used in recording them. Their contents and arrangement, however, can be varied. A standardized arrangement places first, for the record, the time and place of the meeting and a list of members present and absent. Then the contents are arranged chronologically according to the progress of the meeting. Numbered paragraphs or subject headings may identify the points discussed and action taken. Most minutes are arranged chronologically because then all the secretary has to do is to write or type the report from the notes taken at the meeting in the same order. This becomes a time-saver for the one responsible for the minutes.

To rearrange the minutes by subject headings requires evaluation and judgment on which is important, what is relevant, and what should be emphasized. The reorganized material, nevertheless, presents a more interesting and useful report, for the person referring to the minutes can see at a glance the information he is seeking for decision or action.

Minutes must be accurate, complete, and clear. Reports, important ideas, motions, and opinions should be credited to the individuals contributing them. Emphasis should be given to such items as responsibilities delegated to members of the group and action that is to be taken after the meeting. Then, when a member receives his copy (assuming they are distributed, and they should be), he is reminded of the duty he is to perform. This emphasis and distribution help in the proper functioning of the group.

In a company in which several committees and departments operate separately and discuss their plans, policies, and projects, the minutes serve as an invaluable tool to the executive in coordinating the work of the company. Aside from their value as records and their use in the group's functioning, this is their chief value as an informative report.

When a committee has investigated a problem or conducted a piece of research through joint efforts, the committee report follows the same format and organizaton as the short formal report to which has been added a covering memo or a letter of transmittal. For some short, simpler problems or piece of research, a memorandum or letter report may be used, depending on the degree of informality inherent in the situation and existing between the reader and the committee. In either instance, the solution, conclusions, or recommendations must be supported by a logical rationale and evidence to gain acceptance, approval, or action— whichever is demanded to serve the report's purpose.

DICTATING REPORTS

Not every report is written, checked, revised, and rewritten. The type of report and how it is to be used as well as the amount of time available and how well the writer can express himself determine the amount of rewriting. In fact many reports containing information of current or transient use can be dictated, and then afterwards checked for accuracy of facts and data, overall organization, and clearness in accomplishing its purpose. This would be true especially of routine form reports, many memorandums, and some short formal reports.

With a good outline, complete data, and some effort and practice one can become good at dictation. Both the dictator and transcriber work together, thus reducing the cost of written reports by saving time and effort. Good dictation practices pertain to planning and organizing, dictating and transcribing.

Planning begins with an analysis of the situation and getting together the facts, data, and ideas necessary for the report. Arrive at a purpose and determine what is called for to accomplish it. Plan what you are going to say and say it. Assemble all the information. Make a study of it, jot down notes, and reach conclusions. Organize your thoughts. Outline them or mark your notes 1, 2, 3, etc., to indicate the sequence in which you will use them. Set a time for dictation when few telephone calls and people are coming in and out of the office.

In dictating, whether it be to a stenographer, secretary, or a dictation machine, apply the principles of any effective communication and be thoughtful of the other person. Principles of clarity, completeness, courtesy, conciseness, correctness, directness, and objectivity are especially pertinent. Pay special attention to persuasiveness and the use of logical reasoning to support your statements. Visualize your reader and speak with him. Dictate preliminary instructions and then the separate parts of the report. Dictate clearly, indicate punctuation, and spell out proper names and technical terms. Dictate in thought groups by putting words and phrases together, clauses and short sentences. Provide the secretary with your notes and supporting data for reference. She can file them later. Even dictating a rough draft and having it typed triple spaced for changes can be helpful and will save you time.

The secretary who takes dictation and transcribes has had training and has developed skills in shorthand and in transcribing from both notes and machines. The key for her is to listen attentively, ask questions, and look up references and spellings. Reading through the report before beginning to type will give her a perspective of the whole and what she is doing. She should be familiar with the "form" and parts of reports and adapt her typing accordingly. The secretary should proofread and correct her work. The report writer should check for content, organization, and style of expression. The two work together for effective reports that will get the job done efficiently with a minimum of time and effort.

FOR DISCUSSION AND WRITING

1. In its sales training one large corporation hangs a sign in front of the students: "The man who graduated yesterday and stops learning today will be uneducated tomorrow." Discuss the significance of the statement.

2. On the basis of form, organization, style, tone, and reader-writer relationship, compare the various reports used in the everyday operation of a business enterprise.

3. Bring to class memorandums, bulletins, and form reports to discuss their expediency in day-to-day operations.

4. Why is directness in organization and expression of utmost importance in reports used in day-to-day operations?

5. Discuss the factors that determine the kind of report used.

6. Why do most companies prefer that reports begin with either a summary, conclusion, or recommendations?

7. What would you contribute to the conversation if a fellow worker made the following comment to you: "There is simply too much reporting and paper work around here."

8. Discuss the following statement: Form in reports is a means to an end and not an end in itself.

9. Define: Committee minutes, business report, communication process, form reports, and policy bulletin.

10. Become aware of and sensitive to some of the problems around you in your university environment. Observe what is going on and confer with appropriate people. Then prepare a report that will get appropriate action. Some general problem areas existing at most universities pertain to

   a. Registration procedures.
   b. Menus at the dorm or cafeteria.
   c. Conditions in the student lounge.
   d. Part-time student help in the department offices.
   e. Co-ed dorms.

    f. Food- and beverage-dispensing machines.

    g. Bulletin boards in a particular building.

    h. Academic advising policy and/or procedures.

    i. Late library hours.

    j. Work-study curriculum.

11. Assume that a friend from another university is flying in for the weekend. Because of your class schedule, you will not be able to meet him at the airport. Give him directions on how to get to your campus residence, or assume that he is driving and that you will meet him at the student union building. (In either event, he has not been on your campus previously.)

12. Write instructions to an inexperienced driver to help him to parallel park, to start the car on a cold wintry night, and to change a tire.

13. *Reimbursement of travel expenses.* You are personnel manager in your firm and the following provisions are included in your travel allowance policy: private car when company car not available, 12 cents per mile; private car in lieu of available company car, 8 cents per mile; air flight recommended, coach round trip fares; hotel or motel, $16.00; dinner, $5.00; lunch, $3.00; breakfast, $2.00; actual cost of parking, telephone calls, tolls, limousine, and so forth. The company wants to encourage management personnel to attend conventions, seminars, and professional association meetings; to participate in programs; and to speak professionally whenever possible to community, government, and civic groups. Reimbursement of travel expenses is made according to allowable stated expenses. Costs are charged to the department authorizing the travel. Reservations, schedules, and arrangements are the individual's responsibility. Before the trip, an estimate is to be submitted for approval. After the trip, the exact amounts are to be submitted for payment. Payment will be made within a week to ten days. Beginning this November 1st, the company will allow payment in advance up to 75 percent of estimated expenses; will pay conference and convention fees; allow $20 per day for hotel room in cities such as New York, Atlanta, and Washington, D.C.; and will require receipts for meals, lodging, transportation, and conference fees.

    a. Formulate a new travel policy.

    b. Prepare a bulletin for disseminating the policy to management.

    c. To accompany the bulletin, prepare a covering memo in which you get management acceptance of the changes and the new policy.

    d. Prepare a form for reporting estimated and actual expenses for reimbursement. This could also be attached to the bulletin.

14. The following topics call for a report, somewhat longer and more formal than a memorandum report. Select a topic and write the report. You may assume necessary details of a situation giving rise to the report. In most instances, you will need to gather data for an analysis.

    a. The layout of desks, files, book shelves, equipment, and so forth in an office.

    b. The reorganization of a department in a factory or business firm.

    c. Degree requirements in your college.

    d. Recommended purchase of some art pieces for use in the reception room, employee lounge, or _____ .

    e. Relocating the checkout counters in a supermarket or discount store.

15. Your company is planning to purchase a postage meter, a new accounting machine, an electric typewriter, an opaque projector, or some other business machine. One of them will be used in connection with your work. Investigate several brands of the machine and prepare a report recommending the best one.

16. *Excessive talking and visiting among employees.*[4] The home office of the Brighton Synthetic Rubber Company usually hires employees on the basis of interviews and tests. After being on probation for three months and given on-the-job training under the direction of their department supervisors, each person is then considered every six months for a pay increase, but he may be passed over if the department head does not recommend him. If a pay increase is allowed in the plants of the company, which are unionized, the company attempts to make a corresponding increase in the office.

    In the Cost Accounting Department are four women and three men who have been with the company for five to seven years. The senior cost accountant and the factory accountant, who are the supervisors of the department, have been changed twice in the last three years, and in each case, the positions have been filled by younger men from outside the office staff. Management, while recognizing the worth of the older staff members, has felt that the employees in the department were not eligible for promotion.

    This has had a noticeable effect on the work of the women employees of the department; they have been particularly displeased with this action. The department supervisors and the office manager have conferred several times to discuss the excessive amount of talking and visiting that has been going on among the older members of the accounting department. Their topic of conversation is well known to the rest of the office force, and it is feared that it will result in a general morale problem.

    What action should the department supervisors and office manager take? The offending employees could be discharged. The office manager might send a letter to all employees, asking that they refrain from excessive talking and visiting. He could call in the men and women concerned and ask them to discontinue this practice. He might try to break up the "talking and visiting" employees by transferring some of them to other departments.

    Write a report to the office manager of the company.

17. *Location of office facilities.* Industrial plants and offices are usually located in keeping with basic requirements which focus around the following principle: to manufacture and to distribute at the lowest cost and at the same time provide for adequate future growth.

    The Roto Machine Company, located in the center of a large city's industrial area, has an office that occupies the first and second

---

[4] Problems 16, 17, and 18 have been adapted from those by L. M. Newberger, *Collegiate News and Views,* March 1953.

floors of a brick building on a very busy street. The machine shops occupy the rest of the building.

The partitions within the office, the stairway leading to the second floor, and the flooring on the second floor are of wood construction. To conserve space, the hallways are rather narrow. Very clean floors, doors, and walls give evidence of excellent maintenance in both factory and office.

Sixty employees work in the office under the direction of the office manager. Concerned with the usual functions of accounting, payroll, purchasing, and filing, the office receives orders from salesmen and through the mail but does not have many direct contacts with the public.

Mr. Johnson, the office manager, has been been urging executives of the company to move the office to a separate building or to put in concrete floors and soundproof partitions. Management, however, feels that either plan would be too expensive. Although admittedly the office location is not ideal, they feel that increased managerial control is made possible by having plant and office in the same building.

In a report, suggest a plan that will solve Mr. Johnson's dilemma.

a. Can the present location be effectively insulated against noise, dust, and dirt?

b. If a concrete floor is authorized, it would probably have to be covered to deaden the noise and to make it more comfortable to walk on. What type of covering do you recommend?

c. How would you provide for adequate communication between the two floors allotted to the office?

d. What about management's argument that better control can be maintained if factory and office are kept in the same building?

18. *Gift and party policy for employees.* The new office of the Brilliantine Paint Company has been designed to provide pleasant and efficient working space for its employees and at the same time to demonstrate how paint and glass can be used in the construction of a beautiful office building.

Employing over 140 office workers, the company has a reputation for keeping its employees happy and satisfied. The turnover rate is, of course, very low.

The office manager has instituted a policy of providing a farewell party for employees who leave after a period of two years or more with the company and of staging informal gatherings for the office workers who are being married or who have completed certain periods of service with the company. These parties are usually held during working hours in the company dining room. The office manager often gives a short talk and presents the honored guest with a present. The recipient responds, and then cake, ice cream, and coffee are served to everyone present.

It has been customary to collect a small amount from each employee to pay for the presents. The company always defrays the cost of refreshments. Because the staff is growing and consequently the number of gatherings is increasing, it is felt that some definite policy should be established regarding (1) how often parties should be held,

(2) who should be honored, and (3) how the funds used for presents should be accumulated. How would you handle this problem?

a.   You can continue the present policy and procedures.

b.   You can reduce the number of parties and informal gatherings by making it more difficult to qualify as an "honored guest."

c.   You can continue to collect a small sum from each employee whenever the need arises.

d.   You can set up a standing committee to collect a small amount each month. This committee would then be responsible for allocating a uniform sum for each present and for actually purchasing the gifts.

    After deciding what should be done in the Brilliantine Paint Company, prepare

a.   A policy bulletin to be distributed to all office employees.

b.   A bulletin board announcement.

c.   An article on the new policy for publication in the employee magazine.

19. *Building a permanent trade by direct mail.* The Complete Dry Cleaning Service recently opened a cash and carry dry cleaning establishment in a suburban area of the city. The possibility of building a large transient trade was small, and management wanted to build up a permanent trade among residents in the vicinity. Henry Rouford, Jr., the owner and manager, discussed this problem one day with a neighborhood friend, who is a senior taking business administration at the University of Oklahoma, and thus enlisted some help and advice. Jack Thompson analyzed the neighborhood and recommended a direct mail campaign to be used by Mr. Rouford.

    Characteristics of the neighborhood: People living in an area of approximately eighty blocks around the establishment were considered fairly average. About 90 percent of them had a high school education; about 40 percent were college graduates. The husband was the worker, and the wife did the housework and shopping for the family. Families averaged about five members. They had a reasonable amount of leisure time to enjoy movies, picnics, fishing, golfing, boating, tennis, and other activities. They were in a middle-income class, incomes ranging from $12,000 to $18,000 per year. Every family had an automobile, and in some cases two. Homes were considered nice and were single residences. People bought medium-priced clothes and took pride in their appearance. Most of them fitted into a professional or technical worker group. The men were largely office workers with titles, salesmen, and managers and worked a forty-hour week. Public and private conveyance was used for getting to work each day. Nearly every family in the area took an annual vacation, usually during the summer months for about two or three weeks, one of which was generally spent in traveling. Vacation trips were taken within a 2,000-mile radius and by automobiles.

    The direct mail campaign: Mr. Thompson suggested using postcards for mailing pieces, sending out 3,000 each month to people in the area. Their names and addresses were to be obtained from the city telephone Red Book. The cards were to be addressed for only three months at a time to avoid incorrect names and addresses, since people moved in and out of the designated eighty-block area. He estimated this could be done for $380 a month—$180 for postage (third-class) and $200 for printing the cards in two colors and addressing them. He further suggested that on each card there be a cartoon character to get attention and to suggest something that occurs in a particular month or a reaction in relation to clothes cleaning. Also on the card would be a few lines of copy to bring out some selling point, such as prompt service, expert work, or dependable service, and the name, telephone number, and address of the business. He proposed copy and drawings for six cards and suggested that duplicate cards could be sent as long as four months intervened. This reduced the cost of printing, for there would be a lower rate for 6,000 of a kind.

Card number 1 to be mailed in December and June to suggest winter or summer vacations.

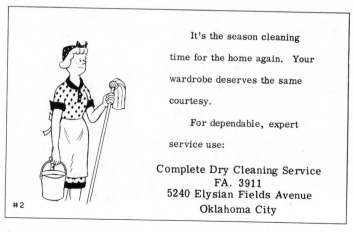

Card number 2 to be mailed in April and September, for they are considered big cleaning months.

No need to complain about

poorly pressed clothes.

Get expert service.

Send them to:

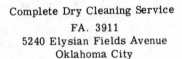

Complete Dry Cleaning Service
FA. 3911
5240 Elysian Fields Avenue
Oklahoma City

#3

You don't need to rob

your savings to pay for expert

cleaning service when you deal

with:

Complete Dry Cleaning Service
FA. 3911
5240 Elysian Fields Avenue
Oklahoma City

#4

Oh! It's a wonderful feeling to

know that your clothes are in

skilled hands at economical prices.

  Wouldn't you like a wonderful

feeling?

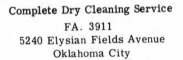

Complete Dry Cleaning Service
FA. 3911
5240 Elysian Fields Avenue
Oklahoma City

#5

Cards number 3, 4, and 5 to be sent out during any month.

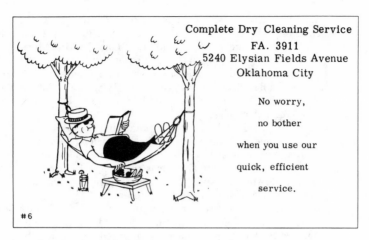

Complete Dry Cleaning Service

FA. 3911

5240 Elysian Fields Avenue

Oklahoma City

No worry,

no bother

when you use our

quick, efficient

service.

#6

Card number 6 to be mailed during summer months.

Assume that you run a small independent advertising agency. Mr. Rouford has brought you the six mailings as presented here and has asked you what he should do. He wants to know whether he should use these cards or not, and if he does use them, what changes should be made to improve them. He also has asked you to suggest any other advertising that could be used to help him build a permanent trade. Present your suggestions in a report to Mr. Rouford.

20. *Handling personal work in the repro shop.*[5]   Personal work in most in-house reproduction shops is a pain in the neck for some people. Individuals active in church work, organizations, service clubs, and civic and political affairs want to have work done in the reproduction department for these groups. Others want personal letterheads run, bridge scorecards, and song sheets. The operators like to do work for their friends. Executives think having personal work done is a privilege that goes with their rank. All of this costs the company supplies, work time, and salaries.

Mr. Marshall Howard, reproduction department manager at Withrow Manufacturing Company, is really in a dilemma. Just the other day he became acutely aware of the problem in his office through a series of incidents.

Sam Jones, personnel director, came in at 4:00 P.M. to have a two-page policy statement run, 100 copies, which had to be distributed to all department heads first thing the next morning. All the presses were loaded; several jobs were in process in which every minute counted. Sam was told it could not be done until the next day. He was very disgruntled and word of this got to Mr. Howard, who checked and found that one of the offset presses was tied up doing a brochure for the Presbyterian Church to promote stewardship; this was at the request of Mr. Henry Floyd, Director of Public Relations

---

[5] Adapted, with permission, from Howard A. Floyd, "Personal Work in the Repro Shop," *Reproductions Review*, November 1970, pp. 12, 14.

and chairman of the church committee. Sam likewise did a little checking on his own and discovered that the day before there was idle time on one machine and that Tom Jenkins, the scout master of troop 468, walked in with a scout newsletter at 4:00 P.M. and walked out almost immediately with the requested 200 copies. No small wonder Sam was disgruntled! "Why can't company work get done when it needs to? It should come first," he complained to the reproduction manager.

As Marshall Howard was pondering the problem and thinking that management should resolve it, his wife telephoned him: "Darling, I simply must have those song sheets for the young people tonight to practice their Christmas carols for the program coming up. And while you are having them run, remember my bridge club meets Wednesday and I need the tally scorecards."

His wife had no more than hung up the telephone when he was called to the office of the sales manager. (The week before Mr. Cardson had received some personal work returned with a note from Marshall Howard that explained that personal work could not be done in the office.) Now Mr. Cardson confronted Marshall Howard with, "I can't understand why your shop can't do this program for the regional meeting of the Marketing Association. Where I formerly worked, the repro shop always did work for me. I've a good notion to report you up the line."

Howard told him he would have no objection to being reported up the line, but asked, "Did you ever consider taking home a briefcase stuffed with several dozen pencils, ball-point pens, note pads, file folders, typewriter ribbons, and other items?"

Cardson quickly replied, "I most certainly would not do anything like that."

Howard then said, "What makes you think that this printing of the convention program is not in the same category? You want to use the company paper, spend company money on mats, ink, time and labor spent in printing, collating, etc. A briefcase full of office supplies or full of reproduced work for an association—both represent a company investment."

The reply was revealing: "Do you know I never have thought of it that way. Paper does have a monetary value. It's so commonplace we fail to put a value on it. This could be a serious problem."

"Indeed it can be and is."

"I shall be glad to help you do something about it."

After the conference with the sales manager, Marshall Howard decided to get some cost estimates and to find out to what degree personal work was being done and specifically the nature of it. Over a two-week period he came up with the following data. Ten percent of the work load was personal work which fell roughly into four classifications:

a. Material employees want reproduced for civic organizations, charities, and churches. Employees who want this type of work contend that the company contributes to charities and that any reproduction work would be the same as a contribution.

b. Work requested for service clubs, election campaigns, civic groups,

P.T.A.s, Boy Scouts, and so forth. The argument for doing this work is based on the fact that the company encourages employees to become active in such groups; thus the company should subsidize their efforts.

c. Material for golf and country clubs, fraternal groups, bridge clubs, social groups, and so forth. People desiring this type of work contend that doing this centers around the fact that a number of other employees are also members or are involved. Some feel it is right to have such work done.

d. Personal-personal work such as scoresheets, letterheads, song sheets, and scores of other items strictly for the individual's use. Argument here is based on precedent. What is done for one should be done for all.

Howard further estimated some cost figures. Roughly estimating a total of 20,000,000 copies annually reproduced in the shop, 10 percent would be 2 million copies. Assuming that an average run is 200 copies, then 10,000 originals have been handled. With the average cost $1.50, this, then, has cost $15,000. But this is not the complete total, because how much of the work required special stock, ink, or handling? How much required collating and bindery operations? Additional costs may increase the total from 25 to 100 percent, making a range of $18,750–$30,000. And what about the loss in having to do company work rush, postponed, or not at all?

With all this evidence and the happenings of the past three weeks, Marshall Howard wondered how he could continue operations in the Reproduction Department with things as they are. Some shop managers just close their eyes and ears to personal work and believe that they have no problem or that the cost is so small that making an issue of it would not be justified. Some shops are interested only in production and not what comes in and out.

Analyze the problem and write a report to Marshall Howard on what action he should take and how to implement it. You might include in the report any pieces of communication that should be used in carrying out your proposed recommendations, suggested media to be used, and channels.

21. The Bank of Denver is confronted with publicizing their new Insured College Loan Plan in order to get student takers. Here are some facts about it.

The importance of a college education in today's specialized world is greater than ever before. All too often the opportunity for higher education is denied the aspiring, capable student for purely financial reasons. The college loan plan makes it possible for the student to attain his fullest intellectual growth without putting a strain on the family resources.

Specifically, this is a plan which spreads the payment of all normal expenses for a full college course over a period of up to six years. Further, assurance of college completion is provided by credit life insurance, at no extra cost, on the life of the parent or guardian. In the event of death of the sponsor, the insurance proceeds pay in full any remaining loan balance.

A parent, guardian, or family member who works or resides in the Denver area may apply for a loan to cover the cost of a student's educational expenses.

The Insured College Loan Plan may be used to cover the cost of attending any college or university of the student's choice. One to four years of college work or similar periods of postgraduate study may be financed by this plan.

All normal costs, including tuition, room and board, special fees, books, or any other costs directly related to the educational program may be covered by the loan plan.

To summarize, the Bank of Denver's Insured College Loan Plan (1) permits budgeted monthly payments for college study instead of large semiannual cash outlays; (2) spreads cost of education over a period longer than the course of study; (3) covers entire cost of education by one, low-interest loan; and (4) guarantees completion of education in event of the borrower's death.

Here is how the plan works:

1. Select the college or university to be attended and determine the amount of money needed for the contemplated course of study. This sum may include tuition, room and board, laboratory fees, books, or other costs directly related to the educational plan and cover periods of study from one to four years.

2. After your application is approved by the Bank, the sponsor signs one note to cover all the expenses of the entire course of study. The amount of the first semester's cost is paid by the Bank at the beginning of the tuition year and the remainder of the loan is placed in the Insured College Loan Plan Commitment Account at the Bank. Future payments are disbursed from this account at the beginning of each semester.

3. Budgeted monthly payments begin one month after the loan is completed and continue until the loan is repaid. These payments may be spread over a period of up to six years for a four-year course.

4. Life insurance protection is arranged without medical examination to guarantee the student's continued education in case of the death of the sponsor.

5. The loan agreement may be terminated at any time. In this event, the balance in the Insured College Loan Plan Commitment Account will be applied to the unpaid balance of the loan, if any, and monthly payments will continue until the loan is repaid.

Terms for the Insured College Loan Plan are flexible. They can be arranged to cover a full four-year college program, with repayments budgeted over as long as six years, or can be made to cover a shorter period of study.

To apply for an Insured College Loan or to secure additional information about the Plan, contact any office of The Bank of Denver, write to the Personal Loan Department, or call JAckson 2-8585.

Here are typical examples of the low-cost, Insured College Loan Plan:

No. of College Years	To Be Repaid in (months)	Amount You Need ($)	Monthly Loan Payments * ($)
4	72	10,000	213.99
3	48	4,000	110.53
2	36	2,000	71.93
1	12	1,000	97.73

* Payments include the cost of credit life insurance.

There are several possible media and ways for getting the message to the public and to students. In a report to the Director of the College Loan Plan give your suggestions and attach some of the possibilities such as a brochure, newspaper advertisement, news release, letter to students, and radio or TV announcement. Wouldn't you also need to present your rationale so he can accept your ideas?

The following quotation from Joseph Addison somewhat sums up the attitude of the Bank of Denver toward education:

Education is a companion which no misfortune can depress, no crime can destroy, no enemy can alienate, no despotism can enslave. At home a friend, abroad an introduction; in solitude a solace and in society an ornament. It chastens vice, it guides virtue, it gives, at once, grace and government to genius. Without it, what is man? A splendid slave, a reasoning savage.

APPLYING PRINCIPLES
FOR UNDERSTANDING
AND PERSUADING

3

THINKING IN REPORT PREPARATION

UNDERSTANDING THE PROBLEM
    Analysis of the Situation
    Analysis of the Problem
    Analysis of the Reader
    Defining and Limiting the Problem

REPORT PLANNING

LANGUAGE

ATTITUDE TOWARD THE READER
    Characteristics of Good Tone
    Techniques for Developing Good Tone

STYLE
    Characteristics of Style
    Principles of Unity, Coherence, and Emphasis
    Using Subject Headings

DEVELOPING QUALITIES OF STYLE ESSENTIAL TO UNDERSTANDING
    Clearness
    Completeness
    Conciseness
    Consistency
    Correctness

TECHNIQUES FOR EXPRESSING FACTS AND IDEAS
    Developing Topic Sentences
    Using Structural Paragraphs

INTERESTING AND PERSUADING THE READER
    Attention- and Interest-Getting Devices
    Narration and Description
    Logic
    Argumentation

FOR DISCUSSION AND WRITING

THE REPORT'S MESSAGE MUST BE UNDERSTOOD, and the reader must be persuaded to action. How can a person accept the message in a report if he has not understood it? And how can he react favorably to it or implement its recommendations if he has not, in addition to having understood it, become interested and been persuaded of the data's validity and the necessity for action? The purpose of this chapter is to discuss the principles and practices of good report writing. We shall consider how understanding the message is dependent on the report writer's careful planning and thinking; how language, style, and tone affect the report; and how to write effectively to achieve understanding of the message and to persuade the reader.

THINKING IN REPORT PREPARATION

One of man's most vital human characteristics is his ability to think. Before submitting a report, the writer will work step by step, systematically, through several stages of development. At each step he will constantly apply creative and logical thinking, and, as he works, he will be forming and practicing good work habits.

The following steps in report investigation and preparation represent a logical, systematic approach:

1. Seek a full understanding of the problem and situation.
2. Plan an investigation.
3. Gather all facts and data; create ideas.
4. Organize and interpret material, create further ideas, reach conclusions.
5. Propose and consider all possible solutions.
6. Conclude which solution is best.
7. Determine action for putting solution into effect.
8. Outline material for presentation.
9. Write up the report.
10. Revise, proofread, type, and edit the report.

Creative thinking implies using ingenuity to think of alternative solutions to a problem. It is the power to visualize and understand by looking at different points of view and approaching a problem from many angles. It is not only the ability to generate new ideas but also the ability to foresee, plan, and look ahead and to search constantly for a better way.

Logic is the study of the structure of thinking. In proving a proposition and bringing out relationships among ideas, we rely on a logical structure to help make the line of argument a valid one. Drawing conclusions from premises, extracting universal truths from individual cases, inferring particulars from general laws, and using statistics, surveys, and mathematical equations—all call for reasoning and logic. Reasoning is used to evaluate and to select ideas best suited to our purpose, to achieve harmony and order in our thinking, to sift the significant from the irrelevant, to compare and to choose for optimum results, and to adhere to the problem or subject at hand.

One of the best ways to describe the use of creative and logical thinking is to describe the report writer who is a careful thinker in his investigation for and preparation of reports:

1. He is deeply motivated and not a person with lots of "easy" solutions for problems.

2. He is filled with curiosity and asks questions that lead to new and productive answers.

3. Continually adopting new assumptions or trying to renovate some old ones, he develops new guesses, new theories, new symbolic word maps.

4. He makes predictions from assumptions, facts, and theories.

5. He understands relationships, cause and effect, comparison and contrast; weighs the pros and cons; and sees all sides to a question.

6. He looks ahead, seeks action, and is not afraid to take chances, for he has thought through his problem, solution, and presentation.

7. He has the drive and competence to demonstrate the validity of his ideas and reasoning and to face criticism of himself and others.

Some people define all thinking as problem-solving. John Dewey essentially does this in listing logical steps of problem-solving: determining the problem, collecting facts and data, analyzing and hypothesizing, drawing conclusions, devising solutions. Alex Osborn does the same in listing his seven steps of the creative process: [1]

1. Orientation—pointing up the problem.
2. Preparation—gathering pertinent data.
3. Analysis—breaking down relevant material.
4. Hypothesis—forming alternatives by way of ideas.
5. Incubation—letting up, to invite illumination.
6. Synthesis—putting the pieces together.
7. Verification—judging the resultant ideas.

[1] Alex Osborn, *Applied Imagination* (New York: Scribner's, 1953), p. 125.

Osborn's seven steps can be reduced to four steps directly applicable for the report writer:

	Report Investigation	Report Presentation
Preparation:	This includes understanding the prob-lem—gathering, selecting, and or-ganizing information, data, and ideas. At the same time a logical consideration of facts and ideas and a logical reaching of conclu-sions are necessary.	This includes reviewing all the ma-terial and reasoning with the idea of presenting it to someone else for his use.
Incubation:	This is a problem-searching period in which all possible alternative solu-tions are gathered.	In this stage the material is orga-nized into the framework of a particular type of report for a particular reader. It would in-clude outlining material for final presentation.
Illumination:	At this stage a sudden insight into the solution appears; the writer de-termines which solution is best and why.	During this period new insights de-velop in which pieces of infor-mation fall together as the first draft of the report is written.
Elaboration:	At this stage action for putting the solution into effect is worked out, and the solution is further devel-oped.	This step involves completing and polishing the report—revising, typing, and editing. Final creative refinements take place.

UNDERSTANDING THE PROBLEM

A problem is a situation that requires a definite decision or action to achieve a desired outcome. Not all reports, however, are written from problem situations; some are merely developments of particular subject matter. However, even in most subject-matter-centered reports a problem can be found. When the situation or subject is examined and the source of difficulty or a question is found, then the problem can be defined. Thus a first concern of understanding the problem is learning how to recognize problem situations. This can be done by setting goals, imagining an ideal situation for comparing and evaluating, observing what is taking place, listening to others, asking questions, and reading to profit from experiences of others.

Sometimes the problem may be stated in a general way by whoever authorizes the investigation and report. He may do this in a letter of authorization or in a personal conference. In these cases the researcher would determine the problem by analyzing the letter or by asking ques-tions during the conference. Problems may also be suggested at committee meetings or group conferences, and an individual may meet a problem in connection with his own job and need a solution. A study of the situation giving rise to a problem will help the investigator to see it in proper perspective and to discover its different elements.

Analysis of the Situation

In analyzing a problem or its causes, the researcher begins at its core. In every situation there are people involved, events or action taking place, and both physical and psychological conditions and environment to be considered. In some problems the issues stand out clearly; in other problems the issues may be complex and obscure. A review of all factors involved will help to point out the basic problem and the approach it requires. Parts of a problem may be isolated and analyzed separately to find their relation to each other and to the central problem. Reactions of people to each other and what is happening should be examined from different points of view. A series of questions about each element may be listed to ensure complete investigation of each and to ascertain the data required and the means of getting them.

An analysis of the situation will also help determine the purpose and objectives of the report. The writer should understand how the report will be used in order to decide what he should do and why. He needs to survey all the facts known at the outset and determine what necessary facts are unknown.

Analysis of the Problem

When the writer has sufficient knowledge of the problem, he can break the latter down into its several elements, outlining them wherever possible to provide the framework for his investigation and later the presentation outline of the report. If he is unfamiliar with the subject matter, he will first need to gather some information about it for understanding the type and nature of the data needed to arrive at a solution.

The problem is also analyzed by accurately phrasing the title and in defining the scope, limitations, and contents of the report. The title naturally designates the subject matter of the report, indicates the nature of the contents, and attracts the reader's attention. Both the problem and its cause help to establish the scope and limitations. From analysis one can also set up a purpose and decide on the type of report to write. These considerations are further discussed in a section on defining and limiting the problem.

Analysis of the Reader

Consideration must also be given at this point to the reader's present attitude. Is he neutral? Is he antagonistic? Is he biased in his views? Will he be favorable to the solution? Knowing the reader's attitude will help the report writer determine his approach to the subject and decide how he can best present his material to accomplish the report's purpose.

The present familiarity of the reader with the problem or subject matter must also be considered. Just as the writer's experience with the problem determines the data he must gather, so also the reader's experience determines, in part, what the writer must present in the report. A reader who is familiar with the situation and the need for a solution does not want to wade through those details in a report, nor should he, for he is ready to consider a proposed solution. On the other hand, a reader who knows little or nothing about the problem needs to be briefed on the situation and the details giving rise to the problem and to the report.

The investigator should also know whether he is writing for a single reader or a group of readers, as well as the use that will be made of the report. Is the report, for instance, to be used by the advertising director of a firm to decide whether or not to advertise by direct mail, or is it to be distributed to members of a board of directors to help them set next year's budget? Is it a problem-solution report with recommendations to be carried out or an informational report for public distribution?

Defining and Limiting the Problem

The problem is generally defined by the person requesting the report. In some cases a description of the situation is given and the investigator is asked to make a statement of the problem. It is then stated in terms of the facts giving rise to it.

The purpose is the long-range goal that the report seeks to accomplish. The objectives are the immediate goals or steps that must be attained to reach this final goal. For instance, the purpose of a report may be to show how to reduce the cost of a certain operational process. In such a report the recommendations will present ways in which the cost can be reduced. An objective, however, will be to examine present operations to find out whether changing them would actually reduce costs. This would have to be done before any recommendation could be made. Both the purpose and the objectives would be supplied in defining the problem.

The scope sets the boundaries of the report. It indicates the extent of the material covered, the quantity and nature of the data. A report on the investigation of the annual reports of Swift and Company from 1955 to 1970, for example, sets the boundaries of the study by naming the fifteen-year period, the company, and the type of report. Within those boundaries certain limitations apply. The investigation might deal only with a study of how the reports promote good public relations. This would be a limitation of subject matter. Often reports are limited to only one or more aspects of a broader subject.

Other limiting factors that often apply are time, cost, procedures available, and the qualifications of the researcher. If you are asked for a report in two hours, you certainly will not do the job you would do if you had a whole week. Yet you would get the job done and on time. If you are allotted $10 for an investigation, your course of action would differ from the course followed if you were allotted $500, yet in either case you would arrive at an answer. Likewise, if you are asked to evaluate something which you are not qualified to pass judgment on, your criticism will be limited by your lack of knowledge or experience.

In addition to a problem's definition in terms of its purpose and objectives, scope, and limitations, it must be differentiated from other problems in the same field. Suppose a personnel director has a lateness problem among his office workers, who are reporting late for work in the mornings and who are extending their midmorning and midafternoon coffee breaks. He must recognize his problem as part of a larger one —employee morale—and must distinguish between it and other morale problems, still dealing with it as a part of the general morale problem.

The more fully the researcher understands his problem, the better able he is to plan and carry out his investigation and present his findings. Defining the problem is merely selecting elements of it which will guide the thinking and planning of the investigation and the report. An analysis of the situation, the problem, and the reader is a basis for determining such elements as need, purpose, objectives, scope, limitations, and divisions of subject matter, which in turn are used as a basis for choosing procedures for collecting and organizing the data. After defining and analyzing the problem, the researcher is ready to formulate his working plan, which is simply a plan of what he proposes to do and how he expects to accomplish it.

REPORT PLANNING

Successful reports are well planned. Planning consists of setting up definite procedures for conducting an investigation, for handling its results, and for writing the report. The purpose of planning is to establish policies pertaining to the objectives, scope, cost, time limit, and outline of the proposed report. Planning clarifies the thinking and work of the researcher and provides him with a guide for conducting his investigation and presenting his findings in report form. The basis for any report planning is the analysis of the situation, problem, and reader, for the determination of one point of procedure usually leads to another.

The working plan for the investigation and the report accomplishes two major purposes: It charts the investigation, and it clarifies the researcher's thinking. It may also be submitted as a proposal to seek approval of the project before work is continued. Usually it takes the form of an outline, but sometimes when it is being submitted for approval, it is written as a letter. In some companies it may entail filling in the blanks of a printed form provided for this purpose.

The proposal plan will include as many of the following elements as are applicable to a given report problem:

1. Statement of the problem.
2. Need and use of the report.
3. Purpose and objectives.
4. Scope and limitations.
5. Divisions of the subject matter.
6. Methods and procedures for gathering data.
7. Tentative bibliography.
8. Methods of organizing data.
9. Digest of impressions.
10. Tentative general outline of the report.
11. Statement of expected results or tentative conclusion.
12. Statement of cost and time required.
13. Definition of terms (specialized use and technical terms).
14. Work-progress schedule.

Determining the sources of data and planning how they will be used are important decisions, and Chapter 6 on researching the data, facts, and ideas discusses several methods of collecting data for solving a problem. After one knows the nature of his data and how he is to get them, he can decide how to organize them. Even while he is collecting material, he can be organizing; doing both processes at once will save time. (This is one reward for careful planning and foresight.) The tentative outline of the report can be formulated as soon as the author has analyzed his problem and broken it down into its basic elements. At this point it may consist of only the major topics arranged in orderly sequence. Or the author may break the topics down further into as many subdivisions as possible, thereby clarifying minor problems for the researcher and simplifying his task of drawing up a final outline later.

Whether or not tentative conclusions can be drawn up will depend on the author's knowledge of the problem or subject and how far along he is able to carry his thinking and preliminary work. He should avoid setting up a tentative conclusion if, in directing his effort toward it, he overlooks factors which may prove it false or inadvisable. It should be merely something he is working toward, and all factors and data in the case should be examined, even if in the end he reaches an opposite conclusion to the one he had expected to reach. The work-progress schedule is used to plan work and budget time proportionately to make sure the project can be completed in the allotted time.

Because the same elements are included, the working plan can be used as a basis for outlining and writing the introduction to the report. The chief difference is that the plan is *what was proposed* and the introduction is *what was done*. Therefore any changes that took place will naturally be reflected in the finished introduction.

Although submission of a working plan is not always called for, the report writer must at least think through the problem situation to secure an understanding of it and where he stands in relation to it. This will indirectly force him to formulate an approach to the problem and to point up areas in which he may or may not need further data. One solves a problem and writes a report based to a great extent on his accumulated knowledge and past experiences in handling similar or like situations. Many decisions are made, problems solved, and reports presented dealing with everyday situations without having to conduct an investigation or carry out a time-and-effort-consuming project. In such instances, a formalized working plan or proposal is not warranted. One simply moves from his thinking and understanding the problem (skipping the formalized working plan and research steps in report investigation and preparation) to organizing and interpreting facts, ideas, and data. Here thinking plays an important role in reasoning and reaching conclusions. Then the reporter moves on to planning his material for presentation in the report, and language, style, and tone greatly affect his presentation.

LANGUAGE

As a means of communicating thought, language consists of a set of symbols used uniformly in ways agreed upon by a group of people who are thus able to communicate with each other. Words are symbols, and clear thinking itself requires words. Words are names given to objects and actions to convey meaning to others. Developing the ability to analyze thoughts and to select the right words for transmitting them improves communication.

One basis for understanding language and communication is derived from the psychology of perception. This is the concept that a person does not "see" the real world but only his image of it. The brain, in receiving nerve impulses only from the sensory organs of the body, constructs an image of reality, which is what appears to be; what we see is not what is really there but our image of it. There are three kinds of reality which we may perceive:

1. Events, persons, and things we have direct contact with.

2. Events, persons, and things we have read about, been told about, or have inferred from our experience with them.

3. Events, persons, and things we have dreamed about or imagined—images created without any reference to any external event or the like.

Our image of reality, then, is influenced by what exists in external reality and what goes on within us, such as our emotions, feelings, and habitual thought processes. To determine what is reality and make our image correspond to it as closely as possible, it is necessary continuously to check concepts against facts. S. I. Hayakawa uses the analogy of a *map* and the *territory* which the map describes to explain the relationship between our image of reality and reality. Words become symbols for an event, person, or object that they represent and are not in themselves the event, person, or object for which they stand. Difficulties in communication arise because words are not directly related to objects. The words you write may not convey the picture you intended. This is true because one word can bring several ideas to mind.

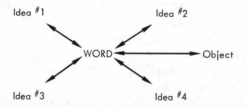

Words should be selected for their denotations and connotations. The denotation is the idea the word expresses, and the connotation is the idea the word suggests. The denotation is the recognized, standardized meaning of the word as given in the dictionary; it has been agreed upon by usage and has withstood the test of time. Connotation, on the other hand, is the impression, feeling, or emotional overtone a word calls forth. It is the effect the word has because of the reader's experience and association with it; thus the connotative meaning may vary greatly from person to person. The purpose of a report must be considered in order to determine when words should be used to express meaning or to impress the reader. Definite, exact words express clear, exact meanings. Abstract nouns tend to be vague and general, for they are less direct and less forceful than concrete nouns. When abstract terms are used, they should be qualified by illustrations pointing out their characteristics.

The following conversation points up the need for saying what we mean:

HE: Stop frying those onions. You can smell them all over the house.

SHE: But I'm in the kitchen.

HE: What's that got to do with it?

SHE: What do you mean *I* can smell them all over the house when I'm only in the kitchen. Where are you?

HE: In the bedroom.

SHE: How do you know they can be smelled all over the house when you're only in the bedroom? Anyway, I'm not frying onions.

HE: Then, who is?

SHE: Nobody. Heat is frying them. I just put them on to fry.

HE: Well, turn off the gas.

SHE: It wouldn't help to turn the gas off because the onions are frying in the electric fry pan. You mean turn the heat off, don't you?

HE: Yes. I guess I do.

SHE: Why don't you say what you mean? [2]

Simplicity is a dependable guide. Words should be selected that will be clearly and easily understood. Technical and unnecessarily detailed explanations should be avoided. Familiar terms rather than unusual words are preferred, short rather than long words, concrete rather than abstract terms, precise rather than vague words. Superfluous words waste time, obscure meanings, and lack force. Roundabout expressions should also be omitted. There is no need to use several words to say what one will say. Indirect expressions such as the following should be omitted: *it was found that, it can be seen that, it is obvious that, it appears that.* Words such as *however, it is,* and *there are,* placed at the beginning of a sentence, generally have little value, although sometimes they are used there for transition. Likewise, words that express the imperative, such as *must, ought to, have to,* and *demand,* are often psychologically bad, and when they are, should be avoided. Words that waste time and space are *in order to, in regard to, due to the fact that, in connection with,* and other hackneyed expressions. Unless jargon is used in a specialized sense and adapted to the reader in an informal, personal report, it should be avoided, because it usually is fuzzy and unintelligible.

Excessive adjectives likewise indicate lack of strength. To habitually say "The true facts are these" will arouse suspicion when we profess to tell "the facts." When a "decision" is always qualified by "definite," what is a "decision" by itself? If a part is always an "integral part," what is a "part"? Adjectives used to make meanings precise are good; used to make meanings emphatic, they weaken the whole effect. The same is true of adverbs. To say "I really believe that" introduces an element of doubt which causes the listener to question the statement.

In a forty-two-page army supply bulletin recommending a fifteen-day low-calorie diet, one of the sentences suggested the diet "is applicable for use of personnel who have consistently put on weight due to the consumption of a ration of higher caloric value than required by their physical activity." [3] Why couldn't the sentence simply read, "The diet is for those who get fat because they eat too much"? One of the most frequent errors in business writing made by executives is overimpressiveness. An executive can think and talk clearly, but when he sits down to write or to dictate, he too often desires to show how smart he is and writes not only to get ideas across but also to prove how profound he is with his vocabulary. Skillful use of a diversified vocabulary will help reports convey messages clearly when simplicity is a guiding principle.

Selection of words is critical in communication. Words need to be precise. Using simplicity as a guideline will mean choosing

1. The short over the long word.
2. The familiar over the impressive word.
3. The specific word over the abstract.

What a reader understands is influenced by the frame of reference or context in which the words are used. The reader evaluates and interprets words, phrases, and facts within his own personal frame of reference, tempered by his understanding and experience, which have not necessarily been the same as the writer's.

Referent is a term used to identify the thing a word represents. Some words have clearly understood referents—California, Chicago, Bible. Others have referents difficult to understand—home, suburbia, justice, literature—for the writer and reader have not had the same association and experience. When we use words without clear referents, their context must provide the meaning by furnishing a common frame of reference for both the writer and reader. Here the use of abstraction is a creative and essential tool to aid understanding.

The semanticist's concept of abstraction is the process of selecting, from all possible qualifying details that may be used to give meaning to a general term, those necessary for conveying the intended meaning. The writer constantly adds and eliminates details to give his reader those necessary for understanding. Ground rules issued by the Federal Trade Commission in the use of the word *guarantee* in an advertisement indicate the application of abstraction to increase understanding.

The advertisement shall clearly and conspicuously disclose: what product or part of the product is guaranteed, what characteristics or properties of the designed product or part are covered by or excluded from the guarantee, what, if anything, anyone claiming under the guarantee must do before

[3] Wilbert E. Scheer, "Words," *Office Executive,* November 1961, p. 20.

the guarantor will fulfill his obligation, the manner in which the guarantor will fulfill his obligation, the identity of the guarantor, full details if the amount of refund is based on a pro rata basis for time the product was used, whether when word *life* is used the guarantee applies to life of the person or life of the product.[4]

Regulations in business and government similar to this will force an awareness of semantic issues in using our language.

ATTITUDE TOWARD THE READER

Because a report is read and acted upon by a person just as human as the report writer, the writer needs to understand the reader as an individual. This requirement involves an understanding of the psychology of everyday life, an abiding interest in people, and an understanding of human behavior. Much of the time we look upon communication as a one-way concept—from sender to receiver. We become concerned with ourselves instead of being aware of the way the reader reacts to us and our words. We tend to be self-centered and subject-centered instead of writing within the framework of the reader's interest, needs, and understanding. We give the impression that we are the authority who is giving the answers instead of involving the reader in the discussion. Prejudices may exist at both ends and need to be reconciled. The reader is interested in the effect our recommendations will have on him, and ideas can be presented from his point of view. Even arguments and disagreements can be avoided by concentrating on facts, ideas, and reasoning. Courtesy and tact should be remembered, for a positive, helpful, friendly tone toward the reader is always conducive to understanding.

Characteristics of Good Tone

Tone reveals the author's attitude toward his subject and reader, his frame of mind in writing the report, his way of thinking, and his method of gathering data. The writer who is thorough in his investigation, attends to details, and thinks logically will naturally have a complete report, paying attention to pertinent details and arranging his facts in logical sequence. The unbiased writer presents his message impartially. An effective tone must be objective, impartial, tolerant, sincere, fair, and honest. The writer strives to exhibit these characteristics at all times. Emphasis should be on the facts and what they indicate. Tone is adapted to the reader's point of view and to the purpose and type of report. In

4 "Are We Bankrupting our Language?," *Printers' Ink,* May 4, 1962, p. 61. Reprinted by permission of *Printers' Ink* and Harry Maynard.

informal, short reports, when the reader and writer are personal friends, an informal, personal tone may be used. In formal, long reports or in cases when the reader and writer are not close friends, a formal, impersonal tone is followed. At all times the writer must exercise keen judgment in his evaluation and interpretations. He should present a definite, positive, impersonal treatment of facts, making clear distinctions between facts, opinions, and assumptions. He must be thorough, accurate, and dependable. An inquiring mind, the ability to see a job through to completion, the skill of writing correctly and persuasively, and the ability to reason clearly are personal characteristics of the writer which contribute to an effective tone.

Techniques for Developing Good Tone

An objective tone is reached by observing facts as a disinterested observer and eliminating personal feelings and prejudices. Further objectivity is achieved by recognizing relationships between facts and ideas and exercising sound judgment in reaching conclusions.

An impartial tone is expressed by weighing and discussing both sides of an issue. Considering advantages and disadvantages of a solution to a problem helps in deciding whether to recommend it. Being tolerant of all viewpoints, letting the facts speak for themselves, also indicates impartiality in a report. Inspiring confidence that the material presented is accurate and valid goes a long way toward convincing the reader of the writer's impartiality.

Writing in the third person keeps the writer apart, emphasizes the results, and reflects an impersonal tone in the report. Some companies and organizations have adopted a policy requiring use of the third person, which enables the writer to present a detached attitude. In an informal, short report, however, when the reader and writer are personal friends, an informal, personal tone may be adopted and the first person used. For long or formal reports, and especially if the reader and writer are unacquainted, it is best to use the third person consistently. Of course, a good principle to follow is to adapt the report to the reader and purpose. Even in some long, rather formal reports, for instance, the reader can relax a little from the conventional third person by a change of pace. Generalizations and results should be stated in the third person. The reader can be advised, though, in the second person, and the writer can bring in his personal observations and views, when appropriate, in the first person. In using all three persons, it is important to strive for naturalness without sounding egotistical, subjective, or commanding. When an awkward situation arises from constant use of the words *author, writer,* or *one,* or when a passive construction is weak and vague, it is better to use *I* than the third person. All shifts in person should be consistently and judiciously accomplished. In a report such as the company's annual report to stockholders and employees, the second person is effectively used to bring the reader into everything being said. It is not "the company" and "the dividends" but "your company" and "your dividends," not "we" and "our" but "you" and "yours." Here person is used to achieve a tone other than an impersonal one and is adapted to a specific purpose in line with that particular type of report. Most reports based on results of an investigation and used to solve a problem or to make a decision for management should retain a third-person, impartial tone.

A formal, objective tone characterizes the opening paragraph of a student report on "Professional Job Opportunities in Advertising":

> The possible job opportunities in advertising and closely related fields are numerous and are growing at a continually rapid rate. In 1917, for example, only 30,000 people were employed in advertising; by 1960 this had increased to 150,000; and by 1970 to 300,000 people.

Likewise the tone is formal and objective in the opening paragraph of a report on the common market, "Decision of the Decade":

> In the past few years there has appeared on the economic scene a fast-growing young giant which could well shape the future of Europe and the rest of the world, politically as well as economically. The European Economic Community or "common market" is the rising power that poses a tremendous threat as well as a marvelous opportunity to the United States today. Without a doubt, the United States must join, but paradoxically they cannot, or rather will not, join. This report is devoted to explaining the paradox, evaluating the possible alternatives, explaining what has been done, and predicting what will happen in the future.

In contrast, the following paragraphs from two student-written reports exemplify an informal, personal tone:

> I spent a summer abroad in the beautiful coastal country of the Netherlands with a Dutch family living in Zaadam. The father was an economist, and I learned many of the problems facing the economy of the country.

> In choosing my future career, I considered many aspects of a myriad of job opportunities, weighed tangible and intangible factors, and made many value judgments. After determining what I want in life, what interests me, and what I can do daily without getting neurotic or static, I chose the job and life of the corporate executive.

Facts and figures are desirable in the present tense. A statement of fact or a result *was* not true merely yesterday but *is* still true today. The present tense indicates this accuracy of statement. The use of exact titles of persons, places, and things also helps to convey accuracy in the report and to gain the confidence of the reader. Likewise concrete, vivid illustrations and the active voice of verbs make the data stand out, enlivened and strong as they should be, giving them dignity and sincerity and adding to the general tone of the report.

STYLE

Applied to factual writing, style consists of the techniques the author uses in writing a report. It is the expression of the writer's ideas, his manner of perceiving and thinking, and it reflects his sense of humor and the degree of his self-confidence. It should inspire confidence and respect for what he has written. Some of the techniques applicable to achieving good tone are also used to accomplish an effective style. The third person, for example, creates not only an impartial tone but also an impersonal, matter-of-fact style, while the first person produces a personal, intimate style.

Characteristics of Style

A simple, straightforward, direct style is used to present facts. The reader expects to get to the heart of the subject immediately. He usually does not want to waste time on nonessential preliminaries and unimportant data. He is eager to get to the point and find out what the conclusions and recommendations are rather than be kept in suspense. A good "rule-of-thumb" principle to follow is, *Have something to say, say it directly, and stop.*

A persuasive style convinces and induces action. Accuracy of the investigation and a convincing presentation of its results entail presenting the pros and cons of a point and relating the facts. Tabular and graphical methods of presenting figures, statistics, and facts are used rather than verbal exposition alone. Illustrative material, examples, pictures—all emphasize the data and convince the reader as well as make things easily understood. The use of graphic presentation is a stylistic characteristic of most reports and, as one of the methods for presenting data, warrants special treatment in the following chapter.

In developing your writing style, consider these general guidelines:

1. Write to express, not impress.
2. Keep the reader's interests in mind.
3. Anticipate his questions.
4. Get to the point as quickly as possible.
5. Use a direct approach.

6. Keep sentences short.
7. Use simple words.
8. Be concise. (Conciseness is the soul of clarity.)

Principles of Unity, Coherence, and Emphasis

To achieve understanding, the report writer uses an effective style which should be direct, straightforward, interesting, persuasive, and readable. This requires careful application of the principles of unity, coherence, and emphasis, along with the skillful use of language and the essentials of understanding. Unity denotes the state of being one. An orderly arrangement of ideas flowing into other facts or ideas and progressing to conclusions helps achieve unity and is an aid to coherence. The elements of sequence and motion make the report move forward in a definite direction toward accomplishing its purpose. There are two aspects of coherence—relatedness and clearness—and to be coherent a report must hang together. Careful planning and outlining lend coherence to the report as a whole. Emphasis gives importance to particular ideas and facts and indicates their relative value to each other and to the report in general. The following suggestions should prove helpful to the writer in applying principles of unity, coherence, and emphasis to his reports.

Unity

1. Apply unity to sentences, paragraphs, sections, divisions, or the entire report.
2. Have each unit of thought express a single idea.
3. Include everything pertinent to one clearly defined purpose, giving consideration to what the reader already knows and to what he needs or wants to know about the subject.
4. Lead the reader in a definite direction from one thought to the next toward the single purpose.
5. Indicate in the title and in the summary the unifying theme or main idea of the whole report.

Coherence

1. Apply it to sentences, paragraphs, sections, divisions, or the entire report.
2. Make relationships readily apparent.
3. To show subordinate relationships use

because, since	cause
as, more than, rather than	comparison
although, even if, though	concessions
if, in case, except	condition
where, whence, wherever	place

to, so that, in order that	purpose
so that, so . . . as, such . . . that	result
after, when, ever since, until	time

4. Interlink sentences so thought flows smoothly.

5. Arrange sentences in clear, logical order and relate them through use of pronouns, transitional words, repetition of ideas, and parallel structure; also link paragraphs similarly and use topic sentences and topic paragraphs for controlling central ideas.

Emphasis

1. Arrange important points in important positions—the beginning and end of a paragraph, section, or division of a report.

2. To arrange for emphasis consider the relative value of the idea for the reader and the purpose of the report.

3. Place main ideas in main clauses of a sentence.

4. Place the main point in a short, direct sentence.

5. Develop a main idea fully. The more details used, the more illustrations given, the fuller development of the point, the more emphasis is given.

6. Repeat important ideas and use parallel construction for a series of items on a list.

7. Arrange text spatially for visual clarity and emphasis:

a. Indent.	e. Set off items.
b. Leave white space.	f. List points.
c. Use capitals.	g. Use spot tables.
d. Underscore or italicize.	h. Use topic headings.

Using Subject Headings

For easy reading and understanding, the text material of a report is usually divided into sections and subsections. Subject headings indicate the content of each section and the degree of relationship between sections. Headings should be descriptive in content and parallel in construction. They may be numbered and lettered as in outlining, or numbers and letters may be omitted. A great deal of flexibility in the selection and use of headings is desirable, but a certain amount of standardization must be maintained for consistency and understanding. One way of setting up headings follows.

FIRST-DEGREE HEADING

When it is necessary to have headings of five different degrees of importance, one generally accepted sequence is shown here. Note that the main heading above is centered and that it is written in all capital letters.

It may be underscored or not. Headings of the first three degrees should have two clear spaces above them and one space below.

Second-Degree Heading

The second-degree heading is written in initial capitals and lower-case letters. It is underscored only if the main heading has been.

Third-Degree Heading

The text starts two spaces below the heading, at a standard indentation. Note that there are two spaces between this heading and the last line of the preceding text.

Fourth-Degree Heading. This heading is followed by a period, dash, or colon. It is indented with a regular paragraph indentation. The text begins on the same line as the heading, which should be underscored.

The Fifth-Degree Heading is made by underscoring the first words of the sentence. This means rearranging the sentence so that the key word or words are at the beginning of the sentence. Note that each of the key words underlined starts with a capital letter.

Not all reports will contain subject headings. They are used for the convenience of both writer and reader in getting the report's message understood. The longer the report in length, the more complicated the problem or subject, and the more formal the situation, the more necessity there is for using subject headings. In fact, in some short, informal reports they could detract from the natural flow of ideas and facts rather than directing the reader's thought trend. Only in very lengthy, complicated reports would there be need to use all five degrees of headings. Generally the writer will use only the first degree or at most two or three degrees—in which case he can vary the headings he uses and may use what is shown here as third or fourth degree as his first and second.

DEVELOPING QUALITIES OF STYLE ESSENTIAL TO UNDERSTANDING

To make for easy reading and understanding, the report must reflect qualities of effective communication such as clearness, completeness, conciseness, consistency, and correctness. It behooves the writer to develop his style to accomplish this end.

Clearness

Writing clearly simply means writing to be understood rather than misunderstood. At the outset it depends on careful, efficient planning. Planning the investigation, planning the organization of the data, planning the writing of the report—all ensure a logical, easy-to-follow arrangement of text material, in which all sections are connected and ideas and thoughts flow smoothly from beginning to end. One major way to achieve clearness is to arrange the material in a report by writing from a well-planned outline.

Transition by words and phrases, sentences, paragraphs, or a natural flow of ideas is another important aid to clarity, because it points out relatedness of parts of the report. Using subject headings which indicate both main divisions and subdivisions of the material is a mechanical but effective means of ensuring clearness.

Careful attention to layout and display possibilities, such as typing and spacing subject headings, tables, charts, and other forms of graphic presentation, promotes clearness as well as interest. Alignment and indentation in listings indicate subordination of ideas and facts. Principles of parallelism should be applied in listings and subject headings. If a sentence is used for one item in a list, sentences should be used for all; if a participial phrase is used for one item, participial phrases should be used for all.

Clarity is also secured through the language used. Concrete, simple language can be understood by all readers. When a report is intended for a reader with technical knowledge, special and technical terms may be used, but when it is intended for a layman, terms must be made clear through definition. The definite word to express a single idea should be carefully selected and adapted to the reader.

Inaccuracy of expression should be avoided. Likewise, dangling modifiers and pronouns with antecedents not clearly expressed or not agreeing in number and person should be avoided. When a split infinitive has the quality of good natural expression, it may be used. If it is awkward, then it should not be used. Long introductions and descriptive passages and overuse of quotations usually result in a lack of clarity. The same is true of nonessential details. Specific details, however, when pertinent, are an aid to clearness.

There is a direct relationship between clearness and completeness, on the one hand, and completeness and conciseness, on the other. Completeness ensures clearness and should not be sacrificed for conciseness.

Completeness

Completeness means comprehensive treatment of the subject or problem at hand and results in clear, persuasive writing. If all points and explanations are sufficiently detailed, no misconception will follow. Evidence must be precisely stated; the significance of the facts in relation to the problem must be shown. The treatment of each section of the report must be complete or the reader will not have an understanding of that particular section or a basis for understanding what is to follow. The analysis is a basis for the conclusions, and the conclusions are a basis for the recommendations. All must be used to accomplish the purpose of the report.

In working for completeness the writer must consider his reader. For the reader who is familiar with the problem, few details are needed. They may be recognized and their relationship pointed out without being included. For the uninformed reader, complete explanations and interpretations are necessary. If the treatment is comprehensive, the reader will find answers to any questions he might have about the material presented.

Completeness must be adhered to in all elements of the report: complete title page, complete table of contents, complete tables, complete bibliography, complete footnote entries, complete index.

Conciseness

Writing concisely requires that every thought be expressed in as few words as are consistent with writing completely and clearly. By culling the insignificant facts and treating the significant points, conciseness can be achieved. It means more than mere brevity, because conciseness involves the omission of unnecessary points. Some awareness of the reader's knowledge of the subject will help in recognizing those points which are so unimportant or familiar to him that they can be omitted or properly subordinated.

Conciseness is also secured through economy and careful selection of words. As few words as possible should be used to give complete, clear meanings. Whenever possible a word should be used instead of a phrase, a phrase instead of a clause, a clause instead of a sentence, a sentence instead of a paragraph. The process of condensing, however, should not be carried so far that the message becomes general and loses its meaning. Words should not be wasted, irrelevant and repetitious details should be omitted, and hackneyed words and phrases should be eliminated. Definite terms should be used rather than general or abstract words. Long parenthetic and digressive remarks should be avoided. The use of the passive-voice construction requires more words than the active voice and may obscure the meaning. Long, rambling sentences use words needlessly and should be recast. Sometimes, however, long, well-knit sentences should be used, since variety of sentence length stimulates interest.

Conciseness also depends on careful revision. Checking, criticizing, and rewriting a report before its final typing ensure not only conciseness but also all the other qualities of effective writing. Writing, revising, and editing are treated in Chapter 9.

From time to time *Winners and Sinners,* the internal house magazine of *The New York Times'* news room, has directed attention to wasteful locutions. These wordy phrases, although customary and inconspicuous, subtract from the directness and sharpness of writing. The following are some specimens; in each instance the wasteful locution is underlined and the suggested remedy is in parentheses.[5]

1. One of the reasons (one reason) for the cut is the drain on dollars. . . .

2. A joint communique was issued after the conclusion of (after) talks between Indian and Pakistan delegations.

3. The general debate came to an end (ended) after a series of sharp clashes. . . . Variations of this one are put an end to and brought to an end.

4. This is due largely to the fact that (because) the public agencies concerned . . . have given their approval.

5. All of them, with the exception of (except) Waldrop and Bonko . . . will be able to play tomorrow.

6. In the meantime (meanwhile), the spokesman indicated, West Germany would do whatever it could. . . .

7. At the present time (at present, now, or, as in this sentence, no qualifier at all) there appears to be little hope for. . . .

8. Students will have to complete nineteen units of work instead of the present eighteen in order (forget it) to qualify.

9. The case in question (forget it) occurred at the Bethlehem, Pa., plant.

Conclusion: Examine critically every frequently used phrase and consider every one guilty until proved innocent.

Consistency

Maintaining report uniformity by conforming to a predetermined pattern is being consistent. The writer must be consistent in the form and style he uses and in his methods of presenting his message to the reader.

[5] Quoted by permission from *The Reporter of Direct Mail Advertising,* September 1960, p. 46.

Consistency in form includes uniformity of typing details such as margins, indentation, degrees of subject headings, listings, tabulations, numbering of pages, footnote and bibliography entries, and the like. Consistency in mechanics of writing means following a set pattern concerning abbreviations, hyphenation, capitalization, use of numerals, spelling, and punctuation. Consistency likewise must be followed in presenting graphic material. If curves are to be compared, the same scale must be used throughout their plotting. Chart "A" must always be referred to as Chart "A" and not "a" or "1." Consistency can be achieved by setting up all tables in the same form and by using the same units of measurement. It must likewise be maintained in making comparisons and in reasoning through to logical conclusions. Each section of factual material must be consistent with other parts of the report or the reader will be confused. Contradictions must be avoided. Sticking to one trend of thought at a time and following thoughts in agreement with one another result in consistency.

Correctness

Correctness is accuracy; it is the result of competent judgment and conformity to an accepted conventional standard. It involves a careful checking with the standard to find out if there is freedom from error. Accuracy should begin with the first step of report preparation and be carried out to the final stage:

1. Analysis of the problem.
2. Planning the investigation.
3. Collecting data.
4. Analyzing and interpreting the facts.
5. Reaching conclusions.
6. Formulating recommendations.
7. Outlining the material for presentation in the report.
8. Writing, revising, and rewriting the final copy.

Correctness applies to both subject matter and the manner in which it is expressed. The data not only must be correct but also must be exactly stated and used to show accurate reasoning and reaching of conclusions and recommendations. This also involves careful selection of words and conformity to rules of grammar, spelling, and punctuation. Correctness helps convince the reader that the report is accurate, that it is based on sound judgment, and that its recommended action should be taken.

All the qualities of effective writing—clearness, completeness, conciseness, concreteness, consistency, and correctness—when applied, are invaluable aids in expressing facts clearly, interestingly, and persuasively.

TECHNIQUES FOR EXPRESSING FACTS AND IDEAS

Developing Topic Sentences

By indicating the essential thought that is developed in the whole report, chapter, section, or paragraph, the topic sentence clearly, accurately, and forcefully guides the writer in presenting his data and later enables the reader to understand it. The sentence, "The differences in initial costs of the four trucks are due to several factors," for instance, concisely introduces the ideas that follow. The reader expects an enumeration of the factors and an explanation of them.

The topic sentence of a paragraph may be placed at the beginning, end, or middle or it may be unstated. The reader, however, must be able to understand it. Stated at the beginning, it lets the reader know what logical development to expect; stated at the end, it serves as a conclusion or summary and leaves the reader with the idea that the topic has been treated completely. Placed in the middle, ideas point to it and go from it. For emphasis it may be stated in the beginning and restated at the end. The important point is for ideas to flow from or into the topic sentence, or both.

Used to express the main idea of a report or of a division of it, the topic sentence comes near the beginning and is sometimes referred to as the thesis sentence. A series of topic sentences are then used throughout as thoughts and facts are further developed. Sometimes topic sentences are expanded into topic paragraphs, which are used for the same purpose. The sentence "The present Federal Income Tax laws should be changed," used as a thesis sentence, would be placed first in a report. The next three sentences listed here could be developed into paragraphs comprising the rest of the report. Each sentence would serve as a topic sentence for its part of the report.

1. Tax rates are overly progressive and deter investment and growth.

2. Exemptions and loopholes have eroded the tax base and made the tax less progressive than generally assumed.

3. Income tax limits the attractiveness of executive careers and efforts.

In addition to indicating the subject matter, a topic sentence generally shows how the subject matter is to be developed. The sentence "Two plans are provided by the lessor for purchasing gasoline and oil" indicates that a number of details or a comparison of the two plans will be made in developing the subject of the topic sentence. Or again, "All services provided by the Dixie System are provided by the U-Drive-It Company" leads the reader to expect a comparison of the services of the two companies.

There are a number of methods of developing thoughts in presenting factual material. Many of the methods of developing paragraphs, such as by details, comparison, cause and effect, illustration, and logical reasoning, are, of course, just as applicable in reports as in other kinds of writing. The logically developed paragraph, which consists of a summarizing topic sentence at its beginning, followed by a series of details, evidence, and examples illustrating the main thought and a concluding statement reached from reasoning through the discussion of facts, is effective for reports. At times there is a deliberate and intentional violation of paragraph unity for clarity and emphasis, especially in memorandum, letter, and other short reports. Thoughts are broken into small units. There may even be one-sentence paragraphs. When this is done extensively in longer reports, a section of the report, rather than a single paragraph, becomes a unit of thought. Principles governing the development of a paragraph and the flow of ideas are merely applied on a larger scale. Thoughts in a report may be developed and expressed by any or all of the following methods.

By Details.   A unit of thought may be divided into parts with details given about each part, thus developing the main ideas in logical order. Details may consist of exact numbers, specifications, specific points, definite facts, structural details, and details of action. They help the reader to understand an explanation or to visualize what is being said. Details ensure complete understanding by providing concrete substantiating evidence, and by being vividly presented, they add interest to the material. When presented in itemized lists, they add emphasis.

By Comparison.   Discussing points of likeness and unlikeness of similar ideas or objects is comparison. Discussing dissimilar objects or ideas and emphasizing the points of difference is contrast. The two may be intermingled or used separately. The respective elements might also be listed in a columnar arrangement. In any case, by comparison and contrast the relationship of points is shown.

The treatment of both subjects being compared must be similar, as indicated by the following outlines comparing personnel policies:

I. Personnel policies
    of White Brothers Store
    A. Hiring
    B. Absenteeism
    C. Conferences, etc.
	I. Hiring policies
	    A. White Brothers Store
	    B. Smith Brothers Store
	II. Absenteeism
	    A. White Brothers Store
	    B. Smith Brothers Store

II. Personnel policies
    of Smith Brothers Store
    A. Hiring
    B. Absenteeism
    C. Conferences, etc.
	III. Conferences
	    A. White Brothers Store
	    B. Smith Brothers Store

In using comparison and contrast a good illustrative device is *analogy*. Between two essentially unlike things or ideas several points of similarity are indicated for the sake of illustrating one in terms of the other. Analogy thus adds vividness, clarity, and interest. One must select two objects sufficiently alike to be actually comparable and yet different enough to make the comparison meaningful through the contrast. The device is especially useful in description and analysis.

By Illustration.   The general idea stated in the topic sentence may be illustrated by a single incident or by a series of examples. Anecdotes, events, and everyday occurrences are types of examples, which may indicate the application of the general idea, thereby creating an understanding of it. Illustrations, such forms as pictures, charts, and graphs, as well as word pictures, may be used for the same result. Both illustrations and examples are best used in explanation and argumentation, for they give clear proof of the evidence at hand. Taken from a special report, "The Hows and Whys of Put and Call Underwriting," in *Forbes'* December 15, 1961, the following shows use of illustration by example:

> Being whipsawed is the option writer's supreme, but rare, indignity. A writer is whipsawed when he loses twice on the same contract and it only happens to a man who writes "straddles." Straddles are contracts which give the buyer two options: one to buy the stock, another to sell it. Thus the writer has two chances to lose.
> For example: Suppose he writes a straddle contract under which he agrees to sell 100 shares of a stock at 70 and to buy it at 70 for a premium of $700—both good for 90 days. Then assume:
> A. The stock rises ten points and is called. The writer has to buy the stock in the market at $8,000 and sell it to the contract-holder for $7,000. Loss: $1,000.
> B. Still within the 90 days, the stock turns around and drops to 60. He has to fulfill the contract by buying the stock from the contract-holder at $7,000 when it is worth only $6,000. Second loss: $1,000.
> To sum up: As against a premium of only $700, the writer has taken a loss of $2,000.

By Analysis.   According to *Webster's New Collegiate Dictionary,* analysis is the "separation of anything into constituent parts or elements; also, an examination of anything to distinguish its component parts or elements, separately or in their relation to the whole"; or "a form of statement . . . exhibiting the results of a process of analysis." In making a preliminary analysis of a problem (prior to the investigation for data), the situation is analyzed by breaking it down into its component parts to determine the problem involved. Then the problem is broken down to determine what aspects need investigation and analysis.

In writing up the report, analysis is the result of resolving anything into its elements. A point is broken down into its parts, which in turn are examined or traced to their sources to discover some general principle or truth. The analytical process involves partition and classification. The systematic arrangement of facts into groups or categories based on some common denominator or relationship is classification. The enumeration of a class into its component parts is partition. Suppose you are writing a report to determine which brand of accounting machines your firm should purchase. You would first analyze each of several brands. The information you obtained would be grouped according to the make of machine it pertained to—this would be classification. You would also want to analyze each machine by its own individual parts or characteristics; this breakdown would be partition. The type of problem you are dealing with will determine whether you use classification, partition, or both.

Analysis is used in dealing with data from an investigation. It interprets facts and figures by explaining their significance and their relationship, thereby enabling a conclusion from phenomena or statistics. In a direct way this is done by classification or partition; indirectly, however, it is done by effective use of comparison and contrast, illustrations, cause and effect, inductive and deductive reasoning, and other techniques for expressing facts and thoughts.

By Definition. Although analytical paragraphs make up the bulk of a report, other forms of expository writing are also important in presenting material clearly, interestingly, and persuasively. Definition is especially helpful for clear understanding of the problem and the report. The problem, aim, scope, limitations, and technical and special terms all require definition if the reader is to have an adequate background of information for completely understanding a report. Thus most defining is in the introductory section of a report. The definition of a term, however, may be given when it is first used. Technical terms are defined unless the reader already has an understanding of them, and special terms are defined according to the limited sense or particular meaning the author wants to convey.

A definition consists of three parts: the *term* to be defined, the *genus* or class or concept to which the term belongs, and the *differentiae* or characteristics which distinguish it from other members of its class. Some pertinent principles for using definitions in a report are

1. Employ clear and direct language. (Words simpler and more familiar than the term being defined should be used.)

2. Express the concept in *terms* other than those involving the one to be defined. ("An annual report is a report issued annually" is mere repetition, which should be avoided.)

3. Be sure the *genus* is large enough to include all members of the term. (This will ensure exactness and clearness.)

4. Make certain that the *differentiae* completely differentiate. (Essential and secondary characteristics may be given.)

5. Avoid terms such as "is when" and "is where." ("An informational report is where the author informs the reader" is meaningless.)

The purpose of definition is to establish a common concept of idea, process, or object. This may be accomplished in a single sentence or statement, or the definition may be expanded into a paragraph by enumerating a number of differentiae, explaining the differentiae, or discussing the meaning or use of the term. A general statement, for example, would define the aim or object of a report; an explanation of how the report is to be used to accomplish this purpose would be an expanded definition. Likewise the report's scope might be stated in a single sentence and the sentence developed into a paragraph by discussing, in specific detail, the breakdown of the problem into its elements, which are later analyzed. The treatment of the subject in a particular report, for instance, must be differentiated from other possible treatments of the same subject matter. The following paragraph illustrates the way in which purpose, scope, and limitations of a report may be combined into a single paragraph defining all three:

> The purpose of this report is to determine whether the Royal Supply Co. should rent its trucks instead of owning them. The results of this report will decide what policy the company will follow in 1974. The analysis of the present system covers the costs of the four Jeep trucks now owned by the Royal Supply Co. The two largest rental agencies in the New Orleans area were likewise examined for cost of renting and operating Ford, Dodge, and Chevrolet trucks. The report is limited to cost figures as they apply to the New Orleans area. Although cost is the most important factor considered, other factors, such as convenience, reliability, and the like, are given consideration. As a result this report covers the overall desirability of each of the three possible systems.

In using expanded definition, descriptive details may be given, specific examples narrated, comparisons made, or explanations of causes and results presented.

By Logical Reasoning. Logical reasoning is a form of clear thinking which must precede all effective writing. It may be expressed simply by stating reasons in explaining an idea, object, or action. One may reason from a cause or source to its result or vice versa, showing the relationship between the two elements. By a series of observed events or a mass of collected data the reader is led from one position to the next until a conclusion is reached—this is *inductive reasoning*. By examining sufficient phenomena until a pattern emerges, a conclusion is formed to explain the pattern.

In *deductive reasoning,* the writer begins with a widely accepted generalization or pattern and evaluates particular cases to determine whether they conform to it. The original premise must be precise and accurate. For reports designed to persuade or to offer recommendations, deductive reasoning can be very appropriately used.

Some form of logical reasoning is used in criticism and evaluation. Here a set of standards might be applied to the procedure or process being evaluated and conclusions reached as to what is good or bad. Advantages and disadvantages may be weighed to determine which course of action should be followed.

The nature of the material and the method used in interpreting it in a report—whether it be by details, comparison, illustration, or logical reasoning—will largely determine the arrangement of thoughts as they are expressed.

The order of presenting the results of logical thinking, for example, depends on whether it is the result of deductive or inductive reasoning. In arranging facts inductively the details, facts, and interpretations are presented first. The conclusion is inferred from them, tested, and then stated at the end. In contrast to material presented in this order is the line of deductive reasoning, which presents first the conclusion, then its application to the situation at hand, and finally the original premise restated as a conclusion.

A technique commonly used in analysis is to begin with a concept of the whole idea and proceed to the several that compose it. This creates clear, logical development. A topic idea presents major divisions first; these divisions are analyzed separately and, in the end, may be brought together as a summary.

A similar principle involves leading a reader from familiar facts to unfamiliar information; in this way the reader is prepared to understand the new data confronting him. Ideas may also be presented according to importance, with the least important idea first and the most important one last, or vice versa.

When dealing with events or other facts that involve dates or a step-by-step process, a chronological arrangement of ideas is followed. The material is presented in the order in which it occurred. This method is especially useful in narrating procedures in the history of a problem or subject. In addition to a *time* sequence, a *space* sequence may be used to describe the relative position of parts; this method is best suited to describing a machine or structure. The important principle to follow in writing effective reports is to arrange ideas and facts according to some predetermined method or methods.

Using Structural Paragraphs

Structural paragraphs will guide the reader as he progresses through the report. They provide the framework around which the facts are presented, thus pointing out relationships of paragraphs and sections.

An introductory paragraph gives the reader a clear preliminary view of the subject matter as a whole. In the introduction of a report, for example, a statement of the problem or subject is pertinent. Then in the introductory paragraph of each section of a report the writer presents the subject matter discussed in that particular section. Essential points or generalizations are often summarized as an introduction to save time for the reader as well as to inform and interest him. Sometimes the introductory paragraph indicates a plan of what is to follow. It may show the division of the material; for instance, $A = a + b + c$. A discussion of each component of A would then be in order. At other times an introductory paragraph may resemble the lead paragraph of a newspaper article. It is easy to read a report rapidly and clearly when lead headlines and paragraphs give the gist of the material at a glance.

Transitional paragraphs clarify the relationship of paragraphs or sections to each other and to the report as a whole. Because they look backward and forward, they point out the relationships of the parts of the report and leave the reader not only with an understanding of facts at hand but also with a clear feeling that he has moved forward. Often a pertinent comment or a reference to both previous and subsequent ideas or facts is sufficient. If there is a logical flow of facts and thoughts, transitional sections are not necessary. This is more likely to be true in short than in long reports, because of the closer relationship among topics discussed.

In providing the framework of the report, structural paragraphs let the reader know what is going to be said and why (introductory), relate sections which present the facts (transitional), and finally tell the reader what has been said (summary). A summary paragraph, if presented at the beginning of a report or section, is also introductory; it introduces the reader to what is to follow. If used at the end of a section, it sums up what has been said. In setting forth the main points brought out in the analysis of facts, the final summary also reasons from them to the conclusions.

Reducing structural paragraphs to a formula basis, the writer may state his problem in an introductory paragraph by breaking it down into its components: A (the problem) $= a + b + c$ (its component parts). He then proceeds to discuss a in a section of the report. After analyzing $a = 1 + 2$ and discussing the facts pertaining to a, he is ready to move on to b.

Before he can do this, however, he may want to summarize the main points he made about a and also to relate a to b. He would thus use summary and transitional paragraphs. The same procedure would be repeated for b and c. Thus facts and their discussion are presented, and a cumulative progression of thoughts is made. Afterwards a final summary would bring all the main facts together: $a + b + c$ (component parts of the problem) $= A$ (its solution). The final summary then would serve as a basis for the conclusions which would follow.

Structural paragraphs provide the framework for writing a report, and well-developed topic sentences fill in the framework with facts, ideas, and data until the report is solidly built. Because the report delves into the meaning and significance of factual information in relation to other facts and interprets them to reach conclusions, exactness of knowledge, orderly arrangement of data, and careful planning are necessary for the reader to understand what has been written. In the everyday operation of any business firm, numerous situations arise which require simple, quick conveyance of information as well as immediate action.

INTERESTING AND PERSUADING THE READER

It is not sufficient in today's busy world for a report's message to be understood. Demands upon a reader's time and effort are so numerous that in most instances readership is dependent on the ability of the report's message to capture the reader's attention. Many reports are written to be read by several people, and the more readers there are to be, the more necessary it is to get their attention and interest. Because reports are used as a basis of decisions and recommend action, it is also necessary that they convince the reader. This calls for appropriate handling of evidence, proof, and supporting evidence in proving a point, conclusion, or recommendation.

Attention- and Interest-Getting Devices

"How does this affect me?" the reader usually asks after reading a report. This is probably the most important single question to remember, especially when writing reports to employees.

An employee picks up a company report; he reads that the company is spending $545,656 per year on company benefits, and the story states that this expenditure is made solely for the employees' welfare. The company naturally expects employees to feel somewhat grateful after reading this. However, the chances are that the individual employee understands little from such a statement; to Jim Garrison, office janitor, the figures mean nothing. If the story had been written to show that the company was spending $925 per year on *each* employee for employee benefits, it would have had much more impact; Jim Garrison has a mental image of $925, for he can visualize what that amount of money will buy—suits, washing machines, or groceries. He could see what the company is doing for *him*.

If a report tells about a new product that the company is adding to its line, the story should be written not only about the product itself but also about how the addition of this product will affect the employee's pocketbook and working conditions. For example, the headline of a report in one employee magazine read as follows: "HOW OUR COMPANY HAS GROWN . . . AND WHAT IT MEANS TO YOU."

Foremost in any employee's mind is this question: "How does this affect me?" If the personalization is not presented so that the employee can understand how the story affects him, he probably will not read it. Nor will he retain any of the information if he does read it.

Personalization is one way of getting attention and developing reader interest. The simple technique of asking a question and giving an answer accomplishes the same purpose, for it arouses curiosity, moves the reader forward, and provides him with something he wants to know.

Pictorial headlines as subject headings lead the reader from point to point. Short, active, direct nouns and verbs are important in headings. It is good practice to follow the advertising caption writer's principle of getting attention and interest or the journalist's technique of writing newspaper headlines that emphasize what, who, when, where, how, and why.

Attractive form and layout also serve a purpose. Short sentences and a variety of sentence structures play their part.

Narration and Description

Narration appeals to the reader, for it creates the illusion of the reader's experiencing the events disclosed. To enliven otherwise dull, uninteresting material and to create a lasting impression on the reader, narration is best used in reports written for the public or for employees, when getting the reader's attention and interest is highly important. It is also used often in sales promotional reports but rarely in problem-solving reports for management.

To use narration for a practical purpose in a report you may

1. Introduce the subject by a brief narrative incident—humorous or thought-provoking, but related to the idea—leading the reader pleasantly into the main subject of the report.

2. Give an account of the procedures used gathering the data and in organizing it for the report.

3. Provide the reader with a history of the problem so he will have a basic understanding of the present situation in view of the past.

4. Intersperse relevant narrative incidents throughout to maintain reader interest and to illustrate points, making them understandable and vivid.

5. Tell a story, and in expanding and interpreting it clarify the points in the report.

6. Present plans for carrying out a suggested project or recommended action.

Narrative technique demands the ability to create an illusion of reality. It uses characters, setting, and plot. In using narration the writer may make use of personal references, conversation, and events. The report moves; the reader is told where he is going and why; active words move him along; a chronological recounting of events helps him to experience them vicariously; he arrives at the same conclusions as the author and agrees with his recommendations.

Occasionally, when all data can be arranged by time sequence, the entire report is narration from beginning to end. This is most likely to be true in giving an account of a process or activity. The report might begin with a summary of the story, letting the reader see the purpose, extent, or direction of the narration. Then details would be related for understanding and interest as the story unfolds from one step to the next. Short sentences emphasize events and action, and the facts build up to a climax. In the end a summary would be used to bring together the main points or the conclusions drawn from the narrative.

Although description is used in literary writing almost entirely for entertaining the reader, explaining feelings and emotions, and describing places and objects, in factual writing it is used chiefly in setting forth and explaining phenomena observed, and only secondarily for entertainment—when it is used for enlivening material. In the *Richmond Times-Dispatch* and *The Richmond News Leader* research report on "Households Reached by Radio and Television," description is used in explaining the procedures used in the survey.

SURVEY DATA

Cumulative Sample. This is our twelfth consecutive semiannual survey of broadcast audiences in Richmond. In all twelve surveys, there have been an aggregate of 56,108 effective telephone calls. This is equal to more than one-half of all telephone homes in the metropolitan area.

Method. Coincidental telephone interviews by an independent survey agency. Trained operators were used under an experienced supervisor who personally verified about 5 percent of all completed calls.

Sample. Selected by systematic random sampling from the Richmond telephone directory.

Questions. Do you own a TV set? Is the set turned on? To what station? What program is on? Who is the sponsor? Is your radio on? To what station? What program is on?

Period. Calls were made from 8:00 A.M. to 10:00 P.M., Monday through Friday, during the week beginning January 8, 197–. Almost seven inches of snow fell between midnight and noon Wednesday, closing all schools in the area on Wednesday, and many of them on Thursday. Thursday and Friday were very cold, with temperatures ranging from three degrees to the upper 20's. The President delivered his State of the Union message at 12:30 P.M. on Thursday.

Sample Size. A total of 4,852 effective calls were made, which is equal to about one out of every 20 telephone homes in the metropolitan area. Approximately nine out of every ten homes in the area now have a telephone.

Sample Tolerances. The extent to which our two-hour audience percentages might vary from those that would have been reported in a completed census of all telephone homes in Richmond is indicated in the following table:

Reported Size of Audience	Sampling Range + or –
1%	0.8%
5	1.8
10	2.5
20	3.3
30	3.8
40	4.1
50	4.2

The mathematical chances are 95 in 100 that all such percentages shown herein would not differ by more than the specified range from the true average if the latter were ascertained by a full census of all telephone homes.

Here specific details have been selected and arranged so that the reader visualizes the procedures and develops a sense of the importance of the data thus determined. Two principles in using description were thus applied:

1. Leading the reader from the known to the unknown.
2. Giving the reader a sense of the importance of the material described.

Other principles of description, more applicable in describing a piece of equipment, device, property, or data than a procedure, are

1. Letting the reader see the whole, then the related parts, then the whole again.

2. Anticipating the reader's questions and answering them.

3. Making comparisons.

4. Using illustrative material such as examples, diagrams, and photographs.

In describing a piece of equipment in a report recommending its purchase, the first principle just listed would be applied by creating a general impression of the machine. It would be named, its use or general purpose stated, the general appearance described, and perhaps its main working principle explained. This would give the reader a concept of the machine as a whole. Then what the reader wants or needs to know about the machine would be answered in specific detail (second principle). The machine's outward, then inner, appearance and mechanism could be explained and its various parts described. The machine could be compared with other similar machines (third principle) and illustrative material used to picture in detail the machine's parts or function (fourth principle). The writer's feelings and emotions would be left out, for he is using objective description to set forth his facts even though he has enlivened them by applying some descriptive techniques.

Logic

Motivating the reader to action requires logic in handling evidence, proof, and supporting statements. A clearly written report indicates sound reasoning and reliable data, for the writer had to reason through his material to present it logically.

Every statement taken from some other writer and all data gathered must be questioned by the report writer. He must evaluate the authority of the person and seek to answer questions such as

1. How well is the authority known?
2. Is he unbiased? Reliable? Honest?
3. What were his sources of information?
4. What has been his experience and knowledge?
5. Do others agree or disagree?

He likewise questions the authority of statements and facts which he obtains, seeking answers to questions such as

1. Are they accurate and reliable?
2. Are they up-to-date?
3. Are they pertinent and essential?
4. Are they representative? Typical cases?
5. Is information the result of observation? Experience? Investigation?
6. Are data sufficient for conclusions?

The report writer avoids hasty generalizations in his own thinking by making sure he has sufficient data for drawing valid conclusions. When using inductive reasoning, he studies an adequate number of specific cases as evidence and picks out the general trend or conclusion to which they point. When working from an assumption, he discovers adequate supporting facts and instances to prove it a workable one. When reasoning deductively, he makes sure the major premise is an inclusive statement and that the middle term, if in a syllogism, is in the minor premise, a specific application of the general premise.

Many fallacies of reasoning occur not only from lack of sufficient data but also from lack of adequate definition of the question, failure to understand the situation, and consideration of something as a cause which is really an effect of another cause. The way to avoid such fallacies is to think logically and critically. By so thinking we pass judgment, draw an inference, reach a conclusion, or form an opinion by thinking over and through the matter. We reason and we evaluate. We also weigh all evidence, see pros and cons, study advantages and disadvantages, make comparisons, and test conclusions.

Because the reader of a report will also question the authority of the author and his facts, statements, ideas, and conclusions, the writer should let the reader know the authority of his material and his procedures in conducting an investigation. He should present his material logically so the reader can reason along with the writer and arrive at the same conclusion. Thus the writer presents not only evidence but also his reasoning and supporting facts when appropriate. He helps the reader avoid hasty generalization by giving sufficient data, by judiciously using accurate, reliable evidence, and by generalizing only after typical, representative cases have been examined. There is no hasty jumping to conclusions when we have considered *all* the evidence, have seen the *whole* picture, and have examined the relationships of its parts.

General statements, which often confuse or antagonize, and ambiguity, which is relative to context and reader, can also be avoided. A word or statement is ambiguous in usage when the reader is confused in choosing between alternative meanings, any of which would seem to fit the context. The writer can prevent generalities and ambiguities by taking the following precautions:

1. Stating ideas definitely, not indefinitely.
2. Being exact, not vague.
3. Using words that are explicit as well as connotative.
4. Qualifying general statements.
5. Using illustration and example.

The writer should employ discretion when using quotations. The following are some helpful rules:

1. Avoid frequent and long quotations.
2. Paraphrase when appropriate.
3. Quote when the statement is particularly apt or well phrased.
4. Quote when the idea is not generally accepted or is original.
5. Quote when authority is needed and recognized.
6. Quote accurately and exactly.
7. Give credit in footnotes.

Quotations are useful as supporting statements and proof, but they call for judicious selection and application so the reader can distinguish between fact and opinion, ideas and interpretations.

Notice how the following memorandum report begins by stating the situation and ends by asking the reader his decision. The major portion of the report uses logic in presenting facts which point up a conclusion.

OFFICE MEMORANDUM   Date: January 8, 197–

To: Second Vice-President Clair

From: Superintendent Arthur C. Mandell

Subject: Policy 00 000 000—DB # 000 000
          John Doe

Please note the correspondence with the attached application and request by the insured and beneficiary for payment of the cash surrender value.

Attorney Phelan ruled on the question on June 29. When the letter from the beneficiary's attorney was received on July 5, the file was referred to Attorney MacArthur in Mr. Phelan's absence on vacation, and Mr. MacArthur has referred it to me saying, "This appears to be a completed surrender. However, before proceeding further we should ascertain how much money the Company has at stake in the controversy and whether it is worthwhile to defend."

The difference between the cash surrender payment and the death benefit payment is $207.50. Obviously, the amount involved would not warrant litigating. Furthermore, there is no special principle involved that would justify proceedings with litigation regardless of the cost. It has been said, and perhaps properly so, that this was a contractual surrender; that as there was a meeting of the minds, it is a completed transaction. However, it will be noted that the policy was lost and the insured could not comply with one condition of the contract; namely, surrender of the policy. In lieu thereof the Company accepted an affidavit and agreement signed jointly by the insured and beneficiary. Despite the fact that we "accepted" this agreement in lieu of the policy, we required that the beneficiary join in the request for the cash surrender value; and when we drew our check, we included both the insured and beneficiary which we normally would not do.

In the circumstances, it might be said that this was a noncontractual surrender. If we were to take that view, then in line with General Counsel Gammill's recent ruling, it would not be a complete transaction until our settlement check was placed in a United States mail depository, and then only provided the check had been so deposited before the death of the insured. In this case, the insured died on June 6 and the check was issued by the Company on June 7.

It would seem to me that having in mind all the factors involved, we should reverse our position and pay the death benefit amount in lieu of the cash value. Will you say if you agree?

Arthur C. Mandell

Superintendent

What do you think Mr. Clair should do in this case? Does he have a logical presentation of facts on which to base his decision?

Argumentation

One type of logical reasoning often used in report writing is argumentative exposition, because in almost every report factual and reasoned proof is presented. Argumentation is especially invaluable in recommendation reports.

Argumentation in reports is concerned with the presentation of facts and evidence to prove a point, conclusion, or recommendation. A neutral or antagonistic reader must be persuaded by argumentative proof to accept the action which the report recommends. The argument must be calm, reasoned, and businesslike. It should not be opinionated, biased, emotional, or unfair. Evidence presented must be weighed and evaluated; reasoning followed must lead to sound conclusions. In this manner the reader can be convinced of the validity of the proof and will accept the action suggested in the report.

When argumentation is dominant in the report, four steps taken in the argumentative process might be used as a basis for organizing the entire report:

1. Discussion of the problem.
2. Explanation of the main issues.
3. Submission of the proof.
4. Conclusions and recommendations.

The discussion of the problem should point to a need for a change or improvement, or should state a proposition or recommendation. The main issues are determined by their importance and use and often are a breakdown of the proposition into the factors calling for discussion and reasoning. Proof may be factual or reasoned. Factual proof consists of facts, opinions, figures, and conclusions. Reasoned proof is the result of the use of logic. Up-to-date, pertinent facts must be given. When opinions are cited, they should be those of authorities. Statistics, tables of figures, and the like present concrete evidence. All facts are used to reach conclusions. Reasoned proof consists of inductive and deductive thinking, an examination of causes and effects, comparisons and analogies, and treatment of both sides of the question, similarly leading to conclusions.

Accompanying factual and reasoned proof, persuasion attempts to influence action. Here the author indicates an open mind and fairness which appeal to the reader's intellect and emotions. Every consideration is given to winning over the reader. Anticipated objections should be presented and refuted. The entire report should marshal its data to convince the reader to accept the recommendation.

FOR DISCUSSION AND WRITING

1. Analyze each of the following situations.[6] Determine the nature of the problem or problems, and phrase them in either question or answer form. What action would you take? Why?

   a. A large dairy company was about to begin a conference on employee relations and public relations. The top executives from various departments were seated in a large private room of a downtown hotel. The door at the far end opened, and a secretary hurried over to the vice-president in charge of employee relations, seated at the head table.

   "Mr. Jameson wants to know if you could possibly okay this memorandum on vacations before the conference starts," she said breathlessly. "It must—you know—it really ought—to go out today."

   The vice-president frowned. Simultaneously, he put on his glasses and got out his ball-point pen—the one with the red ink.

   "Good Lord!" he said. "Does he have to write three pages on this?"

   He began to read—changing words, deleting, and making marginal comments as he went along. His frown deepened. At the head table, the chairman of the conference cleared his throat. He was about to introduce the president, who would make the keynote speech. The vice-president fretted and fumed. He had covered only a page and a half of the three typed pages. As the chairman stood up, the vice-president ripped off his glasses and glared at the frightened secretary.

   "Miss Smart, the rest will have to go the way it is," he snapped. "I don't have time to go over the whole thing now."

   As she dashed from the room, he turned to the vice-president in charge of advertising on his right and said, "Jameson has sat on that memo for three weeks. Now he expects me to approve it in

6 "Profits in Prose," *Harvard Business Review*, January–February 1961, pp. 105–107.

two minutes in a place like this! Isn't there some way we can teach these guys how to write?"

"I wish to God I knew the way," the other said solemnly.

A few weeks later the report the vice-president had partially revised was issued. Jameson had written it with plenty of abstract polysyllabics for dignity, passive verbs for avoiding responsibility, and long sentences for obscurity. The message was a simple one, but Jameson never used one word where he could use three. The vice-president had clarified what he had gone over; he had simplified the vocabulary and shortened the sentences. He had been in the process of making it clearer, easier, and quicker for the company's employees to read and understand.

b. The next episode took place in a very large department store. The executive vice-president in charge of advertising and public relations was staring at a blue-penciled type proof. Then he hoisted his expensive English shoes from his desk top and flung the proof down in their place.

"People can certainly raise hell with a piece of copy when they start changing words," he said, "especially when they haven't the dimmest idea of what they're doing."

He was scornful and angry. And he had reason. For five years he had repeatedly proved himself to management as a brilliantly creative advertising director—as one who could himself write copy that wooed the public like a love song. Now, at the beginning of a public relations campaign of great importance, the president and the general manager had suffered an attack of blue-pencilitis all over his copy. They had introduced unintentional word repetitions. They had substituted dull, plodding words for words that were crisp and fresh. They had recast the sentences into a monotonous pattern. Having no conception of style, pace, color, and warmth in a piece of writing, they had blunderingly sacrificed all these. And, as a result, the clarity as well as the enticement had vanished from the copy.

"All right," the executive vice-president said. "If that's what they want, that's what they'll get."

c. Again, in an advertising agency, the account executive was trying to explain to the publicity writer what had happened to the news release.

"But they've taken all the juice out of it," the publicity writer complained. "It's as dead as a boiled duck!"

The account executive lighted his pipe and thoughtfully rubbed his crew cut before answering. "You see, Bill," he said in his most pacifying tones, "the President thought it might be sort of a good human touch if we got in something about his interest in salmon fishing. You know people like to know that railroad presidents are. . . ."

"What the public wants to know is when they are going to fix that roadbed so it won't be like riding over cobblestones! They want to know when they can read their papers again without having them bounced out of their hands. They want to know when a woman who is six months pregnant can ride the line without having a miscarriage."

"But, Bill, you know how it is when J. B. wants to get a little human interest about himself into a story. Why. . . ."

"Look, Joe, I've worked on newspapers. I know what the public wants to know at a time like this. And I know how to tell it to 'em so maybe they'll be nice and patient for a while longer. And you don't do it by philosophizing about the white-water streams of Maine in a lot of phony, ten-dollar words. Salmon fishing—for God's sake!"

But the ten-dollar words and the fishing saga stayed in. They were relished by the President, his family, and a number of his good friends at the Hawks Hill Hunt Club.

2. Discuss several controversial subjects of current interest. Define what makes them controversial and current. Phrase the subjects in question form. Pick out the issues involved and the different points of view from which each should be examined. Your instructor may also ask that you outline and give a short talk on one of these subjects, or that several of you plan and present a panel discussion on the subject, or that you discuss your position with supporting data in a memorandum report—persuading the listener or reader to accept your conclusion.

3. The following excerpts from an article [7] by Mayor Lindsay of New York City bring to light several problems facing the United States. How would you state the major problem? What relationship to it do the other problems have? What should be the mayor's approach or attack?

I wish I could afford to speculate about the 1970s and the 1980s, taking the long view of national goals: decent medical care for every citizen, the end of poverty and drug abuse and pollution, a guaranteed chance for a higher education, and a guaranteed job. But, for a mayor, there is another, more immediate question. My city now faces an urgent fiscal crisis—and across the country, cities and suburbs that in the past have at least muddled through today wonder whether they can do even that. Not since the Depression have the goals of states and localities been so readily summed up in one word—survival.

And the immediate question of local survival will determine the ultimate outcome of our national hopes. By the year 2000, the United States will be an urban and suburban country of 300 million people. Nine out of ten Americans will live in metropolitan areas. The city is all that we can see. For better or for worse, our fate will be found in our own streets and neighborhoods. The cities are the future. If we lose them, we lose the chance to realize our best hopes.

4. Bring to class a business report and discuss its use of principles for understanding, its attention- and interest-getting devices, and its use of logic and argumentation.

5. Narrate a personal business experience. This could be used to bring

[7] John V. Lindsay, "National Goals: Survival Is the Issue," *Saturday Review*, Vol. LIV, No. 4 (January 23, 1971), p. 46.

out the need for planning and thinking before communicating, or to show some of the causes for misunderstanding in reporting, or to illustrate how persuasive techniques really work for you.

6. Describe one or several of the following processes:
   a. Note taking in a meeting.
   b. Proofreading a report.
   c. Dictating a memorandum.
   d. Bibliographical research.
   e. Planning a report.

7. Make a visit to a manufacturing company, or a broker's office, a bank, or an automobile repair shop. From your observation, report what you saw. Describe the climate and environment, the people, and the action taking place. Can you reach any conclusions from your observation? What? Why? Write up your observations in a memo to your instructor.

8. On beginning work as research director in the Blank and Blank Corporation, you discover that the clerical staff is very inconsistent in typing reports. Prepare a memorandum setting forth some principles and rules of mechanics for their guidance.

9. Your company has announced a suggestion plan whereby an employee will be rewarded for a suggestion that improves production processes or increases the general efficiency of the plant. The suggestion system was announced through notices on the bulletin boards, on slips in the pay envelopes, and over the loudspeaker system. There has been only one suggestion so far. It was a suggestion that a door be swung outward instead of inward, a change that resulted in only a minor increase in plant efficiency. The employee was rewarded with $25. The company is disappointed in the response received and has asked you as editor of the employee magazine to write a feature about the award to encourage suggestions. The company will pay a minimum of $25, and if savings of over $1,000 result, 5 percent of all savings.

10. The following ideas are for short written reports. You will need to assume a situation and supply the necessary details called for.
    a. Should the Young Men's Business Club function politically? How?
    b. Lay out a membership campaign for some organization such as YMCA, Jaycees, or American Association of University Professors.
    c. The owner-manager of a motel needs to promote his motel over the surrounding ones. What gimmicks, policies, services, and the like can he use?

11. In the following case, assume the role of John Gongaware. After reading and thinking about the situation, you will probably have difficulty in arriving at a specific problem. Perhaps there is not sufficient factual evidence given to come to a full understanding of the problem or to reach conclusions, consider alternative solutions, etc. Why isn't there? What evidences are there that indicate John Gongaware's lack of understanding and planning? What additional data, facts, and ideas are called for? How would you approach the situation? What methods would you use for gathering further data? Would these deficiencies show themselves when John sat down to write his report?

Would it be in order to write some general statements about the problem and its different aspects, plan further investigation, and submit all this as a proposal of your approach and plans?

The Hendericks and Smith, Inc. Case

"I'll tell you, I will just not put up with any more of it—and you can tell them so from me. I'm sick and tired of being subjected to a day-to-day administration from 1,000 miles away and I've just about had enough. . . ." Thus spoke Mr. James Hendericks, managing director of Extemco, Incorporated, the North Carolina subsidiary of Hendericks and Smith, Inc. of Wickliffe, Ohio, to John Gongaware, a young consultant who had been hired by the parent organization to study and report on the situation in the southern subsidiary.

Gongaware was, in fact, a Southerner who recently began a two-year study at a Michigan School of Business Administration. In the midst of his program he wanted to go home for a visit but had a lack of funds. He wondered if it were possible for him to earn the funds while making a visit and conceived the idea of offering his services as a consultant to a small heat-treating industry, where he had eight years of summer work experience. With this background and the comparatively small fee he was asking, and his northern-southern background, he believed that the home plant would jump at the opportunity of being able to have this chance for an impartial observer of their Southern subsidiary.

THE VISIT TO HENDERICKS AND SMITH

Gongaware stopped in at Hendericks and Smith for a day on his way south to obtain information about the parent company. He felt it important to understand as thoroughly as possible the problems of the parent company and its attitude toward its subsidiary, so that his report could be tailored to those who would receive and perhaps act on it.

Upon his arrival he found that Hendericks produced the same type of small-job, high-quality product as it had in the past. Though the heat-treating process itself was extremely hot and needed very little skill, the production techniques had to be very skilled, and supervisory people had to be knowledgeable because of the essential role their parts played in larger complex operations. The quality of production was measured down to the millimeter and the length of the heat-treating process to the second. The actual loading and unloading processes were just plain hot and dirty and could be handled by very unskilled labor.

Gongaware gained from the plant an impression of a well-organized and successful company which was confirmed by a tour around the offices. Since the company was situated in a part of suburban Cleveland that had experienced rapid growth, it had not been able to acquire surrounding land at a rate that allowed the physical expansion to match the growth in sales. As a result, there was a severe shortage of office space. Only the president had a private office. The remaining executives worked in groups in noisy and overcrowded rooms. However, despite these handicaps, there was a definite air of efficiency. The executives all seemed to have an ability to concentrate firmly on their own tasks while ignoring the lack of material comfort and quiet in their immediate environment.

CONVERSATION WITH HENDERICKS AND SMITH EXECUTIVES

After his day at the plant and with his knowledge of the company before that, Gongaware had dinner with the three top executives of the firm so he could become aware of what they considered to be their subsidiary's mission and future developments.

The three executives were the president, Harold Hendericks; the executive vice-president, Walter Hendericks; and the sales manager, Roy Cominski. They had scarcely finished ordering before Walter Hendericks said, "Well, I guess I'd better give you a little background information on our North Carolina company. It is at present only a small operation with nineteen employees, not including the three southern directors. They have at the moment two furnaces and four or five production machines and have attained a very reasonable rate of production. The location of the plant is of no importance. We would have expanded right here if we'd have had the land, and we consider the North Carolina plant just an expansion of our facilities here."

"Who's in charge of all operations there?" Gongaware asked.

Walter glanced at Ray Cominski and Harold Hendericks before answering. "That's just the problem. We are at the moment looking for a man to fill the role of general manager, and this has caused us one hell of a lot of trouble."

"What about the directors?" asked Gongaware. "Isn't one of them a managing director?"

"Yes, my son James Hendericks, who has lived with my ex-wife in North Carolina all his life, is the present managing director. He is 38 years old, very well educated, an excellent manager, respected in the community, and has been very successful in his past endeavors. But for some reason he just doesn't handle situations the way we want him to."

"Are all of your directors from the South?" asked Gongaware.

"Yes," Walter replied.

During the rest of the conversation John tried to remember just the items which pertained to Henderick's opinion of the subsidiary. They felt that the real trouble with James was he had become too interested in Extemco and seemed to be in danger of throttling its growth by trying to control every detail of its operations himself. Hendericks has a weekly report sent to them which gives full details of day-to-day production, details of all expenses, and information about sales. All the production workers are local hire and only one of the workers, Dick Stater, an assistant production manager, from the home plant, was transferred when the company started. After the first week, Dick had to come home because of personal problems at home. He was never replaced because the parent plant considered his transfer a temporary one, and he had done about everything he could anyway.

"Am I right in saying that the only Hendericks' personnel who have visited North Carolina to date are Mr. Harold Hendericks and yourself?"

"Yes, but you must remember that James spent close to a year here when we were in the development stages and the subsidiary has only been in operation a little over a year."

"Who is in charge of Extemco matters on this end?"

"Well, that depends on what the problem is. I guess all of us spend a moment or two with Extemco stuff that needs attention. Who actually does it at any one time depends on who can manage to take time off his home plant work. We're pretty thin on the grounds here, you know, and all of us are probably overworked."

It was apparent that the Northerners were very perplexed and John sympathized with them. During his past year in the North, and particularly the last couple months, he had come to undestand very well the northern belief that the average southern businessman was intensely conservative, rather inflexible, disinclined to take risks, and, in general, rather a pale shadow of his vigorous, flexible, dynamic northern counterpart.

GONGAWARE MEETS WITH MR. JAMES HENDERICKS

Extemco is situated in a small town right in the heart of Dixie and everything it stands for. It's located about an hour from John's home, and he planned on spending a couple of days at the plant and a few additional weeks at home vacationing and preparing his analysis of the problem.

As Gongaware slowly threaded his way through a herd of cows being driven along the road just outside Extemco by a straw-sucking farmhand, he reflected that the surroundings in which Hendericks had placed their southern subsidiary could hardly be more unlike their metropolitan Cleveland environment.

Gongaware's first encounter with James Hendericks was exactly the opposite of what he had expected. He wasn't anything like his father in appearance or personality.

There were no formal greetings to be had; James simply shook hands and started telling John what to write in his report to the home plant.

"I think you damn well ought to tell the people in Cleveland that they haven't the first idea how to run a company. They query my judgment of people; they do nothing but complain about our expenses while pouring out money themselves! They refuse to do anything that we recommend because they think they know better; and now, to crown everything, they insist on telling me from over 1,000 miles away whom I should hire to do my job."

"I just can't understand it," James continued. "Each week we send them off a sample of what we have made during the week and always it comes back with a few minor criticisms but nothing else. They just don't realize that we are all working for the same cause. They don't give us any advice. They will never tell us which dimensions of a part are the critical ones, and, above all, they won't send us duplicates of the gauges they use to measure the various parts. As a result we are quite unable to check accurately almost all the features which they criticize, and therefore we can do nothing except continue to send samples which raise the same criticisms."

"Another example is the oil we use to quench heat-treated parts. We still aren't using the right one, just because we can't get an analysis of the oil Hendericks is using. All they tell us is the make and type of oil they use and that's not much use because the oil company concerned doesn't make the stuff down here."

"Why don't you try to develop a new process; maybe they'll add a bonus to your salary."

"What do you mean—'add a bonus'? They don't pay me a damn thing. I took on this because I was Walter's son and that's why I'm doing it now. Family loyalty may seem a lousy reason to you for putting up with all this, but it's the only one. Even though Walter was never a real father to me, I always respected him and still do. Although he's done one thing which upset me a good deal, I reckon that a lot of their stupidity is not his fault."

The following morning John called into Extemco just before leaving. He told James Hendericks that his report would be mailed to the home plant within a week and he should be expecting to hear from them soon after. But as he drove home, John reflected grimly that his job was not going to be an easy one. "The position I have to assume in no-man's-land," he muttered to himself, "is not an easy one. I wonder just how much time I'm going to have for vacationing!"

12. Prepare a working plan on one of the following subjects for a long report. Your instructor may ask that you carry your plan out by submitting the finished report three to five weeks later.

    a. Creative problem-solving in engineering firms.

    b. Should _____ company adopt a profit-sharing plan for its executives?

    c. Improvement of the Personnel Department of _____ (or some other department).

    d. Management's responsibility to society.

    e. Use of increased leisure time.

    f. Professional development for management.

    g. Management training programs.

    h. Consumer attitudes toward department stores in _____ city.

    i. Selection of a plant site.

    j. The foreman's role in management.

    k. The best automobile for a leased fleet of cars for executive use.

    l. Reviving the downtown area of _____ city.

    m. The financial aspect of leasing data-processing equipment.

    n. Comparison of various kinds of loans and lending agencies in buying a home.

    o. Problems in dealing with the older worker.

    p. Problems in dealing with minority groups and the unskilled and semiskilled labor markets.

13. *Planning and communicating changes.* The engineering complex of

a large Midwestern manufacturing company consists of product engineering offices of the operating divisions of the company plus independent pure research facilities. After a two-year period of expansion where the various product offices had increased their staffs, a directive has been received from corporate headquarters to reduce personnel levels.

In addition to the general directive to reduce overall head count in each product office, a specific proposal has come from corporate headquarters recommending elimination of certain financial reporting which is done by the finance departments of the product offices. The proposal will reduce manpower requirements in each product office finance department. There will be additional savings in computer-processing costs. The proposal was forwarded to each product office finance department for comment.

Bill Mathewson, the manager of the finance department of product office A, had encountered similar situations in the past. From past experience he is aware that many times these proposals do not materialize. He decided to say nothing to his employees until more definite direction is forthcoming from corporate headquarters. He had relayed this decision to his supervisors.

In the meantime, employees in finance departments of some of the other product offices had been told of the proposal. Through telephone conversations transacting normal company business with employees of the various finance departments, the employees in product office A learned of the proposal and its implications of reduced manpower.

Speculation ran rampant within the department. Some of the older employees had seen reorganizations within the company before. They knew that a whole department could be done away with at the stroke of an executive pen. Some were nearing retirement age and they knew it would be tough scrambling to find other jobs within the company where they would not lose their retirement benefits. Young men in the department were worried because they knew if supervision adopted a seniority basis for reduction that the younger men would be laid off first.

One week passed. Representatives from corporate headquarters came to meet with the supervisor of the finance department. No official comment was made to employees of the department, but rumors spread that the manager of the finance department had approved of the proposal.

Mike Johns, one of the youngest men in the department, took a day off from work to interview with another firm for a position. He felt that if a reduction were coming he probably would be laid off and he had a better chance to negotiate for a job if he did so before news of a reduction leaked out into the community.

Al Ward, a section supervisor in the department, agreed in main with the philosophy of his manager that after investigation the proposal might not be initiated or it might be altered and modified to an extent that would have little effect on the work force. But he also realized that rumors were circulating in the department and that the men were uneasy. He wished he could say something to the men but was fearful of making the situation worse. If he confirmed the rumor and told his people that the proposal was aimed at reducing the work force but that he felt it would not be implemented, his people would distrust him and the company if in fact it were carried out. If he officially confirmed the rumor, and then the proposal did not materialize, it would cause needless worry and anguish.

Another week passed. All the supervisors from the finance department met behind closed doors all one morning. After lunch, the two section supervisors, Al Ward and Bob West, called their men together. They told their employees that a recommendation was in the offing that would change the manner in which the finance department did business. Reporting of certain costs would be discontinued. This meant that the estimating, budgeting, cost collection, and reporting functions concerned with costs would no longer be required; thus the need for several positions within the department would be eliminated. The section supervisors went on to state that it was not the company's plan to lay off people. However, some men would be asked to transfer to other departments within the product office, and some others might be placed with other divisions within the company. However, the supervisors could give the men no concrete direction as to who would be affected or when.

a. What was faulty in the thinking and planning?
b. Who should take the initiative in working something out at this late date?
c. What should be done now? Why?

Write the report offering your analysis and suggestions.

PRESENTING MESSAGES VISUALLY

IN THE CLASSROOM in which I hold most of my class sessions in communications, there is a flip chart mounted on an easel. Among other items on various newsprint pages are five leading definitions for communication, each on a separate sheet. These are used in discussing what communi-

"Communication does not refer to verbal, explicit, and internal transmissions of messages alone . . . . The concept of communication would include all those processes by which people influence one another. . . . All actions and events have communicative aspects . . . perception changes the information which an individual possesses and therefore influences him."

"The word communication will be used here in a special sense to include all the procedures by which one mind may affect another. . . written and oral speech, but also music, pictorial arts, the theatre, the ballet, and in fact all human behavior."

"In its broadest perspective, communication occurs whenever an individual assigns significance or meaning to an internal or external stimulus."

Flip chart sheets focus attention on the point being discussed.

cation is and, after selecting common elements in each, in arriving at a workable definition. As each definition is shown, students focus their attention on it. Seeing reenforces our oral discussion. Also in the room are an opaque projector used largely for showing and discussing weak and strong points in the students' written reports, memos, and so forth, and an overhead projector on which transparencies of illustrative material can be shown. These are simple means of presenting material visually.

Often much more audiovisual equipment may be found in numerous conference rooms in businesses and industry throughout the country. They are used in visual presentations by committees, departments, and various groups and also in training employees and developing management personnel.

This morning's mail brought from John Hancock Mutual Life Insurance Company a condensation from their annual report. This was a small "Year in Brief" statement sent to policyholders. Among other information and figures it contained a bar chart of "Benefits Paid." The

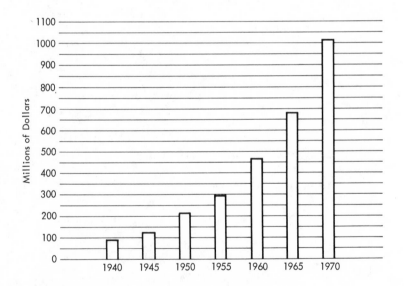

Charts emphasize a point and a trend in a report.

Courtesy John Hancock Mutual Life Insurance Company

chart supported the fact that policyholders were benefiting more than ever and thus created a favorable company image.

Essential to effective communication in business, visual aids convey meaning and specific information which can be readily understood and easily remembered. They emphasize important facts and figures, improve the physical attractiveness of a report, add attention and interest to material, and present supporting data helpful in making analyses and drawing conclusions.

Visual aids include all devices of graphic presentation of information: tables, charts, and graphs and pictorial illustrations such as photographs, maps, and diagrams. They may appear in written and published reports or be used in oral presentations. Sometimes they may require preparation by a draftsman or artist or special preparation for the visual equipment used in showing them. Often mere sketches, however, will be sufficient for communicating ideas, facts, and figures effectively, and many tables and charts can easily be prepared on a typewriter. It is not necessary to be a professional statistician or a skilled artist to use visual aids, but the communicator should have sufficient knowledge of the different types of visual aids to be able to select and use those which will convey his ideas and data and achieve his purpose. The treatment of visual aids in this chapter emphasizes their presentation rather than their construction. Communicating visually involves first an understanding of the idea and why it is difficult for another person to understand it. Second, it involves a knowledge of the media to be used in transmitting it, and then integrating it with other ideas and figures used in the presentation, making it an integral part of the whole.

SELECTING VISUAL AIDS

For a visual aid to lift important information out of the main text in a report and emphasize it so that the reader or listener will not overlook it, for a visual aid to be useful in analyzing data and in getting attention, for it to turn a fact or a figure into interesting information for the reader or listener—it must be carefully selected. The selection of appropriate visual aids depends on

1. The nature and purpose of the report.
2. The intended recipient of the report.
3. The way in which the aid is to be used.
4. The data to be presented.
5. The previous knowledge of the receiver.

The nature and purpose of the presentation are important in deciding which visual aids to use and must be considered in relation to the intended user of the report. Widely distributed reports, such as annual reports, and advertising and promotional material intended to boost the company or the product, for instance, should contain charts and tables which will gain the popular interest and understanding necessary for readership. However, a report used internally to convince management of the wisdom of taking positive action on a recommendation must assemble visual aids as proof that the action is necessary. This can be done in an oral or written report presentation.

Consideration must be given to the type of receiver—to what he wants in the report and to his ability to comprehend charts and tables. Top management may want logarithmic curves to show rates of change, or curves showing the relationship between two variables, and would be able to understand them. For nontechnical readers who would not comprehend ratios, however, the data must be reduced to their simplest terms. For such readers pictorial charts are more suitable. The viewer should be presented with a chart or table containing information that he can grasp quickly and accurately.

After deciding which types of visual aids will accomplish your purpose and which ones will interest the reader and aid him in understanding the message, decide *how* the visual aid is to be used. What special purpose will the visual aid accomplish? What information should it portray? Although visual aids get attention and add interest, their real function is to clarify the material and to support a conclusion. They must effectively display facts and figures. The questions "What significant point do we want the chart to explain?" and "Which chart will best explain this point for this purpose?" should be answered.

In this connection the nature of the data should also be considered. Specific types of charts show certain kinds of data to advantage; certain other data are better presented in tabular form. Are the data chronological in nature? What are their common characteristics? Can the data best be shown pictorially, as a part of the text, or in some other manner to accomplish the report's purpose? The answers to these questions will reveal the nature of the data and will help determine the type of visual aid to use.

Most visual aids are prepared before the accompanying text material is written, the text later being written around them. The opposite, however, can be done. Prepared before the text, visual aids help the author to understand the material with which he is working. Prepared afterwards, the ones which fit the text and purpose must be selected. In either case the writer gives primary consideration to the reader's requirements and to the conditions set by the report and its purpose.

A visual aid must be clear, interesting, and persuasive in communicating. It must clarify, illustrate, or emphasize a point or figure. It must be attention-getting and provide a change of pace. It must save time and be integrated into discussion. In selecting the proper aid, the writer or speaker must consider these requirements, for the purpose of any visual aid is to communicate. There is a wide variety of tables, charts, and other graphic forms from which to choose.

Tables and Their Functions

A table presents data systematically arranged in columns and rows. A series of related facts or a large number of items may be easily seen and followed when displayed in tabular form. Tables are a logical way of analyzing and summarizing numerical and other statistical data. They are invaluable in showing comparisons, trends, and quantities of data. They point up significant facts and make for easy assimilation and interpretation. According to the function performed, there are three major types of tables: general reference, special purpose, and text.

As its name indicates, a *general reference table* presents detailed information for reference purposes. The tabulated results of a questionnaire, for example, show the number and percentage of responses to each question in a columnar arrangement. Points of relationship and comparison of responses can be drawn.

For general reference purposes, tables might be placed in the appendix of a report, or added as a supplemental exhibit in a short report. The general reference table includes detailed data. Since it is not selective, the reader must draw conclusions from it or have significant details pointed out for him by the writer of the report.

The *special-purpose table,* on the other hand, is selective. The reporter may take specific, important points from the general reference table and put them in a special-purpose table for emphasis.

In presenting the responses from a questionnaire study dealing with employers' preferences in application letters, for example, the general reference table may be placed in the appendix, and it would contain *all* the responses to *all* the questions. Then special-purpose tables would be placed in the text, and they would show only the responses to questions dealing with content, form, style, and so forth. Table I emphasizes preferences for the content of application letters.

In Table I, note the usual parts of a formal table. Number and title caption identify it. Headings designate each column. Items are arranged in a logical sequence on the left, and percentages show the response to the right of each question listed. There are other details which are generally followed when using a table. In a long column of numbers, the zero preceding a decimal point may be omitted from all entries except the first and the last. Symbols such as plus and minus signs, dollar signs, and degree signs likewise can be omitted except in the first and last entries. Figures in a column should be aligned by the decimal point.

TABLE I   Employers' Content Preferences in Application Letters

Question	Percentages			
	Always	Frequently	Seldom	Never
1. Do you like the applicant to state in his letter his reasons for leaving a previous position?	81.58	14.92	1.75	1.75
2. Do you desire that the applicant relate his experience to the work of your company?	74.56	14.92	6.14	4.38
3. Do you desire that the applicant relate his education to the work in your company?	75.44	15.79	6.14	2.63
4. Do you want an applicant to include in his letter his average grades in school?	25.44	24.56	29.82	20.18
5. Do you want an applicant to include information on extracurricular activities?	44.25	30.09	18.58	7.08
6. Do you want an applicant to include information on his participation in community activities?	38.94	29.20	22.12	9.74
7. Do you want the applicant to include information on his family's background?	24.11	28.57	31.25	16.07
8. Are you favorably impressed if the applicant shows a knowledge of your company?	52.68	29.46	16.07	1.79
9. Do you want the applicant to state in his letter an expected salary?	33.63	33.63	16.81	15.93
10. Do you like the application to include a request for an interview?	59.09	27.27	10.00	3.64
11. Do you want an applicant to apply for a specific position with your company rather than for just a job?	52.63	34.21	7.90	5.26

Example of Special Purpose Table Used in a Report

The total column is logically on the right, but when it is going to be referred to frequently, it is better on the left. There should be fewer columns than there are items in the left-hand list or stub of the table. For reference, columns may be numbered from left to right on a line below the box head and above the first line of the field (the part of the table that lies to the right of the stub). Items in the stub may also be numbered. Arabic numbers are used. All units in a table should be described in terms of definitely recognized standards, such as feet, dollars, or percentages. Where applicable, variable quantities should be arranged in a scale, increasing from left to right and from top to bottom.

Not all general reference and special-purpose tables present numerical data. Verbal data may also be arranged in columns. Verbal tables are especially useful in organizing and summarizing, as shown in Table II.

The *text table,* or *spot table,* which displays a short single group of facts or figures, is handled like a paragraph inset. Since it is an informal

TABLE II   Verbal Tables Present Information to Save Time and Space
Chemical Prevention of Infectious Diseases

Against Air Borne	
Tuberculosis	—Sanitation in the home
	Cleaning chemicals
	Soaps, synthetic detergents
Against Water Borne	
Typhoid	—Chemical treatment of
Dysentery	water supplies
Schistosomiasis	—Chemical treatment of canals,
	lakes, streams to kill
	molluscan hosts
Against Insect Borne	
Yellow fever	—DDT, other pesticides
Malaria	Atabrine, primaquine, to
Typhus	break chain of mosquito-to-
Cholera	human host transmittal of
Amoebic dysentery	malaria
Dengue fever	
Encephalitis	
Filariasis	
Against Rodent Borne	
Plague	—Rat poisons
Typhus	
Rat bite fever	
Against Milk Borne	
Tuberculosis	—Chemical veterinary medicine
Undulant fever	Chemical disinfectants
	Cleaning solutions for
	milking machinery
Against Food Borne	
Dysentery	—Chemical sanitation in food
Typhoid	plants and eating places
	Chemical preservatives and
	refrigeration to prevent
	food spoilage

Courtesy The Chemical Facts Book, 1960–61 edition, p. 92.

tabulation, no number or title is given to the table. Emphasis is on the facts or figures it displays. The break in the paragraph focuses attention on it. Sometimes two or three significant figures are taken from a longer table and emphasized. The following table, for instance, was derived from the special-purpose table on page 122.

Employers emphatically want the applicant to state in his letter his reasons for leaving a previous position, and to relate his experience and education to the work of the company. Responses to the questions pertaining to contents were

The Harris Concept in Action

Table III

Three Basic Phases (

**Growth in Communications and
Information Handling Equipment Through the
Application of Advanced Technology**

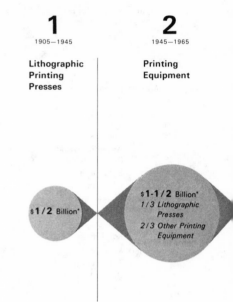

1	**2**
1905—1945	1945—1965
Lithographic Printing Presses	**Printing Equipment**

Harris is a conceptually guided, technologically based company which is accelerating its penetration of the fast-growing market for communications and information handling equipment.

As shown in the illustration, the company established an early technical leadership in the development of lithographic printing presses, then moved into the total printing equipment field on a worldwide basis. It is now working in a much larger, but inter-related market—one totaling $17 billion per year and growing at least 10% annually.

Harris is continuing to expand along conceptual, rather than conglomerate lines, with emphasis on technical leadership and new market penetration. Key guidelines for planning the company's growth are:

Developing and maintaining leadership in applicable areas of technology. This is the basis for retaining domestic strength and expanding overseas market position in printing equipment, for broadening base positions in electronic equipment, and for identifying and penetrating related new markets.

Building the organization and management strength needed to maintain profitable and consistent growth. Prime consideration is given to operating effectiveness, continuity of know-how and skill in the management of technological change.

Adhering to the company's basic business talents. These include engineering, manufacturing and marketing of complex, high-value, standard proprietary products made in comparatively small quantities.

Within the past five years, the company's sales and profits have more than doubled. Of this increase approximately 40% has come from acquisitions. The remainder has resulted from internal product development and market expansion, which are also expected to contribute at least 60% of future growth.

Annual research and engineering expenditures at Harris exceed $50 million. Approximately one-third of this amount is invested by the company to create new proprietary products. The balance represents work for government agencies and commercial customers. Ten percent of the company's 15,800 employees are graduate engineers or scientists. *(Continued)*

2

Courtesy Harris-Intertype Corporation, Annual Report, 1970

3
1965—

Communications and Information Handling Equipment

Printed Communications

$5 Billion*
1 / 3 Printing equipment
2 / 3 Office copiers, duplicators, etc.

Technological Interplay

—Electronic editing and typesetting
—Digital coding of data and graphics
—Equipment automation
—Transmission, processing, storage,
  retrieval and printout of
  digital information

Market Commonality

Advertising
News
Entertainment
Business
Government
Education

Electronic Communications

$12 Billion**
1 / 3 Broadcasting and
  Point to point
1 / 3 Computers and peripheral
  equipment
1 / 3 Aircraft, missile and space navigation
  aids and controls

* Present worldwide markets
** Domestic Markets only—excluding telephone and telegraph

3

	Always	Frequently
Reasons	81.58%	14.92%
Education	75.44	15.79
Experience	74.56	14.92

In this table the white space surrounding the figures displayed also spot-lights them.

Setting up tables for presentation of data is a challenge to the ingenuity of the reporter. Although there are a number of general principles and standards at his command, each set of data presents a different task, and not all tables are set up according to one standard form. Tables must be adapted to the material and purpose at hand.

Note the interesting chart arrangement on pages 124 and 125. Three phases of concept development are graphically represented in a unique way to gain attention and interest and to clarify the accompanying text material of the report.

Charts and Their Functions

A chart is the presentation of data in some visualized form other than tabular. The data are drawn, graphed, or mapped to show relationships at a glance. Charts simplify and clarify facts contained in a report. They reenforce the message, emphasize important points, and impress and interest the reader.

The types of charts used in a report depend on the nature of the data and what they are to depict. A chart contains less detail than a table and usually shows comparisons of only two or three points. Instead of following a tabular arrangement of data as in tables, charts use bars, columns, lines, curves, blocks, and pictorial symbols for visualization. Properly designed, charts tell a story by themselves. Although they should have explanatory notes in accompanying paragraphs to relate their points to the rest of the discussion in the text, they often attract attention and are looked at before the report is read. After the report has been read, they are valuable for a rapid review of important points. When used in conjunction with tables, charts pick up the significant figures for emphasis, and the accompanying tables present the complete numerical data for evidence or reference. The best results of charts are achieved when careful attention is given to their selection, construction, and use. Charts are constructed according to prescribed standards and used to present information that can be grasped quickly and easily.

Bar Charts. Probably the most popular and decorative charts are bar charts. Because they catch the reader's eye and are easily understood,

As communications needs have grown, the scope and sophistication of equipment to serve them have extended far beyond the printing press. Harris is growing and evolving with the market, as illustrated in the 25-year growth chart.

On a broader basis, Harris sees its opportunity in providing equipment to link the minds of men through communication. Annual expenditures in the U.S. for all communications currently total about $150 billion, of which 10% is for equipment. This is approaching one-fifth of gross national product, and is probably the fastest-growing major segment of the economy. Relying primarily on "knowledge" workers such as engineers, scientists and technicians, the communications industries will probably power the growth of the next generation, much as the heavy, mass-production industries provided this thrust in the first half of the century. No matter how far this shift in the total economy goes, nor whether the technology involves coherent optics, microcircuits, digital techniques or the chemistry of ink and paper, Harris plans to be a major participant.

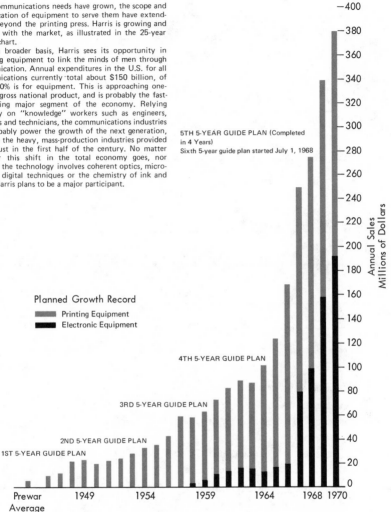

Courtesy Harris-Intertype Corporation

they are used a great deal in advertising and promotional reports—reports written for wide distribution or external use such as the company's annual report. Bars are effective for comparing different items of a specified date, comparing items in two or three respects, illustrating simple, complete facts, and showing the relative importance of items. The simple bar chart shown on page 128 used bars arranged in descending order to

COMPANY OWNED INVESTMENTS

CLASSIFICATION

55.73%	U.S. GOVT. — Direct and Agencies
12.20%	State and Municipal Bonds
11.54%	Corporate and Other Bonds
10.74%	Railroad Equipment
8.15%	Public Revenue Bonds
1.64%	Federal Reserve Bank and Common Stocks

MATURITIES

36.70%	Due within One Year
24.57%	Due One to Five Years
31.28%	Due Five to Ten Years
4.86%	Due Ten to Twenty Years
2.59%	Due over Twenty Years

Simple bar chart.

compare the kinds of investments made and the time periods required for the investments to mature.

Bars may be horizontal or vertical. The *horizontal bar chart* compares several items from the same period or under the same conditions. It measures magnitude horizontally from a vertical zero line at the left. Each bar represents a separate item to be compared for the same condition or time interval that applies to the other items. The *vertical bar chart,* sometimes called the *column* chart, is effective in showing values of a given item over a period of years. The height of the vertical bar or column indicates the percentage or numerical value of the quality measured. The period of time is indicated on the base or horizontal line. Bar charts are used to create a dramatic presentation for public readership.

Note how Harris-Intertype Corporation used a double-colored bar to present their planned growth record for camparison over a twenty-five-year period. The text of their annual report integrates the chart data by reference to it in the first paragraph. The two also make for an attractive, attention-getting page layout, as shown on page 127.

STOCKHOLDERS GROUPED BY NUMBER OF SHARES HELD

73%	24%	3%
1 to 100 Shares	101 to 1000 Shares	Over 1000 Shares

Horizontal bar chart.

A single bar representing 100 percent shows relationships of its parts to the whole and is called the *100 percent bar chart*. It may be horizontal or vertical.

To conserve space and add interest, symbols instead of captions may be used to identify the various bars on a chart. The symbol must be associated with the subject so that each bar may be readily identified. The use of a row of pictorial symbols instead of bars also creates interest and attracts attention. This is the *pictogram* and is used effectively for popular presentation of comparisons for publicity, advertising, and propaganda purposes. Stacks of coins, a dollar bill, geometric figures, and pictures of people, equipment, or machinery are all favorite pictorial symbols and add variety and interest to a chart. A third-dimensional effect can also be obtained.

Line and Curve Charts. By plotting items of data and connecting the points by a line or curve, a *line* or *curve chart* is formed. It is often called a *graph,* and the plotting is most easily done on graph paper. It is especially useful for depicting continuous processes over a time period. Generally more detail can be plotted by lines and curves than can be shown in bar charts. When the emphasis is on movement rather than amount, curves depict the data and their trend. The comparison of several series of items, an amount of change, a rate of change, fluctuations, trends, frequency distributions, time series, and ratios can all be shown by graphs. The charts on pages 130 and 131 show various uses of line and curve charts.

When it is desirable to show the rate of change rather than the amount of change, a *ratio chart* is used. Either logarithms of the values are plotted on an arithmetic scale, or the actual values are plotted on a logarithmic scale, which is the usual procedure because logarithmic paper can be used. The ratio chart should be presented only when the reader is likely to be familiar with it; it is therefore rarely used except for internal reports when it is requested. Because it deals with relative move-

Line graphs emphasize a continuous trend. Several curves on the same scale compare several variables.

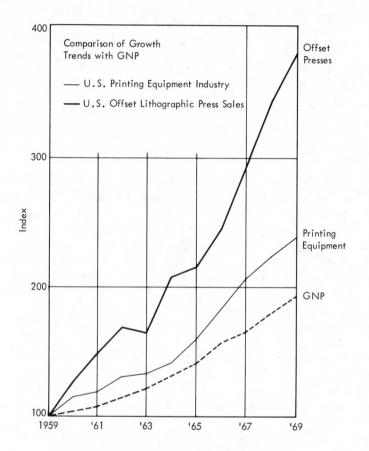

Printing equipment in the U.S. has a 10-year growth rate of 10% and offset presses 14%, both considerably faster than the 7% rate for GNP.

ments, it is helpful in analyzing the nature of changes taking place, making sound management decisions, and predicting future growth.

Pie Charts. A *pie chart* presents data in the form of a circle. The names *sector* and *circle chart* also apply. The pie is divided into segments, which make comparisons with each other and the whole. The sections are labeled and percentages given, or guide lines are used with the information placed outside each sector. Shading or coloring pieces of the pie makes it easier to read. By alternating light and dark, two colors can do the work of four.

Surface charts afford dimensional or pictorial effects with their shadings and attract attention.

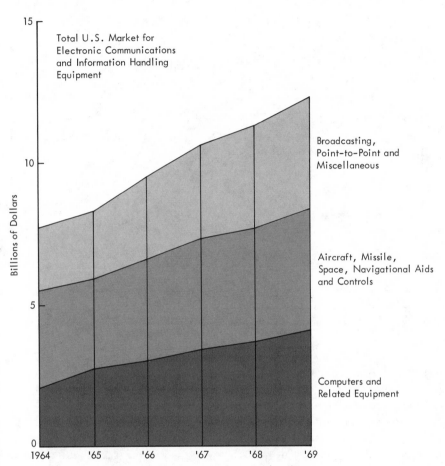

Total U.S. Market for
Electronic Communications
and Information Handling
Equipment

Broadcasting,
Point-to-Point and
Miscellaneous

Aircraft, Missile,
Space, Navigational Aids
and Controls

Computers and
Related Equipment

Billions of Dollars

1964   '65   '66   '67   '68   '69

Sales of electronic communications and information handling equipment in the U.S. have grown at approximately 11% per year for the past five years, with current sales over $12 billion annually.

Lines and curves create impressions quickly grasped.

Courtesy Harris-Intertype Corporation

When many segments are required, pie charts should be avoided or used sparingly. If there are no sharp differences, the pie can be deceptive

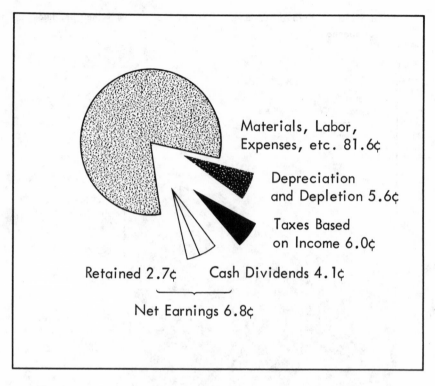

Materials, Labor, Expenses, etc. 81.6¢

Depreciation and Depletion 5.6¢

Taxes Based on Income 6.0¢

Retained 2.7¢   Cash Dividends 4.1¢

Net Earnings 6.8¢

Pie chart.

to the eye. It does not permit true comparison. Because it is so simple and clear, however, it is a good chart to use when the readers of the report are not acquainted with principles of graphing. It appears frequently in reports for the public. A favorite use of the pie chart in annual reports is to show the breakdown of the income dollar as demonstrated above. Often pictures of actual coins or other circular objects are used.

Organization and Flow Charts. Two special charts, not based on statistical information, which are used for reader clarity, interest, and emphasis, are organization and flow charts. An *organization chart* shows the flow of authority, responsibility, and information among positions in a business firm. Starting at the top and branching downward, divisions are indicated by a variety of shapes and shadings with the flow shown by connecting lines. Boxes or rectangles are commonly used and properly labeled. Thus the entire range of organization can be traced through departments to the lowest worker.

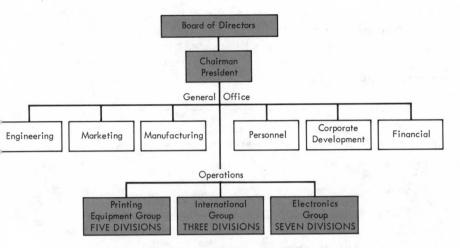

Courtesy Harris-Intertype Corporation, Organization Chart as of June 30, 1970.

Similar to the organization chart in appearance, the *flow chart* is used to show the flow of a product from its beginning to its completed form. The movement of materials, printed forms, and the like through an organizational structure can also be shown as a step-by-step process. These charts are commonly used in production, manufacturing processes, and sales.

Other Charts. The geographic location of commercial data may be shown on a *map* or *cartogram*. The present economic situation in the United States may be plotted by areas or states with shadings, colorings, or cross-hatching used to indicate the characteristics of each area. A key or legend is necessary for clear reading. States that voted for or against a law may be marked off. Details helpful in planning moves from one point to another may be shown. Guides and routes may be marked. Dots and pin points are used to present exact geographic distribution of data and to show density or concentration. Pictures and symbols may be added for human interest. The areas providing source materials for a manufacturing firm, the distribution of the stockholders, and the distributors of a product are frequently shown by maps in annual reports of companies.

Diagrams clarify the relationship of parts and are useful in planning. A floor plan, for example, could be diagrammed showing the proposed location of new elevators and approaches. Then plans could be discussed in the text material. Sometimes blueprints and other scaled drawings are used in a report.

Photographs provide exact knowledge of appearance and are vivid and interesting. Sometimes they are more confusing than enlightening because they show outward appearance only. Yet they are realistic and may serve as concrete evidence or proof. They are used when the reader needs to visualize something that the camera can accurately catch.

A small 3½- by 5½-inch booklet entitled "Are You Safe in the Office?" contained the following double-page spread in its center. Pub-

ALL THE MARKS OF A FIRST-CLASS FIGHT — FOR WHAT?

BRUISED SHINS, MASHED KNUCKLES, CUT AND SCRATCHED FINGERS *HURT.*
TORN CLOTHING COSTS MONEY TO REPLACE. SO —

1. Use handles when closing file or desk drawers or disappearing typewriter desks. Use handles or knobs when closing safe and vault doors.

5. Be sure your typewriter is securely fastened in place. You don't want it to "take off" and jump all over you sometime!

2. Keep file drawers, desk drawers, slides, and locker doors closed when not in use. Open only one file drawer at a time. If a heavy stack tips over on you, you'll be sorry!

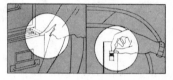

6. Adjust or clean power-driven office machines only when they are stopped. Use all machines only for the purpose intended, and in the way intended.

3. Keep razor blades, pins, pen points, jack knives, shears, hand awls, thumbtacks, spike files, and all other sharp objects in the proper place. Handle them carefully.

7. Wait till the blades stop revolving before moving or otherwise handling an electric fan. Place fans where no person can touch them accidentally.

4. If necessary to pin papers together, insert pin so that point is covered by at least one sheet of paper.

8. Brush up broken glass, wrap carefully and thoroughly in strong paper, and put in a safe place to be removed later. Do not put it in the wastebasket.

Courtesy American Insurance Association

lished by the Association of Casualty and Surety Companies, it uses pictorial illustrations to emphasize what to do in its promotion of safety— and very effectively, too!

PRESENTING VISUAL AIDS IN WRITTEN REPORTS

Proper selection of visual aids to use in a report is merely the first step in ensuring the report writer of their effective use. They must be appropriately presented in the report and related to the problem at hand.

Placement

Tables placed in the body of the report facilitate the reader's understanding of their analysis; placed in the appendix, they are available for reference when needed. Deciding where to put a table should depend on its purpose and use. If it is not essential to the text and adds nothing to it, then it should be in the appendix. Often a long table is placed in the appendix for reference, and information is taken from it and arranged in shorter tables placed in appropriate spots throughout the text. An example of this would be a large table showing the results of a questionnaire survey in the appendix; smaller tables dealing with responses to two or three related questions are taken from it and placed in the text where their significances are discussed.

A table in the text should be as close as possible to the discussion point with which it is used. When typing or printing do not allow enough space for the table on a page, the table should be omitted and the text that follows continued until the page is filled. The table can then be placed on the next page. It is advisable, of course, to continue the text on the next page until the end of a paragraph, unless the table will require a full page.

Large tables should be avoided. When they are necessary, they may be folded into the report to fit the regular page size used. They should be folded from the bottom up and from the outside in. This makes it easy for the reader to open and read them and also serves as a protective measure for the outer edges. Long tables may be continued from page to page. Each page should have the same table number, title, or caption and the word *continued,* in parentheses, should appear at the top of each page after the first one. All column heads should be set up the same as on page 1 of the table. Wide tables may be placed sideways across the page (broadside), with the caption at the left side of the page, which becomes the top of the table. Two facing pages may be used for still wider tables.

Charts are usually placed in the text of the report—rarely in the appendix—since their main function is to depict data in a way that will interest the reader and save him time. Only occasionally are they used as exhibits in the appendix for reference purposes, for they are nearly always a necessary part of the text. Because they are so closely related to the discussion, they should be placed at appropriate spots in it.

A chart is rarely larger than a full page, but when it is, it can be folded in so that it will not extend beyond the page size. Also, it is rarely smaller than one-fourth of a page. This size enables it to fit into the material to which it is related. Small charts drawn on graph paper may be cut and mounted on unlined bond paper and thus fitted in appropriately to the typewritten material. (Rubber cement is the best adhesive to use.) For full-page graphs, graph paper the same size as the report page may be used.

Numbering

Tables are numbered consecutively throughout the report. The exception to this would be a book-length report divided into chapters, in which case the tables could be numbered consecutively for each chapter. Either Roman or Arabic numerals may be used, and often a separate numbering system for tables and other types of visual aids. For example, if the tables are numbered I, II, etc., then 1, 2, etc., can be used for charts. More often, however, the distinction is made by using letters for numbering charts. Sometimes the terms *figure* or *illustration* are used instead of *chart*. Consistency should be followed throughout the report in the use of the term. The number designation of the chart is commonly placed on the same line as the title, and, unlike the number and title of a table, it usually appears either *below the chart,* or as a part of the body of the chart, spaced, for balance and appearance, in one of its corners. The number of the table is generally centered above the title, at the top of the table.

Captions

By typing the title caption of tables in capital letters and the subtitle in lowercase letters, a distinction is made between them. All captions should indicate what, where, and when. They should be specific and concise. The title caption and subtitle apply to the table as a whole and should be descriptive, yet exact. Each column heading, of course, applies only to the material in that particular column by naming the item and the unit in which it is expressed.

Each chart has a title, which is usually typed in lowercase letters and placed with the number below and within the margin limits set for the chart. It can be placed on the chart where it is used similarly to the headline caption in an advertisement. The idea is to attract attention to the chart as well as to let the reader know what the chart contains. Captions are also used to designate units, scales, curves, bars, and the like when appropriate. Only standard abbreviations should be used in captions and then only when space demands their use. Lettering not made on the typewriter should be in India ink. As little vertical lettering as possible should be used. A chart should read from left to right and from bottom up. The title caption sometimes includes the source of data, which may be briefly explained in a footnote placed immediately beneath the title caption.

Footnotes provide supplemental information to a table or chart by explaining or amplifying any one of the entries or headings and giving the source of the data. They are placed at the bottom of the table or chart and are designated by an asterisk or other symbol, which is also used with the item it explains or calls attention to. Footnotes are single spaced and may take up as much, but not more, line length than the width of the visual aid.

Spacing

Tables may be typed in either single or double spacing; whichever is used should be consistently followed. A crowded effect can be avoided by distributing the amount of white space within the body of the table and in setting up the columns. Triple spacing before and after the table will also help to give it an uncrowded appearance. Whenever space permits, there should be a blank line or space between the table number and title and between the title and subtitle or headnote. Also, a space should be used between the headnote and top rule of the table, above and below the first and last lines of the column heads, above the subheadings within the body of the table, above and below each horizontal rule, between the bottom rule of the table and the first line of the footnote, and between the footnotes if there are several.

Tables of only two columns should be set up without rules. Tables of more than two columns should be ruled both vertically and horizontally. A double rule is often used at the top and bottom of the table. A two- or three-column table should be indented from each side margin of the page. A table of more than three columns should take up the entire line length, from margin to margin, and is usually boxed in at the sides.

Plenty of white space should surround charts to set them off from the text material and to present an uncrowded effect. It is well to use wider margins for the charts than are used for the text. Of course, several spaces should be left before and after the chart. Usually charts are boxed in by a single-line border with the title caption and number placed below the bottom border but not extending beyond the side margins of the chart.

WRITING THE DISCUSSION TO ACCOMPANY THE VISUAL AID

Visual aids, which are not ends in themselves but simply means of clarifying data in the report, require explanation and interpretation. Implications of statistics must be discussed; generalizations based on figures should be given.

Tables, charts, and other types of aids should be introduced in the report. The introductory statement should precede the aid, calling attention to it or to some significant point it contains, as:

The results of the test in Table II . . .

or

The data in Table II indicate that . . .

or

A glance at Table II reveals . . .

or

Fifty percent of the readers, as indicated in Table II, ...

Where possible, the visual aid should follow its introduction. In any case, the table or chart should be as near as possible to the material with which it is used.

A complete explanation or analysis of each table should be given. It may include a description of the data and a discussion of the extent to which the figures establish facts and to which they relate to other data, with full explanations of technical terms and details. Attention should be called to maximum and minimum data and to averages, trends, and tendencies. The extremes should be pointed out, exceptions noted, and conditions explained. The discussion is organized by considering, in sequence, total figures, significant figures making up the total, and conclusions drawn.

Most of these points relevant to the analysis of a table also apply to analyzing charts. An important point to remember, however, is that a chart does not require the detailed interpretation a table does, because it presents less detail and is constructed to convey its complete message in itself. However, it should be related to the points mentioned in the text and to other charts and material, and this relationship should be discussed as a part of the text material in the report.

Neither charts nor tables are inserted haphazardly into the body of a report. They are put there for a purpose. To achieve that purpose fully they must add something to the discussion, thus becoming an integral part of the report.

PRESENTING VISUAL AIDS IN ORAL REPORTS

The same bases for determining visual aids to use in written reports apply to oral reports: the material to be communicated, the purpose and use of the aid in relation to the intended use of the report, and the knowledge and background of the audience. Visual aids are planned, prepared, and selected to aid the speaker in getting his message across to the audience. Functions are the same as in written reports—to clarify, to interest, or to support what is being said. Likewise, the speaker can decide to use any of the tables and charts previously discussed, and except for special equipment necessary in showing them, he can prepare them in the same way.

The speaker, and not the aid, should dominate the situation at all times. Each visual aid should be displayed at an appropriate time and made visible to all in the audience. The use of equipment in showing the aid gives an added dimension to selecting and using the visual aids in oral reports and presentations.

Equipment

The most common equipment used in presenting visuals in oral reports are the chalkboard, flip sheets, and felt board. They are the least expensive and easiest to use, for they require very little advance preparation time and effort. Everyone is familiar with the chalkboard. A list of topics, an outline, or pertinent figures and facts can be written on it prior to the oral presentation or as the speaker progresses in his talk. They guide the listener and viewer as the speaker develops his talk. When the speaker writes on the board ahead of time, he and the listeners will not be distracted during the talk, and he will not be turning his back to the audience as he writes. Board material may be covered at the beginning of the speech and uncovered as the speech develops, or the speaker may use a pointer to refer to each particular topic or bit of information on the board as he progresses through his presentation.

A flip chart consists of any number of pages of material fastened together at the top so that when the speaker finishes with a page he can flip it over to the next. It is a device for displaying graphs, charts, tables, and so forth to a group of people as the speaker progresses in his presentation. The size of the paper and lettering depends on the number of people in the audience and the distance from them to the chart. It may be placed on a floor or table easel, tripod, or stand and at a comfortable eye level for easy reading. Flip sheets accomplish a variety of purposes depending on the material they display:

1. To call attention to the title of the talk on the first sheet and to emphasize key words, phrases, or slogans throughout.

2. To show the parts of the whole (perhaps parts that go into a product, or component factors or parts of a problem, or steps in a process, or progression of main and subpoints of an outline).

3. To display charts, graphs, and tables of various kinds such as organizational and flow charts; graphs of company operations; bar or line charts showing sales, costs, and so forth over a period of time; and pie graphs showing comparisons or data displayed side by side for comparison.

4. To present ideas, concepts, and principles in a tangible form.

5. To emphasize organization of topics for the convenience of the audience, indicating transition and headings of new items to be discussed.

6. To keep both the audience and the speaker attentive by reminding them to get back to the topic at hand.

7. To make it easy to refer to a previous point by flipping the sheets back appropriately.

8. To summarize the main points covered in the talk and to point up the conclusion at the end.

Flip sheets have several advantages over other forms of visual presentation. They may be shown in a lightened room. The user can prepare the materials ahead of time, add information on the spot before the groups, or modify his presentation by skipping certain pages or by varying their sequence. He can also stand in front of the group as he manipulates his materials. Flip sheets very readily supplement and support the speaker's remarks. The many types of materials that can be shown and the great flexibility of flip sheets make them most useful for communicating orally and visually.

A felt or flannel board consists of a sizable piece of material fastened to a stiff backing and upon which bits of information on paper may be displayed at appropriate times by adhering to the felt or flannel cloth. The size of the cloth depends on the distance from the viewers where the board is used. Like the flip chart, it, too, may be placed on a floor or table easel, tripod, or stand at a comfortable eye level. It can also be hung on the wall or leaned against the blackboard (if used in the classroom). It has most of the advantages of the flip chart and chalkboard plus the fact that topics and outlines can be built up as the speaker progresses.

The two most often used projectors, overhead and opaque, project images on a screen. An overhead projector provides a bright image on a screen or wall, above and behind the speaker. Its chief advantage is that it can be used in a lighted room, and the speaker can stand in front of the room where he does not have to turn away from the audience. A transparency is made of the material to be projected, and because the speaker has access to it while it is being shown, he can point out details with a pencil or write on the transparency with a grease pencil as he talks. Adding material to the transparency while the audience watches adds to the interest of the presentation. Overlays of additional sheets of acetate with additional information may also be used. Parts of the transparencies can be covered and disclosed at appropriate times as the talk progresses.

Any materials such as charts, tables, graphs, photographs, and outlines can be placed on transparencies for projection. They are easily prepared and with little expense. In fact, the simplest way is to use hand-drawn illustrative material; basically, prepare the chart on a piece of paper, tape the transparency (acetate) into place, and trace the chart on it. Black India ink forms sharp clear lines for drawing and lettering. Grease or China marking pencils may be used. In fact, the grease-pencil marks may be wiped away and the transparency reused. Additional material may be added by his using the grease pencil or felt-tipped pen as the speaker talks. Another method of preparing overhead materials is to use a spirit duplicator in making the transparency. Run a sheet of frosted acetate through the duplicator; it will pick up the dye image that makes the spirit duplicator copy. After the spirit fluid has dried, the surface can be sprayed with a clear plastic that makes it transparent. There are other methods which require more expensive equipment such as the Thermo-Fax DeLuxe Transparency Maker, photographic methods, and various diazo processes. Mounting transparencies and overlays makes it possible to add information during projection and to preserve the transparency for later use.

The opaque projector projects images from material already prepared. It shows printed materials, books, small objects, specimens, pictures, and the like already existing and usable with proper selection and appropriateness to the subject being discussed. The major advantage is in its use of materials already available. No transparencies need be prepared. Typed materials and hand-drawn illustrations such as charts and the like can be projected and viewed as they are explained. The disadvantage is that the projector requires a darkened room and so the speaker loses eye contact with his audience and cannot move about. Attention is focused on the visual shown, however, and the opaque projector is very useful for training and instructional purposes, for instance, to show employees forms to be filled out, photographs of accidents in teaching safety, differences in procedures or processes, analysis and explanation to make a point clear, and financial statements and schedules.

Although materials can be handled as they are, they can be more easily used when placed on a backing of some sort. Mounting the illustration on a stiff piece of cardboard, a manila folder, or the like makes visuals easily handled, prevents their getting creased and dog-eared, and preserves them for further use.

Much more elaborate equipment such as TV and motion pictures are likewise more costly to prepare and use. They become completely audiovisual presentations and are outside the scope of this book. Likewise, the use of slides and filmstrips can be completely used as audiovisual presentations. They can, however, and often are used as part of a total oral presentation in which they supplement by adding clarification and interest to a point, and they provide a means of organizing material in appropriate sequence as it is being talked about. Slides are individual small transparencies mounted so as to be held rigidly in position in a slide projector which transmits the image to a screen. They may be in color or in black and white and can be made by hand. A filmstrip consists of a number of individual transparencies printed on a strip of 35-mm film. Once in the slide projector, the only attention needed is a flip of the wheel for one frame to advance to another. Either can be self-explanatory with title frames and captions on individual pictures. Usually a script is read aloud to accompany the pictures, or a tape recording may provide the information. The speaker may dwell as long as he wishes on a particular slide or frame, which enables him to pace his presentation to fit the audience. A live speech can thus be enhanced by illustrative material on slides. Although slides and filmstrips project similarly on a screen and can be used for similar materials, they differ in their construction.

To give slides as much emphasis as possible in supporting the oral presentation,

1. Do not include too much data on one slide.
2. Present data in small bits.
3. Use only detail necessary to convey the point.
4. Do not leave a slide projected on the screen after it has been discussed.

Contents of a still picture, whether slide or filmstrip, vary according to whether visuals are to carry the bulk of the message or merely illustrate information given orally.

Integrating Visuals in Oral Presentations

Visuals are used to accomplish a specific purpose in an oral presentation. They get attention, add interest and a change of pace, clarify a point by illustration and explanation, support or prove a point by providing concrete evidence, and emphasize what is being shown. To accomplish these functions they must be integrated with the spoken word so a smooth presentation and discussion ensue.

The visual is introduced and brought into the talk or discussion by transitional comments, such as

Note the two extremes as well as . . .

or

A comparison of . . . will show . . .

or

Eighty percent of the consumers, as indicated in . . .

Such comments focus attention on the chart or table being shown visually. Then an explanation or analysis can be given, or a discussion relating the data to other facts and ideas.

Should you be discussing the advantages of one procedure over another, you might list them on a flip chart, and then use a pointer as each one is brought up. Should you be projecting a picture depicting a before-and-after transformation, you might say something like

Let's look now at the conditions in the store before the counters were rearranged. . . . Here note. . . .

To emphasize advantages of a product, you might state the advantage in headline-caption form as is done in advertising and show the product in an action shot in which focus is made on the benefit to the listener (the consumer). This would be especially good for use in a sales presentation, for it would create attention and interest.

There is no doubt about it: Visuals add a focus and impact to oral presentations as well as written reports and can be made to carry the entire message when combined with audio aids. Good visualization includes

1. Proper choice of media.
2. Best use of media and equipment selected.
3. Conveyance of meanings, precisely, vividly, and interestingly.
4. Understood and remembered material.

To accomplish these ends, prior planning and preparation of visuals are necessary as well as a smooth presentation which integrates the visual and the discussion into a meaningful whole.

REFERENCES

For those readers who want to study further the whole area of visual presentation or for those who want further help in selecting, constructing, and using aids which require multimedia equipment, the following list of references is provided:

BROWN, JAMES W., and RICHARD B. LEWIS, eds., *AV Instructional Materials Manual,* 2nd ed. New York: McGraw-Hill Book Company, 1964.

————, RICHARD B. LEWIS, and FRED F. HARCLEROAD, *AV Instruction Materials and Methods,* 2nd ed. New York: McGraw-Hill Book Company, 1964.

————, and JAMES W. THORNTON, JR., eds., *New Media and College Teaching.* Washington, D.C.: DAVI, 1968.

DALE, EDGAR, *Audio-Visual Methods in Teaching,* rev. ed. New York: McGraw-Hill Book Company, 1969.

EASTMAN KODAK COMPANY, *Planning and Producing Visual Aids,* Pamphlet S-13. Rochester, N. Y.

JENSEN, A., *Low Cost Teacher Makes Overhead Transparencies.* Clemson, S.C.: Clemson University, 1969.

KINDER, JAMES S., *Audio-Visual Materials and Techniques,* 2nd ed. New York: American Book Company, 1959.

MARLAN, JOHN E., *Preparation of Inexpensive Audio-Visual Materials.* San Francisco: Chandler Publishing Company, 1963.

MURGIO, MATTHEW P., *Communications Graphics.* New York: Van Nostrand Reinhold Company, 1970.

TECHNIFAX CORPORATION, *A Guide to Overhead Projection.* Holyoke, Mass., 1969.

WILEY, BARRON J., *Communication for Modern Management*. Elmhurst, Ill.: The Business Press, 1966.

FOR DISCUSSION AND WRITING

1. Prepare the visual aids you would use for a talk on one of the principles of business writing, for instance, a pictorial aid that would explain the concept of the "you" viewpoint, or the five c's of letter writing, or different organizational patterns, or forms to follow.

2. Check the "Hints for Improving Your Dictation" or "Improving Your Telephoning Techniques" as presented in Leland Brown's *Communicating Facts and Ideas in Business*, 2nd ed. (Englewood Cliffs, N.J.: Prentice-Hall, Inc., 1970) or the sections on dictation in *Business Communications*, 3rd ed., by William Himstreet and Wayne Baty (Belmont, Calif.: Wadsworth Publishing Company, Inc., 1969) or some other references. Then assume that you want to prepare a short, concise pamphlet on the subject of dictating or telephoning for distribution to secretaries and middle management to get them to improve their techniques. Decide on visual aids to use and plan the copy and layout for the booklet.

3. Assume that you are scheduled to speak to the secretaries in your company to help them improve their telephoning techniques. Check a reference such as suggested in problem 2 and add your own ideas. Prepare both the outline for your talk and the visuals you would want to use. Would any visual equipment have to be selected also? Your instructor may have you present your talk. The same content and visuals could be prepared for a talk to middle management on improving their dictating techniques.

4. Analyze the visual aids in a corporation's annual report for their content and integration in the text of the report.

5. Select a particular product and prepare visuals and plans for a sales presentation before a group of salesmen to help them sell it.

6. Obtain a copy of a budget from an institution or organization. This could be a fraternity, club, small business, church, civic organization, or the like. Assume that you have to present it to either the executive committee or full membership for adoption. Prepare the visual aids you would use and select the equipment necessary for getting your message across.

7. In making a survey of holders of savings accounts, a bank asked the question "Why do you save?" and received these replies:

Vacation	4 percent
Investment	7 percent
Security	51 percent
Retirement	15 percent
Education of children	17 percent
Rainy day	27 percent
Buy things later	9 percent

Design the chart and write the accompanying discussion.

8. Prepare either a written or oral report on one of the following topics. Assume that your purpose is to help management improve their skills. Include prepared visuals and/or use the necessary equipment in your presentation.
   a. The steps in problem solving.
   b. One of the five functional areas of management.
   c. Clear business letter writing.
   d. Motivating employees.

9. During National Secretary Week, it is customary for various companies, schools, or organizations to recognize the work of secretaries and their roles in operating a business. This is often done by having a luncheon or dinner meeting with a speaker on some topic of professional interest, by holding a seminar, or some similar activity. Dr. Rose Marie Roche, Associate Professor of Business Communication at a southern university, has been asked to present an after-luncheon speech for Secretary Day. The meeting will be attended by secretaries and their bosses from business, educational, and government offices in Atlanta. It will be at a downtown hotel. She has decided to stress human relations in being a secretary, discussing such points as cooperation, consideration of others, capabilities in skills and knowledge required for the job, ability to cope with office happenings, and the like. Wanting to give the presentation a light touch and partially to be entertaining as well as informative, she has thought of the idea of ending with *smile*. No one likes to hear troubles, and it is easier to smile than to frown. Another play on words might be used, such as *work smarter, not harder*. Should she use a flannel board, flip chart, or flash cards for illustrating key words? What kinds of visuals could illustrate her points or concepts? Would you help her out by suggesting visuals and equipment and by preparing the outline for her talk and the visual aids to accompany it? Better yet, why not put all this in a memo report to her? Or even assume that you have been asked to give her presentation and do so before your class (as secretaries and bosses).

10. Write a short report convincing management to purchase new furniture for an employee lounge. Include visuals where appropriate.

11. To enable the university publications committee to determine whether or not they should sponsor the publication of a faculty-student directory, a group of students in the School of Business Administration made a survey to determine the need and the support for the publishing of a directory. The following questionnaire was prepared and passed out in small group interviews of 737 students and 101 faculty members, representing 14 percent of the student enrollment and 9 percent of the faculty at the University.

Student Directory Questionnaire

1. Would you find a student-faculty directory helpful or desirable?

2. In case such a directory were printed, would you pay $1.25____, $1.00____, $.75____, $.50____, $.35____, for a copy?

3. Which of the following groups should be included? (Check each group that you think *should be included*.)
____ all students of the university   ____ all faculty members
____ all medical school students   ____ all nonacademic personnel

4. Should the directory also include the following?
____ officers and members of boards and committees of the university
____ officers of social organizations, clubs, and the like
____ officers of fraternities and sororities
____ any others (List)

5. Which of the following personal data should be included about individuals?
____ college   ____ class or year or semester   ____ home address
____ local address   ____ local telephone number   ____ marital status
Other items _____

6. a. If the cost of the directory could be defrayed by selling advertising to be included in it, would you approve of such inclusion?
____ Yes ____ No
   b. Should the faculty (as well as students) receive free copies in that case? ____ Yes ____ No

7. Would *you* pledge your support to such a venture? ____

PERSONAL DATA:

Students: College ____ Class ____ Age ____ Sex ____ Marital Status____

Faculty: College ____ Age ____ Sex ____ Position or duty _____

All: Local or out-of-town resident _____

The following table shows the responses. Not every question, however, was answered by everyone interviewed.

Recapitulation Sheet of Answers to Questions

	Faculty		Student		Total	
	Yes	No	Yes	No	Yes	No
1.	95	6	694	43	789	49
2. $1.25	13		78		91	
$1.00	47		272		319	
$.75	13		78		91	
$.50	11		106		117	
$.35	7		151		158	
3. All students of university	100		708		808	
All medical students	70		427		497	
All faculty members	100		629		729	
All nonacademic personnel	49		209		258	
4. Officers of boards	59		461		520	
Officers of clubs	52		426		478	
Officers of fraternities	50		411		461	
Any other	5		5		10	
5. College	92		615		707	
Local address	93		664		757	
Class or year or semester	72		624		696	
Local telephone number	89		525		614	
Home address	68		498		566	
Marital status	34		220		254	
Other items	2		5		7	
6. a.	80	21	628	109	708	130
b.	73	20	593	130	666	150
7.	70	10	624	98	694	108

The corollary information from the bottom of the questionnaire provided a check on the representativeness of the sample.

Recapitulation Sheet of Corollary Information

Distribution by college		Student	Faculty
Arts and sciences		324	60
Commerce		231	24
Evening college		21	3
Engineering		65	9
Architecture		19	1
Law		42	2
Social work		8	0
Medical		17	1
Graduate		10	1
	Total	737	101

		Student	Faculty and Students	
Distribution by class			Sex	
Freshmen		154	Male	482
Sophomores		162	Female	356
Juniors		178	Total	838
Seniors		211		
Graduate		30		
Unclassified		2		
	Total	737		
Marital status			Residence	
Single		595	Local	202
Married		142	Out-of-town	636
	Total	737	Total	838

Estimates on costs of printing a faculty-student directory were obtained from two printing companies and the University Press.

Estimate on Number of Listings and Pages

4¼″ × 6″ (50 names to page)
    7,500 listings, take 150 pages
    8,500 listings, take 170 pages
6″ × 9″ (80 names to page)
    7,500 listings, take 94 pages
    8,500 listings, take 107 pages

Set up the tables and charts you would use in presenting the survey results to the university publications committee and write the report.

FACE-TO-FACE COMMUNICATION AND ORAL REPORTS

5

FACE-TO-FACE COMMUNICATION AND ORAL REPORTS are musts in business, industry, and government. Every day dozens of opportunities arise for the use of different kinds of oral communication (speeches, interviews, oral reports, discussions, conferences, group meetings, and mere conversation). Men and women in all echelons of administration speak with one person or with many, before groups of varying sizes, directly, simply, naturally, and forcefully. The meetingest, speechingest, conferringest people on earth are businessmen or educators. People face problems as they arise and make decisions at the point of action. In operating business on a day-to-day basis, as many situations requiring oral reports, meetings, and conferences arise as those calling for memorandums and other written informal reports.

This chapter seeks to help you improve your oral communication effectiveness—whether you are speaking informally face to face with one person or more formally with several people in a conference or group meeting or are presenting an oral report to a large audience in a formal speech situation. And the same written and spoken communication concepts, principles, and suggestions apply.

FACE-TO-FACE COMMUNICATION

Face-to-face communication, often referred to as oral communication, is the exchange of ideas, facts, opinions, and feelings between two or more people in a confronting personal situation. As in all communication, words, sounds, and visual symbols contribute through facial expressions, gestures, postures, and verbal language to the effectiveness of understanding and persuasion.

A face-to-face relationship takes place through direct interaction between the giver and receiver of information. This most often occurs in the interview process or within small groups and committees.

Interviews

Interviewing is an information-gathering process that involves at least two persons. Informally, we seek to elicit information in conversation and without a formal setting. Formally, we obtain data for research or reporting to solve problems or influence people. The interview focuses on some specific information for a definite purpose established by the giver or receiver. The interaction evolves around the goals, needs, and motives as perceived by the persons involved. The more formal the interview, the more structure it exhibits.

In preparing for an interview, we need to examine its purpose and function in relation to the situation in which it is used:

Purposes	Illustrative Examples
To disseminate (giving and receiving) information	News interviews, teacher-student interview, TV quiz shows
To solve problems and make decisions	Employment interviews, counseling, grievance, appraisal, parent-teacher interviews
To change belief and behavior	Evaluation interviews, sales interviews, disciplinary interviews
To research and find new data	Consumer surveys, market interviews, author-seeking information (about people, places, or things), opinion and attitude surveys, caseworker interviews

The personnel director, for instance, in an interview with a job applicant wants information that will help him make a decision whether or not to hire the applicant. He is interested in finding out whether or not the applicant can do the job and do it well. He is also interested in finding out the applicant's attitude toward work, the company, and people. At the same time, the applicant is seeking information that will help him to decide whether or not he wants the job. He is interested in finding out working conditions, what he will have to do, what is expected of him, and about promotion opportunities. He also is interested in the company's attitude toward employees and him.

Much of the substance from an interview varies widely according to the interaction that happens. Not all of it is necessarily factual information. Both participants respond in many ways; each one needs to observe the other's responses and relate them to his interpretation and understanding. Each person not only observes gestures, tension, emotions, and physical behavior but also asks questions and listens to what is being said. The art of asking questions is extremely important: The question must be relevant to the purpose of the interview and must relate to the other's frame of reference. It must also require a response.

Much has been written and said about the art of interviewing, but many of the functions of the process are outside the scope of this text.[1]

[1] Several suggested texts for further reading and study: Robert S. Goyer, W. Charles Redding, and John T. Rickey, *Interviewing Principles and Techniques*

It is a part of the larger area of interpersonal communication and human relations and is a subject in itself. Of primary importance in oral and written reports is the use of the interview in research and in finding new data for analysis and drawing of conclusions and for presentation in reports. This usage is discussed in Chapter 6.

Small Groups and Committee Meetings

A group is simply a meeting of more than two people. It can be a collection of persons ranging in number from three to twelve. (Beyond twelve, it ceases to be a small group, and in many communication situations it would become an audience or a crowd of people.) A group meeting is a combination of face-to-face, one-to-one communication and conference, presentation, and speech techniques.

It serves some of the same purposes as the interview, for it disseminates information, changes beliefs and behavior, instructs and educates, seeks solutions to problems and makes decisions, and is used as a research tool for finding new data. It likewise focuses on some particular topic or problem and meets for a specific purpose. Organized responsibilities rest in a chairman or leader, a secretary who takes notes for the record, and each individual participant. A group meeting has advantages over the interview: Several or many points of view are brought into interaction, the ideas and reasoning from several can be more fruitful than from one or two persons, and it is less time-consuming and takes less effort to communicate with several people simultaneously than separately.

Communication establishes common bonds among the members of a group and unifies it. The interaction likewise forms a behavioral claim on each individual in the relationship. As people interact, one expects certain responses in the interaction and depends on it for his own actions.[2] A common concern causes the group to view a problem, or a problem

---

(Dubuque, Iowa: William C. Brown Company, Publishers, 1964)—a paperback study of the interviewing process, including numerous suggestions and cases and covering informational, employment, and persuasive interviewing. John W. Keltner, *Interpersonal Speech-Communication: Elements and Structures* (Belmont, Calif.: Wadsworth Publishing Company, Inc., 1970)—part I deals with the elements necessary for interpersonal speech-communication; part II deals with some of the many structures in which these elements are operational, including interviewing, small groups, and public speaking. Stephen A. Richardson, Barbara S. Dohrenwend, and David Klein, *Interviewing: Its Form and Functions* (New York: Basic Books, Inc., 1965)—methods and principles of interviewing in behavioral-science investigations; emphasis is given to the interview as a research tool, the question and answer process, and the roles and relation of the interviewer and respondent.

2 John W. Keltner, *Interpersonal Speech-Communication: Elements and Structures* (Belmont, Calif.: Wadsworth Publishing Company, Inc., 1970), p. 291.

exists that evokes a common concern. Thus there is a joint focus of interest and attention.

In management, a group or committee may be assigned a specific task to be accomplished. Completing the job will involve decision-making, problem-solving, and leadership processes. As a task group, effectiveness depends upon the group's effort in accomplishing the task at hand. Once the task is accomplished, the group generally is dissolved—unless it has been organized to function on a continuing basis, for one task completed simply leads to another one to be done to work toward far-reaching goals.

Listening, giving orders and directions, stimulating and developing action, asking questions, guiding the process, evaluating, summarizing, and initiating ideas are all ways in which communication functons within the group. The exchange of opinions, ideas, and reasoning; the gathering of facts and data; thinking of conclusions and courses of action are all processes that involve communication, but more important they become helpful steps in solving problems and putting material together in reports. The task may be to gather data for decisions or for a problem solution; it may be to implement a decision or course of action already accepted. It is in the last two areas that groups and committees play a role in oral and written reports. The report presents their findings, the results of their collective thinking and organizing, or their recommendations and implementation for action.[3]

ORAL REPORTS

An oral report is given to two or more people. A highly flexible type of communication, it is used in every phase of business activity. Whenever data, experience, or perspective of subject matter is needed in a hurry, the oral report is an efficient way of presenting it. Problems constantly arise in business to which men say, "If we but knew the facts, we could reach a decision." The function of an oral report, or for that matter a written report, in such a situation is to furnish the facts to expedite action. Oral reports are requested and used at all levels of management, for they save reading time and invite immediate action. The foreman may

[3] For additional reading on small groups, the following three books are suggested: Warren G. Bennis, Edgar H. Schein, David E. Berlew, and Fred L. Steele, eds., *Interpersonal Dynamics: Essays and Readings on Human Interaction* (Homewood, Ill.: Dorsey Press, 1964)—the material covered has direct application to small groups. Ernest C. Bormann, *Discussion and Group Methods: Theory and Practice* (New York: Harper & Row, Publishers, 1969)—a good amount of behavioral-science theory integrated with group methods. Abraham Zaleznik and David Moment, *The Dynamics of Interpersonal Behavior* (New York: John Wiley & Sons, Inc., 1964)—group processes and interpersonal interaction; emphasis on work groups and analysis of problems in face-to-face group encounters.

request an oral report at a weekly meeting; the supervisor may have a foreman present a report at the meeting of the foremen. The reporter and the listeners are face to face for questioning, comments, or discussion. Additional information or explanation, when desired and available, can also be given immediately.

Oral reports may be informational or analytical like written reports. What has been said in this book about the preparation and presentation of written reports pertains to oral reports and good speaking as well. Oral reports require application of the same principles in their investigation, planning, and preparation stages. They present detailed, wanted information and should be complete, clear, interesting, and persuasive as the occasion requires. They also must embody the principles of good speaking, for an oral report reflects the speaker's personality even more than a written report.

Building Confidence

Being realistic about one's speaking abilities and seeking to improve them help overcome mental obstacles encountered in giving oral reports. Self-confidence in giving talks can be acquired by following logical steps:

1. Prepare your talk carefully. Fear of forgetting often results in stage fright.

2. Practice your speech aloud. You know your talk better after you rehearse it. Practice alone, going over your talk again and again, imagining your audience before you.

3. Do not memorize your talk; however, a tape recorder can be helpful in that it allows you to listen to yourself.

4. Check your appearance.

5. When you face your group, wait a few minutes before you start to talk. Think of the members of the group as your friends. They want you to do the job well. Do *not* think about yourself.

6. Begin slowly; do not give up once you have begun. Stage fright disappears after you start.

7. Speak louder than you do ordinarily, at least at the outset.

8. Speak as often as you can. The more practice you get, the easier it is to speak with confidence.

Being natural is one key to being poised and at ease, and asking questions such as the following will help you to understand yourself:

1. What is my outstanding trait—informality, humor, enthusiasm, seriousness, integrity?

2. Is my smile sincere or forced?

3. Do I tell stories well?

4. Are gestures natural to me?

The smaller the group, the more informal the speaker should be. Also, the better he knows the members in the group, the more informal he may be. At all times what the speaker says and does should be appropriate to the demands of the situation, occasion, and audience.

Oral Report Style

Most oral reports report, explain, or instruct and are not likely to entertain or persuade. This does not mean that the speaker should not use an anecdote or a touch of humor or an element of logical reasoning for conviction. It means he should be aware of the major function of the report and use these other elements when they serve an appropriate purpose.

Oral reports should be made easy for the listener to follow. This can be accomplished by

1. Making the purpose known to the listeners.
2. Indicating the structure of the talk (by listing on the blackboard, using a chart, or some other method).
3. Making it easy for listeners to ask questions.
4. Relating points by proper transitions and summaries.

Whenever a report is to be read aloud or presented orally to a group, it should be written in a style that lends itself to an oral presentation. It should be conversational, direct, personal, concrete, and varied. To be conversational is to be natural and casual. Sometimes incomplete sentences, loosely connected sentences, slang, contractions, and other devices help to achieve a conversational style.

Visualizing the audience and speaking directly to them not only helps to be conversational but also aids in directness and personalization. Commands, questions, explanations, and use of first- and second-person pronouns achieve directness. Referring to oneself and personal experiences of the speaker or members of the group make a talk or report personal. Variety is accomplished by a change of pace or tone, by change of sentence lengths and types of sentences. Concreteness is obtained through using facts and words familiar to the listeners and by going from the general or familiar to the specific or unfamiliar.

Presenting Reports Orally

Oral reports are given to directors, managers, committees, conference participants, and other individuals and groups. Often the written report is the basis for the oral presentation. In such instance the report may be read or an oral summary given. In reading a report, complete accuracy is obtained. The reader should avoid a monotone voice and even reading the entire report. Parts, sentences, and phrases can be underlined for reading with emphasis. Reading should be done with spirit, feeling, and understanding. It should be read slowly to be understood; yet some of the less important points can be read faster than others.

When presenting a summary of a written report, an abstract should be carefully prepared. It should cover essential points and substantiate facts, be concise, have carefully selected details, and be effectively delivered. Note cards listing key points will aid the speaker.

When a written report is not read and an oral report is called for, a detailed outline or notes on cards are an asset to the speaker. He uses visual aids and maintains eye contact with the audience and freedom of movement. His delivery is much the same as the delivery of any speech.

Representative of the kinds of oral reports are committee reports, convention reports, and research reports. For carrying out the action of any committee, there are always oral reports of the minutes given by the secretary, reports of the chairmen of committees and of the president, and special reports of members. In each of these, simple, loosely constructed, conversational sentences should be used; transitions and summaries should be smooth; material should be brief but comprehensive in conveying facts; reading should be natural and clear; and rules for effective speaking should always be observed.

Every professional organization has meetings, conventions, or conferences. Participants make reports as called for, and after the convention they report to their local association or their company. It is important to select pertinent information of interest and use to listeners, to give an overall picture of the meetings, to state their purpose, and to summarize what was accomplished.

Research reports present results of a survey, investigation, or professional study. They are likewise factual and may be given to a committee, convention, conference, or before some other group. Here it is necessary to know the audience, choose main issues, interpret factual data, develop one idea at a time for easy comprehension, present new material and a new point of view, and draw conclusions which can be substantiated.

The principles of good oral communication are applicable in any oral reporting situation:

1. Having one's material firmly in hand.
2. Delivering the material to fit the needs and interest of the audience.
3. Matching one's delivery to his personality.
4. Using whatever aids are necessary to accomplish the purpose.

Briefings

A specialized type of oral reporting has come into increased importance in management's decision-making. A briefing is a capsule of information presented by an authority or well-informed person, telling a highly selective or captive audience just what they need to know. It has a well-defined purpose which is readily known by the listeners who share a common interest and goal. The report deals with a particular topic, is fast-paced, and is generally informative rather than persuasive.

The speaker focuses on facts, data, and ideas. Immediate attention is present because of the audience's interest and need to have the information. For this reason the beginning is direct and to the point. There is no time or need to relate a joke, display emotion, or use some other attention-getting technique. The reporter has carefully prepared his presentation; he has done his homework well and advances in a logical sequence which will move his listeners to a decision. As in any report, much of the effectiveness depends on the planning, analysis, and development of the message. A briefing's success is also dependent on the speaker's delivery, and he applies the principles of speech and oral reporting.

SPEECH PRINCIPLES

Principles of effective speaking deal with preparation and content, visual aids, and presentation and delivery.

Preparation

Every speaker must have something to say and know his subject. To meet this requisite, he must work through the stages of speech preparation. Preliminary planning will involve analyzing the speech situation and audience. After such analysis he can decide on his purpose, central idea, limitations, and scope. He can then draft a preliminary sketch or general outline of what he intends to say and start gathering the necessary factual material.

After analyzing the audience, the speaker can select facts and illustrative material that will be interesting, clear, and logical. He will know when to clarify, analyze, introduce new ideas, answer anticipated questions, or explain a process. The experience of the audience will determine what examples and other illustrative material are within their realm. The speaker can select points from the audience's point of view and interest. He can provide adequate factual evidence to substantiate his statements. He will be able to give the audience material that will satisfy their needs and interests. The content of his speech will be meaningful and important, accomplish the intended purpose, and have the desired effect on the listeners.

Other stages of speech preparation include gathering material and creating ideas; thinking through the material to reach conclusions, and when applicable, making recommendations; outlining the speech; making visual aids; and planning the delivery.

Like written reports, speeches have an introduction, body, and ending. The introduction aims to arouse interest, stimulate curiosity, or impress the audience with the importance of the subject. It should also make the group aware of their relationship to the subject. There are six common ways of beginning a speech:

1. Refer to the person who has introduced the speaker, who has invited him to be present, or who has sponsored the meeting. This is a personal reference and it may involve an element of mild, tactful humor—depending on the occasion.

2. Refer to the occasion, purpose of the gathering, or subject of the speech. This should be spontaneous, and it plunges directly into the speech.

3. Paint a vivid, imaginary picture or tell a striking story. This is especially good when the speaker has a keen sense of the dramatic, and the introduction to a speech lends itself to more dramatic subject matter and presentation than the introduction to a written report.

4. State a philosophical truth whenever it is in line with the subject. This is good when a note of seriousness is desired at the outset.

5. Tell a humorous incident or anecdote. It should be appropriate for the group and occasion and have a natural connection with the subject.

6. Use a startling fact or paradoxical statement to evoke curiosity.

Furthermore, an introduction should orient the audience to the subject or problem by clearly stating or implying the purpose, by defining unfamiliar or vague terms, and by setting the limitations and scope.

In the body, the speaker develops the central idea brought out in the beginning of the speech. The speech may be divided into parts and each part explained. The principles of unity, coherence, and emphasis and the principles of interesting and persuasive communication should be applied. The subject matter presented should be appropriate, interesting, and significant. The speaker's analysis and interpretation should be thorough, accurate, and logical. Materials that illustrate and amplify the subject and main points should be adequate, varied, sufficiently detailed, and specific. They should be selected for their adaptation to the audience's interests, attitudes, and knowledge. The speaker should avoid quoting unless the quotation is related, clarifies, interests the audience, or supports a statement. The speaker is obligated to provide transition, summaries, and divisions. There must be a clear progression of ideas; main divisions should be evident and related, and subdivisions should develop the central idea.

The ending of a speech should be carefully timed and the audience made aware of it. Several ways of ending a speech are

1. Give an appropriate summary.
2. Enumerate the main points.
3. Climax the talk with an illustrative story, case study, or specific application.
4. Appeal to the audience to adopt an attitude, particularly if the general purpose is to persuade.
5. Emphasize the importance of the subject.
6. Express the wish for future action. If the aim has been to persuade, urge the audience to take a particular course of action.
7. Come to a logical conclusion from the data presented and state it.
8. Recommend action or give suggestions for the audience to follow.

The ending of a speech must give a summary of main ideas and include effective closing appeals and suggestions.

Visual Aids

Visual aids are planned, prepared, and selected to aid the speaker in getting his message across to the audience. Their function is the same as in written reports—to clarify, to interest, or to support what is being said. Each visual aid should be displayed at an appropriate time and made easily visible to all in the audience.

The following are some visual aids that are commonly used.

Blackboard. List topics, outline main points, or write pertinent figures and facts on the blackboard. They will guide the listener as the speaker develops his speech. Sometimes board material might be covered at the beginning of the speech and uncovered as the speech develops.

Pictures, posters, charts. Use illustrative pictures, posters, and charts, carefully prepared ahead of time. Pictures and posters chiefly add interest. Charts clarify and support statements.

Drawings on large sheets and flip charts. Use flip charts for outlining main points or for showing a series of charts, graphs, and diagrams. They get attention and interest quickly, especially when used to build a point or to symbolically represent facts and ideas.

Slides, movies. Use projectors for showing slides, movies, and the like. The speaker should have someone handle the mechanics of operating the projector and thus free him for his comments, speech, or whatever he is developing. The speaker should view the slides or movies ahead of time so he can concentrate on their relation to what he is saying rather than their content.

Handouts. Distribute handouts so the audience will have something to see now and to refer to later. They show figures, statistics, and other data which would be difficult to comprehend and remember.

Visual aids should be selected and prepared with the audience in mind. They must be adapted to suit the needs and interests of the audience as well as the purpose of the speaker and his message. They should be simple and few in number.

Presentation

The speaker should have a clear conception of the attitudes, sympathies, and interests of his audience to help him maintain a good relationship with his audience, for listeners react to the personality and attitude of the speaker. Subjective qualities, such as the speaker's kindness, honesty, understanding, and character, make favorable or unfavorable impressions on them.

A speaker with a good attitude toward the audience will respect them as individuals, understanding their points of view, meet them on common ground, speak on points of mutual interest, and inform them of important topics. He should never let his attitude reflect boredom or sarcasm. A list of beatitudes for the speaker to follow are

1. Be unaffected and unassuming.
2. Be confident, businesslike, and sincere.
3. Be optimistic, pleasant, and cheerful.
4. Be natural in posture and gestures.
5. Be poised and at ease.
6. Be enthusiastic and interested.

Oral delivery is important for the speaker. His words are selected to convey his facts and ideas; they are selected for their exactness and preciseness and are adapted for the level of the audience. Familiar and descriptive words help the audience to understand and visualize. The speaker should avoid words that evoke controversy or arouse negative reaction.

Pronunciation and enunciation should be accurate and should meet accepted standards. Whenever several pronunciations are acceptable, the one most familiar to the audience should be used. One must open his mouth to speak clearly and distinctly, for lips, tongue, soft palate, and vocal cords adjust for every sound uttered. Energy expended to operate these organs and supply air produces sound. Syllables should be pronounced clearly. Hitting consonants hard makes them come out distinctly, but slurring makes them indistinguishable. Careless enunciation is either the result of laziness in using the mouth, lips, and tongue or the result of physical incapacity, such as cleft palate, missing teeth, and lack of proper dental attention. The speaker should talk loudly enough to overcome noise around him; he should be sensitive to the sounds that might be distracting and speak louder when necessary.

Relaxing and using the voice properly also aid effective delivery of a speech. A pleasant tone and adequate volume are necessary. Volume is adequate when the audience, whether on the first or last row, can hear what is being said. Talking too loudly is just as bad as not talking loud enough, for the audience may feel they are being shouted at and lose interest. There should be variation in volume. This can be achieved by raising and lowering the voice. Variation, however, should be spontaneous and natural; otherwise it becomes mechanical and loses its naturalness. A high-pitched voice creates tension and emotional strain for both speaker and audience. Using the middle range and letting the voice rise and fall at appropriate times avoids tension, creates naturalness, and achieves emphasis and interest. Speaking from the chest rather than the throat gives resonance. A natural, conversational tone of voice is always warm and convincing. It secures the audience's favorable reaction.

One should speak with vitality, not too rapidly and not too slowly, and should also vary the pace. An awareness of the interests of the audience and of the importance of what is being said enables one to change rate appropriately. A change alerts the listener; a slowing down indicates important points, speeding up less important. Speaking about 150 words per minute is an easy and pleasant rate for most listeners to follow.

Slovenly posture reflects careless physical and mental habits. Standing erect, looking alert, smiling occasionally, and walking energetically to the platform indicate orderliness, ease, confidence, and sincerity. Movement of head, face, hands, or any part of the body while speaking is a gesture. Natural and spontaneous movement is good, for it reflects the friendliness of the speaker. Gestures used for emphasis add rather than distract from what is being said. Erect posture commands attention. Leaning, lounging, or slumping detracts from forcefulness and the speaker's enthusiasm.

Looking at individuals in the audience forces the speaker to be aware he is talking to people. He should pick out different areas in a room and face in those directions from time to time. This will help him to be heard in the back of the room as well as to include everyone in eye contact. The speaker thus becomes warm and personal. He will react to the facial expressions of individuals in the audience and his efforts will become more effective and his satisfaction greater.

A prepared speech can be delivered three ways: It can be read, it can be memorized and recited, or it can be given extemporaneously with or without outline and notes. The third method is the best, for it is fresh and vigorous. Notes are best if briefly written on cards and used unobtrusively. It is good practice when using notes to also write out the opening and ending to the speech.

No attempt has been made to cover all the principles of effective speaking in this chapter; however, the suggestions offered should make one aware of what should be done and lead to some self-improvement. Speech courses and speech books cover the material more thoroughly and should be used. Most speech texts include a number of rating scales and lists for self-improvement. The one that follows is from Wesley Wiksell's *Do They Understand You?*

What Is Your Speaker Profile *

	Yes	Not Sure	No
1. Do you have a positive attitude toward your talk?			
2. Do you know why you are giving the talk?			
3. Do you generally study who will be in the group?			
4. Do you check all the physical arrangements carefully?			
5. Do you carefully weigh the amount of material you are going to present, considering the amount of time you have for the presentation?			
6. Do you prepare your talk carefully?			
7. Do you prepare visual aids carefully?			
8. Do you practice your talk aloud?			
9. Do you begin your speeches slowly and confidently?			
10. Do you speak louder at the outset of your talk?			
11. Do you consider your language so it can be understood by the listener?			
12. Do you emphasize the main points so the listener can get them easily?			
13. Do you feel fairly comfortable when you talk?			
14. Do you talk too long?			
15. Do groups seem to accept your ideas?			
16. Do you use any device to evaluate the effectiveness of your talk?			

* Wesley Wiksell, *Do They Understand You?* (New York: The Macmillan Company, 1960), p. 185.

On May 26, 1971, the firm of Dean Witter & Co. hosted a meeting of San Francisco investment officers and invited a group of Amstar Corporation executives as guests. The principal speaker was the Amstar President, William F. Oliver. Afterwards the speech was printed in booklet form for public distribution, stockholders, investment firms, and the like. It serves as a very good illustration here of what is commonly done in applying the concepts, principles, and practices of face-to-face communication and oral reports presentation. As you read it, please notice that:

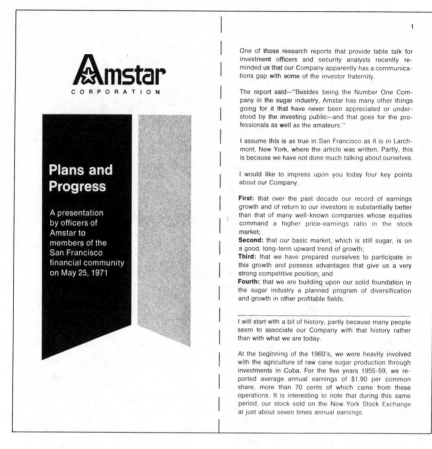

Amstar
CORPORATION

Plans and Progress

A presentation by officers of Amstar to members of the San Francisco financial community on May 25, 1971

1

One of those research reports that provide table talk for investment officers and security analysts recently reminded us that our Company apparently has a communications gap with some of the investor fraternity.

The report said—"Besides being the Number One Company in the sugar industry, Amstar has many other things going for it that have never been appreciated or understood by the investing public—and that goes for the professionals as well as the amateurs."

I assume this is as true in San Francisco as it is in Larchmont, New York, where the article was written. Partly, this is because we have not done much talking about ourselves.

I would like to impress upon you today four key points about our Company.

First: that over the past decade our record of earnings growth and of return to our investors is substantially better than that of many well-known companies whose equities command a higher price-earnings ratio in the stock market;

Second: that our basic market, which is still sugar, is on a good, long-term upward trend of growth;

Third: that we have prepared ourselves to participate in this growth and possess advantages that give us a very strong competitive position; and

Fourth: that we are building upon our solid foundation in the sugar industry a planned program of diversification and growth in other profitable fields.

I will start with a bit of history, partly because many people seem to associate our Company with that history rather than with what we are today.

At the beginning of the 1960's, we were heavily involved with the agriculture of raw cane sugar production through investments in Cuba. For the five years 1955-59, we reported average annual earnings of $1.90 per common share, more than 70 cents of which came from these operations. It is interesting to note that during this same period, our stock sold on the New York Stock Exchange at just about seven times annual earnings.

Courtesy Amstar Corporation.

1. The personal incident introduction ties in directly.

2. The listing of key points adds emphasis.

3. Historical details point up bases for growth, a favorable corporation image, and an advantageous position.

4. The charts presented by Mr. Lamb add proof and support for the company's goals.

5. Having two persons present the material adds a change of pace for the audience.

6. Summarizing comments at the end focus on the plans and progress of the company.

7. The lively question-and-answer period indicates that the presentation was well received and stimulating.

8. The question-and-answer period provided audience participation.

2

3

Also, at the beginning of the 1960's, we were locked into an inflexible capital structure by a corporate charter issued in New Jersey in 1891.

When we inherited this charter, we inherited a real antique. Because of its restrictions, half of our voting stock was in 7% cumulative, non-callable, preferred. In addition, we had no authorized and unissued equity securities and no practical way of obtaining any under the capital structure.

In August of 1960, Fidel Castro seized without compensation our Cuban property valued at more than $80,000,-000. The only offset to this loss of property, and its earning power, was a one-time reduction of federal tax liability to the extent of about $11,250,000.

Our immediate challenge was to compensate for the loss in Cuban earnings and to redeploy assets and redirect strategy in light of the changed circumstances. One step in this direction was to increase our holdings in the Spreckels sugar operations here in California.

We finally broke the stranglehold of the old capitalization in 1963 when The American Sugar Refining Company and Spreckels Sugar Company merged into American Sugar Company. One aspect of solving that particular problem was the creation of $45,000,000 of subordinated debt in partial replacement of the old preferred stock. But that was a far more manageable problem—as we have proved by our progress in reducing this debt over recent years.

Throughout the Sixties we carried out an extensive plant modernization program, increased capacity and prepared for anticipated changes in demand for sugar products. Needless to say, we would not have done this if we were not convinced of the strategically favorable location of our plants and the inherent profitability of our sugar business.

At the same time that we were taking these measures, the recapitalization permitted us to attack one other problem—that we were a one-product company. As you will see, the diversification plans that were laid in the Sixties are now beginning to pay off in the Seventies, helping to

change the character of our business from what it was to what we want it to be.

Of course, Amstar is diversified within the sugar business itself, because we manufacture both cane and beet sugar. Our cane sugar is manufactured in five large seaboard refineries from Boston to New Orleans. Our beet sugar is manufactured by our Spreckels Sugar Division at four California refineries and a new plant in Chandler, Arizona.

A reasonable amount of stability in both these sugar fields is guaranteed for us under the Sugar Act. Under this Act, the government estimates U. S. consumption each year, and assigns quotas to cane producing areas in this country and abroad, as well as to the domestic beet sugar industry.

Since we have an assured raw cane sugar supply at reasonable prices under the Act, our cane business is basically a food manufacturing business, rather than an agricultural business. Cane sugar refining is a complicated chemical process requiring large capital investment. Profits depend, among other factors, on high volume, operating efficiency and good product mix.

On the beet sugar side, which accounts for a smaller part of our sugar business, marketing allotments are assigned to each company based on its producing and marketing history and current inventory. We buy sugar beets from independent California and Arizona farmers who cultivate land under participating contracts tied to the selling price of our refined beet sugar. Our agricultural experts work closely with the farmers to assist with operating problems, to improve agricultural practices and crop yields, and in some cases to help arrange crop financing—all aimed at assuring ourselves a dependable supply of raw material for effective and efficient operations.

Recent trends in per capita consumption in the United States suggest that the sugar business will provide a sounder and more profitable base for our Company than heretofore. Total U. S. refined sugar distribution began to climb in 1968 after averaging about 97.5 pounds per

CONFERENCES

A conference is a speech situation in which any number of people participate. It is a standard method of discussing problems, arriving at final decisions, developing plans of action, disseminating information, and training personnel. *To confer* means to carry together; in a conference, people cooperatively discuss information presented or analyze a problem. A time and place are prearranged. It is a time for analysis and thought. Information or research may be presented. Giving and receiving information are integral parts of any conference. The exchange of information stimulates ideas and thoughts which lead to further enlightenment and solutions.

All business, professional, industrial, and government people par-

4

capita annually for almost a quarter of a century. Last year it reached some 102 pounds per capita, the highest in modern times.

While the percentage increase may seem small, an increase of one pound per capita translates into more than 200 million pounds of annual consumption—and Amstar supplies over a quarter of that amount. Also, the increase in total consumption creates a healthy situation in an industry that is operating closer to capacity than it has for a long time.

One of the factors that has caused total demand for sugar to outstrip gains normally expected from population growth is that an increasing proportion of our population is made up of energetic young people—traditionally the consumers of great quantities of soft drinks and other sweet items. Another is the public alarm over the dangers of additives and impurities in what we eat, drink and breathe. Widespread doubts were created about chemical sugar substitutes when the ban on cyclamates was imposed in the fall of 1969.

Perhaps as much as one pound of last year's per capita increase may have been due to the effects of the reformulation of products, with sugar replacing artificial sweeteners. Despite this nonrecurring factor, we expect demand this year to be close to last year's level and to continue on a historically high per capita level. Projected population growth on this basis would add about 300 million pounds to national demand each year.

In meeting this growing demand for sugar, we have several distinct advantages:

—One is the productive capacity and efficiency of our plants that has resulted from our modernization program.

—Another is our strong brand franchises—the well-known Domino and Spreckels brands of sugar.

—Still another is our unique national distribution system. We are the only company in the sugar business that can distribute in almost all the heavily populated areas of the country.

5

Before I turn to the future and our diversification program, I would like to ask Mr. George F. Lamb, Jr., Vice President-Finance, to show you a few charts.

Mr. Lamb

As Mr. Oliver has indicated, our planned program over the past decade has been to redirect our efforts in response to the consequences of the Cuban revolution, to obtain a more flexible and stronger balance sheet and to improve the profit position of our domestic sugar business—all requisite to the accomplishment of our other corporate goals.

These charts illustrate our progress in these directions—

Chart 1

Growth in U. S. Sugar Distribution
Equivalent short-tons of raw sugar, in thousands

	Calendar 1960	Fiscal 1970	Per Cent Increase
Mainland Cane Refiners	6,484	7,518	+16.0%
Mainland Beet Processors	2,165	3,402	+57.1%
Other (offshore producers, etc.)	611	197	—67.8%
	9,260	11,117	+20.1%

Source: U. S. Department of Agriculture

The first chart shows the picture for the sugar industry as a whole over the ten and a half-year period from 1960 through the first half of 1970, which was the end of our new fiscal year. Total sugar distribution during this period was up 20.1%.

The chart also illustrates the change in the composition of refined sugar supply to the U. S. market which came about largely as a consequence of the severance of diplomatic relations with Cuba. Through amendments to the Sugar Act, Cuban refined sugar was eliminated from our market

ticipate in conferences. Trade associations, staff meetings, board meetings, annual stockholder meetings, committee meetings, union meetings, and news conferences are examples of occasions for conference speaking. There are training conferences, operations conferences, and policy conferences. Any subject, factual or controversial, may be used for discussions.

Conferences seek to inform or to persuade. Each speaker adapts his ideas to the knowledge, prejudices, and experience of his listener. A meeting of several people, in which discussion takes place and questions are asked and answered, is a group conference. In a personal conference, two or three people take part, as in the interview. Because of the informality of the occasion and relationship of speaker, listener, and message, conversation is of the usual type. In group conferences various types of speeches may be presented; some of these may also be adapted to personal conferences:

6

7

—to the direct benefit of the cane sugar refiners. On the other hand, the domestic beet sugar industry was given a larger basic quota and a larger share in future growth in consumption as well. Thus, while total refined sugar distribution increased 20.1% during the period, cane sugar distribution increased 16.0% and beet sugar distribution 57.1%.

In recognition of these potential changes in the distribution pattern, we increased our investment in Spreckels Sugar Company, as Mr. Oliver mentioned. We also revised our overall capital expenditure programs to give greater emphasis to increases in beet sugar productive capacity, as the next chart will show.

Chart 2

Rates of Growth in Amstar Capacity, 1960-1970 Compared with Growth in U. S. Distribution

Amstar Daily Productive Capacity	Per Cent Increase (Calendar 1960 Through Fiscal 1970)
Cane	28.8%
Beet	89.2%
Total U. S. Distribution	
Cane	16.0%
Beet	57.1%

The second chart shows that Amstar's daily productive capacity over the decade went up substantially more than total U. S. distribution, both for cane sugar and beet sugar. On the cane side, we began operation of a new and highly automated plant in Boston and made substantial additions to capacities of our Baltimore and New Orleans plants. On the beet side, we started up a new plant in Mendota, California, and built a new factory in Arizona financed by industrial revenue bonds. Our beet sugar factory at Manteca, California, was substantially rebuilt and its daily capacity increased.

Chart 3

Amstar Plant Productivity

	Refined Sugar Distribution (cwts.)	Number of Employees (at end of period)	Refined Sugar Distribution Per Employee (cwts.)
Calendar 1960	44,942,000	6,633	6,775
Fiscal 1970	54,837,000	5,992	9,151
	+22.0%	−9.7%	+35.1%

The third chart shows that during this period of plant expansion the effective productivity of our employees actually increased 35.1%, thanks to the greater efficiency of automation. You will note also that our distribution increase is 22.0% as compared with the growth of 20.1% in total U. S. distribution shown on Chart I.

Chart 4

Amstar Increase in Plant Investment Per Employee

	Net Plant Investment	Number of Employees	Net Plant Investment Per Employee
January 1, 1960	$118,329,000	7,124	$16,610
June 30, 1970	$174,322,000	5,992	$29,092
	+47.3%	−18.9%	+75.1%

The fourth chart shows that net plant investment per employee went up 75.1% over this period. As of the end of the last fiscal year there was an investment in plant of $29,092 for each Amstar employee. If the remaining lease commitment for the Arizona beet sugar plant is added to net plant investment, the investment per employee would exceed $32,000, which is a very high figure for any industry.

Instructions
Oral reports
Sales talks
Discussion policy
Research report
Problem analysis

Goodwill talk
Inspirational talk
Introductions
Acceptances
Welcome
Telephone speaking

In each of these types, general purposes stand out, such as to exchange information, to analyze and reach conclusions, or to solve problems.

Organization

Most conferences are of an informal, democratic, round-table type. A conference leader presides and keeps the discussion going, but everyone participates. Each conferee is willing to take a fresh point of view and to hear other opinions.

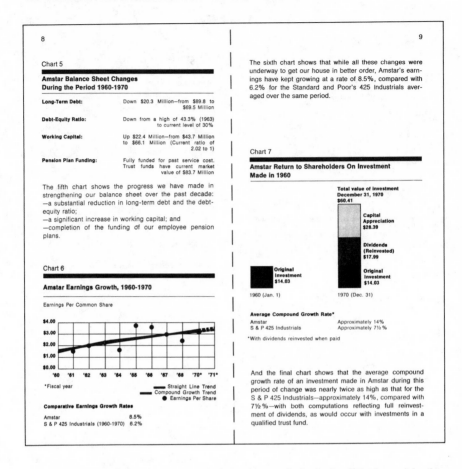

8

Chart 5

Amstar Balance Sheet Changes During the Period 1960-1970

Long-Term Debt:	Down $20.3 Million—from $89.8 to $69.5 Million
Debt-Equity Ratio:	Down from a high of 43.3% (1963) to current level of 30%
Working Capital:	Up $22.4 Million—from $43.7 Million to $66.1 Million (Current ratio of 2.02 to 1)
Pension Plan Funding:	Fully funded for past service cost. Trust funds have current market value of $83.7 Million

The fifth chart shows the progress we have made in strengthening our balance sheet over the past decade:
—a substantial reduction in long-term debt and the debt-equity ratio;
—a significant increase in working capital; and
—completion of the funding of our employee pension plans.

Chart 6

Amstar Earnings Growth, 1960-1970

Earnings Per Common Share

$4.00
$3.00
$2.00
$1.00
$0.00
'60 '61 '62 '63 '64 '65 '66 '67 '68 '70* '71*

*Fiscal year

— Straight Line Trend
— Compound Growth Trend
● Earnings Per Share

Comparative Earnings Growth Rates

Amstar	8.5%
S & P 425 Industrials (1960-1970)	6.2%

9

The sixth chart shows that while all these changes were underway to get our house in better order, Amstar's earnings have kept growing at a rate of 8.5%, compared with 6.2% for the Standard and Poor's 425 Industrials averaged over the same period.

Chart 7

Amstar Return to Shareholders On Investment Made in 1960

Total value of investment
December 31, 1970
$60.41

Capital Appreciation $28.39

Dividends (Reinvested) $17.99

Original Investment $14.03

Original Investment $14.03

1960 (Jan. 1)   1970 (Dec. 31)

Average Compound Growth Rate*

Amstar	Approximately 14%
S & P 425 Industrials	Approximately 7½%

*With dividends reinvested when paid

And the final chart shows that the average compound growth rate of an investment made in Amstar during this period of change was nearly twice as high as that for the S & P 425 Industrials—approximately 14%, compared with 7½%—with both computations reflecting full reinvestment of dividends, as would occur with investments in a qualified trust fund.

The number of people in the group and their familiarity with the subject or problem determine the organization of the conference. In small group-chairman conferences the subject is introduced by the chairman or a designated group member, and everyone contributes to the following discussion and conclusions. For large group conferences, the entire group may be divided into smaller discussion groups and their reports brought to a general conference meeting. Sometimes larger conferences are organized more formally and are centered around one or two speakers who are experts on the subject and problem at hand or who present divergent points of view for consideration. After the speech or speeches there are questions and discussion from the group. Either the speaker or a conference chairman may preside and lead the question-discussion period. This kind of discussion is commonly called an open forum; material is presented and then the meeting is thrown

10

Mr. Oliver

I have mentioned diversification as one of our goals for the future, but we can already point to substantial progress, with respect to both internal and external diversification.

On the internal side, one example is our Food Service Division, which started out selling sugar packets and today distributes annually many billions of individual portion units of sugar, jams and jellies, salad dressings, salt, pepper, mustard and catsup to hotels, restaurants, schools, hospitals, airlines and industrial feeding establishments.

With the imminent completion of facilties in Salinas, California, this division will be the only supplier in this field with coast-to-coast production capabilities.

Another promising area of internal diversification is development of special purpose, sugar-based products for industrial use—products in which we have a proprietary interest.

For example, we have developed and have been marketing a product we call Amerfond fondant sugar. With this product, it is possible for a baker or confectioner to produce—rapidly and without cooking—high-quality fondants, creams, fudge and cordial fruits, icings and frostings. Customers using this product obtain substantial savings in labor and equipment costs as compared with conventional processes.

We also sell a compaction material called Di-Pac that pharmaceutical manufacturers can use to produce a vitamin pill or other type of tablet by a simple stamping process. The former process required the manufacturer to run the equivalent of a candy factory.

Another new Amstar development is a "fermentation broth" with a sugar base which provides substantially improved yields over media formerly used by pharmaceutical companies.

In our acquisition program, we are looking for opportuni-

11

ties with above-average growth rates in situations where we can add some strengths. For example, the Hoffmaster Company, which we acquired a little more than six months ago, makes and distributes high-quality disposable paper products used in the same fast-growing "meals away from home" market that is served by our Food Service Division.

We have the capability to produce Hoffmaster products in our own paper and printing plants in Connecticut and South Carolina now serving our sugar business. This could reduce freight costs between Hoffmaster's Oshkosh, Wisconsin, operations and the population centers of the Eastern seaboard.

Our Duff-Norton subsidiary produces a widely used line of jacks, hoists and actuators for the construction, manufacturing and utility industries. We have made one acquisition already to complement this business. Duff-Norton has shown a good steady annual growth rate.

These activities in industrial equipment, together with our operations in paper and individual portion food service products, accounted for more than 15% of earnings from operations in fiscal 1970. We believe that this is a good beginning in our continuing efforts to strengthen and diversify the earning power of the Company.

Taking all things together we are pleased, but not complacent, with what we consider to be a healthy mix of business—one that has permitted us to enjoy good earnings gains during a period of economic recession.

We plan to continue to use the solid base of our sugar business to accomplish the objectives of growth and diversification that we have set for ourselves over these past few years.

I hope these remarks have made a little clearer to you what Amstar is all about and why we are confident of its future.

open to the audience. Such procedure can be followed with large or small groups.

Another kind of formally organized discussion is the panel discussion. Several people present different phases of the same subject or problem and thereby cover the important issues or points. Members of the panel may then question one another, or the audience may ask questions and take part in the general discussion. The chairman is the discussion leader, introduces the speakers, opens the discussion, and relates the subtopics and questions. He attempts to tie in the different points and to summarize the major ones. Members participate according to the conference procedures set up and their understanding of human relations.

An effective conference will have an approximately arranged time and place, free discussion and participation, preliminary thinking, clear

12

Question Period

After the presentation by Mr. Oliver and Mr. Lamb, the following questions were asked by the financial officers and analysts, and answered by Mr. Oliver or other Amstar officers present.

Q At what level of capacity is the sugar industry now operating, and at what level is Amstar operating?

A "Capacity" is a difficult term to define, and would have to be defined differently for cane sugar refining than for beet sugar processing. Cane sugar refining is a continuous process and uses a nonperishable raw material. A typical operating cycle is one of 5 or 5½ days, with 1½ to 2 days shut-down. At least one cane refiner, however, has a traditional cycle of 10 consecutive days of operation with 4 shut-down days.

In the case of beet sugar processing, operations are continuous, without shut-down, during the period that sugar beets are being harvested. The limitations on utilization of capacity are imposed by agriculture and weather. Here again there are variations in operations—such as pile storage of beets in areas where the weather is cool enough to prevent significant deterioration of the perishable vegetable, or partial processing of beets to a concentrated juice stage for further processing after harvest is completed.

In very broad terms, I would estimate that the industry is operating at about 85% of its capacity. However, recognizing the seasonal nature of sugar demand and the limitations of storage capacity for both raw materials and finished products, the industry could not operate at 100% of theoretical capacity as usually defined.

We have built up our daily productive capacity in cane refining more than others in the industry, both to meet seasonal demand more easily and to anticipate growth in consumption. Consequently, in cane sugar, we are currently operating at a lower rate of annual capacity than some other refiners.

In our beet sugar operations in California, production this

13

fiscal year will be close to practical capacity and will set a difficult target to surpass in the future. On the other hand, we are working to increase beet sugar acreage for our plant in Arizona where excess capacity exists during certain periods of the year.

Q Does higher per capita sugar consumption present any health problem?

A There are many countries of the world where annual per capita sugar consumption is some 20, 30 or even 40 pounds a year higher than in the United States. World sugar consumption generally has increased more than in the U. S., with great variations between locations and age groups. Consumption in the Soviet Union, for instance, went up from less than 30 pounds at the end of World War II to about 90 pounds today. The Scandinavian and Arab countries have higher per capita consumption of sugar than we do in the U. S. Only about 25% of U. S. sugar consumption today takes place in the home. The rest is taken up by industrial users, the largest of whom are the soft drink makers. Speaking in general, we wouldn't expect U. S. per capita consumption to go very much above present levels. We have no reason to believe that consumption at these levels presents any problem to a normal, healthy person.

Q What percentage of total U. S. sugar consumption is accounted for by soft drinks?

A About 22% of total U. S. sugar consumption is accounted for by the soft drinks market.

Q On the subject of diversification, what is Amstar's goal in terms of percentage of earnings originating outside the sugar business?

A We would like to see something in the order of 25% of our earnings coming from other fields, as compared with about 15% in fiscal 1970. In fiscal 1971 our percentage of earnings from sugar will actually go up because of favorable conditions for us in this area of our operations. We're not unhappy about this.

Q Are you looking toward diversification in any particular areas?

A We're looking for opportunities in areas with better than average growth. Expansion of our existing food service

presentation of material, and a feeling of mutual responsibility by the leader and participants.

Planning

For a conference to be effective, careful planning is necessary. The conference leader must formulate the purpose of the conference and objectives for the conferees; he must arrange the time and place, select the conferees, announce the meeting, organize conference materials, and prepare visual aids.

Making physical arrangements includes reserving a well-lighted, ventilated, quiet room. Seating in the room must be planned. A U-shape arrangement of tables and chairs is best unless the conference group is large, and then the formal arrangement of seats in rows facing the front of the room is used so the panel members or speakers will be seen and

14

activities or Duff-Norton operations would fit this definition. We're determined to use diversification as one way
to increase our stability of earnings and our rate of earnings growth.

Q With reference to recent price cuts on grocery sugar in
the Midwest area, do you regard these as an indication
of imbalance in supply and demand or of some other
factor?
A We do not look upon this price action as being related in
any way to an imbalance of supply and demand. For example, we do not anticipate any weakening of industrial
sugar prices in that area. In fact, we are reasonably confident that a good marketing climate will prevail in the
industry generally.

We believe that the price action was an attempt to narrow
the spread in grocery store shelf prices between an
advertised brand and private label sugars. If our own
experience in the eastern U. S. market is typical, the
desired result will not be achieved. You will note that all
competitors in the area immediately met the announced
price reductions.

Q What is the background of private label sugar and who
are the principal suppliers today?
A The practice of private labeling of consumer products was
well established long before it appeared in the sugar
industry. In our case, the first producers of private label
sugars were offshore and foreign producers who had a
refined sugar quota in the U. S., but found difficulty in
marketing industrial sugars as users converted to bulk dry
and liquid sugar facilities.

With respect to competition in the Midwest, discussed in
the previous question, the principal suppliers of private
label sugars are two Gulf Coast cane refiners. In the
Atlantic Coast area, virtually all brand name refiners sell
some private label sugars, including ourselves to a mod-
est degree. On the Pacific Coast, our Spreckels Sugar
Division is a principal supplier.

Q Has the private label business leveled off?
A It would appear that the rate of growth of private label
sugars is diminishing although the absolute level is still

15

on the increase. Furthermore over the last 15 years, the
total grocery sugar market has become smaller—dropping
from about 40% to about 25% of national sugar distribution. As a consequence, the industry profit on brand sugar
sales has become a less significant element of total
profits.

The offset to this change in historic relationships is the
increase in per capita consumption and the improvement
in profit margins on industrial sugars—which constitute
75% of national distribution.

Q What is your policy with respect to dividends?
A As you all know, dividends are a matter for determination
by the Board of Directors.

This Company over the years has paid out a high proportion of its net income to its shareholders. The quarterly
dividend rate was raised only about six months ago, with
the first payment at the current 42½¢ rate on January 2
of this year.

As we progress toward achieving our corporate goals—
both with respect to further diversification of earning
power and achievement of a more appropriate price-
earnings multiple than our stock now commands—it may
be to the advantage of our shareholders to retain a larger
portion of earnings for use in the business than has been
our practice.

heard. The leader can be in the open end of the U, and a blackboard
and easels for displaying charts can be placed behind him. The leader
should also arrange for writing materials, ashtrays, and visual equipment. His purpose here is to look after the comfort and welfare of the
conferees and to provide the appropriate climate for free discussion.

The leader may select the topic or problem or it may be selected
for him. He must think about the subject, however, to formulate his
own ideas. His preliminary thinking will also enable him to formulate
and state the purpose, objectives, limitations, scope, and pertinent facts.
He may pass these on to the conferees prior to the meeting to allow
them to do some preliminary thinking and gather facts and ideas ahead
of time, or he may inform them at the beginning of the conference. His
organizing material for the conference will include as needed:

1. Discussion outline to be distributed or to be put on a blackboard or
flip chart.

2. List of main topics to be in view of all.
3. Facts and figures to be displayed on charts or a blackboard.
4. List of questions to be used.
5. Preparation of visual aids.

Planning will also include selecting the conferees. Those who are vitally interested and concerned will be chosen, and within a company usually those on the same organization level will be considered. The ideal number is from ten to fifteen; however, as few as six to eight and as many as twenty can participate easily. After the conferees have been selected, they should be notified of time, place, subject, purpose, and scope and asked to prepare themselves.

Leadership

In addition to the responsibility of planning the conference, the leader must set the climate, open the meeting, lead the discussion, and close the conference. A friendly, cooperative atmosphere should prevail among the conferees and the leader. The leader may encourage frankness and objectivity. No hard feelings, antagonism, or disagreeable attitudes should exist. Each participant should feel free to speak his opinion and be willing to listen to the opinions and ideas of others. Only in this type of permissive climate can there be a true sharing of opinions, facts, and ideas. The conference leader's friendly, informal, cooperative attitude toward the group members can set the tone for the entire conference meeting. A leader who possesses a spirit of fairness, avoiding sarcasm, prejudice toward an idea or person, anger or irritation, will have a positive influence during the meeting, for the members will recognize that he is seeking the general good of the group toward accomplishing its goals.

In opening the conference the leader will begin promptly, put the group at ease, and state the purpose of the meeting and procedures that are to be followed. In some conferences and discussions the leader is little more than the presiding chairman; he introduces the speakers and grants permission to the members to ask questions at the end. In round-table discussions and other conferences, however, he carries out a set program and guides the thinking of the participants or audience.

He may initiate the discussion by presenting pertinent facts or by explaining the problem situation that is to be discussed. He might also begin the discussion by listing the topics of the subject, the aspects of the problem to be solved, or the factors that are involved. These will be aids for him in regulating and controlling the amount of discussion. He will seek to get participation of all members and to stimulate their thinking. He might do this by bringing the problem close to the group, involving them in it, and helping them to consider all angles. He will reduce, cut off, or eliminate digressions, keeping the discussion going in some direction or following some logical pattern. At the same time he should not do too much of the talking or tell others what to say. At times he must reconcile differences, clarify areas of disagreement, and reduce conflicts. He should strive to achieve a healthy balance among members, giving equal opportunity for participation and making sure the group uses its own human resources.

The flow of ideas during a discussion in a conference should not be merely from the conference leader to the participants but also from participant to participant. In cross exchange everyone gets to speak his point of view and present his ideas. The discussion is lively and good rapport is established from the give-and-take.

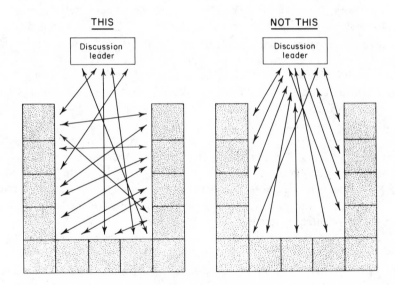

In closing the conference the leader should tie together loose ends, summarize, connect relevant points, and emphasize main points. Here again he will seek the cooperation of the group, getting suggestions from them which he may list on the board. He will also have the group make decisions whenever appropriate. He may evaluate what was done and said in terms of purpose and objectives reached during the meeting, closing with a note on what is yet to be done or the idea of "where do we go from here?"

The conference leader exercises overall leadership ability, and his success can be measured by the total impact on the group and how effective a job he did. A good conference leader will recognize the value of good speaking techniques and apply them throughout the conference session, and he will understand the purpose of the meeting and work toward accomplishing it. He should

1. Be a clear and rapid thinker.
2. Be able to express himself with ease.
3. Be objective.
4. Have analytical ability.
5. Be patient.

6. Be tactful.
7. Be poised.
8. Have a sense of humor.
9. Be courteous.
10. Know when to talk and when not to.

Discussion

Depending on the purpose of the conference, discussions may be informational, exploratory, problem-solving, or persuasive. Information is necessary for understanding subject matter and problem situations and for making decisions. Each level of management uses information. Decisions are passed down to the different levels of management concerned. Thus conferences expedite the dissemination of information and foster togetherness, teamwork, and group participation. Completeness is an important principle. Points should be clarified by concrete applications, specific cases, and statistics.

Exploratory discussions are held at conferences to determine what decisions mean to a particular group, division, or department of the company. At such a meeting, contemplated action is stated and interpreted, implications for subordinates are explored, questions are answered, and suggestions are sought. Often exploratory conferences are held to uncover a problem situation. Instead of presenting the problem and seeking a solution to it, the conference seeks answers to such questions as "What is the problem? Do we have a problem? Will this cause a problem?" Whether or not a problem exists and the nature of a problem that does exist are explored through group discussion by those concerned or involved in the situation.

In problem-solving discussions, participants draw conclusions after discussing the problem and all data involved, make decisions on the basis of facts known, and work out solutions to the problem. Their resulting action may be recommended to another person or group for approval or carrying out. They may suggest a set of regulations or instructions for one particular group. Most conferences combine aspects of informational, exploratory, and problem-solving meetings. The leader should know what kind of meeting he is running and direct the group accordingly, keeping the purpose before it and helping the group function efficiently. Not only are problem-solving meetings useful in providing solutions but also in improving relationships between management and the employees, among the employees, and between the company and employees. It is an effective communication procedure for expediting action and maintaining favorable relations. Useful conferences are often held in these problem areas in a company:

Safety	Election of leaders
Job methods	Vacation schedules
Production rates	Night shifts
Distribution of equipment	Absenteeism
Arrangement of work areas	Coffee breaks
Promotion of new products	Hiring policies
Promotion policies	

Few discussions during conferences are persuasive and argumentative. Sometimes, however, an executive who advocates an administrative change or policy is called on to defend it before his colleagues, superiors, or the public. He should focus discussion on the main issues and support his position with evidence and logical reasoning. He should advance all arguments and anticipate and refute objections. He should relate the issues and consider several courses of action. A friendly, impartial sense of fairness and a willingness to listen will avoid antagonism and irritation in most situations.

In any discussion at a conference, it is important to apply the principles of effective speaking and communication. Many principles and techniques of business report writing also apply, and although this chapter has not treated comprehensively the subject of oral reports and conferences, it has sought to help the reader who is confronted with an oral communication situation and to point out how the principles and techniques of business report writing may be applied. For further work in speech and oral communication, books on those subjects should be consulted.

A LOOK BACKWARD: A MOVE FORWARD

Completion of this chapter in *Effective Business Report Writing* marks the completion of your study and applications of the concepts, principles, and illustrations of report situations in which the job gets done on a day-to-day basis in most companies and institutions.

You should have accomplished the following: an increased understanding of the role of reports in the communication process and in a business enterprise; a knowledge and experience of working with situations calling for short, informal reports; a mastery of skills and techniques to achieve understanding and persuasiveness; and an increased ability to think through a problem, to analyze data, and to reach a conclusion and solution. Accordingly, you should be a more effective decision-maker and communicator, through reports—orally, visually, and in writing.

Usually either the data and facts for reporting are inherent in the problem situation, or the ideas and facts are drawn from the reporter's previous experience and past knowledge. As a businessman, however, you cannot be concerned merely with the elements of administration and operation of a firm nor can you make all decisions and policies nor solve all problems from the data at hand. Investigative research is needed, and longer, more formal reports present the results to ensure wise decisions. The next chapters, therefore, present a logical sequence of report investigation and presentation to help you to gain insight and practice with business research methods and familiarity and understanding of formal report presentation. This likewise should enable you to develop your abilities to think, plan, analyze, and interpret, to make decisions, and to solve problems—and thus become a much more effective communicator through reports.

FOR DISCUSSION AND WRITING

1. Prepare an oral report on one of the following topics:
   a. Increasing the college curriculum in business administration to five years.
   b. Avoiding slum areas in major urban centers.
   c. Making freeways out of tollways.
   d. TV instruction for higher education.
   e. Teaching machines and programmed material for college students.
   f. Government aid for higher education.
2. Assume that as personnel director you have been asked to recommend to the executive committee a new pension plan, hospitalization plan, or some other fringe-benefit plan for employees. Prepare and present your report orally.
3. Give an oral report on a business research study that was made to learn the trends and the future of a comparatively new field, such as electronics, plastics, synthetic rubber, or a synthetic material (nylon, orlon, dacron).
4. Assume that you are a general manager and have been asked to give a summary report on some division of the company—finance, production, marketing, personnel—to the executive committee. Your material may be obtained from a company annual report or from interviews with appropriate personnel in a specific company.
5. Assume that you are president and present a summary of your annual report to the board of directors. Use some kind of visual aids.

6. Have two or more speakers present arguments pro and con on "Graduate vs. Undergraduate Education for Business" before the class. Have a chairman introduce the speakers and subject. Afterwards he might lead the class in a discussion, and another member summarize the main points and any conclusions. This same procedure could be followed for any controversial topic or subject of current interest.

7. Select a report in *Consumer's Research;* condense it and convert it to a style in which it can be presented orally. Present it before the class. Use charts.

8. Hold a panel discussion on how to make a success in business.

9. As director of industrial relations in a nonunion plant, plan and conduct a conference on the subject of handling grievances. Members of the class should participate as foremen in the plant. A major objective of the conference may be to help foremen recognize grievances and their symptoms and to cope with them successfully. In such a conference the importance of dealing with grievances might be emphasized by discussing results of poor handling, and the foremen should be guided in developing methods for effective handling. Grievances will have to be defined.

10. Interview businessmen about their use of conferences in the company. Report your findings to the class.

11. As supervisor of management training in your company, plan and conduct a conference on leadership. Members of the class should participate as a group of management trainees. Your purpose may be to develop leadership among the trainees. You may use speakers or panel members for presenting material to the group.

12. Assume that five members of the class have been appointed by the university student council to deal with a school problem. Have them hold a conference before the class and come to some definite agreement on a solution. Later, write up the plans for presentation to the student council.

13. Hold a panel discussion on "What's Wrong with Schools of Business in Educating for Professional Leadership in Business, Industry, and Government." This could be followed with a general discussion or question period.

14. Assume that you have the position of assistant to Mr. X, who is treasurer of the XYZ Manufacturing Company, maker of a diversified group of products, including both producer and consumer goods. Late in April 1973 he hands you the following data and asks you to prepare a brief (five- to eight-minute) talk for him to give at the annual stockholders' meeting early in May. The condensed statements should also be made available to the stockholders and distributed at the meeting. His instructions follow: Explain in *simple terms* the present (as of March 31, 1973) financial condition of the company and point out any *significant* changes in the company's financial condition as revealed by either the profit and loss statements or the balance sheets. Because many stockholders are not familiar with financial terminology, make your remarks both *accurate* and in simple, ordinary language for easy understanding. Prepare and present your *talk*.

Balance Sheet (Figures in Thousands of Dollars)

	Mar. 1972	Sept. 1972	Mar. 1973		Mar. 1972	Sept. 1972	Mar. 1973
Assets				**Liabilities**			
Cash	28	30	28	Loans—bank	13.2	12.8	12
U.S. govt. securities	24	26	24	Accounts payable	30.4	30.2	30
Accounts & notes							
receivable	50	50	47.4	Income tax accrued	24.6	28	22
Inventories	88	90	89.6	Other current	15	16	16
Other current	4	4.8	5				
Total current	194	200.8	194	Total current	83.2	87	80
Property, plant, &				Long-term debt	38	39	40
equipment	212	220	228				
Less reserves for				**Equities**			
depreciation	94	98	102	Capital stock	90.2	90	90
Net property, plant,							
& equipment	118	122	126	Retained earnings	122.6	128	130
Other	22	21.2	20	Total net worth	212.8	218	220
Total	334	344	340	Total	334	344	340

Profit and Loss Statement (Figures in Thousands of Dollars)

	Jan.–Mar. 1972	Apr.–June 1972	July–Sept. 1972	Oct.–Dec. 1972	Jan.–Mar. 1973	12 months ending Mar. 1973	Jan.–Dec. 1972	Jan.–Dec. 1971
Net sales	132	138	132.8	129.4	122	522.2	532.2	500.4
Cost of goods sold	102	108	104	103.4	96	411.4	417.4	392.4
Gross operating income	30	30	28.8	26	26	110.8	114.8	108
Selling, administration,								
etc., expenses	16	16	16.2	18	16	66.2	66.2	63
Net operating income	14	14	12.6	8	10	44.6	48.6	45
Other income or ex-								
penses, net	0	0	.2	.6	0	.8	.8	1
Net profit before income								
tax	14	14	12.8	8.6	10	45.4	49.4	46
Income, excess profit tax	8	8	7	3.4	5	23.4	26.4	24.4
Net profit	6	6	5.8	5.2	5	22.0	23	21.6
Less dividends paid	2.6	2.6	2.4	3.6	2.6	11.2	11.2	11
Net to surplus	3.4	3.4	3.4	1.6	2.4	10.8	11.8	10.6

15.   Form groups of five to carry out the following conferences. The leader should call the group together to decide on conference plans prior to presentation before the class.

a.   Plan and conduct a policy conference on what should be the responsibility of your company in relation to the United Fund, Red Cross, and requests for financial aid by similar organizations.

b. Plan and conduct a conference for training the foremen in your company on the technique of instructing workers.

c. As head of the public relations department in your company, plan and conduct a conference with your staff members on what you can do to improve good will in your community.

16. Prepare a memorandum containing suggestions on the following case study:

Improving the Oral Communications in the Jones Processing Company

Low morale in the Jones Processing Company seems to be directly caused by difficulties in the company's communication system. Weaknesses exist in the various meetings and interviews used by the company in their communication program.

Company Meetings. There is a chain-of-command meeting once a month. The president of the company meets in conference with several major officials. Important topics are discussed and each official is assigned to a certain project. To solve problems, the designated official can assemble the subordinates who report to him. In this way necessary information can be transmitted to department heads, who in turn transmit information to the working force. The employee-supervisory meeting should be a foundation for a strong and efficient communication system. These meetings are on company time and expense. They are held bimonthly and usually last an hour. Each foreman meets with the workers under him to establish an informal, friendly relationship. The meetings are usually unplanned, and the foreman encourages the workers to introduce any topics they desire and to ask questions. Attendance is on a voluntary basis. Social-recreational meetings consist of anything from a small social gathering to an outdoor picnic or party. They are financed and planned by the company to provide an informal friendly working relationship. The company does not hold an open-house affair.

Company Interviews. The company uses employment interviews to establish good relations by fostering interest in the company. The interviewer represents the company and needs proper training and company enthusiasm. The induction period is trying at times for new employees, and induction interviews help employees adjust to their jobs and the company. Merit rating is used to rank individual employees according to their skill. Ratings are discussed with the employee by the supervisor. The worker thus is informed of his progress and encouraged to continue his good accomplishments. Counseling interviews also are held for aid in solving personal problems, but they are only available on a part-time basis.

There are several questions that arise: Are there too many or too few meetings and interviews? How can meetings and interviews be used to accomplish desirable objectives? In what ways can the present system of oral communication be strengthened?

RESEARCHING DATA, FACTS, AND IDEAS

6

BUSINESS RESEARCH is a search for new data and information necessary for planning future business activity; it influences employment and services offered. It results in new products, new production methods, new markets, greater production efficiency, and better ways of keeping up with competitors. Questions arise that must be answered; problems must be solved. It is up to management to find the answers and the solutions. Business research is needed, and business reports present the results to ensure wise decisions and action.

TYPES OF RESEARCH

For practical purposes all research can be divided into two main types: pure research and applied research. Enormous amounts of money have been spent on atomic research with the purpose of increasing knowledge. It has been research for the sake of research and not for an industrial or commercial purpose. Some results, however, have been applied and found useful. Most of the country's present economy and technology have been based on pure research.

Most research conducted by business is applied research; however, some firms maintain extensive pure research programs. Applied research aims to solve an immediate problem or to find an answer to a question. Essentially every aspect of business could be the object of research, but in most firms the major research areas coincide with the functional areas of operating a business: finance, marketing, production, and personnel.

Areas of Business Research

Financial research deals with the questions and problems of financial planning and controlling. A firm expanding into a new modern plant must ascertain the best ways of securing additional funds. A firm may seek to determine the best use of surplus funds, capital investments, or ways to produce funds beyond production and operation costs.

Financial research seeks to protect and improve the financial conditions of the firm.

Market research is the most publicized area of business research. It deals with products, sales, and distribution. A large bakery had to decide whether or not it should change its wax paper bread wrapper to one of either cellophane or plastic material. As part of its research, the company made a survey to find out homemakers' reactions to the three kinds of wrappers under consideration. Results showed that the homemakers preferred wax paper and revealed the reasons for their choice. Some areas in which market research is applied are

Advertising and sales promotion analysis	Analysis of pricing
Consumer surveys	Comparison with competitors
Analysis of sales methods	Sales forecasting
Studies of brand preferences	Potential market study
Opinion research	Distribution
Analysis of packaging	Sales territories

Research concerning product improvement and the development of new products or new processes is also necessary for progressive management of a business. Cost reduction and changes in manufacturing a product more efficiently, reducing the time involved for speedier operation, using new materials, improving the workmanship—these are areas of concern in production.

Personnel research is significant because of the role the employee plays in industry. Any data relevant to employees are important to management. Personnel research is concerned with behavior and interpersonal relationships, with attitudes and problems of motivating workers, with selection and placement, and with the welfare and advancement of employees:

Analysis of labor market	Personnel records
Job analyses and job evaluations	Safety
Employee testing	Wages and salaries
Employee training	Labor laws
Working conditions	Grievances
Morale	Union relations
Fringe benefits	Collective bargaining
Recruitment	Absenteeism
Retirement	

The Scientific Approach

The scientific approach to research aims at a systematic working from known data to a search for the unknown. It gets results that can be verified and are accurate. The research is conducted objectively by the researcher. Data are facts; they are either true or untrue, either valid under a particular set of conditions or invalid. Research should be as complete as money, time, and effort will permit. Conclusions are drawn from the facts by logical reasoning. After the researcher understands his problem, what is known, and what he needs to find out, he can begin gathering his data.

Data are either primary or secondary, depending on their source. Secondary data are obtained from bibliographical research, governmental agencies, or company records and reports; they have already been gathered and published. Primary data are gathered directly by the researcher from questionnaires, interviews, observation, or some other source. They are usually used to calculate trends and percentages, point up logical conclusions, or formulate hypotheses, which are in turn verified or tested.

THE RESEARCH DESIGN

The research design represents the investigator's plan of attack. It follows his thinking about the problem situation, follows his analysis and understanding of the problem, and sets forth his plan for the report investigation and presentation—much of which was discussed in Chapter 3 and which you have applied to short, informal report problems. The important points for consideration here are

1. *Stating the problem.* This can be in question or statement form with emphasis on need or purpose or a question to be answered. It gives direction to the researcher's thought processes. It also can be a working hypothesis or tentative conclusion which the researcher uses to guide his search for data to prove or disprove it. The generalization may or may not apply in all instances, and he must test to find out.

2. *Listing the areas to be covered.* Breaking down the subject into component areas for study shows the researcher what gaps he needs to investigate to fill in data called for. Sometimes these areas are simply factors that must be considered in making a decision or arriving at a problem solution. They may be built into the problem situation and thus become criteria for evaluating conclusions or solutions. They indicate areas in which data must be collected for consideration.

3. *Selecting the appropriate research methods.* By checking what is known from previous knowledge and experience and what is given in the problem situation, additional data become apparent. It is then a decision on how to go about collecting data, what research tools and procedures will provide it. One or several research methods may be used in any one report: bibliographical research, questionnaire surveys, interviews, observation, or experimentation.

4. *Writing the proposal.* This is the same process as discussed under the working plan in Chapter 3. The emphasis is on what data are needed and the proposed plan for research to obtain them. This should be couched in terms of results and their effective use.

Notice how the following proposal emphasizes the areas to be covered, data needed, research methods for collecting data, and includes two tentative questionnaires to be used for surveying company supervisors and employees. A tentative bibliography was also included in the original copy, although it is not reproduced here.

Proposal for a Report on
Current Employee Motivating Practices

Prepared primarily for the department manager, the report should provide the supervisor with a better understanding of effective motivating practices and should become the basis for establishing changes in policies in management-employee relations.

The problem.   Often managers become so involved with meeting schedules and solving problems that they overlook the desires, feelings, and attitudes of subordinates; consequently, some employees become bored, lose initiative, and develop apathy and resentment against management and the company. Employees want recognition and more say in what they do and how they do it. This raises an important question: Is there a need for changes in the motivating practices of supervisors? What changes should be made?

Purposes and objectives.   The purposes of the report are to examine and evaluate current motivating practices of supervisors within several component areas of the United Motor Company, to determine the effectiveness of current practices, and to recommend changes that will improve the employee's attitude and performance. This will be accomplished by

1.   Analyzing motivating techniques presently used by supervisors.
2.   Determining current industry trends and comparing these trends with present practices.
3.   Determining and comparing employee response to current supervisory motivating practices.

Scope and division of the problem.   The study will include a thorough investigation of trends and accepted practices throughout industry. In addition, the various aspects of the company situation will be analyzed to determine

1.   Attitudes of the employee toward his job, supervisor, and company.
2.   Attitudes of the supervisor toward his subordinates, upper management, and the company.
3.   Employee reaction to his supervisor's managerial methods.
4.   Employee feelings as part of the team, and whether he is given the opportunity to decide how things are to be done.
5.   Techniques the supervisor uses in motivating his subordinates.
6.   Other factors that influence motivation.

Sources of information.   Information relating to current industry trends in motivating practices will be gathered through bibliographical research, while information relating to present supervisory motivating practices will be gathered through questionnaires and personal interviews.

QUESTIONNAIRE FOR EMPLOYEES

This poll is being taken to obtain research data for a project in Business Report Writing at Eastern Michigan University. It is for statistical data only and will be held in confidence. Please do not sign your name.

1. Do you feel your supervisor treats you fairly?

    YES_____   NO_____

2. Do you feel your supervisor treats all employees equally?

    YES_____   NO_____

3. Are you given encouragement by your supervisor?

    YES_____   NO_____

4. Does your supervisor keep you well informed on job-related matters?

    YES_____   NO_____

5. Do you feel free to go to your supervisor at any time?

    YES_____   NO_____

6. Do you feel your supervisor is objective when considering you for a promotion or additional training?

    YES_____   NO_____

7. Does your supervisor allow you to make decisions?

    YES_____   NO_____

8. Does your supervisor set realistic objectives or due dates?

    YES_____   NO_____

9. Does your supervisor value your opinion?

    YES_____   NO_____

10. Do you feel your supervisor has the background and experience necessary to perform his job?

    YES_____   NO_____

QUESTIONNAIRE FOR SUPERVISORS

This poll is being taken to obtain research data for a project in Business Report Writing at Eastern Michigan University. It is for statistical data only and will be held in strict confidence. Please do not sign your name.

1. Does the company provide guidelines to help you obtain peak performance from your employees?

    YES_____   NO_____

2. If not, do you have your own methods?

    YES_____   NO_____

3. Do you value the judgment of your subordinates?

    Most of them_____   Some of them_____   None of them_____

4. Do you afford your subordinates freedom to direct their own efforts within the scope of their assignments?

   Always_____   Sometimes_____   Never_____

5. Do you allow your subordinates to make decisions?

   Most of them_____   Some of them_____   Not at all_____

6. Do you set objectives for your employees?

   Always_____   Sometimes_____   Never_____

7. Do you encourage your employees to surpass their normal level of achievement?

   Always_____   Sometimes_____   Never_____

8. Do you keep your employees well informed on job-related matters?

   Always_____   Sometimes_____   Never_____

9. Do you treat employee problems on an individual basis without applying a double standard?

   Always_____   Sometimes_____   Never_____

10. Do you delegate responsibility?

   Always_____   Sometimes_____   Never_____

11. Which of the basic needs do you feel your employees are working to satisfy?

   Basic (food, shelter, etc.)_____   Egotistic (self-esteem)_____

   Security   _____   Self-fulfillment   _____

   Social (group acceptance)_____

Tentative conclusions: It is anticipated that the investigation and research will show evidence that

1. Supervisors within the area of study do not always follow the established industry-wide motivation practices.

2. Employees, generally, feel they are not being recognized or are not given opportunities to make decisions or judgments regarding their work schedules or problems.

3. There is a need for changes in present motivating practices.

Work-progress schedule: The investigation and report will be completed and submitted by April 8, 197_, according to the following work schedule:

*March 4, 197_* — Strategy planned and research design formulated.

*March 11, 197_* — Progress to date; decide on printing and distribution of questionnaires; bibliographical research underway.

*March 18, 197_* — Complete bibliographical research and survey, tabulate survey results, organize and interpret data, make visual aids.

*March 25, 197_* — Complete outline and rough draft of report and critique for content and organization. Integrate visual aids.

*April 1, 197_* — Review draft and visual aids. Write final draft.

*April 8, 197_* — Complete final report and visual aids for presentation.

BIBLIOGRAPHICAL RESEARCH

The process of using printed materials as sources of information is known as bibliographical research. Data, facts, and ideas may be found in company records, reports, bulletins, and pamphlets and in periodicals, books, and newspapers. Everyone in business, whether he owns his own small firm or is an executive in a large corporation, should know current trends and developments and what others are doing and saying before he can make decisions on policies, and bibliographical research becomes invaluable for each of the following reasons:

1. To provide essential data for the solution of a problem or to give information on a particular subject.

2. To indicate what others have done and how the investigation fits into the general pattern of knowledge.

3. To show findings and opinions of authorities in the field.

4. To reveal whether or not the study has been accomplished already, and if so, to indicate any possible need for further investigation.

5. To give an understanding of the subject background.

The American Steel and Wire Company, for example, made a survey of the attitude of their employees toward the company magazine, *Wireco Life.* A simple postcard questionnaire was prepared and enclosed with each copy of a current issue of the magazine. To interpret the results the editor needed to draw upon his general knowledge of magazine publishing as well as his knowledge of the company. Moreover, it was necessary for him to be familiar with what other companies were doing with their employee magazines. With an understanding of how the problem was related to his general knowledge of the field, he could interpret the results significantly. In this case bibliographical research was helpful to find information on employee magazines.

In another instance a firm was considering whether or not to expand its facilities. The answer to its problem required an investigation of the expansion possibilities. Naturally, facts about the financial condition of the firm, its policies, the physical plant and equipment, marketing methods, and labor conditions had to be obtained. It was also necessary to find out the competitive position of the company within the industry and to determine national and regional trends and the future outlook. Bibliographical research helped supply this information.

Solving a problem and writing a report involving bibliographical information calls for seven major steps:

1. Compiling a working bibliography.

2. Evaluating, eliminating, expanding, and organizing the working bibliography.

3. Reading and taking notes.

4. Analyzing, interpreting, and organizing material from notes.

5. Integrating note material with other facts and ideas for reaching conclusions.

6. Outlining and writing the report.

7. Preparing a final bibliography.

Compiling a Bibliography

For the investigator using bibliographical research, the first step is to compile a bibliography consisting of a list of printed materials on his subject or dealing with his problem. The list, which includes such facts as the author, title, and publication details for each reference item listed, serves as a guide in the investigator's research and is helpful in directing his reading of essential and significant printed material. As a part of the finished report, the bibliography becomes a listing of sources which the investigator used in making his study, and it may serve as a guide for the reader of the report if he desires further information on the subject.

In the beginning the objective in compiling a bibliography is to get a complete list of all available material on the subject being considered. One quick and easy method for doing this is to record the information about each source on 3- by 5-inch cards. After the bibliographical items have been recorded, the cards may be arranged according to the subject matter of each. Thus cards on one aspect or phase of the study are grouped together for guidance in reading. After all data have been collected, the cards listing books are placed in one group, those listing periodicals in another, and so forth. Then each group is arranged alphabetically for typing the final bibliography to accompany the report. An example bibliography card for a book accompanies this discussion.

Notice the information included on the card. The number in the upper right-hand corner is the library call number, facilitating immediate location of the book. The designation in the upper left-hand corner is the subject division under which the information, when it is obtained, will best fit. It will also serve as a guide for reading at one time the sources on a given subject division. The author, title, publisher, and place and date of publication are needed for making a footnote entry and the final bibliographical entry. Knowing the total number of pages makes possible a budgeting of reading time. Sometimes only a part of the book will need to be read, such as pages 142–50, in which case those pages would be designated. The investigator's personal comments are given in the lower

```
┌─────────────────────────────────────────────────────────────┐
│                                                               │
│   Mechanics of Style                          0000.0          │
│                                                               │
│                                                               │
│   Erwin M. Keithley                                           │
│   and Philip J. Schreiner                                     │
│                                                               │
│                                                               │
│   A Manual of Style for the Preparation of Papers and         │
│        Reports                                                │
│                                                               │
│                                                               │
│   2d edition, 1971              Good, comprehensive           │
│   South-Western Publishing Co.  treatment.  Standard          │
│   Cincinnati                    guide to follow.              │
│   80 pp.                                                      │
│                                                               │
└─────────────────────────────────────────────────────────────┘
```

Bibliography card for a book.

right-hand corner. Usually the comments will contain an appraisal of the book or indicate the way in which the material may be useful.

A bibliography card for a magazine article differs from the book card only in the publication facts. Compare the illustration above with the following sample magazine card. Cards for any other reference materials likewise differ from a book card only in the publication facts included.

```
┌─────────────────────────────────────────────────────────────┐
│                                                               │
│                                        0000.0                 │
│                                                               │
│                                                               │
│   Johnson, Robert A.                                          │
│   "Computer Communication"                                    │
│   The ABCA Journal of Business Communication                  │
│                                                               │
│   vol. 8 #3            Clear explanation of communi-          │
│   Spring 1971          cation functions of computers.        │
│   pp. 39-46            Man-to-computer, computer-to-          │
│                        computer, and computer-to-man         │
│                        communications.                        │
│                                                               │
└─────────────────────────────────────────────────────────────┘
```

Bibliography card for a magazine article.

Another method of recording a bibliography is to use a notebook or sheets of paper instead of the 3- by 5-inch cards. Although the process, in general, is the same as the card system, there is one big disadvantage in using a notebook. Alphabetizing and rearranging the list for practical use is difficult and time-consuming.

In compiling a bibliography the researcher checks available sources in the library for articles, books, and other printed material on his subject. Both general and special indexes, as well as prepared bibliographies, are helpful aids.

The following indexes to periodicals should always be checked, for they are the best sources for current articles and data on a subject:

The Industrial Arts Index for articles pertaining to business, industry, and commerce. First published in 1913, issued monthly, and cumulated quarterly and annually until 1958. All subjects covered; over 200 specialized technical and business magazines indexed, including publications of a number of technical societies and associations in Great Britain, Canada, France, Germany, and the United States, as well as publications of the U.S. Bureau of Foreign and Domestic Commerce.

Business Periodical Index for articles pertaining to fields of business. Accounting, advertising, banking and finance, general business, insurance, labor and management, marketing and purchasing, office management, public administration, taxation, and specific businesses, industries, and trades. Succeeded *The Industrial Arts Index.* First published in 1958. Issued monthly and in a bound cumulation annually.

The Applied Science and Technology Index for articles pertaining to the sciences, industry, and technical fields. Likewise succeeded *The Industrial Arts Index* in 1958. Together with the *Business Periodical Index* provides a wider coverage of subjects and an index of more magazines than were formerly found in *The Industrial Arts Index.*

Applied Arts Index for articles on architecture, engineering, and applied sciences. Issued monthly, cumulated annually since 1957.

Reader's Guide to Periodical Literature for articles of a popular and general nature. Over 100 magazines indexed. Monthly supplements issued and cumulated semiannually and annually.

Poole's Index to Periodical Literature for articles written in magazines from 1803 to 1916. Of special significance in doing historical research.

The International Index to Periodical Literature for articles pertaining to the humanities, social sciences, and science. Type of magazine indexed similar to those in *Reader's Guide;* however, not confined to those in the United States. First published in 1907, issued monthly, and cumulated periodically into bound volumes.

New York Times Index for newspaper items. Gives a complete coverage, is published semimonthly, and is cumulated annually. The only index to newspaper items.

The four locators for a book are the best sources for compiling a list of books:

The library card catalog lists books in the library by author, title, and subject.

H. W. Wilson Company's *Cumulative Book Index* indexes all books published in the United States. It is issued monthly and cumulated semi-annually and annually.

The *United States Catalog* lists all books published prior to 1928.

Publishers' Weekly is a book trade journal listing and describing books published each week. It is published by R. R. Bowker Company, 1180 Avenue of the Americas, New York 10036.

There are also a number of special indexes in particular fields which should be checked. The names of the following indexes are self-explanatory:

The Accountants' Index	*Engineering Index*
Agriculture Index	*Index to Legal Periodicals*
Art Index	*The Management Index*
Education Index	*A World List of Scientific Periodicals*

The United States Catalog of Government Publications is issued monthly, and the December issue carries the year's index. The selected list of U.S. government publications, which is issued bimonthly, is free for the asking.

Numerous lists of printed materials on a large variety of subjects have been prepared. Some are typewritten, others printed; some are mimeographed or reproduced by some other method. They vary in length from one to twenty or more pages. A number of them may be obtained by writing the U.S. Library of Congress, Washington, D.C. Many libraries subscribe to services which provide bibliographies. The *Public Affairs Information Service Bulletin* is an example of such a service for libraries. The *Bulletin,* which is issued weekly and is cumulated five times a year and annually, lists books, pamphlets, government publications, reports of public and private agencies, and periodical articles related to economic and social conditions, public administration, and international relations. Each reference is classified by subject and author. It includes not only materials printed in the United States and in English-speaking countries but also those printed in English in foreign countries. Started in 1915, it has always been a cooperative clearinghouse of public affairs information and can be obtained by subscription from its publishers, the H. W. Wilson Company.

Another publication of the H. W. Wilson Company, *The Bibliographic Index,* is a cumulative bibliography of bibliographies sold on a subscription service basis. It is published semiannually with a bound cumulation each December. There are five larger cumulated volumes—Volume I (1937–42), Volume II (1943–46), Volume III (1947–50), Volume IV (1951–55), Volume V (1956–59). The arrangement is by subject, but under each subject, books and pamphlets are listed by author and periodicals by titles. The index includes some foreign periodicals. Complete or comprehensive bibliographies are starred.

Various associations, collegiate schools of business, and libraries publish lists. Representative are the Business Information Bureau of the Cleveland Public Library, the Newark (New Jersey) Free Public Library's Business Branch, the Alpha Kappa Psi Fraternity, and the Amos Tuck School of Administration and Finance of Dartmouth College. They select the leading works in each subject field of business.

Not all libraries contain every printed bibliography listed here, nor is the list complete. The ones mentioned, however, are all valuable and may suggest others. The researcher will find most librarians very helpful in suggesting sources for references.

Evaluating the Bibliography

After a complete listing of all sources of data has been made on cards, the next step is to evaluate the bibliography. This is accomplished by considering the authors and the material they have written. By finding out about an author's educational training and experience, business connections, and previous publications, the investigator can estimate his qualifications for writing. *Who's Who* is one source of information; another is the *Book Review Digest* for the year in which the book appeared. Other published reviews of books also contain information about the author.

An explanation of the text itself, including a look into its prefatory matter, will give such facts as the date and place of publication and the purpose of the book. A quick perusal of the table of contents and of the book itself will disclose the extent of coverage on the subject, whether or not the author is an accurate observer and reporter, whether or not the material is biased, the basis for the facts presented, and the method of presentation.

The author and text may be checked while the bibliography is being compiled or after it has been completed. In either case an entry for each book should be made on a bibliographical card as illustrated on page 191 if the card system is used; otherwise the entries may be made in a notebook. Sources which are judged unreliable and not pertinent should be so marked or discarded. The list should be arranged according to subject headings. The next research step, then, is to read all sources pertaining to each phase of every subject according to the headings on the cards.

Recording Bibliographical Data

When reading to secure information for a report the reader will find the following suggestions helpful:

1. Visualize the facts. Connect words to the facts to which they refer.
2. Understand dictionary meanings and connotations of the words.
3. Examine factual statements and figures for their accuracy and logic.
4. Distinguish between vague and definite statements, between hasty generalizations and careful judgments, between opinion and accuracy.
5. Scan material for important points found in topic sentences.

In reading, notes are taken for later analysis and use in presenting facts and drawing conclusions in the final report. Cards are preferred for recording notes. They may be of any size convenient for the reporter to handle. Each card should contain only one fact. It should be classified under a subject heading indicated in the upper left-hand corner. A specimen note card is shown here.

```
Subject heading
  Sub-head


     The note itself_____

   _____

   _____


     Source: _____ Page reference _____
```

Note card.

Subject headings are indicated for later use in classifying and organizing data. While the material is being read, source and page references should be made for footnote entries later in the report. Instead of writing out the source, however, a number may be used, which would then be placed on the corresponding bibliographical card. Sometimes colored cards are used to indicate division of material.

Loose-leaf notebooks, or even half-sheets of paper, may be used for recording notes. Their advantage is more space for recording details. This can also be a disadvantage, however, if the reader tends to record several facts on one sheet. He will later have difficulty in arranging his notes when he outlines and writes the report.

There are several methods of taking notes: direct quotation, paraphrase, précis, outline, or summary. A direct quotation must be recorded word for word to avoid misinterpretation or changing the author's meaning. Omissions of words should be indicated by ellipses (. . .). The whole must be enclosed in quotaton marks. To paraphrase is to express, interpret, or give the meaning in other words. The précis, on the other hand, is an exact, sharply defined statement. However, specific phrasing of expressions and style used by the original author should not be copied, consciously or unconsciously, in the précis. A summary usually indicates the main idea or point of view of the author but is stated in the language of the notetaker. An outline also records the main points but shows the relationship of several ideas. In taking notes frequent use of quotations, especially long quotations, should be avoided. It is usually best to record information in the form of brief summaries. After one has read and recorded the data from bibliographical sources, the next step is to classify, organize, and interpret the facts. Then one is ready to outline and write the report.

The Final Bibliography

The final bibliography is a complete listing of the printed materials used in preparing the report. It is placed at the end of the report, sometimes as part of the appendix. The bibliography compiled as a guide for the investigation is a basis for the final bibliography. After the data have been recorded and sifted to determine which should be used in the report and which should be discarded, it is evident which sources should be listed in the final bibliography. From the bibliography cards he has accumulated, the researcher selects the ones containing entries for all sources used in writing the report. These are then classified according to the type of source represented. All cards from books are placed together, as are all those from magazines, encyclopedias, directories, and other sources. Cards in each group are then arranged alphabetically by the last name of the author. If the author is not known, the title of the source is used for alphabetizing. Sometimes instead of being divided according to the type of source, bibliographies are arranged by topics, with alphabetical arrangement by author or source under each topic. This procedure is useful in indicating sources used for each subject. It is not often used, however, because it creates repetition and is difficult to organize. The forms of entry must be consistent throughout the bibliography. Suggestions and examples are shown in the reference section, pages 411–414.

The following bibliography lists the articles used in the report-proposal example, pages 186–189.

BIBLIOGRAPHY

Articles

MEYER, H. H., and M. SORCHER, "Motivating Factory Employees," *Production,* January 1968, pp. 50–53.

MEYER, P. J., "How to 'Turn On' Your Employees," *New Jersey Business,* May 1969, p. 80.

MILLER, MUNGO, "Understanding Human Behavior and Employee Motivation," *Advanced Management Journal,* April 1968, p. 47.

POLLOCK, T., "The Gentle Art of Motivation," *Production,* May 1969, p. 201.

"The 10 Commandments for Leadership," *Supervisors,* April 1970, pp. 3, 4.

QUESTIONNAIRE SURVEYS

Questionnaires are used to obtain information on behavior characteristics, to gather opinions or attitudes, and to obtain facts. Finding out what a group of people thinks or feels, and why, gives a necessary basis for making decisions pertaining to them. Knowing what a person does and why, how he reacts, and general characteristics of a group is important in understanding an individual person or a group of people as well as any business problem connected with them. Surveys using questionnaires give these kinds of data. Questionnaires are also used to obtain specific facts known by only a few, who have special knowledge or experience.

A few years ago, management in Standard Oil Company of California felt the need for an employee survey to help improve effective two-way communication between the company and employees. They used a questionnaire survey to determine present communication effectiveness and practices. Five of the sixteen questions follow:

    12. How well do you feel your Company keeps you informed about the Company's activities?
        □ 1. Always keeps me informed
        □ 2. Usually keeps me informed
        □ 3. Sometimes keeps me informed
        □ 4. Seldom keeps me informed

    13. I get *most* of my information about our Company from: (Please check *one* only.)
        □ 1. Notices on bulletin boards
        □ 2. Articles in *The Standard Oiler*
        □ 3. Letters to me at home
        □ 4. Talks with my supervisor
        □ 5. Employee handbook ("You and Your Company")
        □ 6. Group meetings
        □ 7. Newspapers
        □ 8. Fellow employees
        □ 9. Other (Please specify) _____

    14. I would *prefer* to get most of my information about our Company from: (Please check *one* only.)
        □ 1. Notices on bulletin boards

☐ 2. Articles in *The Standard Oiler*
☐ 3. Letters to me at home
☐ 4. Talks with my supervisor
☐ 5. Employee handbook ("You and Your Company")
☐ 6. Group meetings
☐ 7. Newspapers
☐ 8. Fellow employees
☐ 9. Other (Please specify) _____

15. Your Company is interested in knowing how you feel about your opportunities for expressing your ideas and obtaining answers to your questions. Do you feel free to go to your immediate supervisor and discuss: (Please check *one* answer to *each* part.)

	Always	Usually	Sometimes	Seldom
a. Questions about your job	☐ 1.	☐ 2.	☐ 3.	☐ 4.
b. Ideas and suggestions	☐ 1.	☐ 2.	☐ 3.	☐ 4.
c. Personnel practices	☐ 1.	☐ 2.	☐ 3.	☐ 4.
d. Complaints	☐ 1.	☐ 2.	☐ 3.	☐ 4.
e. Personal problems	☐ 1.	☐ 2.	☐ 3.	☐ 4.

16. How do you feel about the amount of information your Company gives you on: (Please check *one* answer to *each* part.)

	Not Enough	About Right	Too Much	No Opinion
a. Company's expansion plans	☐ 1.	☐ 2.	☐ 3.	☐ 4.
b. Company's financial problems —income, expenses, and profit	☐ 1.	☐ 2.	☐ 3.	☐ 4.
k. Information on employee benefit plans	☐ 1.	☐ 2.	☐ 3.	☐ 4.
l. The American business system in general—how it operates	☐ 1.	☐ 2.	☐ 3.	☐ 4.

The questions asked for facts, opinions, and preferences. The answers were of definite concern to management and directors of personnel or industrial relations. Over 42 percent answered "always" and over 41 percent "usually" to question 12, which shows that there is need for improvement. The response to question 13 indicated that a large majority get their information from *The Standard Oiler,* bulletin boards, and fellow employees. In answering question 14, however, they indicated they prefer, in addition to *The Standard Oiler* and bulletin boards, meetings, talks with supervisors, and letters at home. From a survey of this type it can readily be seen that questionnaires can be a useful management tool.

Information obtained from questionnaires helps management in making decisions and establishing policies necessary to run the business. Answers to some of the questions used in the Standard Oil survey, for instance, provided an objective measure of personnel administration at the supervisory level: others showed places where the communications program needed improvement and suggested possible changes. Information from questionnaires benefits management in building mutual understanding among departments and groups and in coordinating and integrating the work of all.

In marketing, questionnaires may be used to gather information concerning the uses of a product, consumer approval of changes, brand preferences, brand purchases, potential market, and the testing of a product—all useful in putting products on the market, appraising attitudes toward products, improving products, and distributing them. Surveys of buying habits and motives and of the readership of advertisements and advertising media contribute to the evaluation of advertising and help in selling a product.

Finding out the attitudes of the general public, consumers, employees, stockholders, management, and the government toward the company, product, or individuals, and educating them in the direction of favorable opinion or approval are important aspects of public relations work. The attitudes of each and the interrelation of the different groups can be determined by questionnaires and used as a basis for mutual understanding and harmony among the various publics and for educational campaigns.

Public opinion polls and employee-attitude surveys measure public confidence in the business, labor unions, and advertising; they determine opinion toward a specific problem such as a labor dispute, toward a person such as Ralph Nader, or toward a specific industry; they find out the stockholders' attitudes toward management and corporation policies; they reveal what the worker thinks about his job and his company; and they measure job-security attitudes.

The method of distributing questionnaires is the basis for classifying them as mail, personal interview, or telephone interview questionnaires. Although the emphasis here is on the mail questionnaire, principles of phrasing and organizing questions and of selecting the sample apply to all types of questionnaires.

The mail questionnaire is the most widely used survey technique, for it can reach a large number of people scattered over a large area—in most cases people who could not be reached any other way. Although it does take time to plan and execute, the time the respondent takes to fill it out is less than he would spend if he were being interviewed, and the questioner's time is also saved.

1. Questions can be answered at the convenience of the respondent.
2. The respondent has a chance to deliberate and look up information.
3. People generally will take care in filling out written information.

4. The bias of an interviewer is eliminated.
5. Specific segments of the population can be reached.
6. The respondent need not be identified.
7. Questions can be standardized.

Generally the mail questionnaire is less costly than interviewing. Time and labor are spent in preparing, mailing, and handling the questionnaires, but that is all. The cost per mailing is low, but the cost per return may be high. If fewer than 10 percent reply, the cost of mailing has been increased ten times over what it would be if there were 100 percent returns. Percentage replies usually range from 2 to 30 percent; however, it is common to obtain 75 percent or better returns from a highly selected, interested mailing list.

The disadvantages of the mail questionnaire lie in the difficulty in securing replies and in the nature of the answers. If the response is too small, the data will not furnish a true picture. It is also difficult to obtain a representative sample. The sample sent may be representative, but the returns may not necessarily include all elements of the population. Often questions are inadequately answered. The answers to some questions may be meaningless, and some questions may remain unanswered. Complex or confidential information is not readily given on mail questionnaires. Most of these disadvantages can be corrected by using a carefully planned, well-prepared questionnaire and by proper selection of the sample or mailing list.

Preparation of the Questionnaire

First of all it is necessary in preparing a questionnaire to understand the subject matter in the light of the purpose of the investigation. Because questions are drafted to seek the desired information, the data necessary and how they will be used should be determined. The list of basic elements of the problem or main issues involved can be used as a basis for making an itemized list of data to be requested. Questions are then worded so that they will best obtain the information needed.

Phrasing of Questions. Questions must be absolutely clear. They should allow only one interpretation and should mean the same to everybody. Phrasing them in concrete, specific terms helps. Technical and unfamiliar words should not be used. The question should indicate the form the answer is to take, such as "What make car do you own? _____" Questions should not be ambiguous. Using words with only one meaning or possible interpretation ensures clarity. Likewise, negative phrasing should be avoided; state the question in positive terms. Each question should include only a single subject. General opinions should be avoided;

specific facts should be sought—information the respondent will have readily available.

If an opinion or attitude survey is being made, ask for opinions on specific points or attitudes about particular things. Ask for reasons for preferences, seeking to find out "why" in each case to understand better the response given.

Questions that begin with *what, when, where, why, who,* or *how* force thought and generally receive definite answers. Leading questions should be eliminated; they are usually worded to suggest an answer which, if given, may not be representative. A question similar to "Did you see this advertisement?" for instance, will be answered "yes" by 50 to 75 percent of the respondents, regardless of whether or not they did.

Questions that call for "yes" or "no" answers should include a "don't know" possibility. Conditional answers should also be provided, such as "If _____, would you _____?" Short, direct questions will save the reader's time. He will also be more likely to understand the question and to respond to it. Questions dealing with behavior should be objective and stated as unemotionally and as impersonally as possible.

If much time and effort are required for respondents to get the facts, few people will respond. Whenever possible, questions should ask for facts that are either quickly recalled or readily available; this will prevent guesswork. Objectionable questions should be avoided. The questionnaire is not the best way to get confidential or inside information. The respondent, when asked for personal information, should be assured that it will be handled confidentially. His name and any identification may be omitted from the questionnaire.

Form of Questions. In deciding on the types of questions to be used, one must consider not only the nature of the information and the respondent's time but also how the answers can be tabulated. Check lists are popular because they are easily and quickly checked. A statement or question is given and a list of possible answers or items follows to be checked:

> Check the items you had for dinner today:
> ☐ Soup
> ☐ Salad
> ☐ Vegetables
> ☐ Other (please state)

Useful in measuring attitudes or preferences is the question calling for a ranking of items:

> Indicate in order of preference the qualities you consider necessary in a secretary by placing 1, 2, 3, and so forth before the quality:

☐ Neat appearance
☐ Punctuality
☐ Good English
☐ Speed in typing
☐ Neat work
☐ Other (please state)

Of course, closely related to a check list is the mulitple-choice question:

As a group to work with, my fellow employees are
☐ As fine a group as I could want
☐ A good group
☐ Fair
☐ Unsatisfactory

This particular example also allows for intensity of reply, as does also:

Do you make use of your credit card when shopping in stores where this service is offered?
☐ Always
☐ Frequently
☐ Seldom
☐ Never

Another form of question is the one calling for a simple "yes" or "no" response:

Does the use of a credit card save you time in shopping?
Yes_____   No_____

This is naturally the easiest type of question to ask, to answer, and to tabulate.

A question may also ask for a single fact:

About how much money did you spend on groceries last week?

or

What is your favorite method of preparing tuna?

Unless a question calls for a specific fact, it is sometimes difficult to tabulate the answers:

Please list your objections to_____.

or

What do you think of_____?

Sequence of Questions. Questions should be arranged in proper sequence to enable a continuous flow of thought from the beginning to the end of the questionnaire. This will make answering easy for the reader, which means a better response to the questionnaire.

Either a logical or a psychological arrangement may be followed. A logical sequence gives full consideration to the subject matter of the questions, which must be covered thoroughly, and the chain of thought moves unbroken from one question to the next. The psychological order, on the other hand, gives full consideration to the respondent. The first questions are easy, the reader then proceeding to the more difficult ones. Some transition is used between questions to keep his interest stimulated.

Personal questions are buried somewhere in the middle of the questionnaire, as are those which may reflect on the respondent's intelligence and those which are likely to be of little interest to him.

In dealing with motives, the first questions should call for "surface" replies and lead to the more important underlying points. The "why" should follow the "what" in such a series of questions. The total number of questions should be as low as possible to gather the needed information. Questions of similar nature may be combined or grouped together and superfluous ones rejected. A well-arranged questionnaire, even if long, will not seem so to the respondent if he is interested in the subject matter, if questions can be answered quickly, and if the flow of thought is continuous.

Makeup of Questionnaires

Elements of a Questionnaire. Notice the parts of the following questionnaire. The heading, which established contact by identifying the source of the questionnaire, is followed by the title, which tells the reader its subject matter. Instructions, simple and clear, are given next. Numbered questions follow with spaces for checking appropriate responses. Comments are asked for at the end. Corollary data are called for as a basis for cross-tabulating the answers to analyze the influence of such factors and as a means of checking the representativeness of the returns from the sample taken.

Sometimes the name and address of the person replying are sought. More often no place is provided for this information, and in some instances the request "Please do not sign your name" is placed at the top or bottom of the questionnaire. This assures the respondent that his name will not be used in connection with the answers, and he feels more free to give his answer because of this assurance that the information will be treated confidentially.

Eastern Michigan University—College of Business
Survey of Job–Interview Practices

By Business Report Writing Class

In the appropriate spaces, please check your opinion and practices:

Appearance:

1. What is an acceptable hair length? _____Short _____Medium
   _____Long _____Not a factor
2. Should a man be clean-shaven? _____Yes _____No
3. Is a beard acceptable? _____Yes _____No. Is a mustache acceptable?
   _____Yes _____No
4. What is an acceptable length for sideburns? _____Short
   _____Medium _____Long
5. What type of dress is acceptable?
   _____Conservative _____Latest style _____Not a factor
6. Are miniskirts acceptable? _____Yes _____No

Personal:

7. Does age have an effect in considering an applicant?
   _____Yes _____No
8. What type of marital status is preferable? _____Single _____Married
9. Is the applicant's willingness to travel an asset in his favor?
   _____Yes _____No _____Not important
10. What draft status is acceptable?
    _____Exempt _____Student exemption _____1-A _____Veterans
    _____Not a factor

Education:

11. Does a master's have any priority over a bachelor's degree?
    _____Yes _____No
12. Would you accept a BA over a BBA degree? _____Yes _____No
13. Is a BA given equal consideration with a BBA degree?
    _____Yes _____No
14. Are college grades a factor in your selection? _____Yes _____No
15. How important is class standing? _____Extremely _____Important
    _____Unimportant
16. Is the quality image of the school considered? _____Yes _____No

Extracurricular Activities:

17. What is the importance of organizational membership?
    _____Extremely _____Important _____Not important
18. How important is athletic participation?
    _____Extremely _____Important _____Unimportant
19. How important are hobbies? _____Extremely _____Important
    _____Unimportant
20. Do you react _____ favorably or _____ unfavorably to participation
    in peaceful demonstrations, protests, etc.?

Character Traits:

21. How important is a clear speaking voice, good vocabulary, and grammar?
    _____Extremely   _____Important   _____Not important

22. How important is the individual's ability to communicate?
    _____Extremely   _____Important   _____Not important

23. Should the applicant carry the discussion? _____Yes _____No

24. Does nervousness count against the applicant? _____Yes _____No

25. How important is a pleasing personality?
    _____Extremely   _____Important   _____Unimportant

General Information:

26. How do you rate experience?

	Extremely important	Important	Unimportant
Full-time job			
Part-time job			
Related			
Not related			

27. Does a résumé increase an applicant's chances? _____Yes_____No

28. Should the applicant ask about salary? _____Yes _____No

29. Should the applicant indicate a prior knowledge of the company?
    _____Yes _____No _____Not important

30. Should the applicant send a thank you afterwards? _____Yes _____No

31. Should the applicant follow up the interview?
    _____Yes _____No _____By letter? _____By telephone?

Please Check Corollary Information:

Approximate number of employees
at your location: Type of industry:
_____Under 100   _____Manufacturing
_____100–499   _____Wholesaling
_____500–999   _____Retailing
_____1000–1999   _____Service
_____Over 2000   _____Other

Your method of handling interviews:

_____Your interviewers go to college campuses
_____Applicants go to your company for interviews
_____You pay applicant's expenses
_____You don't pay applicant's expenses

For a summary of the survey results, check the following:
_____Yes _____No

PLEASE USE THE REVERSE SIDE FOR COMMENTS.

Questionnaires should be made as neat and attractive as possible. Care in making up the questionnaire calls for equal care in completing it. Charts, diagrams, and pictures are sometimes introduced to create attention and interest. These take up considerable space, but if the reader is interested, he will not notice the length. In long questionnaires a booklet is sometimes used. Although this creates an attractive appearance, the processing of the data afterwards can be awkward and time-consumng.

Use of Covering Letter.   The preceding intervew questionnaire was mailed with the following covering letter.

Dear Sir:

    As an interviewer, I am sure you are interested in how students conduct themselves during interviews.

    For this purpose, the students in the Business Report Writing class, Eastern Michigan University, have made up a questionnaire to determine your likes, dislikes, and reactions to applicants during the interview.

    Spend a few minutes, please, fill out the questionnaire, and return it to us in the enclosed envelope. A summary of the results will be available on request.

    We appreciate your cooperation.

                Very sincerely,

                Leland Brown
                Professor
                Business Communication

LB:be

Enclosures

The covering letter should explain the questionnaire and sell the recipient on filling it out and returning it. It should be short and tactful. It should give a reason for the questionnaire and state the purpose of the reply. His cooperation should be sought by stressing the benefit to him or others and by appealing to his sense of pride or self-interest. Sometimes a little sincere flattery will help. A copy of results may be promised or some premium or reward given as a special inducement.

The letter might also include general instructions pertaining to the questions and to returning the form. It is good practice to state a time limit and urge reply at once. Appreciation should also be expressed, and when confidential data are sought, the reader must be assured they will be handled confidentially.

The following questionnaire, on a postcard, is brief and to the point:

Dear Dealer:

    Will you take one minute to give us your very candid advice on an important question?

    RCA and other manufacturers often ask us, "What do you consider to be the most effective form of advertising for our product: magazines--newspapers--television--or radio?

    No one is in a better position to answer that question than you, on the basis of actual experience.

    Will you help us, therefore, by checking and mailing the attached card today.

    Thanks very much for your assistance.

                   Cordially,

In terms of its effectiveness in producing sales, I rate the value of product advertising in the different media as follows:

(Please check only one block for each.)	Mag-azines	News-papers	Tele-vision	Radio
Most Effective------	( )	( )	( )	( )
2nd Best-----------	( )	( )	( )	( )
3rd Best----------	( )	( )	( )	( )
Least Effective-----	( )	( )	( )	( )

Signed...

Company.......................................

Address.......................................

Postcard questionnaire.

Testing and Revising the Questionnaire. The questions and questionnaire should be checked and tested, revised, and finally mailed. The scope and sequence of the questions should be checked for thoroughness and logic. The wording of the questions must be clear. The questionnaire should be as brief as possible. A study of the questions may call for eliminating several or combining and adding others. The instructions should be examined for clarity. The format, spacing, numbering of questions, indentation, and other technical features should also be considered.

When the questionnaire is ready, it may be tested in a small number of interviews or mailed to a sample group before being mailed for the survey. This gives some idea as to the clearness of the questions and instructions and to the soundness with which the sample was chosen. It also aids in further revision, should weak points still show up in the questionnaire.

Sources for Mailing List

Questionnaires seeking information are usually directed to those whose connection with the subject is known through their position or through their contributions to magazines and discussions. Then a mailing list is obtained and questionnaires are mailed to each name on the list. The following are sources for compiling a mailing list:

Censuses	Graduates of schools and
Telephone directories	colleges
Subscribers to public utilities	Members of organizations
(other than the telephone)	Professional directories
Automobile registrations	Clients of social agencies
List of voters	Clients of public agencies
List of customers	Payroll lists
Credit lists	City directories
Subscribers to magazines	Tax assessor's list

Planning the Sample

When a survey of a large group of people is made, questionnaires are not mailed to everyone; only a *part* of the total group is chosen for sampling on the assumption that a representative number of responses is indicative of the whole. Sampling is used extensively in making market surveys, public opinion polls, and employee surveys in which it would be almost impossible to reach the entire population. Two major problems are involved in planning the sample—selection of the kind of sample and determination of the size of the sample.

To select the sample the investigator must first study the nature of the population. What groups does it contain? What characteristics do they possess? If the sample is to be a true reflection of the entire population, each individual must be assured an equal and independent chance of inclusion in the sample.

Care must be taken to assure the sample's being representative and unbiased. Sampling may be random, stratified, or proportionate—depending on the method of selection. For an employee survey, for instance, the payroll list would contain the entire group under study. For the sample, individual names on the list could be selected at equally spaced intervals, such as every tenth or twelfth name. That would be *random* selection. But would every significant element be included? Would the sample contain employees at all the different salary levels? Both men and women? Employees of all age groups? Of every nationality?

Would it not be more representative to divide the employees into categories and select names from each group? Then each group would be assured of being represented in the sample. This would be *stratified* sampling. If the investigator also controls the selection so that characteristics of the whole group are represented proportionately, the sample is also *proportionate*. The proportionate sample is used only if a specific class will affect the responses or conclusions. If age groups would have no bearing on the conclusions, for example, then it is not necessary to have proportionate age group representation; stratified or random sampling would be sufficient.

To determine the size of the sample, one needs to consider his purpose. If it is to find out whether or not the layout of an advertisement emphasizes certain sales points of a product, a check with a few people who know advertising will give the answer. If it is to learn why the odor of a deodorant offends, a few dozen women can tell; the information would be the same as if several hundred were asked. When the purpose is to generalize on the attitudes or opinions of a large group of people, however, the sample will have to be large. An adequate sample is one that is large enough for generalization about certain characteristics.

The size of the sample varies with the problem, for a sample should increase with the number and variety of the categories it includes. A sample should also increase as the required accuracy of the results increases. The increased size of the sample reduces the errors of chance.

The returns from a stratified sample are tested to see if all categories are included; if they are, the sample is valid. For a proportionate sample, each class represented in the returns is represented in proportion to its occurrence in the entire group. Because it shows the characteristics of the respondents, the corollary information from the questionnaires is used in checking the validity of both stratified and proportionate samples.

The normal percentage returns on most mail questionnaires is from 10 to 15 percent. With a carefully selected mailing list, however, and a questionnaire of general interest, returns often will reach 75 percent or more. When they reach approximately 80 percent, the findings are reliable without further testing, because answers from those not responding would have little effect on the total responses. The basic principle here is the same as that involved in the cutoff method of measuring the reliability of the sample. A stabilization point is determined for the responses beyond which no more returns need be considered.

In applying the cutoff method, the total number of questionnaires is divided into several sets, which may be equal or unequal in number. The percentage of "yes" answers to a question is computed. As additional sets of questionnaires are added, the cumulative percentage is derived. When the questionnaires make very little or no change the responses are said to have been stabilized; a cutoff point has then been established. Since there probably would be less than 2 or 3 percent fluctuation either way, the sample is reliable.

Another method of measuring the reliability of the sample is to analyze subsamples. The total number of questionnaires is divided into two or three groups of equal size. Standard errors of deviation are computed statistically for each group, and differences are analyzed for significance. If there is little difference, the sample is reliable.

There are other statistical measures which may be applied in testing the sample and which investigators without a background in statistics may find in books on the subject.

Tabulation

After the returns of questionnaires have been received, they are evaluated and sorted, and then tabulated so that generalizations may be formulated and trends spotted. They may be tabulated by hand or by machine. When there is a large quantity of data (a sample of several thousand or more), when a large number of cross-classifications are needed, or when repeated studies are to be made, it is desirable to use machine tabulation.

The process of classifying, evaluating, and manually tabulating data is included in the next chapter on organization. Machine tabulation is highly technical and requires specially trained personnel for its effective use. Special electrically operated tabulating machines sort cards into groups, count data, and print the totals. Univac Division of Sperry Rand Corporation, International Business Machines, and Burroughs Corporation have machines designed to count a large number of items rapidly. In coding, either a clerk reads the information on the source document and punches the proper code number on a card, or the information is processed through a special machine. The questionnaires are coded in such a way that responses can be punched on a card of the appropriate size and weight to be run through the machine. The cost is prohibitive for small counts, but is correspondingly low for large ones. The greatest advantage of machine tabulation is the ease and rapidity with which it cross-classifies. This would, of course, be unnecessary and confusing for small operations but efficient for large ones.

Tabulation accuracy is assured by machines. Both the elimination of transcription errors and their pinpointing in enumeration are possible.

Other advantages of machine tabulation include early results, duplicate files for filing in a different sequence, flexibility of sequence listings, unlimited statistical analyses within the scope of punched data, and saving in cost and time.

INTERVIEWS

The process of securing information directly through a conversation with an individual is an interview. It involves conversing with a purpose other than personal satisfaction. It allows for a direct exchange of information, and the interviewee's voice, facial expression, gestures, and general behavior all contribute to this exchange of information.

Interviews are used to determine objective facts, such as events, conditions, practices, policies, and techniques. They are also used to gather subjective data, such as attitudes, preferences, opinions, tastes, or emotional reactions. Sometimes their purpose is to discover why or how an individual responds as he does or has a particular attitude or opinion and to enable the interviewer to understand clearly the facts he obtains from the interview and to analyze his information accordingly.

At the very outset of an investigation an interview may help in defining the problem and in planning the investigation. The person who authorized the report might be interviewed, as might those involved in the situation giving rise to the investigation. An interview may also be used to win cooperation from and to establish working relations with persons involved in the problem being investigated. The interview should be avoided as a method of obtaining general information or of securing facts that are commonly known or can be obtained from other sources, such as company records, committee meeting minutes, and other written documents. It is an effective method of determining facts known to a single individual or group of people, and it is also worthwhile when the revealed data are the opinions of experts. A consensus of opinion can thus be obtained, and facts which vary from person to person or from one situation to another can be determined. Several special advantages of the personal interview over the mail questionnaire are

1. The interviewer can, to some extent, control the situation.
2. He can interpret questions.
3. He can clear up misunderstandings.
4. He can secure fully and accurately the most representative replies.
5. He will receive first-hand impressions which will throw light on the data procured by his questions.

Directors of industrial relations, personnel specialists, lawyers, social workers, psychiatrists, reporters, salesmen, vocational counselors, and employment managers all use the interview. There are three special aspects of business in which interviews are used a great deal: in marketing studies, in personnel work, and in industrial relations. Special books dealing with research in each of the fields should be consulted for full treatment of the subject.

It is necessary to ascertain in market analysis the existing and potential sales possibilities of a product. Consumer preferences, when known, are used as a basis for advertising and sales promotional plans. Salesmen, advertisers, manufacturers, and dealers use the data. Surveys provide a consensus of opinion and attitude which can be put to effective use.

Personnel specialists and business executives use interviews as a means of keeping informed of business conditions and relations. Through interviews they learn to know the employees and can establish proper contacts. Interviews are not used so much here to solve a business problem calling for an investigation and a report as they are used to achieve some other business purpose. Important examples are the employment interview used in hiring men, the vocational guidance interview used to help the employee adjust to his job or to place him properly on another job, or the exit interview used when a person leaves a job to go elsewhere. These situations do not necessarily call for a business report, yet each makes use of the personal interview.

Problems in personnel that call for reports in their solution do arise, however. Suppose a firm has a rapid turnover of its employees and wants to stabilize its working force. It will need to find out why people leave the company; it will need to know something about the attitudes of the employees toward present working conditions and policies; it will need to investigate the hiring procedures. Interviews can be used as a source of information in each of these situations.

For the industrial relations director the interview reveals the attitudes of his employees. It is a valuable morale builder, because it gives the employee a chance to "get it off his chest" and helps build goodwill. The interview enlightens management by giving it an insight into the human nature of its workers.

Kinds of Interviews

There are two kinds of personal interviews—fact-finding interviews and depth interviews. In the *fact-finding interview* the investigator may seek either objective or subjective information, or both. The information he obtains is usually in answer to direct questions, which may be general or specific. For example, suppose an interview is being held to determine the employees' attitudes toward their working conditions. The question might be asked: "Are your working conditions conducive to efficient work?" The answer may be a "yes" or a "no." A survey of a representative number of employees would give a consensus of opinion among the workers in the company. But how beneficial would the consensus be? In the *depth interview,* also known as the open-end or intensive interview, the interviewer would seek to find out why the respondent answered "yes" or "no." He would try to ascertain what conditions were considered conducive to efficiency and why, what changes the worker would like to have made and why. He might do this not so much through the use of direct questions as by getting the worker to talk about the subject and by drawing him out on the points on which information is desired.

The chief difference between the fact-seeking interview and the depth interview is the degree of intensity to which the interview is carried out. The depth interview begins where the other ends. After a fact or attitude has been determined, the depth interview gets behind the fact or attitude to discover motives and causes. The depth interview is thus more time-consuming than the purely fact-seeking one, but is more enlightening.

Sometimes interviews are conducted over the telephone. Such interviews are useful for opinion polls when a limited number of questions can be asked and are certainly more inexpensive than the personal fact-finding interview or the depth interview. The *telephone interview* permits wide coverage of either particular or general groups, and a representative or random sample may be obtained. As a method of research the telephone interview has been widely used in the field of radio audience evaluation. Questions on the product being advertised are frequently asked, as are questions as to whether or not the radio is turned on, and to which program and station.

The following list summarizes the merits and disadvantages of the telephone interview:

Advantages	Disadvantages
1. Quickest of survey techniques	1. Not necessarily representative
2. Low refusal rate	2. Cannot gather detailed data
3. Memory factor eliminated	3. Element of observation eliminated
4. Interviewers easily trained and supervised	4. Limited information can be asked
5. Approach and questions easily standardized	5. Credibility of person calling low
6. Low cost	6. Little time for orientation and reaction
7. Geographical distribution of sample easily controlled	7. Task of checking too time-consuming
8. High returns	8. Respondents antagonistic

No matter which kind of interview is conducted there are a number of general procedures and techniques which should be followed for obtaining the best results.

Procedures in Interviewing

Prior to the Interview. It is necessary that the interviewer think through his problem and formulate in his own mind the factors involved so that the interview can contribute to its solution. He will need to master the subject with which the problem deals and to understand fully the background of the situation giving rise to it. This is a part of the preliminary planning of the investigation. Then prior to interviewing, the investigator must review these phases of his planning and understand how the interview will accomplish what he is seeking. Part of the interviewer's knowledge and background in the subject must come from bibliographical research. He must also recognize and eliminate his own personal bias, feelings, and prejudices so that he will have an open mind and can be objective during the interview. If a survey of a group is being made, a sufficient sample must be secured to assure its validity and its representativeness. The procedures outlined earlier on using the questionnaire can be applied in making surveys through interviews.

The interviewer needs to list the questions he plans to ask if he is interviewing a group, because he will want to ask the same questions in the same way at each interview. Consideration should be given to both general and specific questions, to questions which may be asked directly, and to those which may be brought in indirectly or casually. An exact knowledge of the purpose of the interview and what it should accomplish is necessary. A well-thought-out list of topics and questions is the result of an advance knowledge of the main points to be discussed. Advance planning should also include a consideration of the approach to take in the interview.

To plan his approach, the interviewer should find out information about the person or group of people to be interviewed. He can do this in the case of an individual by checking in *Who's Who* or some other source of biographical information, by finding out something about the individual's position and work and what he may have written, or by asking others about him. Any group to be interviewed must be analyzed according to its characteristics. Information on the interviewee will also help the interviewer to explain the purpose of the interview in terms of the interviewee's experience and interest, thus getting him interested in the subject of the interview. Such information will enable the interviewer to adapt his questions to his purpose and to the interviewee. In the depth interview he will be able to lead the interviewee into a freer and more nearly complete discussion than would otherwise be possible. Consideration should also be given to controlling the interview, to keeping the conversation on the subject or problem at hand.

In a survey, when a large number of interviews is being conducted, it is sometimes appropriate to secure and show letters of recommendation or of introduction to make the interviewee feel that the interview has the proper backing. This procedure is followed also when only a few people are being interviewed, especially when interviews have not been arranged in advance, which is the case in conducting surveys or in taking polls. If a few people are being interviewed for information, it is customary and courteous to arrange an appointment in advance. This will let the interviewee know what is wanted and will enable him to get ready for the interview. It will also assure the interviewer that time will be allotted to the interview. A busy executive will not be likely to sit down for thirty minutes and give information on the spur of the moment; his time is too valuable for that. He has his day planned and does not always have time for an unscheduled interview to help someone else.

An appointment for an interview may be made by letter, by telephone, or by a personal office call. The last is too expensive and time-consuming to use often. The telephone has the advantage of expediency. With all three, however, it is necessary to tell the interviewee who the interviewer is and what he is doing. Interest should be created so the interviewee will be willing to be interviewed. A selling job must be done. It can be accomplished in much the same way as the covering letter to a mail questionnaire sells its reader on responding. The same points, such as showing how the reader can benefit, letting him realize the importance and need for the interview, and motivating him to action, should be followed. At the end of the letter or telephone conversation specific arrangements should be made, suggesting or designating a time and place for the interview.

During the Interview. The logical way to begin is to introduce oneself and to explain the purpose of the interview: "I am Jonathan Gogetter, a senior at Podunk University's College of Business Administration. I have come here to find out your practices in interviewing job applicants."

In fact, the purpose can be explained in such a way that the interviewee will appreciate it in terms of his own experience and interests and will reveal the desired information. A psychological approach to the interview might be to engage the interviewee in casual conversation, getting him to talk freely and then leading into some main point of interest for discussion. Again, the interviewer might first seek to create a desire on the part of the interviewee, and then show how this desire can be fulfilled by the investigation.

During the interview the interviewer should

1. Gain the cooperation of the interviewee.

2. Listen sympathetically to personal opinions; be frank, sincere, pleasant, and friendly.

3. Gain and deserve the interviewee's confidence.

4. Keep control of the interview and center interest on the interviewee and what he has to contribute.

5. Ask general and specific questions to guide the interviewee to discuss facts freely and thoroughly.

6. Introduce topics of conversation which will call for significant facts desired.

7. Get the full meaning of each statement or answer given.

8. Give the interviewee the opportunity to qualify his answers.

The conversation might be guided by pertinent statements of the investigator. He might introduce his questions so that they will interest the interviewee. The latter should be permitted to tell the story his way; afterwards he can supplement it by answering questions. As questions are asked the answers should not be implied. The interviewee can be made to realize his responsibility for the facts and the importance of accurate information. Sometimes a casual suggestion that certain statements can be verified will encourage him to be accurate: "Could you give me a copy of the memorandum for checking the cost figures?" or "I am assuming that Mr. Johnson will verify the expenses." The interviewer should watch for new leads for information or for additional information. Sometimes the opportunity comes toward the end of the interview; sometimes it is in the form of a casual remark.

The information secured from an interview must be recorded at once. It can be done during the interview or immediately afterwards to avoid omissions and inaccuracies in recording data. In recording his facts, the interviewer should

1. Understand all that is said, discerning significant points.

2. Record testimony, recognizing inaccuracies and recording specific answers to questions.

3. Distinguish between observed facts and facts reported by interviewee.

4. Distinguish inferences from facts whether observed or reported.

5. Check percentages, figures, and the like to report facts accurately.

6. Distinguish attitudes and opinions from facts.

7. Record explanations for opinions and attitudes, getting all the necessary facts.

When making a survey the interviewer usually records the answer to each question as it is given. Often a checklist will be used for this purpose, making tabulation easy later. On the other hand, in some depth interviews note-taking might hamper the interviewee, in which case all information must be recorded immediately afterwards. The question sheet itself may be used in recording answers to prearranged questions. Note cards should be used to record general information or facts revealed during the interview. The procedure followed in recording interview facts on note cards is the same as that for recording notes from bibliographical research discussed earlier in this chapter. Separate facts should be recorded on separate cards, with subject headings indicated on each card.

After the desired information has been obtained, the interview should be brought to a logical close. Care should be taken to complete the interview within the allotted time. The interviewee should be led to feel that he has made a valuable contribution and that his efforts and the information he has given are appreciated and worthwhile.

After the Interview. Although the interviewee has been thanked at the close of the interview, he will still appreciate a thank-you note. The interviewee should be led to feel that his interview has built goodwill for future business relations. Just a brief letter, thanking him for his time and effort and letting him know that his contribution was useful, is all that is necessary. This should be done within two weeks after the interview.

If data were not recorded during the interview, they should be recorded as soon as possible afterward. The interviewer should also take stock of himself and the interview. He will want to relate his results to his objectives and problem. He will want to review the interview critically. This will enable him to discover his weaknesses and to improve at the next opportunity. If he decides that he wants to quote the interviewee directly, he should secure permission to do so. He may even want to have the quotation checked or verified by the person he is quoting. After an important interview he may also want to secure a confirmatory statement of significant facts. This will enable him to check figures, statistics, and other information for accuracy and authenticity.

A list of interviews should be maintained for making necessary acknowledgments in the report and for inclusion in the final bibliography. Cards are used to record entries similar to those on bibliographical cards. The necessary information includes name, position, company, address, date, and place of the interview.

The Role of the Interviewer

Because of the nature and purpose of the interview as a research method, the interviewer must always maintain an impartial point of view. His role is a difficult one, for he must be continually on the alert and always tactful, friendly, and pleasant. He should like people, and people should like him. A neatly dressed person who is confident and business-like in his manner and knows when to smile will be likely to create a favorable appearance at the beginning of the interview. He must remain calm and collected throughout, never giving opinions or voicing approval or disapproval of the interviewee's ideas.

He should also be accurate and honest in recording data and in filling in answers to a questionnaire. Characteristics of the ideal interviewer listed by Mildred Parten in *Surveys, Polls and Samples: Practical Procedures* include the ability to evaluate people and situations quickly and correctly, the ability to talk easily with all types of people, keen powers of observation, a regard for details, persistence and thoroughness, conscientiousness and reliability, a ready wit, a good memory, an inquiring mind, and an interest in research and ideas.[1]

Interviewing is an art which can be acquired and developed. When surveys and polls are taken, a number of people are usually selected to do the interviewing, since the undertaking is too large for one person to handle. Interviewers are selected for the characteristics mentioned and then are given some general training and specific instructions. The purpose of the general training is to give some background in survey work; the purpose of the specific instruction is orientation to the survey being undertaken. The instructions usually include a statement of the purpose of the survey; a list of interviews to be made, including how, when, and where; instructions for handling the questionnaire; the approach to use; and how to identify oneself. These points must be understood also by the independent researcher who is conducting his own study.

The interviewer is also an observer, but he must keep his observations apart from his interpretations. The findings are recorded, tabulated, and analyzed for relative importance and usefulness.

It is important for the interviewer to plan his interview and to follow procedures and techniques that will assure him of reliable data. Information that has been secured from a single individual is recorded on note cards and examined for reliability in the same way as bibliographical data—by checking the source and by examining the facts themselves.

Information from a number of interviews, however, can be expressed in quantitative terms. Thus its reliability and validity can be tested by statistical methods. The responses to questions are tabulated and examined to formulate generalizations or conclusions. A test of reliability would be a test for adequacy of the sampling. Responses from two sets of interviews under comparable conditions secured by the same interviewer or another interviewer can be put into quantitative form, and

---

[1] Mildred Parten, *Surveys, Polls and Samples: Practical Procedures* (New York: Harper and Row, Publishers, 1950), pp. 138, 139.

coefficients of correlation can be computed statistically as a measure of the data's reliability. The coefficient of correlation between data from one-half of the interviews and data from the other half can also be used. The same statistical tests used for testing the reliability of the results of the mail questionnaire can be applied here; likewise the same tests for the validity of data may be applied. The standard error of deviation is used to test the validity of data secured from both interviews and mail questionnaires. Finally, although it is sometimes impractical to apply statistical measures to facts secured from interviews, data can always be scrutinized for consistency, accuracy, and logic.

OBSERVATION

Observation is a chief source of securing first-hand information, and it is often combined with other methods, especially with the personal interview. Just as an interview in its simplest form is conversation with a purpose, so observation in its simplest form is seeing with a purpose. It is recognizing and recording information pertaining to objects, events, and people that are seen. To determine the amount and nature of the flow of traffic one can stand on a street corner and observe the cars that go by, noting the model and number of automobiles, the licenses, the drivers, and the like. In a grocery story one can determine brand preferences by observing the customers as they buy certain brands off the shelves. On the production line in a factory one can observe the procedure being followed to find out the steps in the production process. Through observation the investigator gains information first-hand; it is in the realm of his experience. He not only observes but also forms a mental impression of what he has perceived. Information thus secured is recorded and analyzed for drawing conclusions.

Types and Uses

There are two kinds of observation—uncontrolled and controlled. In *uncontrolled observation* the observer views things as they are. In the case of observing a worker at his job he would watch him under normal working conditions to see how he performed his tasks. The worker's reaction to his job would also be noticed. Impressions and facts would be recorded. In *controlled observation* the observer selects pertinent data for observation and controls the conditions under which he observes. He might standardize all but one of the factors to be observed. He sets the stage and then observes what happens.

Controlled observation is experimental research. It is commonly used in the scientific laboratory. The scientist carries on an experiment and records his findings, which are observations under controlled conditions. For business purposes controlled observation is used in testing. One way to decide whether or not to buy a certain piece of equipment is to install it temporarily and observe it at work. Before proceeding with an advertising campaign an agency will want to test it. A company interested in devising a new package for one of its products will test several possibilities for their results before deciding on which package to use. Mailing lists likewise are tested, as are sales promotion devices and advertising media to determine which ones to use.

Both controlled and uncontrolled observation use memory. Objects or actions are observed and understood through mental impressions that are preserved through memory and recalled for a purpose. The difference lies in the control the observer exercises over the situation and the conditions under which he observes. Both types of observation are used for similar business purposes. In marketing, pertinent facts about consumers, products, competitors, and the market are observed, reported, and analyzed. In the operation or production phases of a business, processes, problems, procedures, and techniques are observed. In personnel or industrial relations an individual's actions and responses are noted and analyzed. The observer can use a psychological approach to a problem. Sometimes it is necessary to examine something and describe it. Observation is thus the chief source of information used in examination reports. Sometimes the investigator must observe how something is done in a firm other than his own. He makes a field trip and observes the procedure. Observation can also be used in making surveys, particularly those to determine brand preferences. Instead of asking the customers what brands they buy, the observer obtains permission to see what brands they have on their pantry shelves.

One chief advantage of the observation method is that it requires the observer to report behavior rather than interpret it; in this respect it tends to eliminate the observer's personal prejudices and biases. On the other hand, the method is limited, for it reveals only those motives which are expressed in overt acts of behavior. Another disadvantage is that the observer may be so impressed with an exceptional piece of data that he thinks it occurs frequently, or he may be so concerned with finding what he is looking for that he sees it even when it is not there and overlooks other pertinent information.

The observation method for surveys is costlier and slower than the interview or questionnaire. It can, however, lend itself to statistical treatment for reaching conclusions in a survey and can be used for considering subjective data objectively.

Procedures in Observing

Careful planning for observation is just as important as it is for an interview. The observer must have a clear and complete understanding of the problem and of what he is to observe. He must determine not only the main points to look for but also the details, and he should know how they are interrelated and fit into his subject. In some instances he will jot down an outline of what to observe. To know what to expect, he will also try to foresee people's reactions and their relation to the incidences he will observe. Prior to the observation the observer must also assume the proper mental attitude and maintain it. It is important that his mind be free of all prejudice and bias. He should cultivate an inquisitive attitude and keep an open mind.

During an observation the observer must concentrate on what he is doing. It is necessary for him to keep his mind on the subject and to be interested in it. If he has thought out things ahead of time and has listed important points to observe, he will have a guide to follow. He should first observe as a whole the object or person, and then take in the details. This will help him see things in relation to each other and to the problem at hand, as well as give the proper perspective to the facts observed. In most instances it is better to observe one thing at a time. The purpose is to get all the essential facts, excluding the irrelevant ones. In making a survey a questionnaire might be used, and the observer will record the answers to the questions, taking down other pertinent data observed. Otherwise he will follow the same procedures for recording notes as outlined in the discussion on bibliographical research, making use of note cards and indicating subject headings on the cards. Notes may be recorded while observing or written as soon afterwards as possible.

Human elements must also be considered in observing, for the observer feels as well as sees. He should, however, make a clear distinction in his notes between what was seen and what was felt. He should strive to report behavior as it is rather than as it may be interpreted. Therefore he must observe accurately, impartially, and thoroughly, so that his facts will be reliable and applicable. When interpretations are given they should be recorded as such.

Results from observations are evaluated, edited, and incorporated with other facts if recorded on note cards, or they are edited, tabulated, placed in tables and charts, and interpreted along with other statistical data if the purpose has been to observe a number of occurrences as in conducting a survey. They are then organized along with similar data for analysis and presentation in a report.

OPERATIONS RESEARCH

One of the newer research techniques being adapted to business today is operations research. It is an organized effort of a number of people to consider all possible factors, alternatives, and their consequences for arriving at a solution. It began and was developed during World War II by the British as a technique for determining the effective use of military forces and equipment. A team of experts pooled their ideas and efforts to ascertain the best bombing target, the best location for radar equipment, or the best route for supply ships and other means of transportation. In essence, then, it is a team approach to researching a problem or to making a decision.

Operations research is simply what its name says—it is research on operations. It deals with processes common to several functional areas on the assumption that one problem affects the others. It seeks to integrate the findings and ideas from those in various operating areas into one entity.

In business a team composed of economists, marketing and financial specialists, and the like, are assembled. Each specialist examines the problem from his particular point of view, discovers as many alternative solutions as possible, and evaluates the course of action of each. All alternatives are then presented and weighed, and the best possible solution to the problem is found. This technique involves a direct application of creative and logical thinking to problem solving.

The usefulness of the team approach to operations research is controversial, for most business firms cannot afford the luxury of a team of varied disciplines. A few teams once formed have been disbanded. A person with the responsibility of obtaining a soluton to a problem through operatons research can consult representatives of other disciplines as he deems necessary.

Although the advent of the computer has provided a fast and versatile tool for operations research, most problems can be solved without it.

Various mathematical techniques can also be used to find the best solution. When all possible solutions are programmed for computer use, they are assigned relative values, and all possible combinations of factors influencing each are also programmed and given values. The computer comes up with an answer on the basis of the effects the factors have on the solutions presented. This technique is applicable to many business problems, and it may gain widespread use by management. The Operations Research Society of America is a professional group dedicated to refining the process, imparting solutions to problems which it has solved, and furthering operations research in business.

FOR DISCUSSION AND WRITING

1. You have been asked to make a marketing survey of buying habits for frozen orange juice in the supermarkets of your city. The results are to be used in your sales and advertising program. Prepare the questionnaire that you would use. Would you plan to use mail, telephone, or interview procedures for the survey? Discuss the merits of each before making your decision. Or would you use observation research? Why?

2. It will be of interest and importance to find out what research is being done in each of the following areas:

   a. Motivational research.
   b. Information theory.
   c. Game theory.
   d. Industrial psychology.
   e. Communication theory.

   Prepare an annotated bibliography on one of the suggested areas. Also plan to present your findings on one of the areas as an oral report or part of a panel discussion. Your instructor may divide the class into groups to cover all five areas, or he may have you submit a memorandum report.

3. Write a report evaluating and recommending professional magazines in your major area which you think should be included in the new library in your company.

4. A statement on the "Social Responsibilities of Business Corporations" was released mid-summer 1971 by the Committee for Economic Development. An editorial in the July 24, 1971, issue of *Saturday Review,* page 32, says the statement puts it this way:

There is now a pervasive feeling in the country that the social order somehow has gotten out of balance, and that greater affluence amid a deteriorating environment and community life does not make much sense. The discontinuity between what we have accomplished as producers and consumers and what we want in the way of a good society has engendered strong social pressures to close the gap—to improve the way the overall American system is working so that a better quality of life can be achieved for the entire citizenry within a well-functioning community. . . . Inasmuch as business exists to serve society, its future will depend on the quality of management's response to the changing expectations of the public.

Central to the CED report is an inventory of activities that American corporations can fruitfully pursue in order to satisfy these expectations. The areas include: education; employment and training; urban renewal and development; pollution abatement; conservation and recreation; culture and the arts; and medical care. No one doubts the resources and expertise that business can bring to these problems. The difficulty is that, in assuming new societal responsibilities, business almost inevitably must sacrifice some short-term profits.

Not all corporations are equally committed to social improvement. The CED's answer to this difficulty is

If corporations cannot deal individually with major social responsibilities such as pollution because of competitive cost disadvantages, and if they are unable to cooperate in resolving such difficulties, then they logically and ethically should propose and support rational governmental regulation which will remove the short-run impediments from actions that are wise in the long run.

Questions are being raised and issues are being discussed. Efforts are also being made to protect the environment, to aid education, and to employ the disadvantaged.

Prepare a report (written or oral) on the problem. The subject will have to be limited. Interviews, questionnaires, surveys, and correspondence in addition to bibliographical research, could reveal what practices and evidences there are that prove corporations are taking a position on social responsibilities, what that position is, and what is being done about it.

5. Prepare a report on trends in a particular industry. This should include figures and factual data pertaining to employment, wages, types of work, past history, and potential growth. It could be oriented toward a study of a specific company within an industry and an analysis of its potential growth and position for making an investment decision.

6. Prepare a report on your choice for a career. (This might give statistics on employment and salaries, qualifications, supply and demand, and professional opportunities for development and advancement.) Include your rationale for your decision. Would you advise others likewise to enter the same field? And for the same reasons?

7. Talk with someone in a business firm, such as the head of marketing, production, finance, industrial relations, or some other function. Ask him to tell you about a pending problem of fairly broad scope in his company. Prepare to describe it to the class. After class discussion, decide what information and data would be needed for solving the problem:

a. From outside the company—such as government data, trade journal information, prices of machinery, facts about competition. Then prepare a bibliography and decide on other means for collecting the necessary outside facts.

b. From inside the company. Then prepare a list of questions to be asked during interviews or conferences and decide what data can be collected by other methods.

Your instructor may have you carry out the business research necessary for working out a solution. This project may also serve as a basis for your writing a long, formal report to be submitted three to five weeks later or at the end of the semester.

8. Write the covering letter and a return postcard questionnaire that could be used in making a readership survey of the employee magazine in your company. Of the company annual report.

9. Your company wants you to make an investigation of employee morale to determine ways in which it can be improved. Construct a questionnaire and make plans for its use in surveying the feelings and attitudes of the employees.

10. Your college wants to launch a program of informing its students. Just as the well-informed employee is an efficient, cooperative producer, so the student informed of the activities, purpose, objectives, and organization of his college is cooperative.

   a. Prepare a questionnaire to be used in a student survey to determine what the student knows, wants to know, should be told, and how he is to be informed.
   b. How could the results be used?
   c. Make the survey and report on the findings.

11. Make arrangements for your class to visit a company in your community. It may be the newspaper plant, a large business office, an advertising agency, a manufacturing concern, a bank, a large department store's offices, or a distributing company. Before making the visit, plan what to observe, how and why, and what questions to ask. After your return, write up your notes in the form of a memorandum report. Can you draw any conclusions or suggestions for improvement of what you observe?

12. Interview a businessman who is successful in the field in which you are most interested and write up the results. Before making the interview, you will want to plan it carefully and decide what information to seek from him. Afterwards send him a thank-you letter.

13. Go into a store, office, or similar place where people are working and write up the results of a procedure that you observe. Recommend any changes that would increase efficiency of operation.

14. If you were obtaining data for each of the following report subjects, what research method or methods would you use? Why? How?

   a. Consumer attitudes toward the _____ Department Store.
   b. Viewing habits of the TV audience of station _____.
   c. The selection and placement process of executive trainees for _____ Company.
   d. Locating a small business such as a coin laundry, jewelry store, sewing machine center, electrical appliance repair shop, shoe repair shop, or ice-cream bar in a suburban shopping center.
   e. Readership study of _____ magazine.
   f. The need for frozen food lockers in the _____ section of the city.

15. Given the problem of determining the qualities considered necessary in a secretary, prepare a questionnaire and covering letter to be mailed to a particular segment of businessmen such as personnel directors, representatives of top management, executive vice-presidents, or office managers.

   This can be a class project or a committee assignment if your instructor wishes. It can be varied by changing *secretary* to *accountant, advertising copywriter, computer programmer, executive trainee, salesman,* or some other position. The mailing list (sample) can also differ.

16. Given the problem of deciding what professional and trade associations you should belong to when you graduate, interview several professors and businessmen to gain information about the groups they belong to. Several possible associations are

Administrative Management Association	American Statistical Association
American Accounting Association	International Council of Industrial Editors
American Business Communication Association	International Communication Association
American Economic Association	National Association of Accountants
American Finance Association	Operations Research Society of America
American Management Association	Public Relations Society of America
American Marketing Association	

Report to the class which ones you plan to join and why.

17. Given the problem of deciding what brand of paint a company should use for its new warehouse, prepare a list of questions to ask each dealer about his brand. Select three brands for consideration, gather appropriate information, and prepare a memorandum report.

18. Many of you who are students today at colleges of business administration will be tomorrow's business leaders. Questions such as the following provide answers useful to students and instructors in their work together:

a. To what sources of information do you turn when seeking answers to business problems?

b. What magazines are most helpful in providing instructive material for classroom use?

Make a survey of the faculty in your school to determine what, if any, general business and news magazines they recommend to students in connection with their courses, and which, if any, they find most helpful. Make a survey of business school students to determine what, if any, general and news magazines they find most helpful and which ones they turn to for source material. Results from the two surveys should be analyzed and compared, and conclusions should be drawn. Make the surveys, either by questionnaire or interviews, and present your findings in a short report.

A similar survey could be made of businessmen to determine what magazines they read regularly or occasionally and to find out which ones are most helpful as sources of information. Such readership studies would be useful also to magazines and advertisers. Why? Several general and news magazines are

Business Week	*Newsweek*
Fortune	*Time*
Harvard Business Review	*U.S. News & World Report*
Nation's Business	*Forbes*

19. Many schools of business administration seek to determine if the curriculum is meeting its objectives and needs of the students. They send questionnaires to selected or randomly chosen groups of alumni, and the results show courses that have been most helpful to alumni on their jobs and to what degree. Dr. H. C. Edgeworth reported on such a study sponsored by the School of Business, Florida State University, Tallahassee. The questionnaire on page 227 [2] was mailed to Beta Gamma Sigma (Business Administration Honorary Fraternity) mem-

---

BETA GAMMA SIGMA
OPINION SURVEY

Name _____

Address _____

Year of Graduation _____ Major _____ Degree _____

Employed by _____

Your present position _____

Number of employers you have had since graduation _____

1. In terms of your business career, please rate the degree of benefit in each of the following subject areas offered or required by the School of Business.

	Considerable Benefit	Some Benefit	Undecided	Little Benefit	No Benefit
Accounting	_____	_____	_____	_____	_____
Business Law	_____	_____	_____	_____	_____
Communication	_____	_____	_____	_____	_____
Economics	_____	_____	_____	_____	_____
Finance	_____	_____	_____	_____	_____
Management	_____	_____	_____	_____	_____
Marketing	_____	_____	_____	_____	_____
Quantitative Methods	_____	_____	_____	_____	_____
Risk and Insurance	_____	_____	_____	_____	_____

2. Which subject area do you feel has been the most beneficial to you in your business career? _____
Should more courses be offered in this area? _____

3. Which subject area do you feel has been the least beneficial? _____
_____ Should the offerings in this area be reduced? _____

4. Do you feel the School of Business should be changed to a School of Business Administration? _____

If you care to make additional comments, please do so, using the back of this page.

bers who had graduated from 1963 through 1967. Make up a similar questionnaire that will reflect the courses and curriculum in your school. Select a mailing list of alumni and follow through on your investigation by tabulating the responses, drawing up charts and tables, reaching conclusions, and recommending changes. The Florida State survey reported an 80 percent response (147 returns out of 183 sent), which was very gratifying.

20. Suggested topics for a bibliographical research report:

   a. The plight of the graduate teaching fellow in colleges and universities (low pay, lack of recognition, etc.).
   b. Does sensitivity training solve or cause problems?
   c. Are lower educational standards a result of black student enrollment quotas?
   d. Are present narcotic laws fair? What, if any, changes should be made?
   e. What of man's future existence with artificial insemination?
   f. To believe or not to believe (in God)?
   g. Is war ever justified?
   h. The effects of the four-day week on productivity, morale, absenteeism, etc.
   i. Can business change its goals to meet "save the environment" demands?

2 H. C. Edgeworth, "Curriculum Feedback," *Collegiate News and Views,* May 1971, pp. 13–15.

REASONING
WITH DATA

7

ORGANIZING

    Classification

    Qualitative Data

    Quantitative Data

    Tables and Statistical Measures

INTERPRETING

    Reaching Conclusions

    Formulating Recommendations

OUTLINING

    Types of Outlines

    Forms of Outlines

    Outlining Systems

    Checklist

FOR DISCUSSION AND WRITING

THE INVESTIGATOR, after he has completed his research and gathered necessary facts and ideas, faces the problem of organizing and interpreting his data to have meaning and significance to him in formulating conclusions and recommendations. He then must outline his material for effective presentation to the reader in achieving his purpose. This chapter, then, deals with these three stages of report preparation.

ORGANIZING

Classification

The first step in organizing data is sorting and arranging like data into groups. This process is usually referred to as classifying data, and it may take place during or after gathering data. There are four kinds of data: qualitative, quantitative, chronological, and geographical. Facts and ideas on a subject are qualitative. They are recorded in the form of notes resulting from bibliographical research, interviews, letters, experience, observation, or even experimentation. Data expressed in terms of figures and adaptable to statistical treatment are quantitative. Easily recognizable because they refer to quantities or amounts, they are usually the results of questionnaires, although information from interviews, observation, and the like sometimes consists of responses which can be tabulated. The other two kinds of data—chronological and geographical—are self-explanatory. Geographical data are classified according to areas or regions, and chronological data are arranged according to a time sequence.

The purpose of classifying data is to group like with like data. The investigator can find out whether he has secured all his data and can discover relationships between groups of information. After classifying, he continues the process of organizing and interpreting. The type of data he is working with, however, will determine the procedure, and any one report may contain several kinds of data all brought together into a meaningful whole and used for reaching conclusions and making decisions.

Qualitative Data

Assume that you have read extensively on background material on fringe benefits and have a number of recorded note cards; the first step will be to arrange the cards together according to the subject headings placed in the upper left-hand corner of each card. Then it is a simple task to consider all your notes on one subject and the relationship of each subject-area breakdown to the other topics. Examination of the notes in relation to the purpose of your investigation and significance to the problem at hand will also provide fruitful interpretive ideas. Looking for common denominators will also enable you to combine topics and create subtopics.

Let us consider further how this works. In your study of company practices and policies concerning employee benefits, your bibliographical and company research resulted in a large number of notes on the following policies: accident, hospitalization, credit union, jury duty, military duty, sickness, pay advances, sick leave, profit-sharing, surgical expenses, guaranteed annual wage, maternity leave, stock purchase, terminal leave, life insurance, seniority wage increase, merit rating, dismissal pay, vacation, pension plan, and suggestion plan payment. After grouping notes on each subject, examine each group for significant relationships to other topics. This will reveal several benefits that are closely related. Seven deal with absences or leave from work. Because this is a fact they have in common, it becomes the common denominator for combining the seven groups under "leave-type benefits." Thus you combine and subdivide:

Leave-type Benefits—Jury duty, military duty, sick leave, maternity, terminal leave, dismissal pay, vacation.

Another group of policies pertain to insurance benefits. There are six of these:

Insurance Benefits—Accident, sickness, surgical expenses, hospitalization, life, pension.

The other common denominator is monetary-type benefits:

Monetary Benefits—Credit union, pay advances, guaranteed annual wage, profit-sharing, stock purchase, seniority wage increase, merit rating, suggestion plan payment.

Your qualitative data have been organized under common subject headings, and you can place other data under each of these headings.

Another method is to arrange facts and ideas by following a pattern of reasoning. Inductive reasoning calls for marshalling specific instances or details to point up a conclusion; it involves going from the specific to the general. Reasoning step by step from one fact to another is useful to the researcher, because he can see the relationship of the instances or details in proper perspective as he draws his generalizations and validates his conclusions. Reasoning deductively requires clear statements of premises, recognition of common points of relationship, and understanding of definition and classification. It involves going from the general to the specific and is especially useful in argumentation and in drawing conclusions from proved premises or hypotheses.

One can also arrange facts and ideas by the type of relationship they hold to each other—temporal, topical, causal, or spatial. Arranging material on the basis of a temporal relationship lends importance to the time element. Although it emphasizes points mentioned first and last because of their position, equal stress may be given to each item. A time sequence also helps to relate steps in a process and to give historical perspective to events. The employee benefits mentioned earlier followed a topic relationship. Several items were alike and formed part of a whole or larger topic. A causal relationship emphasizes need for a change. It indicates what has happened and the result of a particular action. A spatial relationship facilitates comparison by tying data to a particular location or space.

Quantitative Data

Quantitative data must first be examined and checked for accuracy and pertinency. The following question should be asked and answered in the affirmative about each piece of data: "Does this fact help accomplish the purpose of this study?" Quantitative data also should be examined and tested for their reliability by statistical procedures. The data may be checked for proportionality to determine whether or not they are representative, or the standard error of deviation may be used. The purpose in examining the data is to find out whether they are valid and to what degree. Unreliable and nonpertinent data are then discarded. The next step is tabulation, which enables one to compare, analyze, and evaluate responses. The type of responses called for in answers on a questionnaire determine how to set up a work sheet for tabulating results. For example, all questions demanding a "yes" or "no" answer may be checked together on one sheet, and likewise questions requiring an "always," "frequently," "seldom," or "never" response may be tabulated on one sheet. Corollary information, whether at the beginning or end of a questionnaire, must also be considered as variable factors for cross-tabulation. Tabulate questionnaires by counting and recording the responses in the proper places on work sheets. Dividing questionnaires into groups at the outset—male and female, or according to some other categories derived from the corollary information—will make checking each group easy; then totals may be reached. When the work sheets are completed, a single master or recapitulation sheet is made up from them, showing the number and type of responses for every question. Sometimes the recapitulation sheet is arranged with the same headings as the work sheets, the only difference being that the totals and not the actual counting is shown. All of this can be programmed for the computer and machine tabulated.

After the recap sheet is made up, data are reexamined for their significance and relationship to the problem. This step is very similar to the corresponding one in organizing qualitative data in which the investigator considers the significance of his data as a whole. This precedes his breaking them down into their parts or grouping like data together into a broader category. It is partially an interpretative process as well as an organizational one. The chief difference here between handling qualitative and quantitative data is that one must work out a way of presenting quantitative data in tables and determine what statistical measures will make the data comprehensible. For practical purposes the processes of organizing and interpreting quantitative data at this stage are the same. Interpretation requires organization, and organization requires interpretation; the two processes are one.

Tables and Statistical Measures

An analysis of the figures on the recapitulation sheet will often determine how they can be arranged in the form of tables. One compares figures, thinks through relationships of one fact to another, evaluates the importance of the material, and decides upon the significance of his figures. This enables him to group together like figures for presentation in tables.[1] When tables are set up they must be interpreted. Percentages are determined to bring out the relationship of one figure to another. For example, "50 responses out of 392 replies" does not express the relationship as pointedly as "13 percent of the responses," which is more comprehensible. Even the 13 percent expressed in simpler terms could be "about one in eight." Using small, round numbers makes the data more meaningful.

Selecting a central tendency when interpreting tables helps to spot trends. Three statistical averages indicate a central tendency—the mean, median, and mode. The mean is the arithmetical average obtained by

---

[1] See Chapter 4 for information on how to present data in tables.

totaling figures and dividing by number of cases. The median is the mid-point between the upper and lower halves. It represents the case that is in the middle of a list of figures arranged in rank order. The mode indicates the pattern followed most often. It is the point of highest frequency, where most cases occur. The three averages refer to different ideas, and although the mean is the true average, no case is that realistic. It shows what the situation would be if all things were equal. It is the socialistic average of a group. The median, however, does indicate a true picture; there are as many cases above it as below it. It is in the middle of the road. The mode is the pattern established by the occurrence of the highest number of cases.

In considering averages it is necessary to consider the range and the extremes and how they might affect the central figure selected. The range makes the average more significant. Statisticians use standard deviations to indicate the range, but most report readers will not understand their use. The report writer with an advanced knowledge of statistics may employ them for his own interpretation, but he would be likely to use a simple explanation in the final report. In addition to the range, exceptional cases also should be noted for adding interesting sidelights to the data, although they may not be necessary statistically. Interpreting data in a table calls for considering the totals first and looking at the table as a whole. Then an examination of the appropriate statistical measures—the range, the extremes, and the exceptions—should be made. All this is a basis for drawing statistical conclusions. Before final conclusions can be drawn, however, quantitative data must be considered in their proper relationship to the qualitative data. This is a "fitting-in" process, in which the investigator reexamines each type of data in light of the other and organizes each accordingly.

Let us take a look at a situation in which data were organized and used as follows. Six questions on the personnel directors' survey questionnaire dealt with appearance.[2] The percentages for responses here were

Question
1. 17% Short   58% Medium   13% Long   10% Not a factor
2. 91% Yes   6% No   3% No answer
3. 34% Yes   61% No   68% Yes   29% No
4. 16% Short   65% Medium   18% Long
5. 55% Conservative   16% Latest style 38% Not a factor
6. 78% Yes   21% No

A bar chart showing appearance factors was made up, using a different color for indicating each factor.

[2] See page 204.

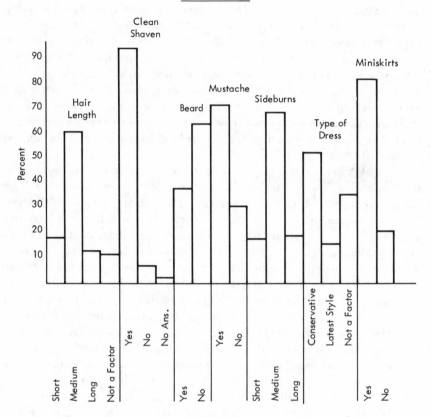

INTERPRETING

The interpretation of the preceding chart for presentation in the report went something like this:

> Personal appearance modes are subject to change and controversy among people. The overwhelming majority of businessmen say they are slow to adapt to changes in appearance. According to the chart depicting the responses of personnel directors in the survey, job applicants should have short to medium-length hair and should be conservatively dressed. Sideburns, however, can be medium length, and mustaches are acceptable. If a young man wants to get the job, however, he will not wear a beard. They are taboo. The personnel directors strongly feel that job applicants should be clean-shaven (with the exception of a mustache).
>
> Apparently what applies to men does not apply to women. Women in the business world can wear miniskirts. Perhaps although the men want men conservatively dressed, they still have a soft touch for femininity.

The researcher considered each appearance factor and the percentages of responses from which he could infer significant points and reach conclusions.

Reaching Conclusions

Conclusions are the result of reasoned judgment from interpreting the data, and they make data relevant to the problem at hand.

The simplest application of inductive logic is to enumerate instances or tabulate responses which will confirm a pattern or trend. Often, such as in the survey results, conclusions will be pointed up. Sometimes causes are examined along with their effects or results. An observed series of events might also establish a generalization.

Sometimes deductive reasoning will be followed. The analyst will reason from the general to the specific, from the universal to the individual, or from given premises to their necessary conclusion. First he might state his proposition, then his reasons to support it, and then the conclusion which reinforces the original premise. Alternative propositions and conclusions may be considered. Analogies prove useful for clarification.

Conclusions, whether derived from deductive and inductive reasoning or reached through statistical measures, are tentative until they are tested and proved valid or true. Then they become final and serve as a basis for formulating recommendations. A check of the data or evidence should be sufficient for proving an inductive or deductive conclusion.

Another test of tentative conclusions is to apply common sense, for they must sound practical and be workable. A real effort must be made to see if all available data have been used and nothing overlooked, noting carefully all exceptions. Sometimes an exception may make the conclusion impractical, or a detailed fact which has been overlooked may prove that the conclusion is unworkable. When the conclusion solves a problem, the researcher must find out how his proposed solution will work out if it is put into effect. In this case he projects his conclusion into the future and, assuming its being put into effect, tests to see how it will work out. If it proved itself workable, then the tentative conclusion becomes a final one.

Conclusions that have been reached statistically can be tested by rechecking the statistical processes and techniques that were used and considering their validity in relation to other evidence and data that were secured. In a questionnaire survey, the conclusions are valid only to the extent to which the sample was representative of the population from which it was taken.

The negative test may also be applied in testing tentative conclusions. Here the analyst assumes that the direct opposite is the conclusion and uses the evidence to prove it. If careful consideration of his facts proves his assumed opposite conclusion, then his original tentative conclusion is not true. The negative test may also be applied to alternative conclusions which are not opposite conclusions. If the assembled evidence supports the alternative conclusion, then a number of alternative conclusions may have to be examined before arriving at a general conclusion with which the alternatives show agreement. This generalization would then become the final conclusion.

Another method of testing tentative conclusions is to use references. The researcher may use bibliographical research to find out whether or not writers agree with him on his findings and conclusions, and if they do not agree, he will seek logical explanations of why they do not. His findings may be referred to others to determine whether or not they can reach his conclusions. He may also consult with others to test the soundness of his reasoning. References might be used further to determine whether or not general business practice or policies agree with the tentative conclusions.

After testing tentative conclusions by applying logic and common sense, by determining whether or not they are workable, by using statistical measures, by applying the negative test, and by using references, final conclusions may be reached. The tentative conclusions that have been proved by testing can be restated as final conclusions. They are the generalizations derived from the interpreted results of an investigation. They must be clear, concise, and definite.

A final check must be made of the relationship of each conclusion to the objectives and purpose of the report. Usually each conclusion will fulfill an objective and will be necessary to achieve the purpose of the report. The original working plan may be used as a basis for this final check on relationships. At this point the analyst should also turn to the statement of his problem or subject and determine whether or not his final conclusions are adequate. If they are, he turns to the next step—the formulation of recommendations.

Formulating Recommendations

Conclusions are the basis for recommendations suggesting action that should be followed. The latter are the logical outgrowth of conclusions which support them and which in turn are supported by data. Just as conclusions fulfill the objectives of a report, so recommendations achieve the purpose of the report. They indicate what is to be done and specifically tell how, when, where, and by whom. To get action, recommendations must be practical and definite. The businessman is not interested in a recommendation that is not reasonable and feasible, nor will he take the recommended action unless it is proved to be the best course to follow.

Before final recommendations are formulated, tentative ones should be tested. Many tests for tentative conclusions are also applicable in testing recommendations. The researcher wants to make sure that his recommendations are logical, workable, and sound. He will check to determine whether or not they accomplish his purpose and present a solution to the problem.

OUTLINING

After the researcher has organized and thought through his data, he is ready to plan his presentation. An outline serves as a further means of organizing material and as a guide for writing the report. A carefully prepared outline facilitates the specific purpose of the report, for it compels the writer to think through all aspects of his data and their relationships and to understand the reader and his use of the report. Business practice often calls for approval of both preliminary and final outlines by the person authorizing the report before the writer continues with his work. Some companies demand outlines so that their personnel will be guided toward presenting clear, logical reports as results of keen analysis of the problem.

An outline divides a report into its major parts and shows the relationship of each subdivision. For this reason it can also serve as a basis for formulating subject headings used in the report and for organizing the table of contents. Consider, for example, the following from a sentence outline:

A. One-floor operation is properly justified for heavy industry, wherein the difficulty of processing heavy materials requires simplification.

Such a main point in an outline may serve as a topic sentence in developing the subject of a section of the report. In that respect it becomes a guide for writing. From the sentence an appropriate subject heading can be selected for a particular part of the report. For instance, "Justification of One-Floor Operation" is a subject heading derived from the example outline heading. In the table of contents the subject heading for the section will be listed with the page number on which it appears:

Justification of One-Floor Operation 10

Another use of the outline is as a basis for writing a summary of the report. A sentence outline, with the addition of transitional words and phrases, becomes a brief, which carries the outline one step further in showing the relationship between ideas. Likewise a sentence outline, with the addition of connectives and presented in paragraph form rather than outline form, becomes an abstract or summary of the report. A part of a report brief in which the connectives have been added to the original outline follows. (The connectives are italicized to indicate the additions.)

II.   One type of executive training program is the multiple-management plan.
A.   It was inaugurated in 1932 by the McCormick Company of Baltimore.

Under this plan,

B.   Three boards supplement the senior board of directors.
1. They are the factory executive board, the sales board, and junior executive board.
2. The junior executive board provides management training for its members.
C.   There are several advantages to this plan,

such as the following:

1. Future executives are given the opportunity to tackle significant company problems, to discuss them freely and openly, to exhibit their judgment and originality, and to meet with senior officers on matters of significance to them;

2.

and

3.

Also

D.   There are several disadvantages.
1. Development of men comes slowly,

and

2. Company action is a slow process handled in this way.

However,

E.   Multiple management develops executive ability at the same time it uses its executive talent.

But

1. Full cooperation is necessary,

and

2. Top authorities must be ready to share authority and responsibilities.

Subject headings converted from the outline brief just shown would appear in the report text on appropriate pages as follows:

MULTIMANAGEMENT TRAINING PROGRAM

Origin

Supplementary Boards

Advantages

Disadvantages

Conclusion: Developing and Using Executive Talent

The fact must not be overlooked, however, that the major use of the outline is as a guide for organizing and writing the report, although its derived subject headings guide the reader for easy comprehension and later reference.

Types of Outlines

The area development division of Public Service Indiana (Indiana's largest electric company), confronted with the task of attracting new industry to the state, decided to prepare facts about Indiana from acreage to zoning, raw material and suppliers available, labor skills, transportation, and so forth. They came up with the following outline, which organized their material and service as a guide for writing the report, published in an attractive slick-paper brochure with an accompanying covering letter.

A case of location
Specialized skills
    The population boom
    The shift in types of employment
    The desire for more localized employment
Access to markets
    Highways
    Trucks
    Railroads
    Airways
    Waterways
Raw materials and sources
    Steel, aluminum, lead refineries
    Rubber and rubber products
    Glass, plastics
    Industrial equipment and supplies
    Natural resources
Now . . . which location?
    North
    South
The case for northern Indiana
    Town sizes and population
    Principal industries
    Railroads, rivers, reservoirs
    Mineral industries
    Raw materials and suppliers
The case for southern Indiana
    Town sizes and population
    Principal industries
    Major manufacturing groups and number of employees
    Railroads, rivers, reservoirs, mineral industry
    Raw materials and suppliers
Recreation, culture, and education
    Recreation
    Education
    Purdue University

Indiana University
University of Notre Dame
Culture
Indiana University
Purdue University
Indiana State University
May we help you?

The preceding outline is topical in its form and specific with respect to the material presented. The form could also have been sentence and the material general in nature. It is also possible and sometimes practical to mix the two forms or to mix the general with the specific by couching main points in general terms with details stated specifically, or vice versa, and by putting major divisions in topical form and all subdivisions and details in sentence form, or the other way around. Consistency must rule. For instance, if the first main topic is in sentence form, all main topics should be. If the main topic is expressed in general terms, all main topics are.

A general outline serves as a guide in organizing material, by indicating general divisions and subdivisions for the report. According to function, there are three main divisions in the body of most reports: introduction, presentation and analysis, and conclusions and recommendations. The purpose of the introduction is to present the necessary background for the reader to understand the report. It may contain authorization or circumstances under which the report was requested, need for the study and its intended use, history of the problem, purpose and objectives, scope and limitations, method of procedure, definition of terms, and a summary of what is to follow. The purpose of the presentation and analysis section is to present facts and their interpretation to the reader. Here the report may be broken down into various factors to be considered, parts of the subject presented, comparisons and evaluations given, and relationships shown. Often several aspects of the same problem are presented. The present situation may be analyzed, indicating the need for changes, and the changes and possible results may also be examined. The purpose of the conclusions and recommendations section is to secure needed action. Conclusions are reached from the analysis of the facts, and recommendations based on the conclusions are then presented.

A general outline may indicate the three main divisions of the report with some subdivision. It does not, however, present all details necessary for developing the outline points. For that reason it serves as a guide but does not give information for writing the report proper. Many reports might follow the same general outline.

Here are some general outline patterns for use as guides in organizing reports. *Logically* a report might be organized as:

I	or	II	or	III
Introduction		Statement of problem		Problem
Main issue		An analysis of problem		Causes
Subdivision		Need for changes		Results
Subdivision		Proposed solutions		Possible solution
Main issue		Discussion of solutions		Discussion
Conclusion		Conclusion		Conclusion
Recommendations		Recommendations		Recommendations

Psychologically a report might be organized as:

I	or	II	or	III
Recommendation		Attention		Conclusion
Conclusion		Interest		Evidence
Supporting facts		Conviction		Alternatives
Discussion		Action		Discussion
Summary				Summary

Variations of the basic patterns might be used:

I	or	II	or	III
Summary		Present situation		Summary—what has been
Nature of problem		Weaknesses		done
Findings		Proposed corrections		Work to be completed
Conclusion		Discussion		Future plans
Recommendations		Pros and cons		
		Conclusions and Recom-		
		mendations		

These are guides, but they can be applied to reports written on any number of subjects. They are general and therefore do not include details. They are organizational patterns or logical arrangements of report divisions.

The psychologically arranged outline presents the material in the order of the significance of points in accomplishing the purpose of the report. Since recommendations are the fulfillment of the purpose and the most important part of the report, they are placed first. Busy executives interested in results and in quick action prefer this order. It points the reader's attention toward the recommendations at the outset, and the rest of the report supports the recommendations. In recent years it has become increasingly popular, because it is based on the reader's needs and his use of the report.

A general outline for a long report, thesis, or book might indicate chapter divisions:

Chapter   I.   The Problem
                   A. The problem and its aspects
                   B. Need and use of the study
                   C. Scope of subject
                   D. Definitions
                   E. Purpose and objectives
Chapter   II.   Previous Research
Chapter   III.   Method of Solution
                   A. Procedure for collecting data
                   B. Reliability of data
                   C. Summary of conclusions
Chapter   IV. ⎫
Chapter   V. ⎬ Devoted to separate aspects of the problem or subject
Chapter   VI. ⎭
Chapter   VII.   Conclusions
                   A.
                   B.
Chapter   VIII. Recommendations
                   A.
                   B.

A specific outline gives the detailed facts not included in the general
outline. Instead of using the term *purpose,* the purpose itself is stated,
such as "to recommend improvements in the sales promotional practices
of the Smith Department Store." The best use of the specific outline is
as a guide for further development of topics in writing the report. The
following outline contains the details which make it specific. Unlike the
general outline it pertains to only one report and thus can be used as a
guide for writing only that report.

An Outline on

IMPROVING COST ALLOCATION ON CONSTRUCTION
PROJECTS

I. Introduction
   A. Purposes
      1. To determine to what extent foremen and supervisors
         could be asked to assist the field accountant in allocating
         costs on road construction projects
      2. To revise the present cost accounting system so that an
         accurate picture of costs can be supplied to the home
         office
      3. To supply accurate cost information to management so
         that they may be able to bid more accurately on new jobs
   B. Scope and limitations
      1. Study of the cost accounting system used in field offices
      2. Exclusion of the cost accounting system used in the
         Ruston office

C. Procedure
   1. Personal experience and conferences with company accountants
   2. Information from company ledgers
II. Method of Setting Up Accounts
   A. Using those used on previous similar jobs
   B. Determining new ones as stated in the contract
III. How Costs Are Incurred
   A. Labor
   B. Direct materials
   C. Indirect costs
IV. Method of Allocating Costs
   A. Guessing
   B. Finding foremen and asking
   C. Using information on time sheets and dray tickets
V. Conclusions
   A. Present method inaccurate
      1. Depends too much on guesswork
      2. Foremen do not know what accounts are used
   B. Management unable to bid as competitively as possible due to inaccurate cost figures
VI. Recommendations
   A. Set up accounts in the Home Office for each project
   B. Supply foremen with accounts pertaining to their work
   C. Include labor breakdown on time sheets according to these accounts
   D. Foremen indicate account to charge on dray tickets for materials and supplies

Usually a report writer will begin with a general outline—depending on the nature of his problem, the type of report, and the reader—and then develop a specific outline. The general outline thus serves as a guide for organizing data. The specific outline will serve as a writing guide, for it shows at a glance the basic information which the report will contain. For more specific detail than is shown, this outline would give facts under each of its subdivisions. However, it serves its purpose as it is, and the same topics, with very little variation, can be used in each case as subject headings and as a table of contents.

Forms of Outlines

The outline just considered is a topic outline. Main points, divisions, and subdivisions have been expressed in words or phrases used as topics; the latter serve as a guide for further development in writing. A topic outline is used when the writer is fully aware of the relationship of each point to the whole problem and to all other points. It enables him to outline his data quickly and easily.

Noun forms are used whenever possible. For both thought and phrasing, parallel construction should be followed. Ideas that are parallel in thought must also be parallel in grammatical construction; therefore corresponding parts of an outline, being of equal significance, must be stated in the same grammatical form. When an infinitive construction is used to express an idea in a subdivision in an outline, the other points of equal significance, and listed under the same division, must also be stated in infinitive form. Likewise when point number "1" is a participial phrase, points "2," "3," and all other points appearing with it under the same subdivision must be expressed in a participial construction. The first word or phrase in an outline point is the key to the construction used.

In a topic outline each point should be a single phrase or idea. Each subhead should support its main head. Points of equal importance should, by their positions in the outline, be given equal rank. Subdivision means division into at *least* two parts. A "1" in an outline calls for a "2," an "A" for a "B," and so forth.

A sentence outline states each point in a complete sentence which may serve as a topic sentence in writing a paragraph in a report. By using a sentence outline, the writer carries his thinking one step further than in a topic outline. He has begun his writing. Sentence outlines are used later as briefs or summaries, whereas a topic outline is later used for subject headings and may be converted into a table of contents. A sentence outline often begins with an unnumbered thesis sentence which states the main idea of the entire report. Norman Shidle, in his *Clear Writing for Easy Reading,* calls this the "peg" idea and would use it as a starting point for all outlines.[3] The "peg" guides and limits the natural flow of ideas that follows. Often it is a brief statement of the problem; sometimes it states the purpose of the report or the solution to the problem. A portion of a sentence outline on the future expansion of the delivery service of the Mid-City Cleaners follows:

II. The management of Mid-City now feels that there is a possibility of further expanding delivery service.
   A. Lakeview route is becoming too large for present driver to handle.
   B. New subdivisions on lakefront offer advantage of easily acquiring many new customers.
   C. Neighborhood trade is very competitive and delivery service offers best means of expanding.
III. Since management desires to limit delivery expansion to lakefront area, a study of present and proposed developments in that area would be beneficial.

3 Norman Shidle, *Clear Writing for Easy Reading* (New York: McGraw-Hill Book Company, 1951), pp. 19–26.

A. Lakeview is rather well developed and serviced.
B. Lakeshore West is only about a year old and is sparsely developed.
C. Lake Vista is rather fully developed and well serviced.
D. Lake Terrace was opened this November and promises to be a very successful and large development.
E. Oak Park is close to lakefront subdivisions and is developing like Lake Vista.
F. With the filling of the former New Basin Canal, area along Pontchartrain Boulevard, from Metairie Cemetery to Lake, should develop fairly well in next year.

IV. Because new route servicing lakefront would be similar to present route serving Lakeview, management intends to use same setup with new route as with present one.
A. Three-day service is given: pick-up on Monday, delivery on Thursday.
B. Driver gets 35 per cent commission on all dry cleaning and 10 per cent on laundered shirts.
C. Mid-City pays all gasoline and truck repair bills on its trucks.
D. Prices for delivery are usually ten cents more per article than shop prices.
E. Expansion of route in area covered depends on driver; new customers who call in are given to driver who services their area.

V. Now that area to be covered and policy to be followed are known, their effects on present shop labor, trucks and other equipment, and management's finances have to be considered.
A. Cleaning and pressing work is done by three employees at present.
B. Of two trucks owned one is used only at night at present.
C. The only expense management feels it will incur is through the addition of more machinery.

Outlining Systems

There are two systems that can be used in outlining: the numeral-letter system and the decimal system. The examples used in this chapter thus far have followed the numeral-letter system.

In the numeral-letter system Roman numerals are used to designate the major divisions. Capital letters show the breakdown of each main part. Arabic numbers indicate the subdivisions under each capital-letter heading, and lowercase letters indicate further subdivisions under each Arabic number heading. For example,

I. First main point
  A. First part in the breakdown of the major division
    1. Subdivision
      a. Subdivision
      b. Subdivision
    2. Subdivision
    3. Subdivision
  B. Second part in the breakdown of the major division
II. Second main point

The numeral-letter system alternately uses numbers and letters. This is known as the principle of alternation. It provides the writer with four degrees of headings at the outset. After the four degrees have been used they may be repeated in parentheses to indicate further subdivision: (I) would be the first division under a. Then (A), (1), and (a) would be used. For instance,

a.
   (I).
      (A).
         (1).
           (a).

This scheme thus permits four additional degrees of headings, making a total of eight. Therefore the numeral-letter system is used a great deal in short reports and for problems that are simple and uncomplicated. In most cases it is not necessary to carry an outline beyond three or four degrees of subdivision.

Other patterns which are sometimes followed in outlining are

```
I.                      A.              1.
   1.                      1.              A.
   2.                        a.              a.
      A.                     b.              b.
        a.                 2.              B.
        b.                   a.              a.
      B.                     b.              b.
   3.                      3.              C.
II.                     B.              2.
```

None of these allows as much flexibility as the pattern suggested earlier. They are, however, practical adaptations which can be used at the outliner's convenience. Regardless of the pattern used, consistency as a principle must be maintained.

All headings must stand out conspicuously. Each one begins on a separate line. When it covers more than one line, the second line begins directly under the first line. Each subsequent subdivision is indented. All headings of equal rank have the same indentation. Relative weights of various points are thus indicated by the system of numbers and letters, as well as by indentation. In the numeral-letter system the numbers and letters used to designate the divisions and subdivisions of the outline are usually followed by a period; however, the period may be omitted. In either case the principle of consistency must be followed. The topics in a topic outline are usually left unpunctuated; however, the writer may use end punctuation if he does so consistently. In a sentence outline each division is punctuated like a sentence.

Although the numeral-letter system is commonly used, it has several disadvantages. When the outliner comes upon a heading numbered 5, for example, he does not know at once whether it belongs under A, B, C, or D, and when he looks back to find out, he still does not know whether it is under I, II, or III. This is a disadvantage both in organizing and in writing the report. Another disadvantage is the limited number of degrees of headings that can be used.

In the decimal system only Arabic numbers and the decimal point are used. The number of degrees may be expanded indefinitely. Every item can be immediately identified in its proper relation to the major subject and subtopics with which it is associated. In the book *Technical Reporting,* for example, Joseph N. Ulman, Jr., effectively used the decimal system for his headings and organization.[4] The points in the outline became his subject headings and table of contents.

Arabic numbers placed to the left of the decimal point indicate major subjects or topics in a report. The Arabic numbers to the right of the decimal point indicate various subdivisions of the topic. The degree of subdivision is indicated by the number of digits to the right of the decimal point. For example,

1. First main topic
  1.1 First item in first degree of subdivision
    1.11   First item in second degree of subdivision
    1.12   Second item in second degree of subdivision

    1.1(10) Tenth item in second degree of subdivision
    1.1(11) Eleventh item in second degree of subdivision
      1.1(11)1 First item in third degree of subdivision
      1.1(11)2 Second item in third degree of subdivision
        1.1(11)21 First item in fourth degree of subdivision
        1.1(11)22 Second item in fourth degree of subdivision
          1.1(11)221 First item in fifth degree of subdivision
          1.1(11)222 Second item in fifth degree of subdivision
  1.2 Second item in first degree of subdivision
2. Second main topic
  2.1 First item in first degree of subdivision
    2.11   First item in second degree of subdivision
3. Third main topic

The sequence of each subdivision is indicated by the numerical value of the digit. When more than nine items are listed within any one subdivision, two or more numerals will be required, and the sequence should be enclosed within parentheses. (However, to avoid the parentheses in the

---

4 Joseph N. Ulman, Jr., and Jay R. Gould, *Technical Reporting,* rev. ed. (New York: Holt, Rinehart and Winston, Inc., 1959).

tenth and succeeding items in the second degree of subdivision, you can show the first item in the second degree of subdivision as 1.101 and proceed: 1.102 . . . 1.110, and so forth.)

It is rarely, however, that more than nine items would need to be listed under any one sequence, and parentheses will seldom be required. The system can be expanded indefinitely as needed, to any degree of subdivision and to any number of topics within any subdivision. This great flexibility is not possible with the numeral-letter system. Another advantage is that every item is completely identified in its proper relation to the major subject or subdivision with which it is associated. For use in arranging note cards, the outline number may be placed on its corresponding note card. Thus the note cards can readily be arranged to correspond to the outline. This provides ease and convenience in writing the report. The report can be written in sections according to the wishes of the author and later assembled in proper order as indicated by the numerical identification of each section.

In addition to these advantages, the use of the decimal system forces the author to consider the position and proper classification of every detail in his material. An outline showing use of the decimal system follows.

Outline of a Report on

THE PRACTICABILITY AND NECESSITY OF PIONEERING
IN COLOR TELEVISION
By Station USDW-TV

1. Introduction
    1.1 Purpose—To determine whether or not Station USDW-TV should pioneer in color telecasting to remain an outstanding station
    1.2 Objective—Evaluation of possible advantages to be gained in light of problems and costs involved in modifying operations for color
    1.3 Scope and limitations
        1.31 Scope
            1.311 Consideration of changes and modifications of departmental operations, equipment and facilities, and personnel and of the relevant costs in each step involved in the transition to color telecasting
            1.312 Consideration of problems in color set production and consumer acceptance
            1.313 Consideration of advantages to be gained—present and future
        1.32 Limitations
            1.321 Lack of sufficient nontechnical material
            1.322 Experiences of other stations not helpful in solving certain problems
            1.323 Subjective valuation of advantages

1.4 Sources of data
1.41 Personal interviews with personnel of Station USDW-TV
1.42 Trade publications
1.43 Other publications
2. Steps involved in transition to color telecasting
2.1 Network pickup
2.11 Equipment
2.111 Requirements
2.112 Costs
2.12 Effect on departmental operations
2.13 Training of personnel
2.2 Color slide and film projection
2.21 Equipment
2.211 Requirements
2.212 Costs
2.22 Effects on departmental operations
2.23 Training of personnel
2.3 Live color telecasting
2.31 Equipment
2.311 Requirements
2.312 Costs
2.313 Obsolescence
2.32 Facilities
2.321 Requirements
2.322 Possibility of expansion of present facilities
2.323 Costs
2.33 Personnel
2.331 Additions
2.332 Training of present employees
2.34 Effects on departmental operations
2.4 Present situation in color television industry
2.41 Production of color receivers
2.42 Viewer acceptance
2.43 Advertiser acceptance
2.5 Advantages to be gained by taking immediate action to begin color telecasting
2.51 Present
2.52 Future
3. Conclusions
3.1 Necessary for Station USDW-TV to plan immediately for transition to color telecasting to maintain its position of leadership
3.2 Practical considerations
3.21 Outweighing of immediate problems of transition by present and future advantages
3.22 Increase in consumer and advertiser acceptance
3.3 Three successive steps necessary for the transition to color
3.31 Network pickup
3.32 Color slides and films
3.33 Live color telecasting
4. Recommendations
4.1 Immediate plans to begin color operations as soon as possible
4.2 Transition in three successive steps

Checklist

An outline which provides an effective means of organizing data and a guide for presenting material must contain the principles of consistency, division, and parallelism. The following checklist will prove helpful in checking an outline for the mechanics involved in applying these principles:

For consistency

1. Are either sentences or topics consistently used?
2. Are equal ideas consistently expressed in either general or specific terms?
3. Are indentations uniform?
4. Are letters and numbers alternately and consistently used?
5. Are symbols for subdivision consistently followed by a period?
6. Is end punctuation used or omitted consistently?
7. Does each heading begin on a separate line?
8. Are second lines directly under first lines?
9. Do headings of equal rank have the same indentation?
10. Are capital letters consistently used?

For division

1. Are all corresponding divisions of equal rank?
2. Do parts make up a unified whole?
3. Are there always at least two parts wherever there is a division? Is there a B for an A, 2 for a 1, and so forth?

For parallelism

1. Are ideas parallel?
2. Is parallel grammatical construction followed? For instance, are points of the same degree of subordination expressed as nouns? Or sentences? Or "ing" words?
3. Are either sentences or topics used for the same degree of division?

FOR DISCUSSION AND WRITING

1. *THE VICE-PRESIDENT'S AGENDA.*[5] An embarrassing look at how not to conduct a meeting. It's embarrassing because most of us have been guilty of participating in a similar time-wasting conference in the past. The discussion questions add structure to the case and remind

[5] This case and the three following case studies have been reprinted with permission from *Training in Business and Industry*, © MCMLXXII, Gellert Publishing Corporation, August 1972.

us to consider planning our next meeting rather than just watching it happen.

DISCUSSION QUESTIONS

1. Make a complete list of problems involved in this meeting and discuss each one.
2. What was handled well at the meeting?
3. Which statements in the text tended to help move the meeting in a positive direction? Which tended to distract or delay the meeting?
4. What is the value of an agreed to meeting agenda?
5. What is good about a fixed meeting time limit? When should it be imposed and enforced?
6. What is bad about a fixed meeting time limit? When should time not be rigidly constrained?
7. How can discussion priorities be established for a meeting? How do we most effectively get attendees to agree and comply?
8. What is the value of summary statements, attendee evaluations of meeting effectiveness, and post-meeting minutes?
9. Discuss the role of the effective meeting moderator or discussion leader.

The participants: V-P & General Manager
Office Manager   Sales Manager
Personnel Manager   Manufacturing Manager
Purchasing Manager
The Place: The Executive Conference Room
The Time: Friday 3:10 P.M.
V-P: Where's our esteemed purchasing manager?
Office: He was on the phone. When I passed by, he nodded. He should be in shortly.
Sales: That man is married to the phone.
Manufacturing: (winking) You don't do so badly yourself, my friend.
Personnel: (smiling) That's right: How about all those Houston calls?
Sales: That's different. I've had problems with the Houston distributor and . . .
V-P: Look, it's after three already and I have to leave by 4:30 for Chicago. We'll start without him. (writing on a chalkboard) There are three items on my agenda for today's meeting:
1. Cash flow problems
2. Excessive tardiness among exempt administrative personnel
3. Final arrangements for the Employee Open House
Sales: How about adding an agenda item? I think we should make a decision on whether or not to open a Seattle distributorship.
Office: I suggest we pick that up at our next staff meeting the Monday after Open House.
Sales: We keep putting it off.
V-P: It's firm for that meeting. In the meantime, draft a thought paper on the pros and cons of the proposed distributorship. Then circulate it so we can analyze it prior to the meeting.

Sales: Well, okay. But how about you? You'll be in Chicago all week. Shall I mail you a copy?

V-P: No, hand it to me at Open House.

Office: Gentlemen, it's 3:20. Perhaps we should get back to our agenda. I suggest we dispose of the easy items first to expedite this meeting.

Personnel: Good. Since I've got the administrative responsibility for the Open House, I'd like to go over the last minute arrangements.

Manufacturing: (interrupting) I *still* feel we need a cocktail hour for employees and guests.

V-P: (angrily) Dammit, man! We settled that last time! No alcohol. It's expensive as hell and some clown from fabrication will end up wrapping his car around a streetlight afterward . . .

Manufacturing: It has been a custom, though.

Office: We settled the issue last time. Let's get back to the unfinished Open House arrangements.

Personnel: (passing around sheets of paper) Here are the items each of you will have to handle.

V-P: (examining his list) Can one of you draft my speech? I'll be jammed solid in Chicago.

Personnel: (tactfully) Sir, I feel that you should handle it personally. You know how heavily you usually edit staff drafts of your speeches.

(Purchasing Manager enters) Purchasing: Sorry I'm late, but that was a very productive phone call. I got Universal Plastics to reduce the unit cost by nine cents in quantities of 5,000 and up.

Manufacturing: Hey, that's great! That means we can substitute the plastic extrusion for the machined aluminum . . .

V-P: (interrupting) That's good news, but we must go on. It's nearly four.

Purchasing: Can you fill me in on where we are?

(Several minutes pass)

Manufacturing: The shop people don't have the problem because they clock in for work. Why don't you use some modified clock-in system for the exempt people as well?

Office: Impossible. Too chicken.

Personnel: We could have the guard at the employee entrance jot down the names of all those coming in over fifteen minutes late.

V-P: That would have the same negative effects once it was known what he was doing.

Manufacturing: Who would know?

Office: Everyone would know the first time you warned an employee about his tardiness record.

Sales: The problem with people nowadays is that they've lost the cost-conscious attitude.

Purchasing: That's right. Why, when I first started in business my boss said . . .

V-P: We've developed some good thoughts but it appears we won't have time to come to a decision. Let's pick this up again at our next staff meeting.

Sales: That will bump our discussion on Seattle.

V-P: No, I'm sure we'll have time for both.

Sales: (shaking his head) I hope so.

V-P: Now, concerning cash flow. Until our receivables are turned around we're going to have to suspend all noncritical expense items not already committed. My signature will be required for any expense items not in payroll, material, or the 400 and 500 series budgets.

Purchasing: Wow! That raises a thousand questions. For example, how about the . . .

V-P: I'm sorry. You'll have to work out the details with accounting. I've got to leave now or miss my plane. Call me in Chicago if you need me.

2. *REQUIEM FOR A GOOD SOLDIER.* There are two issues in this case for the instructor to develop: the utilization of women in the work force, and the deterioration of work output due to lack of promotion and/or challenge in the work.

DISCUSSION QUESTIONS

1. Define and discuss the issues presented in this case study:
   a. How is career development involved?
   b. How is employee counseling involved?
   c. How is the utilization of women involved?
   d. How is manager obsolescence involved?
2. What steps could be taken to bring about positive behavioral change with Alice Beaton?
3. Evaluate and discuss the implications of Clifford Guenther's last decision.
4. What is your organization doing to provide equal employment opportunity for minorities and women?

"How about Alice Beaton?" Zagorski asked. "She's certainly in line for the job. Alice has had all of the requisite training and experience to become a branch manager."

Clifford M. Guenther, president of the Great Plains Savings and Loan Association, rolled a ballpoint pen between his fingers and rocked slowly in his executive desk chair. "I don't know," he said softly, "I really don't know. Give me another rundown on her experience."

Harold Zagorski opened the manila personnel folder and laid it on Guenther's desk. "Six years with the company, but she had been with Pioneer Savings and Loan for almost nine years before they merged with us. She started as a teller and worked herself up to assistant branch manager at the time of the merger."

"We had too many chiefs as a result of merging with Pioneer," Guenther said. "As I recall, we had to temporarily take away her administrative assignment."

Zagorski beamed, "I recall it vividly. I was the one who took over as the assistant branch manager."

"How did she take the demotion?" Guenther asked.

"No problem," Zagorski said. "She was a good soldier."

"A good soldier," Guenther mused, echoing his staff assistant.

"She was very capable and versatile," Zagorski said. "In fact, I relied on her heavily for new personnel training. Many of those green young men she trained are now managers and assistant managers." Zagorski pointed to the personnel folder. "Alice was made assistant manager of our Rialto

Branch four years ago and was seriously considered for the position of manager when Mr. Fillmore retired."

Guenther shook his head. "Regrettably, I had a difficult choice then as well. I had to choose between a capable career woman and an equally talented young man who appeared ready to submit his resignation. In the end I felt that the Rialto Branch was not the right office in which to place our first female branch manager."

"Now would be a perfect time," Zagorski said, "especially in light of recent government orders on the utilization of minorities and women in business and industry."

Guenther winced. "You need not remind me. But promotions must ultimately be based upon qualification and attitude and not on sex or color of skin."

"I agree with that completely," Zagorski replied quickly, "but all other things being equal, why not give the edge to a woman?"

"If that were true, I just might. But all other things are not equal. Not only do I again have several capable candidates, but there have been problems with Alice lately."

"I wasn't aware of that. What's happened to Alice Beaton, the good soldier? I can't imagine her causing problems for anyone."

"That's what I'd like to know," Guenther said. "For the past year and a half I've placed her in several assignments and all of her supervisors have complained of her deteriorating work output and poor attitudes. Several months ago we had to remove her from her role as a new employee trainer and put her on individual assignment."

"What's her complaint?"

"No one seems to be able to put his finger on the problem. I even had her in my office once for a casual chat. I asked her to tell me what was troubling her, but she claimed there was nothing causing her any concern. I mentioned her slipping work performance and she promised she would show an improvement."

"And?"

"Oh, she's improved. I guess her work is acceptable, but that old spark is gone."

"That's a shame," Zagorski said. "Alice Beaton has done so well . . . for a woman."

Guenther nodded, "Yes, it is a shame. I'm afraid we'll have to look elsewhere to fill the open manager position."

3. *ARE YOU CLEARED FOR RUMOR?* What organization operates without rumors? The rumor here is of major importance and morale has sagged. The management solution is a questionable one involving secrecy and business ethics. The questions force us to look at our respective organizational patterns of communication.

DISCUSSION QUESTIONS

1. Analyze and discuss the issues and implications of the cover story planned for use by Rosewood.
2. Discuss the ethics of this management approach.
3. Discuss the implications of secrecy or limited communication from

management to workers even if no deception is planned or intended.

4. How can longer term management strategies be better communicated to the lower members of the management team without disclosing competitive moves or technically confidential data?

5. How effectively are you dealing with unfounded rumors in your organization? How can you do better in the future?

The secretary to the director of administration placed the morning mail on his desk. "Is it true, Mr. Nash?" she asked. "Are we going to close the Fall River facility?"

"Where on earth did you hear that, Edith?"

"It was in the morning paper. Phyllis brought in the clipping and was showing it around."

"You know you can't believe everything you read in the newspaper," Nash said. He tried to be casual. "Sometimes I don't know where those business reporters go for their information."

Edith persisted. "Actually, I heard it several days ago. At first the rumor was that there would be a small layoff at the Fall River plant. The next day the girls were talking about a layoff at this facility too. When I saw today's clipping, I felt I should let you know."

"I appreciate that, Edith, but why are you so concerned? Suppose the rumor were true?"

"As executive secretary to the director of administration, I guess I'm not in danger of losing my job, but the girls in the typing pool are all shook up over it. Many of them need their jobs and would find relocation difficult."

"Tell the girls not to be concerned," Nash replied after a moment of thought. "The typing pool will not be affected."

"There's not going to be a layoff then?"

Nash hesitated. "I didn't say that, exactly. Look, Edith, I can't say any more at this moment. We're having a meeting with Mr. Kirby. Maybe I'll be able to tell you more afterward."

Later, at the staff meeting, Nash was less reluctant to speak out. "Kirby, we've got to tell them *now*. The rumors are getting out of hand."

Malone, director of manufacturing, nodded. "I agree with Nash. Morale is coming apart in the shop. The production people feel they'll lose, no matter which rumor is true. They can see that work is slow here and worse at Fall River. They figure that with the seniority edge at that plant, a lot of workers will be relocated here at the sacrifice of our people."

"It's even worse among the middle management and first-line supervisors," Nash said.

Gerald Kirby, director of operations, waited for the rash of comments from the other managers to end before he responded. "Gentlemen, perhaps you have forgotten the bleak situation we have been facing. Let me review the facts. First, Fall River operations losses continue to mount, and the board of directors wants out.

"Second, Datalox Corporation has agreed to purchase the Fall River facility plus its existing contracts. This not only cuts our losses but provides us with working capital."

"Datalox benefits as well," added Pearson, director of public relations. "They can combine their backlog with ours in the Fall River plant."

"And our people lose their jobs," Nash said.

"That is most unfortunate," Kirby replied. "Datalox intends to shift their personnel to Fall River. Their current plant is only ten miles away. They don't expect to lose many employees."

"Can't they absorb any of our people?"

Kirby shrugged. "A few perhaps."

"So," Nash said, "our next step is to tell the employees there will be extensive layoffs."

"Not quite," Kirby said. "Your suggestion is noble but impractical, Nash. The Datalox move is five and a half months away. We can't afford five months of low productivity."

"What are you suggesting?"

Kirby's tone was deliberate. "I suggest an official news release for tomorrow's paper to contradict the one which got to them yesterday. Read the news release you wrote, Pearson."

Pearson read the carefully prepared article: "Contrary to rumors which have circulated about the sale of the Fall River facility and projected personnel layoffs, Rosewood Manufacturing Company today stated that the facility was to be completely refurbished and re-equipped with modern, competitive equipment. The changes are expected to return the facility to a profitable position in the corporate structure within a year. A starting date for the refurbishing will be announced shortly."

"But that's a lie!" Nash said, "an outright lie!"

"I prefer to call it a cover," Kirby replied. "It's an economically necessary cover story."

Malone was also stunned by the cover story approach. "What happens when it becomes apparent that we are doing no refurbishing?"

"It will be three or four months," Kirby said, "before anyone really begins to question it, three or four months of valuable, productive time. Then we will announce that, after extensive re-examination, we have decided not to proceed and plan to sell the facility."

"It stinks!" Nash said, realizing the decision had already been made. "It's cruel and deceptive."

"Really?" Kirby asked. "And would releasing the 'truth' be less cruel to the economic future of the corporation? I think not, Mr. Nash. Sleep on it, and I think you will agree."

4. *THE MAN WHO WON'T TALK.* The new manager finds a problem worker who refuses to discuss the problem. The issue has been ducked in the past so it is not so easily dealt with in the present. Personal factors may be involved, but how far should a manager go into the personal life of an employee?

DISCUSSION QUESTIONS

1. What is the proper action to take with Deering at this point?

2. Should the supervisor continue to probe Deering's personal life? Why or why not?

3. How do you get a reticent employee to "open up" on a problem which is affecting his work performance?

4. How can the supervisor/manager in general reconcile the dilemma of professional flexibility on one hand and reasonable work rules and habits on the other?

It has bothered me since the day I interviewed for the job of purchasing manager at Stanhill Products. Several times during the interview the employment manager mentioned the Stanhill policy of promotion from within whenever possible. I asked why, if that was the usual policy, they were going outside the company to fill the top purchasing job. I was told that, because of recent staff turnover, no one in the small department was adequately prepared to assume leadership of the group.

That was three months ago. Now I know why they didn't promote from within. The senior buyer, Harry Deering, will probably never be able to assume the job of manager. But that's a secondary issue. What really concerns me is Harry Deering's problem. Whatever it is, he won't talk about it. All I can see are the symptoms, which, in turn, are causing problems for me.

Harry Deering comes to work late every day. Yes, I said *every* day! Sometimes it's only fifteen or twenty minutes, but often it's more like three quarters of an hour. He also takes long lunches and *never* stays overtime.

Being new, and with no prior supervisor to lean on for background information, I waited a couple of weeks before saying anything to him. Then, in a very casual, light-hearted way, I kidded him about his punctuality. He was composed, but his eyes indicated he was upset at my inquiry. Instead of responding to my friendly barbs, he changed the subject!

I'm not a clock watcher. My concern is for total productivity, not the hours a person spends on the job. I recognize that you have to be flexible in managing office and administrative operations. But Deering was *always* late and, although no one else said anything to me, I could tell it was troubling the others in the department.

So one day I decided to simply ask Deering directly why he was continually late, thinking perhaps he might he having transportation difficulties. Again he stiffened when I brought up the subject of his tardiness.

"I don't have a transportation problem or any other problem," Deering said.

"Then why are you late every day?" I asked bluntly.

"I am a professional," he replied. "I am paid for the work I do and not the hours I keep."

"What about the others?" I asked. "Don't you suppose they are concerned?"

"They are clerks and must work by the clock," Deering replied. "I am a professional and am paid for the work I accomplish."

Deering was both right and wrong. We had several clerks employed as procurement assistants and they were hourly. However, the two junior buyers were both exempt personnel, yet maintained regular working hours.

Now if Deering were a marginal worker, I might have a good case for disciplinary action. To the contrary, his productivity is above average and steady. He tends to avoid office chit-chat and, although never rude, spends

most of each day involved in his paperwork or on the phone with suppliers. He leaves the office each noon and, as far as I can tell, dines alone.
Although it's generally a poor practice, I talked to two or three of the
others to determine what they knew of Deering. I found little. He has been
in the department three years and has always been late. No one knew why
the prior supervisor had done nothing to correct the problem. His personnel folder gives his age as 47 and shows that he has been married several years and has one child. There is no record of tardiness noted or any
disciplinary actions.

More recently I began to suspect a medical problem might be involved.
I had asked Deering to join me and several others for pizza one lunchtime.
As usual, he declined politely. But he did mention a difficulty he had with
certain foods, often resulting in loss of sleep.

In my last effort to help Deering I asked if he had seen a doctor about
his stomach.

"No," he replied. "I have not."

"Don't you think it might be a good idea?" I offered.

"I think that is my business," he replied crisply.

What do you do with a guy who refuses to acknowledge a problem he is
creating for me? If there is a reason other than his stubborn professional-
ism for being late, he doesn't want to let me in on it. I don't have any
reason to believe he is an alcoholic, but something is wrong. If I could only
get him to talk about it.

5. The following case study presents the results of a Trading Stamp Ques-
    tionnaire.

Consumers' Views on Trading Stamps

In 197– a survey was made in the Greater Cleveland area by John
Carroll University's Business Research Center on consumers' views
on trading stamps.[6] A total of 370 questionnaires was mailed to individuals living in the residential postal zones of the city and in many
of the suburbs. Individuals who saved trading stamps were asked to
answer the questions and return the questionnaire; nonsavers were
asked to indicate their status but not to answer the questions. Of 370
mailed questionnaires, 341 were returned. Of the 341 returned, 332
declared themselves savers of trading stamps. The national estimate
was that three out of four Americans saved trading stamps.

Questions and responses follow:

1. Name the brand of saving stamps you save:

Eagle	319
S & H Green	226
Top Value	129
Other (11 miscellaneous brands)	37

---

[6] The facts and figures given here are reprinted by permission of Dr.
Frank J. Devlin, formerly director of the Business Research Center, John Carroll
University, Cleveland.

2. What type of redemption arrangement do you consider to be the best?

Department store	261
Redemption store	36
Cash	11
Place of issuance	7
Filling stations	4
No preference	13
	332 total

3. Does the convenience of redemption-center location have any bearing on the kind of stamps you save?

94 Yes   235 No   3 Abstained

4. Do you think that there is any significant difference in the number of stamps needed to fill a book under one stamp plan as against another?

119 Yes   187 No   26 No opinion

5. Do you think there is any significant difference in the redemption value of a filled stamp book under one stamp plan as against another?

112 Yes   193 No   27 No opinion

6. Has stamp saving caused you to favor those merchants who issue the kinds of stamps you save?

194 Yes   138 No

7. Do you think prices are any higher at a place of business that gives stamps as against a direct competitor who does not?

173 Yes   149 No   10 Abstained

8. Have you experienced any irregularities with merchants in the handling of trading stamps?

100 Yes   190 No   42 Abstained

Irregularities cited:

Forget to issue stamps	64
Withhold stamps on some items	21
Give short count	10
Out of stamps	3
Refuse to issue	1
Out of books	1
	100 total

9. Generally speaking, do you think that the stamp movement is a good idea and should be continued?

200 Yes   115 No   17 Abstained

A number of dissenters commented on irregularities in the handling of the stamps by the merchants, the belief that stamps led to higher prices, the bother of saving stamps and pasting them in a book.

Here are some additional facts about trading stamps in the Cleveland area: Eagle stamps had been the traditional trading stamp and were handled by a large department store chain, a supermarket chain, and numerous other merchants. They used the department store redemption plan which allowed savers to select from all merchandise stocked in the store. The Eagle plan required 1,380 stamps to fill a book.

S & H Green Stamps, the oldest existing variety in the United States, entered the Cleveland area the summer of 1960 and were handled by a department store chain, a food market chain, and a large number of smaller merchants including filling stations, drug stores, and a hardware store. They used the redemption store plan which was used with S & H stamps in most sections of the country. They required 1,200 stamps to fill a book and advertised that low number. Top Value stamps had been in the Cleveland area for a number of years and were handled by a food market chain and smaller merchants, but did not have a department store connection. They used the redemption store plan and required 1,500 stamps to fill a book. Top Value also advertised that fewer pages were necessary to fill a book. Other plans required as many as 1,560 stamps to fill a book. Practically all stamp companies attached a $3.00 value to a book filled with stamps.

a. Write a report on consumers' views on trading stamps. You might do this for the merchants of Cleveland who are using the stamp plans, prepare it for publication in a trade journal in the Cleveland area, or present it as a Business Research Center report available to anyone upon request. You will, however, first need to figure percentages, analyze responses, arrange tables, and draw conclusions. You may want to check Chapter 4 on using visual aids in the report.

b. Make a similar survey in your area of consumers' views on trading stamps. Compare your findings with those of John Carroll's Business Research Center. Present your findings in a written report.

6. The following case study presents the results of questionnaire research on discount stores:

Public Reaction to Discount Stores

At present the discount store movement is spreading in many directions.[7] New stores seem to appear overnight, and old-line stores have begun to wave the discount banner. In addition, specialty stores, limited to a narrow line of goods, such as draperies, drugs, or furniture, have appeared. These developments are more true, of course, in some regions of the United States than in others. Total

[7] In its original meaning, a discount store was more or less a self-service department-type store, conveniently located near a residential area. It provided parking facilities, long shopping hours, centralized check out, and discount prices. Emphasis was on merchandise that had a good turnover record.

sales in discount operations, however, climbed to $6 billion in 1971 as compared to $4.5 billion in 1970; and they are expected to pass the $8 billion mark in 1972.

To get a better understanding of the situation, particularly in Cuyahoga County, Ohio, the Business Research Center of John Carroll University undertook a study of discount stores. In early December 1971, 1,029 questionnaires with covering letters were mailed to consumers in Cuyahoga County. The sample included people living in all residential areas in Cleveland and its suburbs. Returns totaled 787. A copy of the questionnaire follows.[8] In the blank for the consumer to fill in has been placed the number of consumers checking the response.

BUSINESS RESEARCH CENTER
JOHN CARROLL UNIVERSITY

(Project: *Discount Stores*)

QUESTIONNAIRE

Please answer the following questions to the best of your ability. There is no need to give your name.

1. How often do you shop at discount stores? (Check one)

   142 Once a week   7 Twice a month 244 Once a month 345 Occasionally 49 Never

2. How far must you travel to shop at a discount store?

   539 1/4 to 10 miles   199 1 to 30 blocks   49 No answer

3. At which discount stores have you shopped? (Check one or more)

   550 Giant Tiger 522 Uncle Bill's 95 Fame   None
   65 Norban   89 Zayre   Other: Revco—86

4. What influences your choice of discount store? (Check one or more)

   98 Appearance of store   221 Parking facilities

   627 Price of merchandise   None of the foregoing

   269 Convenience of location   Other:

5. What type of merchandise do you purchase most frequently in discount stores? (Check one or more)

   182 Clothing 161 Appliances 281 Garden supplies

   132 Medical 246 Toys 273 Auto supplies 134 Sporting goods

6. Do you think that there is any significant difference in the quality of merchandise sold in discount stores as compared with the quality of goods sold in downtown department stores?

---

[8] The questionnaire and responses given here are reprinted by permission of Dr. Frank J. Devlin, formerly Director of the Business Research Center, John Carroll University, Cleveland.

429   Yes   313   No   (Please explain briefly)
                                19 checked both blocks
                                17 gave no answers
                                 9 wrote in "possibly"

7. Would you like to see a limited number of food items sold in discount stores?

170   Yes   591   No   No opinion— 6
                                      No answer —20

8. Would you like to see a complete line of foods, including fresh meats and produce, sold in discount stores?

95   Yes   699   No   No opinion— 6
                                      No answer —17

9. Would you like to see food sold in discount stores if the food section were under the sponsorship of a national or local food chain familiar to you?

284   Yes   470   No   No opinion—10
                                      No answer —23

10. What is your opinion of discount stores in general? (Please answer briefly below and/or on the back of this questionnaire.)

To question number 2, two or three miles were typical answers expressed in miles, and two and three blocks were typical answers expressed in blocks. One respondent indicated "just across the street." To question number 3, names of 58 district outlets were written in. Giant Tiger and Uncle Bill's were of chain-store variety. Revco was a drug discount chain and had been established only a few months. It was the chief "write in" store.

In the tenth question, people were asked to express their opinions in general. Nearly 800 subjective answers were freely expressed. The respondents said discount stores reduce middle-man costs and save shoppers a substantial amount of money, are a good place for low-income families to shop, are fine for item lines in which quality is not a principal specification, and have helped control prices in conventional retail stores. They also complained that merchandise is generally lacking in quality, that Sunday sales are objectionable, and that smaller merchants are being hurt. A few said stores were "junky" and their merchandise was mixed up; some stores were even unclean and unsanitary. Other respondents lamented the lack of personnel to answer questions and help customers.

From the facts obtained, one might be able to establish a "John Doe" to represent the typical consumer who took part in this survey or to reach conclusions for an over-all appraisal of discount stores.

a. Discuss the significance of the results of this survey. What conclusions do you reach? How do the responses substantiate your conclusions?

b. Make a similar survey of public reaction to discount stores in your area. Prepare a written report of your findings.

c. Compare the results of your study with those found by the Business Research Center. Do you have similar conclusions?

d. Present the findings of the Business Research Center in a report to be sent to discount stores.

7. Analyze the following case study; then answer for class discussion:

a. What conclusions do you reach? Explain how you reached them.

b. What would you recommend to Plastics, Inc. as a result of your analysis of the survey facts?

Survey of Plastics, Inc.

Plastics, Inc. is primarily a fabricator of plastic products. The principal end products are illuminated control panels for aircraft. Thus, the most important customers are aircraft companies and companies which subcontract assemblies for the aircraft companies. The products are precision components, demanding in their fabrication a high degree of manual dexterity and attention to detail. This also adds the requirement of machinery capable of working to highly exacting tolerances. Finally, inspection must be of the highest order, and appropriate inspection tools and equipment must be available.

Plastics, Inc., is owned by Mr. E. A. Gassoner. Mr. Gassoner founded the firm, and much of its success appears to be the direct result of his efforts. He is a researcher and an inventor of considerable stature, holding several patents on processes used in fabricating by Plastics, Inc. Mr. Gassoner is assisted in the operation of Plastics, Inc., by a board of directors. This board of directors consists of Mrs. Gassoner, Mr. Henry Allis, and has, at various times, included those intimately associated with the firm—the general manager, the attorney, the labor relations adviser, and others.

Plastics, Inc., recently moved to Terre Haute, Indiana, from Norfolk, Virginia. Several of the Norfolk employees moved with the firm (at the firm's expense) and have established homes in Terre Haute. The remainder of the approximately 90 employees were hired locally and come from Terre Haute or the surrounding towns and countryside in the Wabash Valley. Very few had any prior experience in industry, and quite a number had no prior work experience of a continuous nature.

Plastics, Inc., operates in three buildings. These are in close proximity to each other, and the entire plant is within minutes' walking distance from the center of Terre Haute. Manufacturing, involving the bulk of the equipment and the vast majority of the personnel, is located in a converted dairy building. The various processing rooms are located around a central hub which houses the offices of the shop superintendent, an employee who handles scheduling of fabrication, and an employee who maintains records of the degree to which the schedules are met. The physical layout is reasonably geared to movement of materials. One possible exception to this is the location of the machine shop and lathe department. Lighting is excellent. Some departments have considerable noise to contend with, but there are obvious limitations to any attempts to alleviate this condition. Press operations involve the use of steam equipment, and summer operations may find this an undesirable place in which to work.

Office operations and a research and development laboratory are housed in a converted old county jail, located just across the street from the manufacturing building. The office operations, including engineering, are on the first floor, and the laboratory is on the second floor. Lighting, desks, chairs, and other physical facilities are excellent for the entire office operation. The main office, now housing Mr. Gassoner, might be made to look more prosperous as potential customers do visit the firm in various capacities.

The laboratory is virtually a miniature of the manufacturing operation. One of each of the major tools is located there. This facilitates research and development by keeping experimental work out of the main plant. On the other hand, it encourages use of the research facilities in a straight production status when the manufacturing plant gets behind in its operation or when small "rush" orders are received.

The third building in the operation is a small, newly constructed storage building, of particular importance since it permits concentration of inflammable materials away from the manufacturing plant.

Immediately prior to this survey, Plastics, Inc., had some difficulties within its top management ranks. This culminated in termination of the contract of Plastics' president and general manager. This man's leaving was immediately followed by the resignation of another who had held the post of chief engineer and who, subsequent to the leaving of the president and general manager, had been made manager of manufacturing. Simultaneously, the foreman in charge of the paint and trim department resigned. Thus, at the time of the survey, all authority was vested in Mr. Gassoner, except for that which he had delegated to the office manager. The engineering department was placed in the hands of a man who had been foreman of the route and drill departments, and one of the local female employees, with about four months of service, was made temporary forelady of the paint and trim department.

During the course of the survey the sheet metal shop foreman of the Binder plant in Wichita, Kansas, was interviewed by Mr. Gassoner and Mr. Allis regarding a position in the manufacturing division of Plastics, Inc. Mr. Gassoner had initially considered this man as a potential general manager. However, the interviewee continually emphasized what he thought he could do about production, and the discussion pointed more and more toward a position which might be labeled shop superintendent, production superintendent, or manager of manufacturing. One of the investigators making this survey was invited to participate in the interview. The interviewee's continued emphasis on production, tools, operations, and the like was somewhat disturbing, since the investigator's experience and training suggested that the most important task of a manager is handling people. Several questions by the survey investigator revealed that the applicant was willing to assume the task of handling people and that he was woefully inexperienced. After some discussion of job terms, responsibilities, and other matters, the applicant and Plastics, Inc. agreed to a trial employment of the applicant in the position of shop superintendent. The remuneration agreed upon represents the highest salary now paid in Plastics, Inc., a fact which is known in the typical small plant among all employees not later than 24 hours after the first pay checks are issued.

Despite the confusion entailed in the terminations of contracts, changes in position and status of various individuals, and the hiring of new employees, several conclusions were reached concerning the over-all operation of Plastics, Inc.

Morale is currently quite high. The "core of trusted, loyal employees" who came from Norfolk speak very highly of the attitude of the local employees. There is no evidence that the "natives" feel that the Norfolk group is composed of "outlanders," and this acceptance will probably continue unless the local employees conclude that there is favoritism with respect to communication, promotion, salary, hours, or conditions of work.

Understandably, almost all efforts in manufacturing are devoted to getting out orders; the backlog of work virtually demands this. But, because of their zeal to turn out finished products and their inexperience as supervisors, the foremen are committing some of the cardinal sins of foremanship. For example, since each foreman knows a lot about all the operations, the foreman of one department frequently corrects or instructs in another department.

The "work order" is the major control tool throughout Plastics, Inc. The content of the "work order" is initially established in the bids for business, and if the cost estimating department is wrong, everything else is out of order. As it now stands, the cost estimating department does not require the direct services of an engineer. Estimates of time required and subsequent payroll costs are made on the basis of "standards" which give the time required for each minute operation—drilling a hole, routing a slot, engraving a letter. Unfortunately, these standards are based on operations in Norfolk. With so many employees in an unskilled or semiskilled status, it has been considered impractical to revise these standards as yet. The problem is serious because the attitude of the manufacturing foremen and their subordinates can be seriously affected by what comes out of the cost estimating department. If the estimates are such that they are never met by manufacturing, the foremen and the employees are robbed of success experiences. If the estimates become so lenient that they are easily met, indolence and inattention may easily result.

The problem of foreman control versus standards control is not simple. There are great individual differences in competence among the production employees, and these differences are in more than one dimension. For example, one router may be extremely good in performing operation A and rather poor in operation B, while another router is just the reverse. Given some flexibility in the assignment of work, the individual foreman can influence production tremendously. In its initial stages improvement can probably be best effected through working over existing work orders by the shop superintendent and his foremen. In the long run it should permit the cost estimating and sales functions a greater degree of freedom in situations where highly competitive bidding is likely to occur.

At present, and they are quite new to the job, the functions of scheduling and production control have little real meaning. Scheduling is more or less automatic, depending on status of prior work orders, and production control is simply production recording.

The inexperience of the foremen is a matter of concern. They have no background from which they can draw supervisory techniques and methods. They are eager, but eagerness is not enough.

As mentioned earlier, various management personnel have been greatly impressed with the willingness of the new personnel to learn. The caliber of learning institutions in Terre Haute has not been evaluated as yet. Plastics, Inc. might well look into its selection and employee training program.

In summary, the survey investigator found Plastics, Inc. to be a going concern, despite the confusions of the past week. It will probably continue as a going concern.

Outline and write the report that you, a member of an outside research firm, would present to Mr. Gassoner and the board of directors.

WRITING,
REVISING,
AND EDITING

WRITING

    The First Draft

    Introduction

    Discussion

    Conclusions

    Recommendations

    Checklist for Writing

REVISING

    Checking Content

    Checking Organization

    Checking for Expression, Mechanics of Style, and Form

    General Suggestions

MEASURING READABILITY

    Frequently Used Readability Formulas

    Influence of Readability Formulas on Style

EDITING

PROOFREADING

FOR DISCUSSION AND WRITING

8

By the time the writer has planned and conducted his investigation, gathered data and created ideas, organized and interpreted facts, prepared tables and charts, reached conclusions, formulated recommendations whenever appropriate, and outlined his material for final presentation in the report, he is ready to write. With a detailed outline as a guide, a report will almost write itself, for it is easy to go from one point to another.

A businessman who had difficulty writing reports and was a member of his company's special report-writing class for employees made these comments to the group after he completed the course:

> After I had worked everything out in the outline, I was ready to write. I wrote the introduction by simply stating what I was going to cover and the order in which I planned to cover it. I wrote about the first topic in the outline, for it came first in my thinking. Next I discussed the second topic, for it belonged next in my scheme of reasoning. In the same way, topic followed topic until I was ready to sum up the findings and state my conclusions. After steadily working three hours I had all my ideas and data down on paper. I had written the first draft of the entire report.

WRITING

In writing the report from an outline, the writer focuses his attention on the facts he is presenting and on the reader who will absorb them.

The First Draft

Writing should be done rapidly; in fact, the writer can easily write any short report in one sitting. Long reports he can complete individual sections at a sitting. Getting ideas down on paper in logical order is of the utmost importance, and keeping to the outline makes this possible.

Because good report writing is based on effective organization, the first draft is written to record facts and ideas within the framework of the outline. The writer at this point is not concerned with punctuation, spelling, grammar, and form so much as with the flow and development of facts and thoughts. The correction of mechanical errors comes with revision. A simple easy flow of related ideas is necessary to get the message across to the reader. Each part of the report should prepare the reader for what is to come, and the discussion of each fact should be completed before introducing another.

While writing, the author should keep before him his specific purpose and his audience as a technique by which to measure ideas as they occur. It will help to keep his points in focus, to relate them to each other, and to give perspective and shape to the material at hand. In remembering his reader the writer may unconsciously carry on a discussion with him and be stimulated by it. He can also examine his ideas from the other person's viewpoint and thus will be able to make them more meaningful.

There are times, of course, when the writer will want to depart from his outline, which is merely a guide. When he is expanding it in writing, he will be thinking, and thinking is a chain reaction. One idea will generate another. The outline suggests the sequence and subject matter. Because it does not include the thoughts that will occur to the writer as he develops the points, he is free to depart from the outline when his thoughts do—if they are in line with his purpose.

There are times also when the writer will want to sit and think, go over material, find a fresh approach. This will, however, slow down his writing and should not often be necessary if he has done enough thinking and planning before this time.

The report can be thought through as it is being written from its outline. Experienced, capable writers sometimes can write short reports that require very little revision. They write well naturally, thinking through each sentence and selecting words with care. Most report writers, however, will write a first draft, using all the principles and techniques of style, of tone, and of expressing facts clearly, interestingly, and persuasively that are applicable to the particular report at hand. Then they improve the report through careful revision before it appears in its final form.

There are four general divisions of a report—introduction, discussion, conclusions, and recommendations. They are based on corresponding functions of a report text:

1. To give the background information the reader needs to know for understanding the report.

2. To describe what was done to gather data.

3. To relate the results or findings by analyzing, interpreting, and discussing the data.

4. To state conclusions and/or recommendations.

Introduction

The introduction of a report presents the subject or problem to the reader and gets his attention. Through reading it he becomes interested in reading the report. The introduction must furnish him with sufficient material concerning the investigation and problem to lead to an easy understanding of the rest of the report. It should thus give the reader a general view of the report before he plunges into the details.

Note how the introduction to "What College Students Should Know About Job Interviews" gets the reader's attention.

WHAT COLLEGE STUDENTS SHOULD KNOW
ABOUT JOB INTERVIEWS

Introduction

What do personnel directors require of graduating college students applying for jobs in the business world? Must the applicant have short hair? Does nervousness count against the interviewee? How important is the applicant's draft status? All these questions and many more were answered in a job interview survey done by members of Professor Leland Brown's class in business report writing at Eastern Michigan University. Members formulated a questionnaire and conducted a survey of 150 personnel directors in the Southeastern Michigan area to determine their reaction toward different characteristics of student applicants they interviewed. The results of the survey could then be used to inform graduating college students how to prepare for a job interview.

From the University Placement Office, a list of representatives who interviewed students on and off campus was obtained. To these individuals a questionnaire was mailed. (See appendix A.) Ninety-two replies (61 percent) were returned. They represented companies varying in size from 100 to over 2,000 and including manufacturing, wholesaling, retailing, service and other industries. The attitudes toward applicants were many times surprising.

The questionnaire encompassed six areas: appearance, personal qualifications, education, activities, character traits, and general information. Questions were directed to evaluate what personnel directors look for in interviewing applicants.

Each introduction must be arranged to suit the situation and the reader. A good introduction will set up an orderly path for the reader to follow. The following list of contents is suggestive rather than exhaustive, and few introductions will include all the items:

Explanation of or reference to authorization of the report
Situation giving rise to the report
Author's understanding of the problem
Author's attitude toward the problem
Scope and limitations
Purpose and objectives
Basic principles or theories involved
Methods of gathering data
Sources of information
Procedure in organizing material
Definition of terms
Brief summary of findings or results
Brief statement of main conclusions
Brief statement of chief recommendation
General plan used in developing the solution
General plan of the report

The introduction may contain subject headings such as *purpose* and *procedures* for its subdivisions. Although these are stereotyped headings, they are, nevertheless, significant guideposts for the reader.

The end of the introduction must provide effective transition to the next section of the report. If it ends with an explanation of the general plan of the rest of the report, logical transition is made. It could also end with a discussion of the procedures used to gather data, and then the next section would present the results. A brief synopsis of the findings or a statement of the main conclusions can also make a logical transition.

Note how the introduction makes use of subheads in the report "An Analysis of Communications in a Department." [1]

I. INTRODUCTION

"Every member of management must understand that effective communications is an essential tool of good management; and that part of his job is to relay and interpret appropriate information and news, whether good or bad to his subordinates and superiors. . . ." [*] It is common knowledge that communications are vitally important to all levels of an organization, be the flow of that information upward, downward or laterally across organizational lines. It is important that this communication flows freely and with little distortion of the information. Not only is it important that communications move with minimized distortion, but there must be motivation on the part of subordinates to perform their tasks. A good communications system is the tool or technique to attain these results.

If communications are important to the proper functioning of an organization, is it not important, then, to understand how communications

[*] Lynn Townsend, quoted from ICIE Speech (December 1964) in G. Seybold, *Employee Communication: Policy and Tools* (N.Y.: National Industrial Conference Board, 1966), p. 11.

[1] From a report by Charles Dagleish, Eastern Michigan University.

work within the department in which one works? It is then the function of this research report to investigate the departmental communications.

The organization studied is the Industrial Engineering Department of a large production facility in Michigan. The department itself consists of twenty-three people performing various activities. There are five operational area sections: An indirect or nonproductive group, five employees; product line number one, six employees; product line number two, six employees; a cost analyst section, three employees; a department head, a secretary and a suggestions supervisor. The formal lines of responsibility within the department are as shown in exhibit A below:

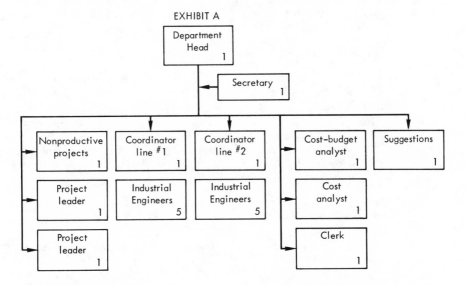

EXHIBIT A

(The number in the lower right corner of each box is the number of employees in each area)

Purpose and Objective:

The purpose of this investigation is to determine the effectiveness of the communicative processes and to gain insight into the communicative behavior exhibited between the various levels of responsibility in a department. Through a research survey various attitudes and other information revealing the formal and informal structures that communications operate within were exposed. These data were then evaluated between levels of responsibility. It was assumed then, that if the overall evaluations show similarities of opinion, that portion of the communicative process is operationally functional with the system.

Survey Procedures:

Questionnaires were used for collecting data on superior and subordinate opinions about the subordinate's job. Four areas of investigation were included: the duties and responsibilities of the subordinates' jobs, the requirements of their jobs, the organizational structure of the department, and finally general questions on department communication.

Subordinate respondents were asked to fill out a questionnaire by either stating their opinions (objective questions) or by listing the various factors making up their job assignments. Superiors or supervisors were then asked similar questions on their opinions or to list items on how they felt about their subordinates' jobs.

The questions were specifically designed to first get the employee involved with thinking about his job by listing the duties entailed. Objective questions were then used to gain insight on his opinion about those duties and responsibilities. Similar procedures were used for handling the requirements and the organizational sections of the questionnaire. The final section dealt with superior-subordinate attitudes toward intradepartmental communications.

Scope and Limitations:

Determining the effectiveness of communications can be very elusive for it is very difficult to investigate and measure opinions or attitudes regarding communications, and there are a great many factors involved in communication. Thus this research project was limited to the four areas of investigation previously stated.

Order of Presentation:

Before questionnaires could be handed out, evaluating and rating procedures had to be set up. These procedures are presented in Section II on Methodology. Section III deals with the findings discussed under the supervisors Joe, Larry, and Jerry. Inferences are then drawn from these findings in Section IV. Finally, recommendations are made in Section V.

In the illustrations of introductions presented here, the assumption is that the report begins with an introduction and ends with conclusions and/or recommendations. For several years there has been a pronounced trend toward reversing the organizational pattern and beginning a report with either conclusions or recommendations; then come the findings and their discussion, and the report ends with a summary, a restatement of the recommendations, or plans for implementing the recommended action.

The latter practice accentuates the need for immediate action and assumes that a great deal of the reader's time is saved by his not having to delve into problem details and allowing him to concern himself with the solution and its implementation. For the same reasons, there are also situations in which the conventional *introduction* begins with a summary of the conclusions or recommendations.

Discussion

The discussion section, as the major part of the report, presents information and data, analyzes them, and interprets them. The writer decides between pertinent data to include in the text and less important information to omit or relegate to the appendix. Meanings, ideas, and facts are made clear to the reader. Comparisons are made; facts are evaluated; significant relationships are drawn. Solutions of a problem may be given with an explanation of advantages and disadvantages. Tables, charts, and other media for presenting figures and data are used. Other illustrative material may be included. Emphasis is on the results and their interpretation. The discussion may lead the reader through the same reasoning process the author used to reach the conclusions and show him that they are sound.

Opposing contentions should be considered to show how the data prove otherwise. The writer should not assume that the reader agrees with a concept unless it is generally accepted. Simple, straightforward statements of facts are most easily understood. Different aspects of the problem are treated in the discussion section. Major subject headings are used to guide the reader. Points may be arranged to suit the subject and reader.

Conclusions

The final section of the report contains conclusions and recommendations. They may be treated in the same section or in separate sections. Conclusions are the result of reasoned analysis and judgment of the data in the report and serve as a basis for recommendations growing out of the study. They may be summary or analytical in nature. If summary, the conclusion section is a recapitulation of the significant points developed in the discussion section. New points are not developed, nor is the analysis carried any further. Concluding statements stand alone, supported by the facts in the discussion section. In an information report the conclusion is nearly always summary. An example of this type of conclusion is the following, taken from a consumer-preference survey made by Swift & Company for the molded pulp egg carton vs. the regular self-locking egg carton:

1. The molded pulp carton is decidedly preferred, both by those having used it (77 per cent of them) and those who have not used it (68 per cent of them).

2.   Protection is the principal reason of preference for the molded pulp carton.

3.   "Hard to open" and "can't see eggs" are the principal reasons for disliking the molded pulp carton given by those who have used it.

4.   Fifteen per cent of those preferring the molded pulp cartons had opening troubles—69 per cent of those preferring the regular type found the pulp carton difficult to open.

5.   Forty-five per cent of those preferring the molded pulp carton liked to look at eggs before buying, compared to 74 per cent of those preferring the regular type. "Want to see size" and "color" were given as reasons why.

If analytical by nature, conclusions are reached through analysis and interpretation of the data. They result from thinking over the facts and are usually discussed in paragraphs. An example follows:

CONCLUSIONS

Up until the final, comparative analysis of sales, there was relatively little to choose between the two cities. Both were certainly well adapted to a location for conducting the pretesting surveys of a small national-scale advertising agency, although at this point Kansas City has probably shown itself to be slightly more representative of the nation than Cincinnati. The analysis of retail sales, however, completely changed the picture.

Original Assumption of Suitability

As has been stated previously, no city's population can ever be expected to represent an average sample of the inhabitants of the entire country. Income, standard of living, and sales almost invariably will be greater than average. Consequently, the only measure of suitability is the extent to which these factors remain in proportion to one another, and hence, the degree of reliability which they have, after making necessary corrections and adjustments in data.

On this basis, Cincinnati would seem quite adequately and satisfactorily suited for use as an advertising "pretesting" ground. Kansas City, in view of its retail sales pattern, is certainly far less suitable, although it could probably be used if necessary.

It should be remembered that these conclusions are based on a current analysis, not a trend analysis, and pertain only to the present time. A period of a few years may completely reverse the situation, or it may be found that the present sales pattern in Kansas City is only a temporary distortion.

Choice of the More Suitable City

After the foregoing discussion, it seems hardly necessary to state that Cincinnati, Ohio is by far the more suitable of the two cities. Its population constitutes a better average sample than Kansas City's, and the result of surveys made there should prove more reliable, in the long run, than those made in Kansas City.

Sometimes facts are presented and analyzed and a conclusion reached in the discussion section; then the writer moves on to another set of facts, their analysis, and another conclusion. In this case conclusions are reached along with analysis of the material. Then in the conclusions section they are all brought together in summary form.

Conclusions may be listed or may be presented in paragraph form. They are usually introduced by an appropriate statement. Sometimes a summary of findings is given first, followed by conclusions.

Recommendations

Recommendations pertain to the action that is to be taken as a result of the report. They are supported by the conclusions, and they are aimed toward accomplishing the purpose of the report. If the purpose of a report, for instance, is to alleviate employee grievances over wage incentive plans, the recommendations will suggest ways that this can be done. Conclusions and results of investigating the problem will support the recommendations.

Like conclusions, recommendations may take the form of a numbered list of details or may be treated in paragraphs. They should answer the questions "What is to be done?" "By whom?" "When?" "Where?" and "How?"

In following a logical sequence for the textual parts of a formal, long report, recommendations are presented last; such has been the case in the discussion in this chapter. They do not, however, always appear at the end of the report. They may be given first, especially in recommendation reports. They are also sometimes treated briefly in the letter of transmittal, preface, and separate summary section. If the reader is likely to react unfavorably to the recommendation, then it should be given last; the report can prepare him for it. If he is already familiar with the data or is chiefly interested in the action to be taken, then the recommendation should be first to avoid his reading through a lot of material.

Checklist for Writing

Rapid writing of all sections in the report text to set down facts and ideas in logical order and sequence still calls for adherence as much as possible to principles of clarity, conciseness, and coherence. The following important questions should be asked and answered as the writer works:

Is it clear?

Can I make it clearer?
Are these ideas in the right order?
Can I arrange a better sequence?
Would an example or case study help?
Would a table or graph help?

Is it concise?

Have I wasted words?
Suppose I cut this, or this, or this?
Suppose I combine these ideas?

Is it coherent?

Does it hold together?
Does it flow smoothly from one idea to another?
Does it read aloud?

After the first draft has been written, the report can then be criticized, improved, and revised before it appears in its final form.

REVISING

The type of report and how it is to be used, as well as the amount of time available and how well the first draft was prepared, determine the amount of revision needed. A memorandum report, for example, containing information of temporary use does not warrant much revision. The report is checked, nevertheless, for accuracy of facts, clearness of expression, and overall organization; is tested to see whether it accomplishes its purpose adequately; and is proofread for correction of mechanical errors in form and typing. This procedure is generally followed for all reports of a routine nature or use and, to some degree, for all short or informal reports written for only one specific reader, usually within the company organization. Whether the report gets its message across to the reader is the all-important test, and time is not always available for revision beyond that point.

A report containing data of permanent value, or one which is to receive wide distribution, certainly warrants time spent in revision. Revision, for such a report, may decide whether or not it is read and in some cases may even increase its readership. Of course any printed report should be carefully revised and edited before publication. It would be foolish to spend money for printing ineffective or incorrect writing.

Revision varies according to the qualifications of the writer. One who writes competently may have few mechanical errors, such as spelling, punctuation, and grammar. One who normally expresses what he has to say clearly, concisely, and interestingly will have little revision of that nature to do. Revising offers the opportunity to correct the deficiencies of the report and the writer.

Revising a report systematically requires reading the report several times, each time checking the report for a different purpose. The reading may be done aloud or silently, to or by someone other than the writer.

Checking Content

Since the first draft of a report is written to set down facts and ideas and expand on the outline, and since it is written rapidly, one of the first checks to make on the subject matter is to find out whether or not it is accurate and complete and whether or not the purpose of the report has been accomplished. In checking the accuracy of the material, the writer should make sure that the problem is accurately defined and that the proper background material is provided for the reader to understand the situation. Is the scope properly limited? The original working plan can be used as an aid in checking the introductory material in the report. A look at the plan for conducting the investigation and making the report will indicate whether or not it was carried out in the first draft, and, if not, whether or not the changes can be accounted for and are improvements.

To further check the facts and data presented, the following questions will be helpful:

Are the numerical data exact?
Do the tables and charts contain accurate data?
Are the tables and charts used appropriately?
Do the illustrations conform to standard practice?
Are the illustrations suitable for the purpose and the reader?
Are the quotations exact?
Are the conclusions sound and logical?
Are the conclusions definite and clear?
Are the recommendations workable?
Are the recommendations an outgrowth of the conclusions?

In checking the subject matter for completeness, the writer should consider whether or not certain repetitions should be omitted or left in for emphasis. Irrelevant material should be deleted, and omitted data or explanations should be added. It is not sufficient at this point to check merely for the facts and ideas presented; it is also necessary to judge how they are presented. Are the comparisons clear? Are the analogies appropriate? Are there sufficient examples and illustrative material for clarity and interest? Is there adequate support or evidence for generalizations and conclusions that have been made?

Additional checking of subject matter should disclose whether or not the main issues stand out in proper perspective and the minor issues are related. What about the flow of ideas from one topic to the next? Is the reader adequately prepared to move forward? Does the report develop logically in one direction? Is adequate transition achieved through transitional sentences, paragraphs, words, and ideas? Will the reader reach the same conclusions as those stated? Do the data prepare him to accept the conclusions and to agree with the writer? Are the conclusions a basis for the recommendations? Do the recommendations fulfill the purpose of the report?

Checking Organization

Closely related to the process of checking the subject matter is that of checking the organization of the report—enough so, in fact, that in most short reports both can be done at the same reading. In long reports, the writer sometimes might want to check the organization before he delves into the subject matter. The overall organization of the report should be examined first, and then the organization of its parts. The outline will serve as a guide in determining the wisdom of the sequence and arrangement of the topics treated. If changes have been made in writing, the writer should decide whether or not they should remain or be changed further.

The organization should be logical and provide general coherence. The report should hang together as a whole; every part should be related and make sense.

Checking for Expression, Mechanics of Style, and Form

After he has checked the subject matter and organization, the writer can examine in detail each paragraph, sentence, and word in the report to be sure that everything is clearly expressed and mechanically correct. The questions—who, when, where, what, why, how much, and how many—should all be answered. Important specific details should be included, since they ensure clearness, interest, and conviction.

Sentences should be checked for their thought and structure. Are the ideas clear to the reader? Are their relationships conveyed by proper connection of the sentence elements? Is there ambiguity? What about the phrasing—does it read smoothly? Logically? Does it sound natural? Simple, short sentences outnumbering more complex sentences contribute to clearness and exactness of expression. Yet there should be a variety of sentence types, patterns, and lengths. For easy comprehension there should be an average sentence length of eighteen to twenty-two words. This is an *average;* there should definitely be a combination of long, short, and in-between sentences, with the short predominating and the average maintained. The longer the sentence and the more complex its structure, the more difficult it becomes to grasp clearly and quickly. Sentences should also be checked for grammatical correctness. Are unity, coherence, and emphasis maintained in each sentence? Does the sentence contain any faulty pronoun reference, dangling modifier, indirect or awkward phrasing?

In checking the words used, the writer should try to substitute a concrete word for each abstract one. The concrete word is within the experience of the reader and will have more meaning for him than the abstract word that deals with concepts which are usually beyond the realm of the five senses. Some abstract terms must be used for want of something better; these should be defined or the concept illustrated by specific details. Complex, bookish, and trite words and phrases should be avoided. Simple, plain, familiar words facilitate comprehension.

Because they are closely related, the checking of sentences and words can be done at the same time. In working for conciseness, for example, both must be considered. The length of the original copy can usually be reduced by shortening sentences, combining sentences, breaking up sentences, cutting out all unnecessary wording and phrasing, and selecting words with exact meaning. As thoughts become clarified and concepts simplified, the number of words tends to decrease. If clarity demands additional explanation or description, report parts will be longer in the revised copy, but the overall length will have been shortened merely by applying principles of simplified writing. This is the best way to save the reader's time.

The more one examines the words and sentences, the more likely he is to notice any mechanical errors in English and typing. In most cases he can correct these at the same time. Simply by being conscious of spelling, punctuation, and grammar, one can perceive many errors. In some cases, however, a reference handbook or dictionary should be used—to what extent depends on the qualifications and experience of the writer.

Since the form of a report is determined by its type, purpose, and use, each of these factors should be considered in checking the form. This might be done while examining report organization, but at this time the writer usually is concerned with a general impression of form rather than with a detailed examination. Does the report conform to a standard form for its type—letter, memorandum, bulletin, or some other kind? What about details of typing form—margins, spacing, footnotes, subject headings, and the like? Has the proper footnote form been used? Is there consistency in form? Are all headings of like degree typed in the same manner? Are proper degrees of relationship shown in the headings? Have tabulations or quotations been set off rather than run into the other paragraphs of the text?

General Suggestions

The purpose of revision is to prepare the report for final typing and distribution. Revision gives the writer an opportunity to correct or rewrite portions and in general to improve and polish the report—all of which may assure its acceptance, increased readership, and resultant action. All corrections may be made in the margins or in the text, or an explanatory symbol may be placed in the margin and the error underscored in the text. The location for inserted material may be indicated

Checklist for Revising

Contents
Fulfillment of purpose
Accuracy and completeness
  Background material
  Scope defined
  Numerical data
  Tables and charts
  Quotations
  Examples and explanations
  Facts and other evidence
  Duplication
  Repetitions
  Irrelevant material
  Conclusions
Main issues
Minor issues
Logical development
Flow of ideas
Emphasis

Mechanical correctness
English
  Spelling
  Punctuation
  Grammar
Form
  Type of report
  Parts of report
  Margins
  Paragraphing
  Footnote form
  Bibliographical form
  Subject headings
  Consistency

Organization
As a whole
Relationship of parts
Position of topics
Sequence of ideas
Transition
Unity

Clearness of expression
Sentences
  Specific facts and details expressed
  Varied sentence structure
  Short sentences predominant
  Average sentence length
  Grammatically correct sentences
  Smooth phrasing
  Use of topic sentences
Words
  Concrete
  Familiar
  Precise
  Simple
  Abstract concepts defined

Adaptation to reader
Level of readability
Tone
Experience and knowledge
Interest

by a caret. Material may be deleted by marking through it or blocking it out. Material to be added may be written on a separate sheet and attached, with a notation made on the original copy as to where it is to be inserted.

After the marked copy has been retyped, it should be proofread for correction of errors in typing and English. Persistent errors may warrant another typing, but this is not usually necessary. If the report is to be published, a list of proofreader's marks used by the publisher should be checked and used in revising and editing it.

A general checklist for revising a report appears on page 286. The extent to which it is used will depend on the writer's experience and abilities, the type and use of the report, and the amount of time available for revision. Not all reports are revised, nor should they be. Most reports, however, can be improved by careful revision.

MEASURING READABILITY

Readability is that quality of writing that provides clearness and interest for the reader. The level of readability is expressed in terms of the general educational level of the reader. For example, a report from management to a group of unskilled employees, who have probably not attained an average educational level beyond the eighth grade, should be written in terms that could be understood at the eighth-grade level of education. Readability formulas have been developed for rating material by measurement of its difficulty. Results determine whether or not the measured material will reach its intended reader. If testing indicates that he will be reached, then the writer, in revising, need not be further concerned with readability. If the writing is too difficult or too simple, however, the writer should lower or raise the level when he revises. The formula merely indicates the degree of difficulty and leaves correction to the writer. After the report has been revised it is good practice to apply a readability test again.

Because it measures readability in a general way for the general reader, a readibility formula is best applied to reports and written communications for a wide audience. Reports from management to employees and from the company to the public, such as policy statements, bulletins, employee handbooks, company magazines, and annual reports, fall into this category. In general, readers will prefer an easier version to a more difficult one and will find it more pleasant to read. If well handled, easy material will save time for the superior reader.

When the report writer and reader are on the same education level, there is usually no readability problem. Most of these reports are of the informational or problem-solving variety; the reader is interested in the information or the solution, and his education level is sufficiently high for comprehension. For these reasons the report will be read. However, for a widely distributed report, readership as well as comprehension may be greatly increased by using a readability formula.

Frequently Used Readability Formulas

No one formula is definitely superior to another, but the newer ones are as accurate as the older ones and in general are easier to apply. The report writer should be familiar with several of them and know how to use them. Although it is impossible to present enough information about applying every formula, two have been selected for discussion here on the basis of their frequent use.

Flesch's Formulas. Rudolf Flesch is more responsible than any other person for popularizing the readability formula. His formula for measuring reading ease is by far the most widely used, and formulas developed since have made use of it. The first Flesch formula, developed in 1943, measured readability by the average sentence length expressed in words, the number of affixes, and the number of personal references.[2] Since it was time-consuming and hard to apply, he revised it in 1948. The 1948 formula, which measures reading ease by the average sentence length and average word length in syllables and measures human interest by the number of personal words and personal sentences, has become the most widely used of his readability formulas. Counting syllables instead of affixes makes testing both easier and quicker.

Attempting to get a measurement of abstraction in writing, Flesch developed another formula in 1950.[3] It is based on the premise that abstract style contains relatively more descriptive adjectives, indefinite pronouns, and subordinating conjunctions than concrete style, which contains relatively more proper nouns, limiting adjectives, finite verbs, personal pronouns, and coordinating conjunctions. Accordingly he determines the level of abstraction by computing the ratio of certain parts of speech. The formula includes a count of sixteen categories of definite words and the average word length expressed in syllables. Because this formula is difficult to apply, it has not been widely used.

Another Flesch formula, published in 1954, uses two criteria for measuring readability—specificness and communicative energy.[4] Specific-

[2] Rudolf Flesch, *The Art of Plain Talk* (New York: Harper & Row, Publishers, 1946).

[3] Rudolf Flesch, "Measuring the Level of Abstraction," *Journal of Applied Psychology*, Vol. 34 (December 1950), pp. 384–90.

[4] Rudolf Flesch, *How to Make Sense* (New York: Harper & Row, Publishers, 1954).

ness corresponds to his earlier criterion of human interest. Specific words, including names and places, are counted. Communicative energy bears a close relationship to his earlier concept of sentence length; it includes counting all punctuation marks except commas.

Gunning's Fog Index. In 1944 Robert Gunning Associates set up a firm for readability counseling. They adapted twenty years of research for the use of business writers. Surveys made in business and industry indicated "more than a third of the writing intended for employees and customers is above college reading level. Writing of that degree of difficulty is usually skipped by both customers and employees." [5] They sought to determine the factors of writing style that could be measured and to what degree each affects reading difficulty. They discovered the seven most helpful factors to be average sentence length in words, percentage of simple sentences, percentage of verbs expressing forceful action, portion of familiar words, portion of abstract words, percentage of personal references, and percentage of long words. [6]

Gunning uses two elements in measuring readability, the number of words of three or more syllables in 100 words and the average sentence length in words. His method, though related to Flesch's reading ease formula, is easier to apply and gives much the same result. One can count

Fog Index	Reading Level by Grade	Reading Level by Magazine
17	College graduate	(No popular magazine
16	College senior	is this difficult.)
15	College junior	
14	College sophomore	
13	College freshman	
	DANGER LINE	
12	High school senior	*The Atlantic*
11	High school junior	*Harpers*
	EASY-READING RANGE	
10	High school sophomore	*Time*
9	High school freshman	*Reader's Digest*
8	Eighth grade	*Ladies' Home Journal*
7	Seventh grade	*True Confessions*
6	Sixth grade	Comics

the hard-word factor about as fast as he can skim the material, since few familiar words are of more than three syllables.

[5] Robert Gunning, *The Technique of Clear Writing* (New York: McGraw-Hill Book Company, 1952), p. 7.
[6] *Ibid.*, p. 32.

The following instructions are for applying Gunning's method of measuring readability: [7]

1. *Determine average sentence length.* Jot down number of words in successive sentences. For long pieces of writing take samples of 100 words. Divide total number of words by number of sentences.

2. *Find the percentage of hard words.* Count the number of words of three syllables or more per 100 words. Don't count capitalized words, words that are combinations of short easy words (like *bookkeeper* and *butterfly*), words that are verb forms made into three syllables by adding *ed* or *es* (such as *created* or *trespasses*).

3. *Figure Fog Index.* Add the two factors (Steps 1 and 2) and multiply by 0.4.

The Fog Index is determined in such a simple, easy way that no formula or device for computation is necessary. The preceding table is for interpreting the Fog Index or readability score.[8]

Influence of Readability Formulas on Style

Readability formulas can be used to the extreme and lead to writing faults. A choppy, childish style will result from writing in too many short, simple sentences, and the most familiar word may not always be the best choice. Even a short sentence may not be clear. Writing within a limited vocabulary range may become monotonous and deadening.

The formulas should be used for measuring the readability level and not as rules for writing. They do not measure the reader's background and interest, nor do they consider many factors that go into effective writing. They do, however, measure readability in a general way for the general reader and help the writer to see his material as the reader will or *to adapt his writing to the reader.*

Most research in readability points to the use of clear sentences and understandable words for making writing readable. Thus emphasis is on clearness in writing, and readability formulas have affected the style of writing to the extent of emphasizing the following principles in writing clear sentences:

Keep majority of sentences short and simple.
Make relationships clear in each sentence.
Vary sentence length and structure.
Use small number of prepositional and infinitive phrases.
Use adequate conjunctions and transitional phrases for smooth reading.
Convey only one or two main thoughts in each sentence.
Let each sentence mean something in relation to other sentences.

[7] *Ibid.,* pp. 36, 37.
[8] *Ibid.,* p. 38.

The formulas have also emphasized the following principles in using vocabulary:

Use familiar words.
Make words meaningful.
Avoid unnecessary words.
Use short-syllable words.
Select nontechnical terms.
Put action into verbs.
Use a variety of words.
Select pictorial words within the reader's experience.
Use concrete rather than abstract words.
Apply concrete analogies, examples, and comparisons when abstract concepts must be given.

EDITING

Editing is basically the same as revising, for its purpose is to correct and improve the report—to prepare and check the final copy. Although editing is often done by someone other than the author, a number of writers edit their own material. The report rewritten from all points noted—with additions, deletions, or corrections—is read again to check and improve it before distribution. If the report is to be published, editing also involves preparing the final copy for the printer. The manuscript is checked first for the accuracy, completeness, and clearness of subject matter, then for overall and sectional organization, and last for correctness in the mechanics of style and form. In most instances after a report has undergone careful revision, all that is necessary is to correct the few mechanical errors that remain and, if the report is to be published, mark the copy for the printer.

Large companies employ editors to polish material written for wide distribution. The amount of work they do on a report depends on the quality of its writing. In some instances they merely correct mechanical flaws, and in other cases technical errors; sometimes they do a complete rewrite job, retaining only the conclusions of the original. Publishers also have editors who correct and mark material for publication. The compositor will then go over it and make his plans. The material is checked and returned to the author for approval or changes. When it goes back to the compositor, he makes the galley proof, which is usually read and corrected by the editor or a proofreader. Page proof is then printed, proofread, and returned for final printing.

Throughout the process of publishing, the editor is responsible to the printer for marking instructions and corrections clearly; to the author for preserving his facts, ideas, style, and objectives; to the publisher for protecting his publication policies and for increasing readership; to the reader for presenting clear and interesting material; and to himself for maintaining his own reputation as an editor. Careful editing is just as necessary for printed reports as careful writing, revising, and checking are for typed reports. Effective writing and revising make the editor's task an easy one and assure the reader a clear, well-written report and the writer the fulfillment of his purpose.

A good working relationship should be maintained between the report writer and the editor, for both are working toward as good a report as possible. Recognizing that they have a common goal, setting up a time schedule and maintaining a cooperative attitude are necessary. It always helps also for them to follow one particular guide or manual for handling mechanics of style and form. This may be prepared by the company or the publisher, or it may be simply a setting down of rules and guiding principles that the author and editor agree to follow. For instance, the *comma before and* in a series may be omitted. The writer and editor must agree to either using the comma or omitting it. Agreement to follow a particular handbook of English might also be helpful.

PROOFREADING

Proofreading is done at each stage of manuscript preparation to ensure correctness. A report which is to be typewritten in its final form requires checking the typewritten page for errors. The proofreader should read the copy as a whole, and then check it for form, layout, and mechanical accuracy. It is not necessary to read for content at this stage. He should read each word and phrase, not sentences and paragraphs. Each word and punctuation mark should be scrutinized, for the aim is perfection. The final typed copy is checked against the draft to be sure they are the same and that the typist has followed instructions. Proofreading marks are used in the copy and in the margins to designate corrections or necessary retyping.

If a report is to be reproduced and copies distributed, proofreading is repeated at each stage of the reproduction process to ensure correctness in the final copies. In mimeographing, the stencil is proofread and checked against the typed copy and corrected before runs are made. In hectographing, the master sheet is proofread and checked; in multilithing, the specially prepared mat is proofread.

For a printed report, galley proofs are checked against the edited manuscript for mechanical correctness and to make sure the compositor has followed the editor's instructions. Notations can be written in the margins for corrections to be made in setting up page proofs. Then page proofs are checked against galley proofs to be sure all corrections have been made and no further errors committed. In both galley and page proof stages, it is easy to skip over misspellings and omissions. Here again the proofreader should examine each word and punctuation mark and check all tables, statistics, and percentages against the copy. Sometimes he may question deletions or additions, or even the way something has been written. Such things should be kept at a minimum in galley proofs and avoided as much as possible in page proofs. In reading page proofs, the proofreader should concentrate on making sure that all corrections indicated on the galleys have been made. He should examine all lines affected to see that no error was made, verify the positions of tables and charts and other visual aids, and check all captions, credit lines, footnotes, and cross-reference page numbers. Compositor's corrections can be costly, especially from page proofs. The time to make changes is from the galleys, for the compositor must only set the new material and drop it into the

PROOFREADER'S MARKS

Mark	Meaning	Mark	Meaning
⅄	Insert comma	⌄²	Superscript (number specified)
V̇	Insert apostrophe		
V̈	Insert quotation marks	⅄²	Subscript (number specified)
⊙	Insert period	#	Insert space
⊚	Insert colon	hr#	Hair space between letters
;/	Insert semicolon	↓	Push down space
?/	Insert question mark	⊏	Move to left
=/	Insert hyphen	⊐	Move to right
⊥	One-em dash	⊔	Lower
⊥	Two-em dash	⊓	Elevate
en	En dash	X	Broken letter
|·|·|	Ellipsis (If preceded by a period there will be 4 dots.)	⌒	Ligature (Æsop)
९	Delete	ⓢₚ	Spell out (U. S.)
◠	Close up	stet	Let it stand (some day)
⑤	Delete and close up	wf	Wrong font
⑨	Reverse; upside-down	bf	Set in boldface type
⋀	Insert (caret)	rom	Set in roman type
¶	Paragraph	ital	Set in italic type
no¶	No paragraph; run in	sc	Small capitals
tr	Transpose (their only is)	caps	Capitals
=	Align	lc	Set in lower case
		ld>	Insert lead between lines

galley. If corrections are from the page proof, he must change the page makeup, and sometimes this involves several pages and the renumbering of pages.

In all proofreading, it is advisable to have someone help. Having two people, one reading aloud from the typed copy, the other checking the galley sheet, works well, since two pairs of eyes are always better than one. The editor usually proofreads material when it comes from the compositor and makes his notations, and then sends it to the author for his proofreading. After the author returns the proof, the editor can go over it again before returning it to the printer.

FOR DISCUSSION AND WRITING

1. The following case study presents problems in relationships of report writers, supervisors, and editors. What would you recommend?

Elliott Oil Company—Case Study

The management of Elliott Oil Company Refinery, Long Beach, California, asked you to investigate the attitudes, beliefs, and feelings of the technical men toward their work situations in the refinery and in the laboratories. Conferences were held, and at the beginning of each interview you said, "I want you to tell me about yourself and your job. What do you like about it? What do you dislike? What changes should be made?" You then would sit back and listen, taking detailed notes. From these interviews you found most grievances centered around communication problems and report writing.

Most information on changes in company policy was disseminated by word of mouth from supervisors to the employee or in group meetings; occasionally a letter or a memo was used. Half of the men interviewed felt that messages were neither complete nor clear. About two-thirds of the men stated they thought the group meetings were a farce—no exchange or discussion took place.

Most written reports were passed up the line for approval and rewritten to satisfy each man's objections until they finally passed the level responsible for sending them outside. Half of the men reported they rewrote material three or four times. Common reasons for rewriting were that the men did not always have complete information and supervisors were concerned with petty details. They would make unnecessary changes which suited them at the moment. These changes generally were not called to the attention of the original writer of the report. Sometimes reports lay on or in a supervisor's desk for almost a year before being sent back to the writer for changes. Material became obsolete, and errors of fact, as well as mechanical errors and inconsistencies occurred in finished reports.

Since men did not sign their reports, they felt cheated of proper credit and unimportant in their jobs. Most projects and reports were assigned with: "This is a rush job; do it immediately." It was hard to

believe everything was *rush*, especially after a report lay in a desk
drawer for six months, became outdated, and then was returned
with: "Bring it up-to-date and make changes I've indicated. This is
a rush job. Get to it immediately." Men no longer felt quality of
work was important; a job simply had to be done in a hurry. Writers
did not feel they were part of a working team with their supervisors
who edited and approved their reports.

2. Assume that you have been asked to set up, in a new company office,
a publishing unit for reproducing reports. Most reports are memorandums, letters, and bulletins, with occasional short, formal reports.
There is a weekly report of about fifty pages of text and ten illustrations that calls for twenty-five copies for distribution. You are to
specify the equipment, methods, and personnel. On what bases would
you make your decisions? You will need to consider various equipment
and reproduction processes, such as printing, multigraph, photography,
mimeograph, hectograph, xerography, and offset. You should also
weigh the advantages of electric versus manual typewriters, offset printing versus typeset printing, and stencils versus typing mats or preparation of special plates. Will you need to estimate cost? Gather your
information and ideas and write the report.

3. B. A. Value, Ltd., a high quality department store in Detroit, Michigan, has an annual policy of having its salespeople wear a sprig of
holly on their suit coat, blouse, or dress during the Christmas season.
This holly distinguishes the salespeople from the customers during a
crowded period; it also adds a personal seasonal cheer. A newspaper
advertisement announces this identifying seasonal touch at the beginning of each Christmas season. During the two past years, some personnel have not been wearing the holly consistently. Because it has
become a tradition with B. A. Value, Ltd., customers expect to find
sales clerks wearing holly.

Salespeople not wearing holly were asked why they failed to follow
company policy. The most popular explanations are as follows:

1. When a salesperson arrived home after work and changed clothes,
he took off the holly and placed it on the bureau. In the morning
rush to get to work on time, the holly was left on the bureau. The
salesperson did not miss the holly until he arrived at work; once the
day's work began, he forgot about the holly again.

2. The sprig of holly is attached to the clothing of the salesperson
by a straight pin. Some salespeople say that the holly dropped off when
they bent over or brushed against objects, and they did not have time
to pick it up or get another sprig.

3. Each morning as the salespeople arrived for work, there was nobody to make sure that they were wearing their sprigs of holly. Since
few people were checking, the salespeople were not concerned if they
wore the holly or not.

4. Many part-time salespeople are hired during the Christmas season; there is also a large turnover of salespeople. Nonpermanent salespeople say that the policy of wearing holly was never fully explained to
them, if explained at all.

Failure to wear the holly has created several embarrassing situations:

1. When customers try to find a salesperson, they ask another customer if he might be a salesperson. After receiving a negative response and failing to locate a salesperson, they become impatient and leave the store.

2. When customers are unable to purchase the Christmas gifts in B. A. Value, Ltd., they depart and look for another store which is less crowded.

3. With the loss of customers, the store sales will drop below the expected or required amount.

4. The salespeople lack the personal touch of Christmas cheer that the store is noted for.

5. Customers reading the newspaper advertisements will be very dissatisfied when they cannot find the salespeople wearing holly.

6. Money will have been wasted on the newspaper advertising if there is no follow-up by the salespeople.

There should be a change in store enforcement of the holly policy. Customers dissatisfied with B. A. Value, Ltd., can also influence their friends to shop elsewhere with them, and there will be an increasing loss of sales. No store can maintain a drop in sales and stay in business and be successful. Over the years B. A. Value, Ltd., has been known as the store with the Christmas spirit. The lack of holly will reduce the personal touch in the spreading of the Christmas spirit. It is important that a store have regular customers. If the regular customers go to other, less-crowded stores, they may never come back to B. A. Value, Ltd. It is almost impossible to find a salesperson in a crowded store. There is tremendous confusion when many customers are all trying to buy something at the same time, and confusion sometimes leads to panic.

Analyze the conditions in the B. A. Value store and recommend solutions either for enforcing the wearing of the holly or for abandoning the idea.

WRITING
PRELIMINARY AND
SUPPLEMENTARY SECTIONS

9

SOMEWHERE ALONG THE WAY as you go through the stages of writing, revising, and editing a report—especially one that calls for a degree of formality and length in a complicated situation—you will want to decide how to dress it up so it will convince the recipient to take action on it.

Generally such decisions are reached during the revision stage so that the text plus additional parts can get that final editing and proofreading. In the previous chapter we were concerned with writing the text, or body of the report, and perfecting it as much as we could. Now assuming that we have refined the report text as much as possible, the decision remains on how we can dress it up by adding preliminary and supplementary parts. Preliminary sections present reference and informational material which explains and identifies the report and the situation for which it was prepared. Supplemental sections follow the report proper and include material of a general and secondary interest for reference and record purposes. Sometimes material too bulky for inclusion in the text is placed at the end in a supplemental section.

The relationship of the writer, reader, and material in the report plus the report's purpose and use in a given situation determine the extent to which one adds preliminary parts to dress it up. It is possible but very unlikely that any one report would contain all the possible parts. The writer should always be selective and use only those parts that are relevant in the given situation.

ADDING PRELIMINARY SECTIONS

Possible preliminary sections from which you may choose are listed in the order in which they would be placed before the report text.

Cover	*Letter of transmittal
Flyleaf	Dedication
Frontispiece	Foreword
*Title page	Preface
Copyright page	Acknowledgments
Letter of authorization	*Table of contents
Letter of acceptance	*List of tables
Letter of approval	*Summary

The asterisks indicate the ones used most frequently. They are illustrated on the following pages, whereas the other sections are merely explained for your understanding and reference.

Cover

The cover identifies and protects the report. Leather, cardboard, heavy paper, or other flexible materials are suitable, or a self-cover from the same paper on which the report text is typed may be used. Sometimes a manila file folder serves the same function. It should contain the title, author, and completion date. If the report is a numbered one, the cover will carry the number. In reports used for internal communication a printed form is often filled out and attached to the outside.

Flyleaf

The flyleaf, a blank sheet preceding the title page, is used only when the report is written for a high official or when a very high-quality appearance is desired. The paper may be of the same stock as the rest of the report but is frequently a thinner paper of better quality.

Frontispiece

Likewise a frontispiece is neither required nor often used. Consisting of a map, an organizational chart, a photograph of equipment, or a visual presentation of the major results, it can add interest or importance to a prominent feature of the report. Although sometimes used in printed reports for the general reader, it is rarely used in internal typewritten reports. When used it faces the title page and often has the flyleaf as a protector.

Title Page

The title page is necessary for long reports and those that are retained for future use. It provides complete identification of the report. Therefore it should include the title, subtitle, author (his position and address), name and address of the person or company for whom the report is prepared, serial designation if in a series, contract or project numbers, and date of completion.

A good title tells the reader what the report contains by both attracting his attention and informing him. Thus it must be complete, accurate, concise, and descriptive—characteristics seldom found in a catchy title.

There is value in conciseness, and when necessary the subtitle can provide details for completeness.

Because the title should indicate the contents of the report, the following suggestions should help in composing effective titles:

1. Use subject and verb.
2. Indicate action suggested by the report.
3. Suggest results or findings.
4. Answer who, what, why, when, where, and how.
5. Indicate scope or limitations.

The title should not contain such unnecessary words or phrases as "a report on," "an investigation of," "a survey of," and the like. Some titles, however, indicate the nature of the report by use of such phrases as "recommendations for" and "the progress of." The subtitle is entirely explanatory or descriptive; it explains and gives details of the subject. It may be as long as necessary.

Complete addresses are given for the author and the person for whom the report is prepared to facilitate inquiries about the report. The date aids in filing and keeping records; it also lets the reader know the recency of the data in the report.

For short, routine, and most internal reports the cover and title page are combined, and a memorandum form arrangement is generally used:

Subject: _____
To: _____
From: _____
Date: _____
Distribution: _____

_____
or

Report on _____
Submitted to _____
Prepared by _____
Date of transmittal _____

If a report is to be published, the title page will follow the arrangement of the title page of a printed book. The printer's type provides a wide variety of faces that can be used for presenting an attractive appearance. Whether it is printed or typed, the title page should be carefully arranged to create a favorable first impression on the reader. Words of the title are grouped, lines are broken, spaces are left—all so that the information can be readily seen and understood at a glance. In typewritten reports, the typist relies on the use of capital and lowercase letters and underlining and spacing to make up an attention-getting title page. Proper balance and proportion must be achieved. The sample title pages immediately following should be carefully noted for their arrangements. Each title page, although arranged differently, contains the same basic information. A formally arranged title page contains full information and follows a set pattern, as shown in the following two illustrations.

Improving the Sales Operational Methods of Audiphone
Company of Raleigh, North Carolina

A Comparison of the Sales Program of Two Companies in
the Hearing Aid Industry as Applied Specifically to
Audiphone Company in Raleigh

Prepared for:

    Mr. Frank L. Fauston
    Audiphone Company
    709 Pere Marquette Building
    Raleigh, North Carolina

Prepared by:

    James Fauston
    School of Business Administration
    North Carolina State University
    Raleigh, North Carolina

January 11, 197–

Formally arranged title page (blocked style).

An informally arranged title page does not contain all the information that is called for in the formal title page, nor does it follow a set pattern of arrangement. In fact it is quite varied, as in the arrangements on pages 304 and 305.

IMPROVING THE SALES OPERATIONAL METHODS OF
AUDIPHONE COMPANY OF RALEIGH, NORTH CAROLINA

A Comparison of the Sales Programs of Two Companies
in the Hearing Aid Industry as Applied
Specifically to Audiphone
Company in Raleigh

Prepared For:

Mr. Frank L. Fauston

Audiphone Company
709 Pere Marquette Building
Raleigh, North Carolina

Prepared By:

James Fauston
School of Business Administration
North Carolina State University
Raleigh, North Carolina

January 11, 197–

Formally arranged title page (centered style).

Copyright Page

When the material is copyrighted, the fact is recognized on the back
of the title page. Included are the date of the copyright, name of the
publisher, and a notation similar to "All rights reserved. No parts may
be reproduced without the permission of the publisher."

Letter of Authorization

The letter of authorization is used to establish authority for and to
state the terms under which an investigation and a report are made. It
precedes the investigation and is written by the person requesting the

Improving the Sales Operations Methods of
the Audiphone Company

James Fauston
January 11, 197_

Informally arranged title page.

The
influence
of
magazine
page size
on
advertising
effectiveness

GALLUP & ROBINSON, INC.   *Advertising and Marketing Research, Princeton, N. J.*

Informally arranged title and cover pages combined.

Courtesy Gallup & Robinson, Inc.

study to the person who is to do the research and report. Usually a report contains a letter of authorization *only* if the letter is desirable as a record. Most of the time authorization is given verbally or the report arises out of the reporter's work, and there is no letter of authorization.

There are two kinds of letters of authorization—general and specific. A general letter merely states the request for the report and suggests arrangements for its execution. In addition to making a request, a specific letter of authorization gives details of the problem situation and of what is to be done. In the following letter of authorization, the problem, the need for the report, a suggested method of obtaining data, the scope and limitations, and the use to be made of the report are all presented. The investigator can begin his preliminary work immediately, for he knows what to do.

AUDIPHONE COMPANY OF RALEIGH
709 Pere Marquette Building
Raleigh, North Carolina

December 5, 197–

Mr. James C. Fauston
263 Audubon Street
Richmond, Virginia

Dear Mr. Fauston:

Several of my salesmen have recently called my attention to deficiencies in the operations of the sales program of the Audiphone Company. With this problem in mind, would you please present a report analyzing the situation and giving your conclusions and recommendations?

Since the hearing aid field is a limited one, you should make your analysis by comparing my sales methods with those of two of my competitors, preferably the Telex Company and the Sonotone Company, both of which have local offices. Please confine your investigation of the activities of these companies to the states of North Carolina and Virginia, as this is the limit of my territory.

In your report, you should cover office selling, road work, and advertising, for these are the main sales methods used in the hearing aid field today. You may find that some policies are made at a national level rather than at a local one, but they should be included in the comparison because of their effect upon local operating procedures. The sales programs of hearing aid companies are not secret; therefore, perhaps the best way to collect the necessary information would be by personal interview. However, any advertising booklets, sales manuals, or other material relating to the problem should be used in making your recommendations.

In an effort to improve our competitive position, these recommendations will be the basis for changing our methods. For this reason, please present the complete report by January 11, 197–.

Yours very truly,

Frank L. Fauston
Manager

Letter of Acceptance

The letter of acceptance is also used infrequently. On rare occasions, however, it is included as a record or for publicity purposes. Because it is an answer to the letter of authorization, it accepts the request to make the investigation and to write the report. Thus it may include plans pertaining to stipulation of money, time, and expense; it may ask for additional information; it may state changes over plans proposed in the letter of authorization; and it may make clear what the investigator proposes to do. Occasionally it includes the working plan or even a preliminary outline; in this case it sometimes requests approval of plans before the researcher proceeds with his investigation.

Letter of Approval

There are two possible functions of the letter of approval. If it is written in answer to the letter of acceptance, it may approve the working plan or the like, so the investigator can begin his study. In this case it is rarely part of the completed report. If the letter is written after the investigation and report have been completed, then it approves the final report and may be included as part of it. In this case the letter of approval is from a superior officer and is written to help the report get proper attention. Sometimes the report, which has been prepared by a subordinate, is submitted to his chief for approval before it is transmitted to a group or an individual.

Once in a while the letter of approval becomes the letter of submittal because it either takes on aspects of the letter of transmittal or is used in its place. A strictly formal report to the public might contain this type of approval, which would usually be formal and conventional.

Letter of Transmittal

The letter of transmittal, which forwards the report, is written after the report has been completed and is addressed to the person or group for whom the report has been prepared. Sometimes it is separate from the report and attached outside to the cover or title page. But usually it is part of the bound report, in which case it may follow the title page, precede the table of contents, or follow the letter of approval.

The composition of the letter of transmittal varies from report to report. It may contain any or all of the following elements and any additional ones that may be appropriate:

1. Reference to authorization.
2. Summary of the report.

3. Scope and limitations.
4. History and background.
5. Acknowledgments.
6. Need of the report.
7. Use of the report.
8. Conclusions and recommendations.
9. Personal attitudes of the writer.
10. Personal opinions of the writer.

The elements of the letter of transmittal are determined by the type of report it forwards, the relation of author and reader, and the existing situation. It should increase the reader's interest and confidence in the report. For this reason a natural, conversational, but dignified, tone is effective. This letter, however, can be written in an informal, personal style, for the author has an opportunity to mention personal ideas which cannot appear in an impersonal report. By being direct and straight-forward he can persuade the reader to accept the report. By developing points of interest to the reader he will get his attention and create a desire to read the report. This may be done by calling attention to points of significance and value to the reader.

When a report has no preface or foreword, the transmittal letter performs their functions. Used in a report which has a foreword or preface, the letter of transmittal merely transmits the report or is used as a covering letter separate from the bound report.

The following sample letter to the Audiphone Company emphasizes the analysis and results of the report and was used with a report that contained a title page and table of contents.

263 Audubon Street
Richmond, Va.
January 9, 197–

Mr. Frank L. Fauston
Audiphone Company of Raleigh
709 Pere Marquette Building
Raleigh, N.C.

Dear Mr. Fauston:

As you requested, I am submitting my recommendations for the sales operational methods of the Audiphone Company. The report is based on the operating procedures of your firm as contrasted with those of two of your competitors in North Carolina and Virginia, the Telex Company and the Sonotone Company.

The analysis shows that the road selling and advertising procedures of the Audiphone Company offer the largest room for improvement. Because of a high degree of control over the policies of the company, you should experience little difficulty in making the proposed changes. Road and rural selling is the most deficient phase of your sales program, from the hiring of road men to their remuneration. The policies of the Audiphone Company toward suboffices and local repair points have been found excellent, for they provide the hard-of-hearing person with necessary extra services.

The high place occupied by the Audiphone Company in the competitive picture is widely recognized, but this is no indication that changes are not necessary. As selling methods progress, the company must progress also; and it is only by change that this can be accomplished. Following the recommendations should strengthen the position of the Audiphone Company in the highly competitive hearing aid industry for many years to come.

Yours very truly,

James C. Fauston

Dedication

Rarely does a business report contain a dedication page. When it does, it is handled in the same way as the dedication of a book. The report would have to be very formal in nature and issued on a very special occasion to call for a dedication.

Foreword

Functionally the foreword accomplishes the same purposes as the letter of transmittal and the introduction. Thus one should complement the others. The foreword establishes contact with the reader and orients him to the report. When the report is addressed to the public in general, the foreword usually replaces the letter of transmittal.

The foreword may contain any or most of the following elements:

1. References to purpose, scope, etc.
2. References to circumstances out of which the report developed.
3. Statement of the writer's qualifications and experience.
4. Indication of the author's interest in the subject.
5. General orientation of the reader to the subject.
6. Reference to the authorization.
7. Acknowledgments.
8. Pertinent comments.
9. References to other related reports.
10. Evaluation of work accomplished.

For practical purposes the foreword and the preface are the same— they are used interchangeably. Discriminating authors and publishers, however, distinguish between them. The foreword is written by someone other than the author, and the preface is written by the author. For this reason a report may have both a preface and a foreword, although it usually does not. The foreword should be written by one who knows the author and his work, because he is able to comment on the author's qualifications and the merit and value of the work—comments which might sound egotistical if made by the author.

Preface

The preface is written by the report's author and gives him a chance to state his opinions and attitudes. It may include his reasons for writing the report, his thinking that led to the report, a presentation of his background and experience, and his explanation of how he intends the report to be used. It is the author's opportunity to talk about himself to the reader.

Often it is informally and personally written. It is not generally included as a part of a report; however, when it is, it may replace the foreword or letter of transmittal.

Acknowledgments

Acknowledgment of assistance of individuals and organizations in gathering or contributing information and in writing or editing the report may be included in the letter of transmittal, preface, foreword, introduction, or a separate section of the report. A separate listing gives greater emphasis. If placed in the letter of transmittal, acknowledgments should not take up more than four or five lines. If they are included in the preface, foreword, or introduction, a paragraph should be given to them. The amount of emphasis desired and the number and length of acknowledgments will determine where they are placed.

Table of Contents

Because the table of contents is a topical outline of the material contained in a report, it facilitates referral to any section of the report by giving page numbers for each topic listed. Repeating the major subject headings and subheads indicates the relationship among divisions and topics. As a rule, however, no more than three degrees of headings are used, for this number is sufficient to give the reader a clear idea of the extent and content of the material in the report. The shorter the report, the fewer the heads that are listed. The longer the report, the more detailed the subdivisions.

The preliminary and supplemental sections, as well as the divisions of the report text, may be listed in the table of contents. Typing the preliminary and supplemental elements in lowercase letters and the major headings referring to the divisions of the report text in capital letters (with subheads in lowercase letters) distinguishes the supplemental and preliminary sections from the report text headings. Here, as in an outline, numbers and indentation help show relationships.

Notice how the relationships have been indicated in the following table of contents from a report on an analysis of the internal communications system of an advertising agency:

TABLE OF CONTENTS

The outline numbers and also the listing of prefatory and supplemental parts of the report may be omitted, as in the following table of contents:

CONTENTS

List of Tables

At various times the list of tables is also appropriately called "Table of Charts," "Table of Illustrations," or the like, depending on whether charts, tables, or pictures appear in the report. It follows the table of contents and lists the tables in consecutive order as they appear in the text. The list is prepared from the table captions and shows page numbers. Thus it serves the same function for the tables as the contents page does for the other material. When there are only a few tables in the report, they may be listed either at the bottom of the contents page or as subdivisions in their appropriate place in the table of contents. In the example that follows, the same form is used as is followed in the table of contents. An appropriate heading is given to the page and to each column.

LIST OF TABLES

Number	Title	Page
I.	Types and Grades of Woods Used in the Manufacture of Selected Products	2
II.	Relative Price Increases in Different Types and Grades of Lumber, 197–	5
III.	Classification of Employees of the National Manufacturing Corporation	10
IV.	Labor Turnover, 197–	19
V.	Age Distribution of Employees of the National Manufacturing Corporation	21

Summary

There is some form of summary in every report. It enables the busy executive to get significant facts without reading through the entire report or hunting for them. The first paragraph of an introduction may be a summary of the conclusions, designed to call the reader's attention to them. A brief paragraph summary of significant points in the report may also be included in the letter of transmittal, foreword, or preface. As a separate part of the report, however, a summary is usually from one to five pages long, depending on the length of the report text. Bound with the other parts of the report, it completes the preliminary elements of the formal, long report and introduces the report proper.

When used separately it may speed action. Twelve people, for instance, may read a copy of the summary and decide on the action to take with only one or two of the group ever reading the entire report. Also, a summary may be published in a book of summaries or in a magazine.

The terms *abstract, synopsis, digest,* and *brief* are all used interchangeably for types of summaries, with few or only arbitrary points of difference. The *abstract,* for instance, is an impersonal, unbiased, noninterpretative, noncritical presentation of essential elements of the report. What the author says is given without evaluation. Although its emphasis is on the results, to which it devotes about two-thirds of its length, it covers the material in the introduction and the ending of the report. In fact, the same organization and style of writing used in the report is adhered to. Thus an abstract has the flavor of the report and lends itself well to printing or other use separate from the report.

A *synopsis,* on the other hand, is generally briefer than the abstract and lacks both the detailed information and the style of the original report. Rather than present a complete summary of the entire report, the synopsis aims to give only its outstanding features. The reader can see by glancing at a synopsis the development of the subject or problem, but he has to read the report itself for the details. In other words, this type of summary tells in general what the report contains and does not give specific information. The following sentence is typical of a sentence from a synopsis: "The results of the questionnaire survey are shown in table form and discussed."

To find out what the results are, one must read the report. The synopsis tells that they are there. Sometimes the synopsis is merely an expansion of the title and is used on the title page as the subtitle. It also is appropriately placed as a last paragraph in the introduction section of the report text.

Since the *digest* is a condensation of the entire report, it is similar to the abstract. The chief difference between the two is length. The report, reduced to three-fourths, one-half, or one-third of its original content, retaining the author's style and other factors, is a digest.

A *brief* is in the form of a sentence outline with connecting words and phrases added, as illustrated on pages 239, 240, and 247.

In all types of summaries, direct, concise writing is used. The essence of each main division should be stated in proportion to its importance in the report. Of course, no information should appear in the summary that is not in the report. In writing a summary one should read the report through, and then pick out its main points. Afterwards the reader can go back for the details, visualizing them in proper perspective. Then he is ready to write the summary. Just as the outline is a valuable guide in writing the text, it also serves in writing a summary. In fact, a sentence outline presented in paragraph form makes an excellent summary.

An example summary section from the report on "The Influence of Magazine Page Size on Advertising Effectiveness" follows.[1] It was placed between the introduction and findings sections of the report.

SUMMARY OF FINDINGS

The over-all results of this study show that there is no difference in effectiveness between advertisements the size of a page in magazines like the Reader's Digest and ads the size of a page in larger magazines.

Specifically, the results reveal no differences in advertising efficiency in terms of the following measurement criteria used in this study:

- No difference in recall
- No difference in communication of sales message
- No difference in persuasiveness
- No difference in relative permanence of impression

Additionally, the data indicate that these general findings with respect to the influence of page size on advertising effectiveness probably hold true among both men and women readers, and for ads in individual product classifications.

SPECIMEN REPORT WITH TRANSMITTAL

A typical example of a report to which only the letter of transmittal was attached is shown on pages 317–21. The letter orients the members of the New York Stock Exchange to the report by enabling them to recall the circumstances under which the report was prepared and the committee responsible for it. The last paragraph of the transmittal calls for action and prepares the reader for what is coming up. Throughout the

[1] Courtesy Gallup & Robinson, Inc., Advertising and Marketing Research, Princeton, N.J.

report text, subject headings direct the reader through a logical flow of plans and recommendations that the committee agreed upon. The table of contents and other preliminary parts were deemed unnecessary, for the nature of the report and familiarity of the readers with it did not call for dressing it up. The personalized use of *we* was consistent with the appropriate degree of informality.

SUPPLEMENTAL SECTIONS

Material of general and secondary interest, or material that is too bulky to be placed in the report text, is placed in the supplemental sections of a report. Here it is used for record and reference purposes, and as such gives supporting evidence to material discussed in the report text.

Appendix

The appendix is a catchall for all supplementary material which, if placed in the body of the report, might disrupt or delay the reading process. The appendix contains record and reference material, such as

Large tables and charts
Copy of the questionnaire used in the investigation
Sample forms and the like used in the investigation
Extensive quotations and summaries
Detailed data for reference
Plans and specifications
Glossary
Mailing list
Recapitulation tables
Letters

Short and simple reports often do not have appendices, nor do all formal, long reports. It depends on how the report and its supplemental sections will be used. Sometimes all material is placed in one appendix section; at other times it is divided and placed in several, such as: Appendix A—Recapitulation Tables, Appendix B—Letter from _____ on _____, Appendix C—Glossary of Terms. The appendix is what the writer wants to make it, depending on how it is to be used by the reader.

Bibliography

The bibliography may be included as part of the appendix or presented as a separate supplemental section of the report. If presented separately, it may either precede or follow the appendix. It lists all the

NEW YORK STOCK EXCHANGE. INC.

ELEVEN WALL STREET

NEW YORK. N. Y. 10005

December 30, 1971

TO: Members and Allied Members

SUBJECT: Transmittal of Report on Reorganization of the Exchange

As you know, last September our Board appointed a committee to consider
the Martin Report proposals for an internal reorganization of the New
York Stock Exchange and to submit recommendations to the Board regarding the governing structure of the Exchange.

No time limit was given to the committee but we had hoped they could
complete their report by the end of the year. Cornelius W. Owens,
Chairman of the committee, a Public Governor of the Exchange and executive vice president of A.T.& T., submitted the report today. Enclosed
is a complete copy of their report to the Board.

The Owens committee has made special efforts to secure the viewpoints
of executives of listed companies and of public investors as well as
the views of the Exchange membership. This has required an intensive
schedule of meetings over the past three months.

Recommendations in the Owens committee report to change the Exchange
Constitution would require action by the Board of Governors, discussion
with the Securities and Exchange Commission, and approval by a membership vote before they could be implemented.

Other members of the committee headed by Mr. Owens are: Robert M.
Gardiner, president, Reynolds Securities Inc.; Joseph A. Meehan, vice
chairman and director, Henderson Brothers Inc.; Henry W. Meers, partner,
White Weld & Co.; William R. Salomon, managing partner, Salomon Brothers;
Robert L. Stott, Jr., partner, Wagner, Stott & Co.; and Albert B.
Tompane, managing partner, Benton, Tompane & Co.

We plan to discuss the report in detail at a special meeting on January
6, 1972 and to schedule a vote on the report at the policy meeting on
January 20, 1972. Membership voting could occur in late February following the usual time period for submission of the proposed Constitutional changes to the SEC.

Ralph D. DeNunzio
Chairman

Robert W. Haack
President

317

REPORT OF
THE COMMITTEE ON
EXCHANGE REORGANIZATION
DECEMBER 29, 1971

INTRODUCTION

On August 5, 1971 William McChesney Martin, Jr. submitted a report on the securities industry undertaken at the request of the Board of Governors which included proposals for an internal reorganization of the New York Stock Exchange.

Following receipt of the report, the Board, on September 16, 1971, appointed Messrs. Frederick L. Ehrman, Robert M. Gardiner, Joseph A. Meehan, Cornelius W. Owens, William R. Salomon, Robert L. Stott, Jr. and Albert B. Tompane to study and submit recommendations regarding the governing structure of the Exchange. Later, Mr. Henry W. Meers was substituted for Mr. Ehrman. At the first meeting of the Committee, Mr. Owens was appointed chairman.

Early in its deliberations, the Committee agreed that the Exchange should be reorganized and that this reorganization might well follow the lines suggested by Mr. Martin. It was, however, clearly recognized that modifications of his proposals might be necessary. This was consistent with Mr. Martin's statement that he was only attempting to identify goals in the public interest without precluding modifications. From the beginning we were in agreement that the interests of the public were paramount. This report sets forth the results of our deliberations and our recommendations for the implementation of this goal of reorganization.

VOTING PROCEDURES

The Exchange is presently a corporation with 1,366 members each of whom has one vote. We have studied the Martin suggestion to convert seats into shares. The thrust of this proposal was to grant wider access to the Exchange and to transfer voting power from individual members to member firms. Access will be provided by the nonmember discount set forth in the Exchange's pending commission schedule. With regard to the transfer of voting power we recommend that all a-b-c members be required to assign their votes to their member organizations by means of irrevocable proxies. This would transfer voting power from more than one half of the membership to their member firms. This recommendation is a first step toward the goal of a more representative voting procedure which should be reviewed by future Boards.

BOARD OF DIRECTORS

The Committee agrees that the interests of the Exchange are closely related to those of the public and that recognition of this fact should be reflected in the governing body of the Exchange.

The Committee is also of the opinion that the present Constitutional language establishing the qualifications for Governors should be broadened in order to obtain the best possible candidates for the Board including representation for public, regional and specialist firms. This results from our agreement that all major segments of the industry must be represented. The Exchange through its network of national and regional firms touches every section of the country in all phases of our business and the specialist system is a keystone of the Exchange's trading mechanism. Except for representation from these three areas, the Committee has not established categories to limit future nominating committees. Our avowed purpose is to have the most qualified men lead the Exchange.

The Committee recommends that members of the Board of Directors who come from New York Stock Exchange member organizations (industry directors) should be the principal executives of their member organizations. To accomplish this, we have set forth as a qualification for an industry director that he be either a principal officer and director of a member corporation or a member of the managing committee of a member partnership or a sole proprietor. We are attempting to obtain for the new Board the decision makers, the men who occupy positions of leadership in their own firms.

All directors, except the Chairman, would be elected by a vote of the membership. All directors -- public and industry -- would be elected for a term of two years and industry directors would not be allowed to serve more than three consecutive terms. Industry directors could, however, be elected again after an interval of at least two years.

The Committee recommends that the Exchange be governed by a twenty-one man Board of Directors. This Board would consist of ten public directors, ten industry directors, and a full time, salaried, Chairman of the Board who would also serve as the Exchange's chief executive officer. He would be required to sever any ties with any member organization of the Exchange or any other business.

The following language - in Constitutional form - sets out the Committee's recommendations for a new Board of Directors:

> The Government of the Exchange shall be vested in a Board of Directors, each member of which shall be a citizen of the United States, and which shall be composed as hereinafter set forth.

> The Board of Directors shall consist of the following: The Chairman of the Board (who shall be chief executive officer of the Exchange) who shall not engage in any other business during his incumbency and who, if a member of the Exchange at the time of his election, shall promptly thereafter dispose of his membership; ten public directors none of whom are brokers or dealers in securities; and ten industry directors, as set forth below, each of whom shall be a principal officer and director of a member corporation or a member of the managing committee of a member partnership or a sole proprietor, of whom not more than three shall spend a substantial part of their time on the Floor of the Exchange:

> a. four directors whose member organizations are engaged in a business involving substantial, direct customer contact, at least two of whom reside and have their principal places of business outside the Metropolitan area of the City of New York;

> b. two directors who are specialists and who spend a substantial part of their time on the Floor of the Exchange;

> c. four directors elected without reference to place or type of business.

NOMINATIONS

Nominees to serve as directors of the Exchange should be selected by a nominating committee which has been elected by a vote of the membership. Initially, in order to make the transition to the new Board of Directors, the Exchange's present nominating committee, subject to the approval of the Board of Governors, should select eight individuals to stand for election as a nominating committee. Four members of this initial nominating committee should be representatives of the public with consideration given to present or former public governors. The other four should represent the major segments of the securities industry and, as with industry members of the Board of Directors, should be principal officers of their member organizations or sole proprietors.

If this nominating committee is approved by the membership, it will be expected to present nominees for twenty directors in the two classes described below, and a slate of nominees to serve on the next nominating committee.

In order that the new Board may have 50% of its directors elected each year and to comply with the legal requirement of an election every year, it is recommended that the initial balloting by the members elect two classes of directors. The first class would consist of five public and five industry directors elected for a term of one year. The

second class would consist of five public and five industry directors elected for a term
of two years. This one year term would mean that some industry members of the first
Board might be limited to not more than five consecutive years on the Board. All subsequent terms would be two years in duration.

In seeking public directors, the nominating committee should consider representatives of
listed companies and other areas which, in its discretion, might supply outstanding directors including financial institutions, such as mutual funds, banks, trust companies
and insurance companies.

With regard to industry directors the Committee will give representation to the major
segments of the New York Stock Exchange financial community.

The initial nominating committee, and all subsequent ones, will be expected to propose as
directors men who are committed to serving the interests of the public and strengthening
the New York Stock Exchange as the public marketplace.

When the Committee has selected its candidates for the Board of Directors, it should also
develop a slate for the subsequent nominating committee. This committee, and all subsequent nominating committees, should consist of eight individuals, four industry and four
public representatives. As with the initial nominating committee and the Board of Directors, industry members must be principal executive officers of member organizations
or sole proprietors and public members may not be associated with a broker or dealer in securities.

After the slate has been agreed upon, the names of the nominees for directorships and for
the next nominating committee will be submitted for a vote of the membership. This procedure will be followed in subsequent years.

To insure that subsequent Boards and nominating committees are responsive to the membership,
our Committee is of the opinion that the present right of the membership to nominate oppo-
sition candidates by petition should not be altered.

All directors should be reimbursed for expenses incurred in performing their duties and
all directors (except the Chairman) should be compensated. We think the compensation
should be meaningful and suggest that to avoid embarrassment the present Board of Governors assume the responsibility for setting the initial figure. We urge the Governors
to arrive at an equitable and attractive retainer which will serve in some way to compensate these men and their organizations for the time they spend in service to the Exchange.

CHAIRMAN OF THE BOARD

At the first meeting of the new Board of Directors, a Chairman shall be elected by the
Board. This Chairman will preside at meetings of the Board and will be the chief execu-
tive officer of the Exchange. He must devote full time to the affairs of the New York
Stock Exchange and must sever any business connections he has at the time of his election.

The Committee is agreed that the selection of this chief executive officer is of the
utmost importance in deriving from this reorganization the benefit we seek for the public.
The Board should immediately appoint a special search committee to find and recommend a
permanent Chairman. While it is not within the scope of our authority to establish a rate
of compensation for the holder of this new office we do feel that to attract an executive
of the caliber that the Exchange required, the compensation should be substantial and
competitive.

The Chairman would be elected for a one year term. He could, of course, be reelected as
often as the Board determined. Whether or not an employment contract is appropriate
would be left to the Board of Directors.

The Chairman shall be a voting member of the Board. He shall, subject to the Board's
approval, appoint such other officers as, in his discretion, are necessary for the efficient operation of the Exchange.

VICE CHAIRMAN

At the first meeting of this new Board and at each annual meeting thereafter, the Board shall select one of the industry directors to serve as Vice Chairman. The Vice Chairman, in the absence of the Chairman, shall preside at all meetings of the Board but will not be responsible - as the Chairman is - for the day to day operations of the Exchange and its staff.

FUNCTION AND RESPONSIBILITY

The new Board of Directors should concern itself with establishment of Exchange policy. In line with this general mandate it shall have the authority to amend the rules of the Exchange as it deems necessary. In addition, the Board shall have the right to propose amendments to the Exchange Constitution and to submit these amendments to the membership for approval. This Committee does not think that the present right of the members to petition for amendment should be changed.

COMMITTEES

We leave to the new Board of Directors the responsibility for the creation and composition of whatever committees it may feel are necessary for the efficient handling of its business. For example, there should continue to be a committee for the floor of the Exchange which would be comprised of member firm representatives on the floor. These committees should, wherever possible, be vested with the power to make final decisions on routine problems which come before them rather than act merely as prescreening bodies which leave to the Board the eventual rendering of a final decision.

CONCLUSION

We unanimously recommend for the Board's consideration these changes in the governing structure of the Exchange. If these proposals are approved by the Board, we would suggest that a task force of staff and counsel be appointed to draft the necessary amendments of the Constitution and of the Rules of the Board to implement these changes. Since that drafting process might develop other questions on these proposals not answered in our report, this Committee offers to continue in existence - at the pleasure of the Board - to consult with members of that task force and to furnish any guidance or other assistance which might be requested.

Respectfully submitted,

Cornelius W. Owens William R. Salomon
Robert M. Gardiner Robert L. Stott, Jr.
Joseph A. Meehan Albert B. Tompane
Henry W. Meers

printed sources used in gathering data and in writing the report. Each source is alphabetized by the last name of the author. Sample entries for different types of sources are shown in the reference section (Appendix B) of this book. If only a few sources have been used, the bibliography will list them together in one alphabetized list. If, however, there are several kinds of sources, then all sources of each type are alphabetized in a subdivision of the bibliography. Thus all books are in one list, all articles in one, and so forth.

Index

The index is prepared after the final typing of the report text and is used only with extensive, complicated, long reports. Arranged alphabetically, the index lists page references to important words, phrases, facts, names, and ideas. Main divisions and subdivisions are also indicated.

In preparing an index, the use of small 3- by 5-inch cards is advisable. On each card one item can be listed with its major heading, subheadings, and page references. Then the cards can be arranged alphabetically and the index typed. The completed index to a report is like the index to a book, and it appears as the last part of the report.

Generally a detailed table of contents serves the same function as an index, and the index is not necessary.

SPECIMEN REPORT

The following report is a typical example of the formal, long report. The preliminary sections give the background of the problem and indicate what was done. In the report text are discussed the findings and conclusions upon which recommendations are based. The example illustrates the fact that not all reports contain all the elements discussed in this chapter but only the ones the writer considers appropriate to his problem and purpose. The report did contain a bibliography, which has not been reproduced here.

CONTROLLING ABSENTEEISM IN THE STYLING CENTER
OF _____ APPLIANCE COMPANY

Prepared For:

Mr. John B. Stevenson, Manager

Personnel and Organization Department
Styling Center, _____ Appliance Company
Cleveland, Ohio

Prepared By:

William C. Knudson

Personnel and Organization Department
Styling Center, _____ Appliance Company
Cleveland, Ohio

May 20, 197–

Personnel and Organization Department
Styling Center, _____ Appliance Company
Cleveland, Ohio
May 20, 197–

Mr. John B. Stevenson, Manager
Personnel and Organization Department
Styling Center, _____ Appliance Company
Cleveland, Ohio

Dear Mr. Stevenson:

The attached report, prepared with the approval of your department, analyzes the absenteeism problem in the Styling Center and offers recommendations for bringing the problem under control. In addition, the report analyzes the absenteeism problem as it exists in the industry and describes several absentee control programs which other companies have found to be effective. Particular emphasis has been placed on the underlying causes for high absenteeism rates, the effects absenteeism has on costs, and procedures for effective controls.

Because the Styling Center's work force consists largely of professional designers and others with specialized skills, the report recommends a "middle of the road" approach and places more responsibility on the supervisor for reducing absenteeism.

The report shows that there is much more that the Styling Center can and should do, and I am sure that if the suggested recommendations are followed, absenteeism in the Styling Center can be reduced to more acceptable levels.

Sincerely,

William C. Knudson

WCK/cp

ii

CONTENTS

CONTROLLING ABSENTEEISM IN THE STYLING CENTER
OF _____ APPLIANCE COMPANY

INTRODUCTION

Statement of the Problem

High absenteeism at the Styling Center has been prevalent for a good many years, but it has been only the past few years that it has been recognized as a serious problem costing the Company thousands of dollars each year. From an audit made by the Company's Industrial Relations Staff in late 1969, it was revealed that the Styling Center's average absenteeism rate substantially exceeds the Company average as well as the national average. This is a challenge to Styling Center management to reduce this high rate of absenteeism so as to increase efficiency and profits for the Company.

Absenteeism among employees appears to be inevitable. People do get sick, have social and personal problems, and differences in attitudes, feelings, desires, and needs. Although the cost of absenteeism through lost time is sometimes difficult to measure, employee absenteeism is costing business and industry millions of dollars each year, and there is evidence that the cost to employers is steadily increasing. Absenteeism from all causes is on the increase, particularly from sickness, in spite of the advancements in medical technology and the improvements that have been made in working conditions, employee benefits, facilities and general technological changes. What then are the underlying causes for high absence rates? How can business and industry effectively minimize the frequency of absenteeism?

Purpose and Scope

The purpose of this report is to aid management personnel of the Styling Center, _____ Appliance Company, in establishing more effective controls for reducing absenteeism to acceptable levels. Past and present conditions were examined and evaluated to uncover the weaknesses or deficiencies causing this high rate of absenteeism. Styling Center and Company absentee rates were determined from personnel reports and letters, while data on industry trends and practices for controlling absenteeism were obtained from bibliographical research.

The research covers not only the problem as it exists in the Styling Center but also the problem as it exists in the industry. A thorough investigation was made of techniques and practices advocated by others and

1

found to be effective in controlling absenteeism. The report includes discussions on general factors causing absenteeism, the costs to the employer, the role supervisors play in reducing absences, and guidelines for establishing effective controls. In addition the various aspects of the present situation at the Styling Center were analyzed to determine

1. What the causes are for the high rate of absenteeism.

2. What has been done in the past to reduce the absence rate and what is currently being done.

3. If there is an established procedure for disciplining the chronic offender.

4. What the current company policy is toward absenteeism.

5. What the procedure is for reporting absences.

6. How attitudes, working conditions, and overtime affect absences.

Absenteeism Defined

In the Company Supervisor's Manual issued to all management and supervisory personnel, absences are termed "leaves of absence" and can be with and without pay, depending on the nature and extent of the leave. An employee is entitled to 18 excused absences a year, 5 of which can be personal business and 13 sick days. Additional time (31 days) will be granted at half pay. What constitutes an absence has not actually been defined in the manual, but it is presumed to be any leave whether authorized or unauthorized.

Some experts have defined absenteeism as the failure of workers to report on their jobs when they are scheduled to work.[1] This could include ill or injured workers, workers who quit without notice and have not been removed from payrolls, and unauthorized leaves from the job.

The Styling Center employees who are absent due to sickness or personal business are required to notify their supervisors each day they are on leave. When an employee will be absent more than five consecutive working days and the reason is known, the supervisor must prepare a "Leave of Absence" form; otherwise Salary Payroll Services will not continue an employee's pay beyond the first five consecutive working days. Whether or not an absence is justifiable is left to the discretion of the supervisor.

[1] Marjorie Brookshire, *Absenteeism* (Los Angeles: Institute of Industrial Relations, University of California, Los Angeles, 1960), p. 3.

2

ANALYSIS OF THE PROBLEM

Absentee Averages

Over the years many labor experts have quoted what they believe to be the average absenteeism rate in the United States. Statistical data have been released showing the average being anywhere from 3% to 9%; however, most authorities place the average at about 6%. The variations in rate are due partly to the method of measurement and the definition of absenteeism rates. What rate constitutes a serious threat to efficiency? One researcher states that any absence rate above 2% is excessive and costly.[2]

In 1969 UAW sources estimated the absenteeism average in the industry to be from 4% to 5%; however, a company spokesman at the same time stated that the average at the _____ Plant was from 8% to 9%, and on the days following payday the rate was from 11% to 15%.[3]

Various experts in the field use different methods for computing averages, which accounts for variances in the rates. Some base averages on the amount of lost time per 1000 hours worked. The _____ Appliance Company has used this method on one or two occasions in the past. For example, Figure 1 shows the Company rate for salaried people during 1967 and compares it to the national average for that year.

Figure 1

Manhours Lost Per 1000 Hours Worked for Year 1967

	Sick Leave	*Personal Business*	*Total*
_____ Appliance	16.4	9.8	26.2
United States	NA	NA	19.2

(NA—Not Available)

Other authorities in the field compute the averages on a monthly basis, including the U.S. Department of Labor, which recommends the following formula for computing average absenteeism rates [4]:

[2] John C. Kearns, "Controlling Absenteeism for Profit," *Personnel Journal*, Vol. 49, No. 1 (January 1970), p. 50.

[3] Paul Pigors and Charles A. Myers, *Personnel Administration*, 6th ed. (New York: McGraw-Hill Book Company, 1969), p. 287.

[4] *Ibid.*

3

$$\frac{\text{(Number of man-days lost through job absence during period)}}{\text{(Average number of employees)} \times \text{(Number of work days)}} \times 100 = \text{Absence rate}$$

The Styling Center, as well as the Company, has used yet another system based on the average lost time hours per employee per year. Although it is difficult to relate the averages based on this system with industry averages, it was possible to compare Styling Center performance with Company performance. Figure 2, reproduced from the Appendix, shows this comparison for the last four years, 1967–1970. This comparison shows that the Styling Center's absentee rate for the last four years has been averaging about 32% higher than the Company average and aptly illustrates the need for reform in policies for controlling absenteeism.

Figure 2

Absentee Comparison—Styling Center vs. Company

(Average Absence Hours Per Employee Per Year)

Year	Design Center Totals	Company Totals	Percent Design Center Variance
1967	58.7	45.2	30
1968	63.3	48.7	30
1969	60.5	46.9	29
1970	63.0	45.0	40

Effects on Cost

Although difficult to compute, absenteeism does cost employers money. No records have been kept at the Styling Center regarding costs, but the cost generally is felt to be considerable. One could generalize and say that the cost equals the salaries paid to employees who are not on the job, but there are other factors to consider. What about fringe benefits, the cost of training replacements, the added overtime which may be incurred, and the costs in loss efficiency? In certain situations and under certain conditions, particularly in group work, a replacement worker, because of his inexperience, could hold up the entire group. Absenteeism can create a lot of little costs that add up to considerable sums.

Some companies have done a great deal of research to determine the cost of absenteeism. For example, the records of a machine manufacturing

4

company showed that on an average day 7 out of every 100 employees failed to show up for work, causing an erratic production cycle.[5] The company estimated that this high absenteeism rate was costing the equivalent of $2 million in sales every year. Controls were later put into effect which saved the company $150,000 in the first six months. In another case a lighting equipment company with 1,800 employees had an average of 108 employees absent each day.[6] They estimated that this 6% rate was costing the company over $213,000 a year in excess payroll and fringe benefits. Through control measures, the absenteeism rate was reduced by 2% and the fringe costs reduced by $71,000 in one year. Another company estimated that between 1957 and 1963 their absenteeism cost was $20.73 per $1,000 payroll.[7] General Electric estimates that it loses $2.00 for every dollar lost in wages due to absenteeism.[8] Finally, the Seventh Industrial Health Conference held in 1954 estimated that absenteeism due to sickness cost the employers in United States industry approximately $10 billion per year.[9]

These examples show why there is need for effective absenteeism controls in industry and business. It is estimated that in a plant of 1,000 employees, a rise in the absentee rate of 1% will cost the company about $150,000 per year.[10] Higher costs mean higher prices for products and a greater expense to the consumer.

General Facts About Causes

Records show that sickness is responsible for most absences of short duration and nearly all absences of long duration. At the Styling Center sick leave accounts for about 75% of the lost time annually, the remainder being personal business. The causes are varied and many of the reasons are not the real reasons; therefore, accurate reports on causes are difficult to obtain. Actual causes can be classified into three groups.[11] The first involves situations external to work relationships such as weather, accidents, and transportation problems. The second involves personal and economic characteristics of the work group such as the age and sex of the employee, his marital status, and the length of time he has lived in the community. Industry statistics show that single men have the highest absentee rates, and then married women, while single women and married

---

[5] *How To Reduce Absenteeism Costs* (N.Y.: American Management Association, June 1967), p. 17.

[6] *How To Attack Absenteeism Costs* (N.Y.: American Management Association, May 1968), p. 7.

[7] Charles J. Sternhagen, "Medicine's Role in Reducing Absenteeism," *Personnel*, November–December 1969, p. 28.

[8] Franklin G. Moore, *Manufacturing Management*, 5th ed. (Homewood, Ill.: Richard D. Irwin, Inc., 1969), p. 380.

[9] Kearns, *op. cit.*

[10] Brookshire, *loc. cit.*, p. 12.

[11] *Ibid.*, p. 25.

5

men have the lowest rates.[12] Also, workers under 20 years of age are absent more than those over 30, rates are higher among new workers than among established workers, and factory workers are absent more than office workers.

The third classification of causes involves situations in the work relationship. It has been found that absence rates among employees are more closely tied to conditions within the company than to conditions within the community. Factors that arise from the employment relationship should offer the greatest challenge to management because absence rates seem to be directly related to the employee's satisfaction or dissatisfaction on the job.[13] Personnel practices are also very important because these practices can affect an employee's desire to work. The manner in which the Personnel Department selects and places workers, reports and checks on absences, establishes policies on hospitalization, and decides on payment of overtime can greatly affect the worker's attitudes toward his job and supervision. Many of the employee emotional disturbances are believed to be triggered by management itself through ill-advised personnel practices and reprimands by supervisors.

What are the underlying causes for the high absenteeism rate in the Styling Center? Working conditions, facilities, salaries, and employee benefits are very good and in fact considered above average; for this reason, it is very difficult to isolate specific causes. One reason for the high absenteeism rate is the general attitude toward taking time off. Many employees feel that the allotted sick and personal business days are due them and so they are going to use them. Others do not seem to recognize absenteeism as any kind of a problem. Supervisors appear to lack self-discipline and do not themselves set good examples.

Investigation of causes shows that Styling Center employees usually work under considerable pressure to meet schedules, and there are usually a great many design changes which have a demoralizing effect on worker attitudes. Also, since the work load fluctuates from year to year and from program to program, there is always a threat of a layoff, which tends to create a sense of insecurity. Above all there is a lack of positive control on the part of managers and supervisors. Discussions with supervisors and representatives of the Personnel and Organization Department indicate that most supervisors lack understanding of the rules to be applied for controlling absenteeism; consequently, there is little or no uniformity in the rules applied.

[12] Moore, *op. cit.*, p. 379.
[13] *Is There an Answer for Lateness and Absenteeism?* (N.Y.: American Management Association, November 1967), p. 20.

6

ABSENTEE CONTROLS

Guidelines for Absentee Control

There are many types of absentee control programs which produce good results. Most programs are variations of one another and incorporate the same general guidelines, but tailored to suit the particular needs of the company. Most experts will agree that the key to any control program is supervision. An effective program needs supervisory support, which can be accomplished through proper training. The basic essentials of an effective program are good records, proper communication, proper disciplinary procedures, and proper follow-through.

In the lighting equipment company cited earlier a control program was put into effect which reduced absenteeism by 2% the first year. In this situation supervisors were made responsible for administering their own departmental programs of review, recognition, reward, and reprimand with close follow-up maintained on employees who were frequently absent one or two days.[14] Each supervisor was required to follow certain preliminary steps to assure consistency in the system. For instance, it was agreed that the chronic offenders would be turned over to the personnel and medical departments for study and recommendation. Guidelines were established as a measuring stick to determine serious cases, and a reward plan was adopted for employees with good attendance. Supervisors were held responsible for making improvements at the risk of jeopardizing their own chances for merit raises. Meetings were held in which employees were told of the seriousness of the problem. Supervisors had meetings among themselves to discuss mutual problems, and a campaign was undertaken to improve attitudes, working conditions, and facilities. The importance of the employee contribution was stressed, and he was made to feel missed and needed. It became standard practice for supervisors to speak with employees after they had been out. These were just a few of the things done, and the results were very rewarding.

Another company reduced absenteeism by establishing clear-cut guidelines that allowed for normal, legitimate absenteeism and discouraged abuses.[15] This company began by redefining the term *absence*. Instead of being counted in days or hours, absences were defined in terms of "occurrences," with six occurrences a year considered normal. An occurrence was considered a continuous period of absence for a single reason and was used rather than hours or days to identify a chronic attendance-standard violator. Supervisors then adopted certain procedures designed to discourage

[14] *How To Attack Absenteeism Costs, op. cit.,* p. 8.
[15] "Curbing Absenteeism," *Supervisory Management,* January 1970, pp. 10-12.

7

chronic offenders from taking so much time off. The supervisors agreed that when an employee approached six absence occurrences within a year, they should immediately discuss the problem with him. Beginning with the seventh absence the employee was requested to produce verification of the medical reasons for his absence. The employee would then be subject to a transfer to an area with less responsibility. Each case was handled on an individual basis since each set of circumstances could be different. Also, more definite procedures were developed for employees calling in. Employees were instructed to notify their supervisors no later than 9:30 A.M. on the days they are absent. Those who failed to do so were required, upon their return, to fill out a form explaining why. A policy was adopted in which an employee's attendance record was added to his annual performance review. Each employee would be given an attendance rating. If an employee received an "improvement needed" rating, he would have one year to correct his problem. If he received an unsatisfactory rating, he would be subject to discharge.

Supervisors, as well as management, found that these guidelines very effectively reduced absenteeism $3\frac{1}{2}\%$.

Most studies show that the best absenteeism control program is the middle of the road approach, neither too punitive nor too liberal. The following basic ten principles are advocated to hold down absences [16]:

1. Pay special attention to the new employee because if he is going to be a problem, his absence pattern will show up in the first six months.

2. Investigate short-term absences with special care because studies show that most long-term absences are legitimate. It's the one- and two-day absences, especially when they fall consistently next to a weekend, that should be watched carefully.

3. Pinpoint the problem area to determine if there is a pattern by pay bracket, by sex, by longevity, or by age.

4. Talk to the chronic offender and ask for an explanation. Be specific about the standards you expect him to live up to.

5. Try to determine the underlying causes because the actual reasons may not be obvious. The employee may have a personal problem or there may be something wrong with working conditions.

6. Give the employee good reasons why he should change his behavior. Let him know how disruptive he is, how he undermines the whole group, and that the same rules must apply to all.

7. Keep in touch with long-term absence cases. If an employee is expected to be out for a long period of time, keep in touch with him because it's good for his morale and allows you to provide for a replacement.

[16] Les Rich, "Ten Steps To Cut Down Absences," *Supervision*, Vol. XXI, No. 4 (April 1969), p. 3.

8. Communicate with management. The information uncovered regarding absenteeism could be helpful to other departments.

9. Take corrective action. Disciplinary or punitive action should be treated on an individual basis, not just as a matter of policy.

10. Keep continuing absence records and don't conceal the fact from employees.

Disciplinary Action

Discretion must be used in disciplining employees for absenteeism because many causes do not lie with the individual employee. At the Styling Center each case is handled individually, as it should be. The consensus is that a penalty in itself has no effect. Most discipline is handled by verbal reprimands. If discussion fails to bring about improvement, the employee is told that his conduct will be shown in his annual performance review. If this fails, transfer is discussed. Although there are no records in the Styling Center showing that an employee has been dicharged because of excessive absenteeism, it would not be out of order to consider a layoff if the employee happens to be a marginal performer.

Normally, the purpose of establishing penalties is to correct the practices of the employee. In some companies penalties vary from a reprimand to demotion, loss of seniority, and layoff of short duration to layoff of a specific number of days. If these things fail, then dicharge may be the ultimate extreme penalty and may be necessary, not to discipline or to set an example, but to protect the interest of the company and its stockholders. Some companies feel that firm disciplinary action is the most proficient method of reducing the absenteeism rate.[17]

Disciplinary action should be consistently administered for the unexcused absence, but in other cases the objective of enforcement is to correct rather than to penalize. Employers are more apt to determine the real reasons for absences and to differentiate in their treatment of corrective measures.

In establishing disciplinary procedures, it is essential that the employer notify employees of impending penalties, that warnings first be verbal and then written, that accurate attendance records be maintained, and that consistency be maintained.

CONCLUSIONS AND RECOMMENDATIONS

Summary of Facts

For the past seven years the average absentee rate has exceeded the Company average by a considerable margin. The Center's absenteeism rate

[17] Kearns, *loc. cit.*

over the past four years has averaged out 32% higher than the Company average for the same period. The greatest difference was in 1970 when the Center's average exceeded the Company's by 40% and reflects a trend that is apt to continue unless positive control measures are taken.

Although the cost of absenteeism is sometimes difficult to measure, the report shows the effects of cost, tangible and intangible. Not only is money lost in salaries, but also money is lost in the payment of fringe benefits and in training replacement help. The intangible costs show up in reduced efficiency and lowered morale.

Since the supervisor is the most important link in an effective control program, management must place the responsibility for absenteeism with the supervisor. Supervisory personnel appear to lack the knowledge and understanding of the rules to be applied, which indicates a need for improved training procedures.

Worker attitude in the Center is a major factor causing the high absenteeism rate but should be verified by additional research. There is much more that the Design Center can and should do to reduce absenteeism to acceptable levels. Evidence shows a definite need for reform and more rigidly enforced policies.

Recommendations

Because of the artistic and professional nature of appliance design, which tends to set the Styling Center apart from other components of the Company, it is recommended that the "hard-line" approach to absentee control be avoided and that a middle of the road approach be followed, placing a greater emphasis on the responsibilities of the supervisor. Specifically, the following action is recommended:

1. Determine if the high absenteeism rate is actually the result of overall general attitude among employees or if particular individuals are responsible for the greatest share of absences. This can be accomplished by a building-wide short-term study of each department. If the records show that absenteeism is rather evenly distributed among workers, it can be assumed that the cause is general attitude. On the other hand, if the records show a pattern in which a small group of offenders account for the majority of absences, then general attitude can be discounted, and instead of resorting to a building-wide campaign to curb absenteeism, efforts can be concentrated on particular groups and individuals.

2. Establish and hold regular training sessions with supervisors. Train the supervisor on how to differentiate between occasional offenders and chronic offenders and show him how to distinguish between real and unreal absences. Encourage the supervisor to challenge employees for specific reasons for the absence and to discourage employees from taking leave for unreal reasons.

3. Hold the supervisor responsible for maintaining acceptable ab-

10

senteeism levels in his department. If acceptable levels are not maintained, reflect this on the supervisor's annual performance review and make this a factor in giving merit increases and promotions.

4. Make it a regular practice to commend those employees who maintain good absence records. Issue letters of commendation, bulletins, or newsletters praising those who maintain good attendance for a specified period of time. Offer theater, baseball, or football tickets to employees who meet certain standards.

5. Establish a set of standards for measuring chronic offenders. The chronic offender must be defined before he can be disciplined or corrected.

6. Develop a definite procedure for employees calling in absent and keep the employees informed as to policies and what is expected of them.

11

FOR DISCUSSION AND WRITING

1. Investigate the internal communication system of a firm and prepare a report on your findings and evaluation. Some suggested points to look for would be those in the Table of Contents, pp. 311, 312.

2. The Household Finance Corporation's Supplies Problems

"Mrs. Peterson, I'm not going to put up with any more of this nonsense. The daily reports are going out today regardless of what type of paper you have to put them on!" Mr. Layton, manager of Household Finance Corp., was very displeased and it was not really Mrs. Peterson's fault. Mrs. Peterson had run out of daily business report forms yesterday. She had complained to Mr. Layton but with little success. He had enough problems without worrying about a sufficient quantity of business report forms.

Mrs. Peterson's entire day had been trying. She was head cashier and responsible for seeing that the secretarial end of the work went out of the office each day. Report forms are ordered weeks in advance of an anticipated shortage. She felt that sufficient time in which to receive a fresh supply from the regional office was given. Yet as she watched, the pile of daily reports dwindled, as did her faith for a prompt delivery of supply forms.

Mrs. Peterson began using reports that showed erasures and corrections upon them. She was one for neatness and really hated sending in sloppy reports, but she had been forced to do so many times. The other girls in the office were advised to use their supplies sparingly, creating more dissent toward the corporation.

She had called offices in other cities close by but no one had any daily reports to spare. In talking to several of the girls and some of the managers, she found that they too were very disgusted with the whole situation. One manager, Dewey Ball, was very distressed.

His experiences with the problem as manager had not improved since he was an assistant. As assistant manager, he continually had to track down all types of forms and supplies when the girls would run out. At first, he blamed the girls for lack of organization. The girls produced carbon copies of letters they had sent requesting supplies. Some were dated as far back as two months or more. As of that time, the order had still not been filled. Mr. Ball asked "WHY?" The head cashier of that office could not answer. She had several calls on her telephone log, sometimes as many as two a week, to the regional office urgently requesting supplies. One thing she noted was that she never talked to the same person twice. At first, she figured that more than one person was connected with supply orders. After several attempts to obtain supplies, she began to feel that she was getting a real runaround. It upset her when she would receive letters reprimanding the use of regular letterhead to file reports. She was perplexed, feeling that dissatisfaction was inevitable.

"You know, Mrs. Peterson, we are doing the best we can with what we have. What else can you expect?" Dewey was really at his wits end. Just this last week he had opened a new branch of Household Finance Corp. It had been an uphill battle all the way. Nothing had gone right for him. He proceeded to tell Mrs. Peterson of his latest experience with the regional office and their system of supply.

The new office Mr. Ball opened had been on the drawing board for several months. All furniture, carpets, and drapes were ordered and installed well in advance of the opening day. The week before the office was due to open Mr. Ball finally received the bookkeeping supplies he was to start operation with. He was greatly displeased when he opened the boxes to find supplies for court proceedings, bad-debt forms, and outside collection sheets. He had not even made his first loan and already had enough supplies to handle an office with a great delinquency problem. This mistake delayed the opening for two days after receiving a few basic supplies from other offices for the opening even to take place.

Mrs. Peterson thanked Mr. Ball for all his valuable information. She felt something had to be done or customer service was going to be seriously impaired. Dissent increased; she felt resentful toward the regional office. This produced a lack of concern for her job and had similar effects throughout the whole of the corporation.

Bill Tate, an outside representative, came stamping into the office. His day began at 6 A.M., calling at delinquent customers' homes before they left for work in the morning. He had certain forms that must be filled out for each call stating the type of contact he made and the results. These cards are very important as they are the backbone of the collection department. "Mrs. Peterson, where are some contact sheets? You know I have to fill them out for all my calls, and I could not find any when I was in earlier this morning." This item had also been on her order list for several months, and Mr. Tate's day was to be hampered. Mr. Ash, their district supervisor, would be very displeased. He is a noted stickler on forms or the wrong use of forms, but when supplies were not available or the wrong forms were sent, it became a common office practice to make do. Fridays were dreaded the most as the supply problem interfered with the weekend wrap up.

A short time ago a memorandum was received by all branch offices. It stated that effective that day a new system of weekly reports would go into effect and that the forms, along with self-explanatory directions, would arrive several days prior to the office's need for them. No package of any type of forms had come into this office in over a month. The regional office had to be contacted concerning this problem, but with Mr. Layton's reluctance. His prior calls had been ineffective and felt to be a waste of time, but he placed a call to Mr. Hood, the regional office's manager, to explain the problem. Mr. Hood was very sympathetic and agreed to do some checking and call back.

Several hours later, Mr. Hood called to inform Mr. Layton that his shipment of the new forms had not been mailed but promised to personally see that they went out in the mail that afternoon. "That is fine, but what should I do about a report for this week? I don't even know what types of figures or information you want." Mr. Hood proceeded to explain the nature of the report over the telephone. This took quite a bit of time. Finally Mr. Layton had all the necessary information for the report required. Mr. Hood had expressed his regret about the nonreceipt of supplies and promised it would not happen in the future. Mrs. Peterson was required to type the report, putting it in some kind of order so that it could be sent to the regional office.

Mr. Layton was informed of the distress in the office and became acutely aware of the problem when a customer, Mr. Burns, came in to borrow more money. He wished to use his car as security. Mr. Layton had Mrs. Peterson prepare all the necessary papers. Everything was ready to sign and then Mr. Layton noticed that there was no lien form included. He asked Mrs. Peterson for the form and she informed him that they were out of it. He asked her to call several of the branches nearby and see if she could locate some. Mrs. Peterson was successful to a degree. A nearby office had extras but it would be the next day before they would get some. Mr. Layton could not make the loan until he had the form. He told the customer to come back the following day.

They were obviously having trouble getting any type of supplies from the regional office who demanded perfection, yet failed to supply the necessary tools. Constant lack of basic forms that were needed daily and the surplus of other supplies became an even bigger problem as the company grew. When the regional office was asked for permission to hire an outside firm to print some forms for use until it could supply the needed ones, the regional office refused. It was also noted that the various conversations with employees in other branches exposed the same problems.

Mr. Layton could see that it was not just his office; the company as a whole was suffering from poor organization on the relatively simple matter of supplies. It was decided that Mr. Hood must be faced with the entire inefficient situation. Monday morning Mr. Layton called Mr. Hood.

"You know this business of ordering and receiving supplies has really gotten out of hand. Pretty soon we will be out of loan contracts and when that happens our business will stop. Contracts are a blood supply needed in order to operate. How come your people in regional office have such little regard for that end of the business?" Layton asked.

"Mr. Layton, how long ago were these supplies ordered? You know it does take a few days for printing, packaging, and mailing," Hood replied.

"Mr. Hood, my head cashier has had some of these supplies on order for more than two months. She has sent written requests as well as calling once a week to see if anything has been sent. Our office is not the only one having this problem; everyone else is too. Mr. Hood, who is in charge of supply?" Mr. Hood could see that this problem was a lot bigger than anyone at the regional office realized. He promised he would check into the problem.

The regional office is a short distance from many of the branches and yet communication with them is very difficult. The home office in Chicago has charged regionals with the responsibility of supplying forms, but this was considered to be a minor function. A regional organization has a manager, three assistant managers, and several department heads. The structural chain of command is fairly well set within this organization. Each assistant has a certain number of supervisors and branch offices under his control. Within the organization itself there are the common departments such as bookkeeping, personnel, and so forth.

The printer has a shop set up in the basement of the building and he does the printing of forms and all supplies for the company as a whole. He is his own boss insofar as how the printing is done. He is responsible to the regional manager of the company. Mr. Robin, the printer, is a very likable and easygoing fellow. As soon as a printing order is given, he sets the machinery in motion. Mr. Robin fills the orders as soon as someone with authority gives his okay. Any one of the assistant managers may do so.

Mr. Hood spent a few hours talking with Robin to get first-hand information on his problems in the printing room. Since Mr. Robin has been told to cut down on expenses, he does not do any printing until he has a rather large order for supplies. Then he prints the amounts requested with a small abundance to make sure he has enough. The president of the company told him not to make a large surplus of any forms as they are always modifying and making changes. Under this mode of operation, no wonder branches are having trouble replenishing supplies when needed. No two offices use the same amount of supplies in the same length of time, but there wasn't any type of count being kept on how much and what type of supply was available. New offices were being opened and no provision for an increase in supplies was made. No one saw to it that supplies were sufficiently increased and sent out to the new branch offices.

Mr. Hood then proceeded to ask around to see who was receiving the orders for supplies. There was no one person delegated to receive mail for supplies so that mail just fell on the nearest desk. It is then up to the person who opens the letter to see that it reaches the printer. No one was responsible and the job was neglected.

Mr. Hood arranged a meeting with the three assistant managers, Mr. Murray, Mr. Mont, and Mr. Kent. Mr. Hood explained why he called the meeting and then told of his findings. The assistant managers were surprised. Each man had been receiving complaints about lack of supplies but never took time to look into the matter.

"The problem is much more serious than I realized. I guess it is up to us to look into the problem and see what can be done. Do you agree with me, gentlemen?" asked Mr. Hood.

At this point they all agreed that something must be done.

What would you suggest?

Prepare the report that would cover this situation.

3. The Small Investor Dilemma

The average investor today is at wits end as how to read the stock market and with good reason. Consider the following: During May

1970, business was generally poor; unemployment was at 4.8 percent, the highest in five years; interest rates were very high; and the government said we are getting out of Indochina, but we had just invaded Cambodia. Students were rioting, and what was the market's reaction? The Dow Jones Industrial Average was down 217 points in the last 12 months and went down over 100 points the next 17 trading days. This seems to be perfectly understandable, but how many can make sense of the following: In February 1971, business continued to be poor; unemployment was up to 6 percent, the highest in nine years; interest rates continued to be relatively high; and the government continued to say we are moving out of Indochina, but we just supported an invasion of Laos. Student unrest still existed, and the market reaction showed the Dow Jones Index up 118 points in the last three months and 240 points in the last eight months.

This seemingly illogical move of the stock market has baffled many an investor. It has also made many an investor bitter, as great losses were sustained by many during these periods. But the apparent and illogical patterns of the stock market is only one of the many gripes of the small investor.

Some former investors say that they will never invest in the stock market again because they feel the deck is stacked against them. Many feel that the corporate world and securities markets are organized and sometimes manipulated to serve the interests of big financial institutions and leave the small investor a victim of forces he cannot control. Many contend that the big institutions that represent great sums of money receive vital information from other companies before the small investor and are able to make critical investment decisions. This enables the big institutions to buy and sell stocks at advantageous prices before the small investor gets wind of the information. This practice of investing on the basis of material information received on the "inside" is in violaton of federal law. However, to a degree, it still goes on.

Another factor that has bred pessimism among small investors is the stock analysis letters that are published weekly by brokerage houses. Investors have relied on these publications in the past, but now the reliability has dropped significantly. The primary reason for this deficiency is as follows: Brokerage firms have been reducing their overhead costs, and while research staffs have been reduced, poor analysis reports have been the result.

The small investor is subject to inequities when depending on brokerage houses for advice on their investment portfolios. The biggest problem is as follows: Brokerage firms are in competition for the big accounts of financial institutions. Therefore they concentrate on servicing the big accounts and have little time or desire to service the small account. This knowledge usually compels the small investors to make their own decisions, and, as a group, they have a habit of misinterpreting the movement of the market. For example, there are numerous cases where an individual has concluded that the stock market has bottomed out and that it is a good time for investing. Sometimes, almost on a random basis, he then selects a stock and finds that this particular stock has not bottomed out and ultimately realizes a loss.

So with much disgust about prior experience, many investors are getting out of the stock market basically because they say it is not any fun losing money. On the other hand, the disgruntled investor is looking for alternatives to stocks as a hedge against inflation rather than putting his money under a mattress. The alternatives to stocks, however, are not so rosy.

One attractive investment would be the purchase of low-risk corporation notes that normally bear a hefty 9 percent interest rate. The problem here is that the minimum investment must be $100,000. United States Treasury bills occasionally yield as much as 8 percent, but the minimum investment is now $10,000. The small investor has been effectively cut out of these investments and can only turn to such things as government bonds, but the yield on these instruments is only 5.5 percent—lower than the current rate of inflation. Annuities are another possible alternative, but inflation nibbles away at the real returns. Investment in land offers a chance for great appreciation, but, often, it is hard to sell and is subject to special management problems.

Equity investments have attracted many individuals. Such decisions to become involved in mutual funds have proved to be anything but breathtaking. Actually, in the psst, the average stocks in the same class have performed better than those stocks selected by mutual funds.

What it amounts to in the final analysis is that all investments have advantages and disadvantages. However, one economist has the answer for the patient investor. It has been cited that a small investment of $1,000 earning a high interest rate of 8 percent would be worth $43 quadrillion 400 years later. It should be noted that the first 100 years are the hardest. Obviously, lack of longevity is the disadvantage. But the risks are everywhere and the best investment alternatives should be researched.

Prepare the report that would cover this situation.

INTEGRATING MANAGEMENT AND EMPLOYEES THROUGH INFORMATIONAL REPORTS

OBJECTIVES FOR EMPLOYEE COMMUNICATION

Making Decisions

Maintaining Favorable Employee Relations

10

EMPLOYEE PUBLICATIONS

Kinds of Employee Publications

Content of Employee Publications

Securing Reader Interest

CREATING GOOD PUBLIC RELATIONS

FOR DISCUSSION AND WRITING

FOR THE PAST FOUR CHAPTERS, we have been concerned with report investigation and presentation, stage by stage as one progresses from understanding the problem through researching the data, reasoning with the data and organizing it for reaching conclusions, outlining the material for report presentation, writing, and dressing up the report for final presentation. The steps are applicable for long reports and complicated problems and also are adaptable to short reports used in day-to-day operation of the company as studied in Chapter 2. In the next two chapters, we are concerned with areas in which reports function in a specialized way—enough so to warrant our special study.

The purpose of this chapter is to give an understanding of how management, employees, and the company are brought together through informational reports. Every company, to be an efficient organization, demands an integrated management team and satisfied, responsible employees, both groups trusting the company and working toward common interests. Keeping personnel well informed helps achieve positive attitudes, loyalties, respect, and teamwork. Informative reports develop an understanding of the aims, objectives, organization, policies, regulations, procedures, problems, and future outlook of the company. They also provide information essential for decision making, determining a course of action, and coordinating the operations of a firm. Company success depends on effective interaction through communication.

OBJECTIVES FOR EMPLOYEE COMMUNICATION

An informed employee is productive, has favorable attitudes toward coworkers and management, and carries a favorable image of the company to people with whom he has contacts outside the firm. The following objectives for effective employee communication, when attained, indicate that informational reports have played an important role in the decision-making process in the firm and that good favorable employee-management relations exist:

1. To aid in achieving the operational objectives of the firm.
2. To improve job performance and satisfaction of employees at all levels of the organization.

3. To understand, accept, and support the company's position on vital economical, political, and social issues.

4. To create and maintain a favorable image with employees and the community.

5. To aid in decision making and control.

Making Decisions

Decision making is simply making a choice—selecting one action from several courses of action. In the process are three major phases: recognizing situations calling for decisions, finding possible courses of action, and choosing among these courses. There are three basic steps in the final phase, when the decision is reached: predicting the outcome of each possible course of action, evaluating the desirability of each action, and selecting the best course of action on the basis of purpose. Informational reports are used to give and receive orders and instructions and to give and receive information necessary for making decisions and solving problems.

The accompanying diagram indicates the scope of management decisions.[1] In area A, such decisions as calculating payrolls and reordering

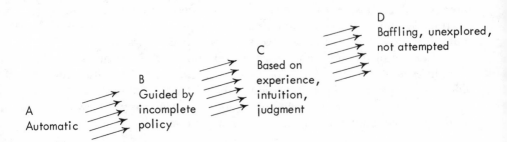

goods are repetitive and routine. Because past procedures, rules, and policies have been established, decisions can be automatic. In area B, decisions are partly circumscribed by corporate policy, but current operating data influence and change them. Examples would be decisions pertaining to employment levels, production schedules, and inventories. In area C, top-management decisions on capital investment, budgets, and union contracts are representative; they not only are based on past policy and operating data but also encompass the experience, thinking, and judg-

---

[1] Jay W. Forrester, *Industrial Dynamics* (New York: The M.I.T. Press and John Wiley & Sons, Inc., 1961), p. 6.

ment of top-management personnel. Top management also pushes on into area D, which presents the challenge of unknown and unexplored areas in industrial management and economic development. Here long-range planning is done, and the firm must be considered in relation to the industry and to the economic development of the country.

Computers and linear programming have made more data available faster, and management is freer than ever before to make decisions in areas C and D. Rapid processing of data and programmed computers solve many problems falling in areas A and B. The computer, however, can put out only according to its input, and management must determine what data will be programmed and how they will be used. Memorandums and form reports convey information and data for programming the computer.

Industrial dynamics integrates the entire firm through its information-feedback system so important in decision making. Computer-processed information, by giving management timely, accurate, and complete data for analysis and evaluation, has transformed management into converters of information into action. Since decision making is the conversion process, the success of a manager depends on what information is chosen and how the conversion takes place. Information flows to him and is used for decisions, which produce action. Policy is a formal statement of the relationship between informational data and resulting decisions; it becomes a rule for others to follow. Communication of information through reports is necessary for decision making and also for relaying decisions to others. Such communication can be achieved through a variety of report media: memorandums, letters, bulletins, short reports, manuals, booklets, magazines, and newspapers.

Maintaining Favorable Employee Relations

Every company wants its employees to work harmoniously with management. Industry realizes that much labor friction results from management's and labor's misunderstanding facts and attitudes toward each other. Unless the company explains its operations, objectives, and problems—unless it confides in employees and makes them feel necessary—the employees are suspicious of the company's actions.

Industry has spent millions of dollars in training programs, recreation buildings, pension programs, hospitals, insurance plans, profit-sharing plans, and many other employee benefits to show employees that the company is genuinely interested in their welfare and that cooperation between management and employees is mutually desirable and profitable.

Through observation, experience, and analysis most companies have learned seven basic points for consideration in creating favorable employee relations and company image:

1. Employees are the most important factor in building a corporate image. They represent the company.
2. There should be no communication vacuum. Employees uninformed by the company may be informed by people unfriendly to the company or may on their own reach conclusions based on ignorance of facts and become suspicious of company motives.
3. Employees not only need to know about the business—they want to know. And they want to feel important to the business.
4. Although employees want to know about the business, they will not pick it up on their own initiative.
5. Facts alone are not sufficient to create faith and belief in the company. The employee needs to be treated fairly and know the company is trying to do right.
6. Faith and belief can be created through good communication.
7. In a large company, the task of informing and motivating employees cannot be left to chance.

These are important premises on which to develop employee information programs: to develop happy, progressive, informed employees with faith and confidence in the company.

Numerous means of communicating with employees can be classified as either oral, audiovisual, or written—recognizing that there can be a combination of any of the three in any given communicating situation and that a communication program to be successful generally uses them all.

Oral Media	*Written Media*
Round-table conferences	Announcements
Small group meetings	Policies and procedures
Staff meetings	Pay inserts
Orientation meetings	Management newsletters
Counseling interviews	Newspapers
Labor-management committees	Magazines
Performance evaluations	Bulletins and booklets
Grievance handling	Letters to employees
Walking the shop and office	Reading racks
Special award meetings	Posters and bulletin boards

Audiovisual Media

Radio	Film strip	Public address
Slides	Chart talks	Sound-action exhibits
Video tape	Closed-circuit TV	Motion pictures

In using any of these media, the following guides are highly important for effective communication: clarity, consistency, adequacy, timing and timeliness, adaptability and uniformity, and interest and acceptance. In accomplishing the goals of effective employee communication, employee publications play the greatest role other than through face-to-face interpersonal communication.

EMPLOYEE PUBLICATIONS

Employee publications is a general term embracing all written and graphic communication between a company and its employees, excluding routine correspondence. These publications may be magazines or newspapers, memorandums or bulletins, booklets or handbooks. They are distributed free to employees, and occasionally companies send them to outsiders for advertising and public relations purposes. In accomplishing the functions of informing, educating, and entertaining, employee publications help unify the employees, management, and company into one group working toward common interests and goals, thus maintaining favorable relations.

The common aim of all employee publications is to inform. One company official expressed it this way: "Employees should be kept informed about *what* the company is doing, *why* they are doing it, and *how* it will affect each one of them." This involves telling employees about the financial condition of the company, its sales and production problems, plans, and achievements. The informed employee is made a part of the company; he can better understand the company's actions and has the desire to cooperate.

Every company wishes to increase the loyalty and morale of its employees by explaining their work in an interesting fashion. Information about the company's product, the source of raw material, and the end use of the product helps employees to realize that they are important contributors to the company's success. An employee will take pride in his workmanship and his company if the story emphasizes his individual importance and the importance of everyone's working as part of a "family" or "team" to get products to consumers.

Also included under educational aims are stories about benefits rendered to employees by the company, such as hospitalization, pensions, and insurance. This is usually done in detail through handbooks, but newspapers and magazines frequently supplement the material by using specific illustrations to emphasize the benefits.

Most employee magazines and newspapers contain items written solely for the entertainment of employees—articles about social activities, sports, and hobbies; woman's pages; cartoons; jokes; news of promotions; and human-interest stories about individuals. In addition, each story in the employee publication, whether educational or informational, should be written in an interesting or entertaining fashion; otherwise, the majority of the employees probably will not read it.

A company may have information, education, or entertainment as the main goal for its employee publications—or, more likely, the publications will have elements of each. Some major aims of employee publications are

1. To give information on company operations, policies, and problems.
2. To draw individuals into closer contact with the company.
3. To make employees feel they are members of a single organization.
4. To help employees understand each other.
5. To keep employees informed on the progress of the industry.
6. To promote safety.
7. To stimulate employees in work.
8. To promote better industrial relations.
9. To make employees understand the principles and philosophy of the company.

Kinds of Employee Publications

Magazine.   The magazine is one of the most common employee publications. Usually published monthly and varying in length from four to fifty pages, it has a separate illustrated cover and is printed on a high-grade, slick paper. The magazine is most effective when presenting company or employee news in feature-story form with illustrations and layout designed to make the story attractive, interesting, and easily understood.

The magazine has the main disadvantage of being expensive to publish and of requiring much time and work. News stories often have less impact in a monthly magazine because the magazine is published after the occurrence of many events. However, editors can counter this somewhat by showing how the news affects the lives of employees.

Newspaper.   When a company wishes to contact its employees with straight news frequently, the newspaper format is usually chosen. It may be issued daily, weekly, semimonthly, or, rarely, even monthly and is most often used by large companies with many thousands of readers. It may be issued to employees and to supervisors separately. Employees accustomed to reading news in their daily newspaper find the company newspaper easy to read because of the similarity. The stories are laid out in columnar fashion with heads; such a layout makes the publication easy to plan and read.

For the very reason that the company newspaper has appearance advantages, it also has disadvantages. The employee is likely to skim over the headlines, read news items selectively, and discard the issue quickly. Since the stories must be short, there is little chance to present informational or educational material in an interesting and complete manner. Each company must decide between newspaper timeliness and sensational appeal and magazine flexibility in style and layout.

Sometimes a tabloid format is used for a newspaper. It contains many pictures, with catchy captions; the stories are extremely short, often written in narrative style. Surveys have shown that the readership of tabloids by employees is usually high, but employees often read them for entertainment alone and remember little of what they have read. There is little room in a tabloid for good articles of an educational or informational nature.

The first page of *Westinghouse News* (pages 352, 353) indicates a good coverage of items of interest to employees as well as a news format.

Bulletin and Memorandum. If a company does not wish to publish either a newspaper or magazine, it may decide to publish a bulletin. These publications are usually from four to eight pages long and may be issued regularly or whenever the company wishes to publicize some particular news. The format may vary between newspaper or magazine, and it may be reproduced by any number of processes—printing, offset, mimeograph, or multilith. The bulletin has the disadvantage of small size, but this may be an advantage to some companies.

A company memorandum is the fastest means of getting information to another employee. Memorandums are short, varying from less than one page to three or four pages, deal with a timely subject, and are easily and quickly reproduced. These characteristics all ensure rapid distribution. When using bulletins or memorandums, the following suggestions are worthy of consideration:

1. Write so the message and meaning will be clear to others.

2. Pretest, often informally, by trying out the copy on a small group to determine clarity and probable effect on the readers.

3. Have someone representing top management read the copy to be certain company policy is followed.

4. Write briefly and concisely.

5. Cover one subject only in each communication.

6. Clearly indicate the subject at the top of the bulletin or memorandum.

7. Use an attractive format.

8. Make the finished reports easy to file for ready reference—perhaps in a loose-leaf binder.

9. Issue special informational bulletins to keep employees informed on problems confronting the company or the employees themselves.

Westinghouse News

Westinghouse Electric Corporation
Pittsburgh, Pa. 15222

Volume 27, Number 8
April 21, 1972

Copyright, 1972

May 15 Raise Adds Over $300 A Year To Most Paychecks

A majority of Westinghouse employees will get a pay raise—amounting to more than $300 a year—on May 15.

Hourly employees will get an increase of 15 cents an hour. Raises for nonexempt salaried employes will be approximately four percent on a bracket basis (with increases ranging from a minimum of $4 to a maximum of $12, depending on individual rates).

The new raises will add approximately $48 million a year to the Company's payroll and will help keep wages of Westinghouse employes ahead of or as good as the average wages paid in local communities for similar work.

The Company has already notified the Pay Board of these increases, in accordance with the Wage Guidelines established under the Phase II Economic Plan.

The general increase next month comes on top of a cost-of-living increase that took effect for most employes last November. That raise added eight cents an hour to the

Company Honors 20,000th Pensioner

For the first time in its history, Westinghouse has 20,000 individuals on its pension roll, and the Company marked the occasion at the recent annual stockholders' meeting by honoring its 20,000th pensioner. He is Michael Doperak, an assembler of switchgear at the East Pittsburgh Plant, who retired April 1.

Pittsburgh as a material handler. He has worked in R-60 Switchgear at East Pittsburgh for the past 10 years.

Calling the occasion "a significant milestone in the history of Westinghouse," Mr. Burnham pointed out that among all the manufacturing companies in the U. S., there are only 191 who have more than 20,000

Westinghouse Off To Fast Start In First Quarter

Following the record year of 1971, Westinghouse is off to a fast start for 1972, Chairman D. C. Burnham reported this month.

Sales in the first quarter of the year were $1,179,300,000, a record for any first quarter in the Corporation's history. Dollars of profit for the first three months were nearly $43 million, another first-quarter record. On the basis of what was left from each sales dollar, the Corporation's profit was 3.6 cents.

Figures for the first quarter last year showed sales of slightly more than a billion dollars and profit of about $34 million. The profit figure was 3.3 cents on each sales dollar.

Relating profit to shares of Westinghouse common stock, first-quarter profit this year amounted to 48 cents. For the first three months of 1971, profit amounted to 40 cents a share.

Orders entered continued at a high level during the first quarter and corporate backlogs stood about 7 percent higher than a year ago.

pay of hourly employes and $3.20 a week or $13.87 a month to the pay of most salaried employes on the basis of a 40-hour week.

In the photo above, Mr. Doperak (left) is congratulated by Chairman D. C. Burnham after receiving his first monthly pension check as Mrs. Doperak looks on.

Just a few months short of having 39 years' Company service, Mike started at the Large Rotating Apparatus Division at East employs on their *active payroll.*

In presenting the check to Mr. Doperak, Mr. Burnham said, "I'm sure that all your fellow stockholders here today join with me in the earnest wish that you will enjoy many happy and healthful years of well-earned retirement."

"The overall picture for the Corporation in 1972 continues to look promising," Mr. Burnham said, "even though in some areas of our business the results have been disappointing.

"Our experience in the field of small household appliances and home electronics products demonstrates again how important it is to have both a good volume of sales and a respectable profit on the sales dollar. Because we did not see our way clear to making good in that business, we have regretfully reached the decision to get out and direct our efforts to other fields where we stand a better chance for success.

"Each of the many types of business we are in must constantly stand up to the test of paying its way," Mr. Burnham said. "As always, the best way to make sure a business can be successful and provide jobs is for each one of us to make it a personal responsibility to put our best thinking and our best effort into every job we tackle."

Personalized Statements Of Benefits Coming

Personalized statements of the benefits you enjoy under the Westinghouse Pension Plan and Insurance Plan will be distributed sometime in May.

The statements, printed at the Tele-Computer Center, give an individual account of what these benefits mean to you and the members of your family. There will be a statement for all employes on the Company's roll as of last December 31.

7 Elected Vice Presidents

S. F. Miketic *H. H. Gray* *C. E. Price* *N. A. Beldecos* *G. F. Mechlin Jr.* *Theodore Stern* *J. T. Stiefel*

The election of seven Westinghouse executives as Vice Presidents of the Corporation has been announced by Chairman D. C. Burnham.

Stephen F. Miketic was elected Vice President, Manufacturing, and Herbert H. Gray, Vice President, Southeastern Region. Five General Managers also were elected Vice Presidents. They are:

Nicholas A. Beldecos, Large Rotating Apparatus Division, East Pittsburgh;

George F. Mechlin Jr., Astronuclear/Oceanic Divisions, Annapolis;

C. E. Price, Industry Services Divisions, Pittsburgh;

Theodore Stern, Nuclear Fuel Division, near Pittsburgh;

John T. Stiefel, Pressurized Water Reactor (PWR) Systems Division, near Pittsburgh.

Before becoming head of the Large Rotating Apparatus Division in 1970, Mr. Beldecos was General Manager for five years of the Bettis Atomic Power Laboratory, which Westinghouse operates for the Atomic Energy Commission. He joined Westinghouse in 1946 at Lester and moved to the Company's Atomic Energy activity in 1952.

A 25-year Company veteran, Mr. Gray was appointed Southeastern Regional Manager April 1. He had been National Field Sales Manager of the Power Systems Company at Headquarters since 1967. From 1963 to 1967, he was Zone Manager for Power Systems Sales, Southeastern Region, and has held field sales positions in Nashville, Chattanooga, Atlanta and Birmingham.

Mr. Mechlin has been General Manager of the Astronuclear/Oceanic Divisions since last November. He began his Company career in 1949 at the Bettis Laboratory. He held a series of scientific and management positions at Bettis and at the Sunnyvale Plant until 1968, when he became General Manager of the Undersea Division.

Another 25-year Company veteran, Mr. Miketic has held a series of manufacturing, planning and general management positions in Pittsburgh, Lester, Chicago and Cincinnati. He was General Manager of the Small Steam and Gas Turbine Division at Lester from 1969 until this past February, when he was named Director of Manufacturing.

Mr. Price joined Westinghouse in 1940 on the Graduate Student Training Program. In 1962 he was named General Manager of the Repair Division. Eight years later he became General Manager of the Industry Services Divisions, which include 60 apparatus service plants and facilities in the U. S.

A native of Germany, Mr. Stern is responsible for the nuclear fuel cycle activities of Westinghouse. After joining the Company in 1958, he held a series of engineering assignments in nuclear power activities before becoming General Manager of the PWR Systems Division in 1969. He assumed his present assignment early last year.

Mr. Stiefel heads an organization that is responsible for the development, design, marketing, engineering, procurement and production of nuclear steam supply systems. His Westinghouse career also began in 1949 at the Bettis Laboratory. He has been General Manager of the Heat Transfer, Tampa, Nuclear Concepts and PWR Systems divisions.

Courtesy Westinghouse Electric Corporation

10.   Locate bulletin boards in prominent spots and keep material on them up-to-date.

11.   Place announcements in readable locations on the bulletin boards.

12.   Emphasize in posters and announcements the role of the company in the life of the community and nation. Include clippings and stories about employee activities and news of a civic and cultural nature.

Memorandums and bulletins generally handle operational information necessary for running the business, making decisions, and coordinating the work of the firm. Magazines and newspapers, on the other hand, communicate not only to inform but also to educate and entertain. They influence employees' attitudes toward their jobs and the company, thus creating a favorable image.

Handbook.   Because of the complex relationship between employees and management, the men who set policies in large companies seldom have a chance to talk personally to employees. Thus handbooks have been designed to explain the company to the employees, to define their rights and responsibilities, and to inform them of company benefits. A handbook fosters in the employee a feeling of security, a sense of loyalty, and a cooperative attitude.

Booklets on many different subjects are prepared in almost all companies, and the cover must be eye catching to appeal to the reader, or the booklet may be discarded instead of taken home and read by family members as well as the employee.

The following is a partial list of subjects frequently found in handbooks:

Vacations	House organ
Personal records, changes	Overtime
Group insurance	Activities (recreational, dramatic,
Company business history	etc.)
Pay day	Canvassing, charity, soliciting
Office hours	Bulletin boards
Holidays	Payroll deductions
Use of telephones	Message from president
Salary, advancement, promotion	Smoking privilege
Suggestion plans	Social security benefits
Absence (how to report, excessive,	Disability, sick leave
etc.)	Cafeteria
Attendance (encouragement of	Wage policy
regularity as aid to production,	General welcome
promotion, efficiency)	Uniforms, dress, cleanliness
Accident prevention	Care of records, equipment
Hospitalization	Company club
Retirement benefits	Workmen's compensation
Resignation, discharge, layoff	Lunch hours
Medical examination	Job security

The employee handbook must be easily read; the content must be expressed in a logical, friendly, and factual manner; and illustrations and artwork must be interspersed to increase interest and readability. An index or table of contents is helpful for easy reference to specific subjects, and sometimes a question-and-answer section reinforces the message. A personalized style and the application of the "you" attitude principle, combined with a human-interest approach, emphasize benefits to the reader and influence his reaction.

Observe the following excerpts from Shell Oil Company's booklet, "Program For Security."

> As a Shell employee you can look forward to income from at least three different sources after retirement. They are
>
> Shell Provident Fund—Paid for by you and
>   Shell on a 50–50 basis
> Shell Pension   —Paid for 100 per cent by Shell
> Social Security —Paid for by you and Shell
>
> Shell considers these three together as a Retirement Program.
>
> The main purpose of the Provident Fund is to permit you to approach retirement age secure in the knowledge that you have a retirement "nest-egg."
>
> Under its terms you contribute up to 10 per cent of your regular earnings into an account which is established in your name. Your Company contributes dollar for dollar and the money is accredited to your account monthly.

Here the "you" attitude gains the reader's attention and interest. The employee is being informed about the company's retirement program and is liking it very much!

Content of Employee Publications

In deciding what will be included in employee publications, the company must balance what the company wants the employees to read and what the employees want to read. Research material indicates employees do not want to read about themselves and other workers; they want information about the company's plans and activities. Such knowledge strengthens their feeling of job security and their pride in belonging to a successful company, for they feel they are part of the firm. An employee who is "in the know" is happy and proud to answer questions from his friends and neighbors about his company's progress, policies, and plans.

The employee is interested in what affects his job. Companies who think their publications are being read and understood by employees simply because they are published and handed out are mistaken.

Because company officials are vitally interested in production, sales, and profit problems, they often assume that the employees are equally interested in the same information. The employee *is* interested, but not in the same way, for he sees these problems from a different viewpoint. Companies who write stories from the management point of view and who publish only information that they want the employees to know are wasting thousands of dollars and man-hours.

To know what will interest employees the editor must listen to employees talk, be a good judge of human nature, and have some broad knowledge of sociology, philosophy, and psychology. What does John Phillips on machine number 14 think about wages? What is on his mind when he reads about a new expansion policy or a company million-dollar profit? What are his basic wants? Employees want to know about office planning, and companies are beginning to tell them something of the plans for the future. If employees know about the strength and weaknesses of the company, they are more likely to be understanding when problems arise that affect both them and management.

An employee publication should be a two-way communication me-

Westinghouse Camera To Show Astronauts During Apollo-16 Flight

The launch of Apollo 16 from Cape Kennedy was slated for April 16—and if all goes as scheduled, you can plan to catch a repeat performance of a walk in space on the astronauts' return trip.

A Westinghouse hand-held color-TV camera similar to those used in previous lunar missions will be used aboard Apollo 16 during the flight to and from the moon. And one of the events to be captured by the camera will be a space walk by Astronaut Tom Mattingly. A walk in space was recorded for the first time on the Apollo-15 mission.

As the spacecraft nears Earth on its return flight, Astronaut Mattingly will leave the Command Module and go to the Service Module to retrieve film from a photographic camera mounted there. Astronauts John Young and Charles Duke will watch the show from their posts in the Command Module.

Westinghouse TV cameras, which have documented for millions of people man's pioneering trips to the moon and the first exploration of the lunar surface, have been used on eight Apollo flights starting with Apollo 9.

Westinghouse TV systems are also slated for future space missions, including Skylab. Aboard the space station eight color cameras will be used to monitor activities and record space experiments.

Company tells of its product in action.

Courtesy Westinghouse News, April 1972

dium—from management to employees and from employees to management. If the editor consistently communicates one way to employees, there will probably be a growing stack of unread magazines in the wastepaper baskets. If an employee has a question about the company or his job, he will not be receptive to any other information until his question is answered. He will respect the company publication more if he feels that it is his medium for communication also. Many companies publish employee questions with answers credited to a responsible official. Open answers will build employee morale and confidence in management. The employees' side of the picture can also be presented by reporting their discussions and conferences with management and by printing side-by-side statements representing differing points of view.

The following is a sample checklist of some categories of company and employee news that might be included in an employee publication:

Employee efficiency   Employee benefits
Company policy   Employee recognition
Business and financial information   Employee welfare
General information about the   General stories
  company   Miscellaneous
Information about industry

Securing Reader Interest

Much of what has been written about securing reader interest in earlier parts of this book applies to employee publication writing. The essential difference is that the usual business report is designed to be read by one person or a small group of persons. Usually these persons want to read the report because it is directed to them personally or because it is their job to read such reports. Employee publications, however, are distributed to large numbers of people who are not required to read them, and the publications will be thrown away unread if the readers are not interested or entertained to some degree. It is the responsibility of the editor to secure readership. Because the editor must interest employees, the style of writing for employee publications is similar to that of daily newspaper and popular magazine writing. Journalism involves objective reporting of facts—who, what, where, when, and why—with little interpretation of the facts. A newspaper reporter collects and reports facts with no intent to influence reader attitudes, except on editorial pages. The newspaper audience is large and varied, and the value of the news lies in its timeliness or sensational appeal.

An employee publication is aimed at a specific group; all its members work for the same company. Therefore only the news that affects those individuals need be reported; such news stories can be written and

Overseas Operations Vital to Growth, Chairman Tells Stockholders

Having manufacturing operations in other countries as well as at home is vital to the continued growth and prosperity of Westinghouse, Chairman D. C. Burnham told stockholders who attended the annual meeting in Pittsburgh early in April.

Mr. Burnham said multinational operation also is vital to the "prosperity of our stockholders and employes.

"To successfully sell overseas," he explained, "we have learned in recent years that we must also be able to manufacture overseas because of the many restrictions which other nations impose on imports. Only through multinational operation can we penetrate and win our share of expanding world markets and keep abreast of world technology.

"What many people fail to realize," he added, "is that this method of operation not only increases our total sales and earnings, but it also creates jobs in this country as well as other countries."

Creates Work in U. S.

Speaking of the recent sale by Westinghouse of five nuclear power plants in Spain, Mr. Burnham said: "While much of the work on these plants will be done in Spain, a large share will be performed here in the United States—a lot of it here in the Pittsburgh area.

"We would not have gotten any of this business if Westinghouse had not been organized in Europe to put together a proposal that was attractive to our Spanish customers from the standpoint of Spanish industry doing part of the job. Without our multinational approach, this big order would have gone not to Westinghouse but to some other company."

As to the outlook for this year, Mr. Burnham said that "1972 has the potential of being another record year for Westinghouse. The economy is slowly improving, consumer confidence is returning, and we look for capital spending to rise. We are prepared to take advantage of these improving conditions."

Robert E. Kirby, President of the Industry and Defense Company, told stockholders that a renewed spirit of civic cooperation could make Allegheny County a showcase of transportation progress. He said he was distressed at the "acrimony" that has developed over Pittsburgh's efforts to solve its mass-transit problems.

Also at the meeting, Chairman Burnham presented a first pension check to the 20,000th person now on the Westinghouse pension rolls—Michael Doperak, an assembler of switchgear at the East Pittsburgh Plant, who retired April 1 after 39 years with the Company. (See photo on front page.)

During the business session, stockholders meeting at the Pittsburgh Hilton elected the following directors to four-year terms:

Harry O. Bercher, retired Board Chairman, International Harvester Company, Chicago; Louis K. Eilers, Chairman, Eastman Kodak Company, Rochester, N. Y.; Alfred W. Jones, Chairman, Sea Island Company, Sea Island, Ga.; Donald F. Hornig, President, Brown University, Providence, R. I.; and Hobart Taylor Jr., partner in the Washington, D. C., law firm of Dawson, Quinn, Riddell, Taylor & Davis.

John W. Simpson, President of the Power Systems Company, was elected to a two-year term on the Board of Directors.

Stockholders voted down three proposals, dealing with limiting to three locations the sites for the annual meeting, limiting charitable contributions by the Corporation, and providing pre-emptive rights for shareowners.

Price, Waterhouse & Co., certified public accountants, were selected by stockholders as independent accountants to verify the 1972 financial results.

Keeping employees informed of company operations and plans.

Courtesy Westinghouse News, April 1972

interpreted according to the way they affect the lives of employees. Because employee publications are usually published more infrequently than daily newspapers, their stories are seldom timely. The news item is written to interpret its impact on the company and employees. Therefore journalism is essentially objective writing; employee publication writing is generally more interpretative, or subjective, writing.

Too many ideas in one story may cause an employee to get confused, lose interest, or miss the major idea completely. The more that is written into a story, the less the reader is likely to read. The writer should restrict the story to one or two major ideas or facts.

A main purpose of employee publications is to present accurate information which will refute erroneous rumors and grapevine gossip. If the publication is consistently accurate, employees will consider it an authoritative source of information. Errors in dates, places, and names can earn a publication a reputation for inaccuracy, and the entire publication may be disbelieved or unread. Accuracy requires double-checking the original copy for inaccuracies of fact and careful reading of the printer's proof.

Everyone likes to hear a good story, and everyone likes to read a good story. The top management of one company was considering the purchase of a competitor's plant to increase its product line. It involved a major expenditure and the executives debated for months. Finally they decided that it was a wise purchase and they announced it in the employee publication. Later a poll revealed that few employees were interested and many had never even read the story. Why?

The story was written as a factual, straight-news release. There was no interest or drama to make an employee take an interest in the story and realize that the purchase would affect *his* job. The editor's writing should catch the employee's attention, hold his interest right to the end, and be clear enough for him to understand.

The editor of *The Lamp* began his story about the importance of ship fueling in world commerce in this fashion:

At 5:06 o'clock on a Monday afternoon, the telephone rang on the fifth floor of the Esso Building in midtown New York.

The Tarpaulin Steamship Company wanted 7,500 barrels (about 1,168 long tons) of bunker fuel oil delivered at eight o'clock next morning to its steamship *Hawser*, lying at Pier 1234 in Brooklyn.

The SS *Hawser* was loading bathtubs, cotton shirts, soup in tins, wrapping paper, and road scrapers for the Far East and was due to sail on the tide at 11:18 Wednesday morning.

After that, things happened fast. . . .

The most important sentences in a story from an attention-getting angle are the first sentences. The writer is competing for the employee's attention with the daily newspaper, radio, television, movies, books, wife, children, friends, and an urge not to read anything requiring effort. The employee will take about five seconds on the story in the hope that it may prove to be of interest. If the opening sentences do not arouse his interest, there probably will not be a reader for the rest of the story, and the publication will have misfired.

The opening sentences are called the lead. They set the atmosphere for the rest of the story; therefore it is dangerous to begin a story with a routine expository style, no matter how well the story is developed thereafter. Create a picture in the employee's mind and set the stage for what is coming. Tell the story in terms of people and not inanimate objects.

An article about old age and survivors insurance published in The Champion Paper and Fibre Company's publication *The Log* was written interestingly. Instead of presenting a set of uninteresting and complicated rules and regulations, the entire story is told in terms of how the laws affect a typical employee. The story begins:

> "Yes, I've got a good job . . . I make pretty good money, and I have a fair chance for promotion.
> "But I haven't done much figuring on the future. How will I be fixed a few years from now? What about when I retire? Or if I die, what will my family live on?"

A story about the facilities of the company library may be dead reading to most people, but a personal interview with the librarian about the library will often develop interest. Use incidents and anecdotes to illustrate principles, rather than dry reasoning throughout the story. If there is no real incident, make up one by using a hypothetical case, such as, "Let's see what the company president does after getting to the office on a typical morning."

The entire Spring 1970 issue of *Michigan Bell*, published by the Michigan Bell Telephone Company, was devoted to vignettes and in-action pictures of thirty-five or more employees. The front and back covers were a collage of what was inside. The first page, serving as a preface-type introduction, contained a statement from President Kenneth J. Whalen:

> We can explain about wages and salaries easily enough, and we have booklets that cover benefits and others that describe the job we do. But how do we get across to new employees the kind of people we are?

The issue then went on to create the image that Michigan Bell is people and to show the kind of people in after-work-hours activities.

The company publication, designed to appeal to a group or groups of people with special characteristics, must be adapted to their needs and interests. This adaptation can be made by giving them information which they can get nowhere else and which is important to them and their well-being in the company. That is the reason for its being published.

CREATING GOOD PUBLIC RELATIONS

The first line for building good public relations is the employee, for employees are the public and represent the company in the public's eye. Company magazines as discussed thus far have been internals—publications for employees. Numerous magazines are also published for both employees and the public and for the public alone—referred to commonly as externals. Shell Oil Company's *Shell Progress* is aimed at the company's service dealers, offering information about products, selling tips, merchandising, and the like. *Steelways,* published by American Iron and Steel Institute, circulates to a wide audience of readers to provide an understanding of the business and economic problems facing the steel industry. The success of external company publications depends on their adaptation to the needs and interest of the publics they are to reach. The principles of communicating information interestingly and persuasively are just as applicable here as in any business report; the only differences lie in the use of the advertising and public relations media available to the company and in adaptation to the readers.

Just as informative reports are an integrating force within the company by bringing together parts of the business into a working organization, so they establish a relationship with labor unions, with suppliers of equipment and machines, and with buyers and sources of products. They promote business activity, and through a relation to government control and public opinion, they are a link with society in general. The company story must be told to the public to help build attitudes and loyalties that will result in favorable impressions and responses. The proper public image for the company and products must be created, the concept of a reliable, desirable product or service must be communicated, and the concept of a firm rooted in know-how and sound business sense must be conveyed. A company strives to produce a favorable disposition by helping the public develop friendly, confident feelings toward the firm. Sales promotion reports, advertising of all kinds, news items, and annual reports help accomplish these purposes.

FOR WRITING AND DISCUSSION

1. You are personnel director in your firm. There has been difficulty with one department in keeping open the flow of communications. An

open-door policy exists in the company, but in this particular department complaints are stopped by the supervisor and go no further, although he does not always handle them satisfactorily. The men are afraid to go over his head, thinking their jobs may be at stake.

Finally, through the grapevine, complaints have reached you. Upon checking them, you find they are well founded. You also decide, after talking with the men, to establish a grievance committee and to set up a suggestion box for the employees' benefit. It is your responsibility to formulate a policy statement and circulate it among the employees. It should cover points such as composition and makeup of the committee, organization of the committee, duties and responsibilities of the members, and functioning of the committee as a group.

You may need to do some reading in books and articles on industrial relations or labor problems to help you formulate your policy, or perhaps you can draw from knowledge you have obtained from a course in the subject.

2.   Bring an employee booklet to class. Discuss its purpose and use. How does its tone and style differ from other types of reports?

3.   Find out the financial or operational history of one firm in your community and write a report showing the progress that has been made.

4.   Standard Oil Company of California conducted an employee poll on the subject of employee benefits communication. Questionnaires were mailed to a random selection of 1,000 employees throughout the United States and Western Canada. Eight were returned undelivered. Out of the 992 basis of the survey, 390 answers were received.

The first question in the poll asked, *"When you have a question regarding one of your benefits, whom do you ask or to what do you refer in trying to get an answer?"* Respondents cited various sources or combinations of sources. The following tabulation shows two rankings of these sources—those cited as "first choice" and those cited as "a source."

Named as First Choice (% of all respondents)		Named as a Source (% of all respondents)	
Supervisor	46	Supervisor	59
Booklets	27	Booklets	42
Personnel office	18	Personnel office	33
Policy manual	2	Policy manual	4.5
Fellow employees	2	Fellow employees	3.5

The second question asked, *"Is there some other source for answering the questions on benefits that you would prefer to use? If so, what?"* Only 20 percent of the respondents named other preferable sources, which would seem to indicate that most employees were reasonably satisfied with existing sources. Most frequently mentioned alternative sources were meeting (3 percent of all respondents), personnel office (3 percent), up-to-date booklets (3 percent), articles in publications (2.5 percent), well-informed supervisors (2 percent), and clearly written booklets (2 percent).

The third question asked, *"During the last few years, have you attended an employee meeting convened primarily to explain and discuss employee benefits? If so, what do you think of this type of meeting?"* Of the respondents, 36 percent said "yes" and 61 percent said "no." These percentages varied quite widely among operating companies; among the fairly large companies represented in the poll, the "yes" response ranged from a high of 89 percent to a low of 25 percent. Of the respondents who said they had attended such a meeting recently, 80 percent felt they were "excellent" or "very informative." Eight percent of the "yes" respondents said they would like such meetings more frequently. About 9 percent of the "yes" respondents offered negative comments, most frequently pertaining to the lack of knowledge of the individual leading the meeting. Of the respondents who had not attended such a meeting, the most frequent comment was that they would welcome the opportunity to attend one (by about 20 percent of the "no" respondents). Some sample write-in comments to this question were

"No. I think this type of meeting is very necessary to keep employees informed."

"Yes. During the past year a Home Office representative spoke to us re employee benefits. This was an excellent presentation but held too infrequently (once in 15 years). Believe more advantageous to have local management more versed and hold these discussions on a twice a year basis."

"Not for over 10 years. I would welcome the opportunity to attend one."

"Yes. I think the idea is excellent and is by far the best method of reviewing information on our benefit plans. During these meetings written material could be distributed at the same time."

"I have never attended one of these meetings and I don't remember any meetings of this type being held in this area. I think it would be a good idea."

"The only time employee benefits have been discussed with me was the first day of my employment."

"Yes. Found it to be very informative. I was appalled to find out how little our supervisor knew about benefits."

"I have not attended a meeting recently, but I do feel that these meetings should be held periodically for new employees and to bring older employees up to date."

"I have not. If there are meetings which discuss Company benefits, I've not been notified. My information comes from correspondence routed through our office."

The next question asked, *"What written material, if any, do you now have either at home or on the job which describes your employee benefits?"* Of the respondents, 79 percent mentioned the individual benefits booklets. Other materials cited by a few were Annual Benefits Report, Pocket Summary of Employee Benefits, Policy Manual, Comments on the Annual Benefits Report, You and Your Company, Administrative Guide for Employee Benefits, and union leaflets.

The fifth and final question asked, *"Do you have any suggestions for improving any of our written materials on benefits?"* Of the respondents, about 40 percent offered suggestions. Most frequently mentioned were the following:

Write booklets more clearly	8% of all respondents
Bring booklets up to date	7%
Combine into one booklet	5%
Explain materials at meetings	3%
Provide more detail in booklets	2%
Use examples in booklets	1.5%
Issue annual report of benefits changes	1.5%
Question-answer column in publications	1%
Improve supervisor knowledge	1%

After interpreting the information resulting from the poll, prepare a report which will present the results, conclusions, and recommendations for applying this information to planning future benefits communication media.

5. Do a report on the relationship of internal communications to employee morale. You may use either bibliographical research or obtain information from a particular business firm.

6. If employees understand the meaning of competition—its driving force as an incentive and how it affects the company and their own job security—they will be more cooperative and productive. Find out what some companies are doing to promote this understanding. Prepare an article on the subject of competition for publication in an employee magazine.

7. How to make employees aware of the need for accuracy and care at every turn of the company's operations is a problem in most plants. What are your suggestions? Prepare an article for publication in the company magazine that may help accomplish this objective.

8. There are many operating problems facing every company which employees should know about and understand—for example, the break-even point. In a memorandum to employees, explain the break-even point or some other operating concept.

9. The following situation presents several aspects of the role of the employee publication in explaining company economics. Prepare a report to the executive vice-president.

The executive vice-president of a large chemical manufacturing plant walked into the office of his manager of personnel relations one morning and said

"John, as you know we've been hit pretty hard by this recession in recent months. Our sales are $1 million off what they were a year ago in the first quarter, and the stockholders are letting us know about it. In spite of the fact that our sales are down, our costs are rising steadily. Now, I've talked over things with the production people and I'm telling you what I told them. The Old Man says that if we're going to stay competitive we're going to have to reduce costs by 8 percent. We're going to have to trim away the fat, John. Now, I'm not ordering you to do this, but one quick way we can save is by chopping out that employee publication in your section. Another thing we might think about is starting a suggestion program on ways to save. A lot of other companies are doing this and seem to be making a success of it. What I'd like to have, John, are the ways you feel your staff can help in this project, and I'd like your suggestions by Friday morning. I'm going to tell you right off that I am going to be looking hard at that publication budget and I'm going to want to see some good justification for keeping it around. Pretty spring weather we're having, isn't it, John? A bit hot, but we can't have everything nice. See you Friday morning."

The personnel manager strolls into his editor's office and tells him exactly what has transpired. He adds, sympathetically, "Now I would like some suggestions from you on how we can go about achieving this 8 percent saving. You know I don't want to lose you, but we're going to have to come up with something positive to recommend."

What are some basic problems in this situation? What action would you take?

10. The following case study deals with receiving and analyzing information for making decisions and formulating plans and with passing on information to others who can thereby understand and carry out the necessary action.

GETTING INFORMATION TO DEALERS

Elliott Oil Corporation, New Orleans Branch

You are Jonathan Marshall, sales manager for the New Orleans Area branch of Elliott Oil Corporation (Exhibit I), and just this morning you received communication from the home office that the new, low-priced gasoline, *Sea Gull,* is to be on the market and ready to sell by November 30, only three weeks hence. Although you have been aware that a new product was to be marketed, you have not yet studied the reports that arrived this past week from the various research departments concerning *Sea Gull.* You decide that this is the day to study the five reports that arrived this past week and to reach a decision as to how the new gasoline may be most efficiently marketed and what will be the best method of informing the 251 dealers of the change in the product line. Since you hope to have analyzed each of the five reports by the end of the day, you quickly set up a work schedule and arrange the reports to be studied in the following order: the market survey report, the product report, the pricing policy report, the physical introduction report, and the advertising report.

The Market Survey Report

After deciding the order in which to analyze the reports, you place the market survey report from the marketing research division of Elliott on the desk, open it, and begin your study.

A chart shows there has been a recent trend toward the use of small foreign cars and compact, economical American automobiles in the past five years. This means that more cars have been operating on less gasoline and that the gas purchased for these small automobiles was almost always "regular" grade. Now, even the big cars are being engineered to operate more economically. This is the main reason Elliott decided to switch from the expensive high octane fuel to a lower octane and less expensive grade of gasoline, *Sea Gull*.

Elliott decided to experiment with *Sea Gull* before actually offering it for sale on a nationwide basis. Market tests were conducted in San Antonio, Texas; Indianapolis, Indiana; New York City; and Norfolk, Virginia. In each of these areas *Sea Gull* was readily accepted, and dealers realized higher gross profits and therefore larger incomes than previously.

One statement in the market survey report made a favorable impression: "A dealer in Buffalo, New York, averaged 685 gallons of gas per day before the testing of *Sea Gull*. His volume rose to 1,483 gallons per day, or 116 percent, after introduction of *Sea Gull*. His average gross gasoline profit before *Sea Gull* was $33, and rose to $60 per day, or an 82 percent increase, during the test."

Also, at the Indianapolis test market, one dealer's volume was up 112 percent, while his profit increased 58 percent.

The Product Report

After finishing the market survey report, you call into your office Mr. E. J. Ellis, the technical assistant manager for the New Orleans Area branch, to discuss the product report. He has technical knowledge of the ingredients in Elliott gasolines.

With the outstanding results of the 90 octane *Sea Gull* in the test markets, higher echelons decided to drop the expensive, high (105) octane fuel, *Sea Wolfe*. However the other two grades handled by nearly every dealer, *Good Ogg* (102 octane) and *New Premium Ogg* (100 octane) were retained. Both *Good Ogg*, or "regular," and *New Premium Ogg*, or ethyl, were upgraded, and the common term "regular" applied to a gasoline somewhere between *Sea Gull* and *Good Ogg*. The *New Premium Ogg* grade received many additives previously contained only in *Sea Wolfe*. The report stated that *"New Premium Ogg* will be higher quality than any other premium gas sold by competitors." Although most people believe the amount of octane indicates the quality of gasoline, additives also increase the quality of gasoline.

Sea Gull is designed to serve older automobiles, as well as many new models, and it is predicted that *Sea Gull* will satisfy "one out of every two cars on the road."

EXHIBIT 1

Area covered by the New Orleans branch office of the Elliott Oil Corporation.

The Pricing Policy Report

After a quick review of the important aspects of the product report, Mr. Ellis is called out on business, and you once again return to the task at hand—study of the pricing policy report, which has been prepared by the marketing research division in Pittsburgh.

The suggested pricing of the three Elliott brands is designed to give the customer a satisfactory price as well as provide the dealer with a substantial profit margin.

The *New Premium Ogg* brand is suggested to sell 4 cents above

Good Ogg, which, in turn, is suggested to sell 2 cents above *Sea Gull.* Of course, the actual price will depend on the particular market condition, but, under reasonably normal conditions, the suggested price policy should permit the dealer to operate at a satisfactory profit. Although *Sea Gull* is priced lower than the other two grades of gas, increased volume should make up for the lower price per gallon.

At the introduction of *Sea Gull,* price spirals, both positive and negative, are expected to occur. This condition is created because *Sea Gull* is a new form of gasoline designed to satisfy budget-minded motorists. Since it is the only gasoline on the market to fulfill this particular purpose and is lower priced than any other grade, other firms will lower their "regular" prices, but *Sea Gull* can still operate successfully 1 or 2 cents below their "regular" price.

These prices are merely suggestive, and in no way infer that the dealer must sell at the indicated price. Elliott, however, feels that its method is the best, if the dealer wishes to be competitive. Prices must be competitive to keep customers returning.

Satisfied that you are gaining insight into the market problems and what and how information should be relayed to the dealers, you decide to take a lunch break.

Mr. Ellis is waiting in your office when you return. "I've just been glancing over the physical introduction report," says Mr. Ellis. "It appears to me that timing of the physical transformation of pumps and tanks is the critical problem here."

The Physical Introduction Report

The physical introduction of *Sea Gull* will require much coordination, organization, and timing of effort if the program is to operate smoothly. Many physical changes must be made at the dealer stations. Basically, four separate alterations must be covered to introduce *Sea Gull* for sale.

All these changes must take place in the ten-day period from November 21 through November 30, for the entire sales campaign will break on the latter date, and *Sea Gull* must be available for sale. Dealers must be advised that, beginning November 21, they are to sell all the *Sea Wolfe* supply, the higher octane fuel being dropped from the product line. Dealers are supposed to have their *Sea Wolfe* emptied by November 29. If their tanks are not empty by that date, an outside pumping crew will extract all the fuel from the *Sea Wolfe* tank. The differences in the price of *Sea Wolfe* and *Sea Gull* will be credited to the dealer's account. Should a dealer sell all his *Sea Wolfe* before November 29, the empty tank will be filled with *Sea Gull,* and the pumps locked until the night of November 29.

Also on November 21, seven paint crews, consisting of two men each, will radiate to the 251 dealer locations from the Natchez, Baton Rouge, and New Orleans areas and spray-paint the 275 *Sea Wolfe* pumps from purple to blue and white, indicating *Sea Gull* pumps.

Within the same ten-day period, thirty-feet-high advertising poles are to be cemented in the ground and signs bolted to them at each of the 251 stations. The *Sea Gull* sign and a set of pricing numerals, costing approximately $50, are to be given to the dealer with instructions to bolt the numerals and grade name on the pole the night of November 29. Also to be distributed to the dealers are two decal emblems for each *Sea Gull* pump and sufficient rustless screws to bolt on the emblems. Again instructions will accompany each set, stating that the emblems should not be mounted before the night of November 29.

Should all be done properly, the program will have an impressive impact, and a new grade of gasoline will appear on the market overnight. Mr. Ellis remarks how important this phase of the product introduction is; proper timing must be a major objective, since *Sea Gull* should be ready for sale when national advertising breaks.

The Advertising Report

Mr. Ellis leaves the office again on business, and you decide to study the final research report, the advertising report.

Elliott plans to introduce the new program on November 30, the same date as *Sea Gull* goes on sale, to gain maximum impact. Elliott will convey its message through several different media. All new advertising will appear on the two Elliott-sponsored television programs, "NBC News Special" and "Here and Now." Elliott will advertise in several major magazines, such as *Time* and *Reader's Digest*. Also, the Sunday newspaper supplement will carry the large-scale ads. Beginning on November 30 there will be two full-page ads spaced one week apart in the leading newspapers.

This is the first, full-impact ad that will appear in the November 30 morning and evening newspapers:

FOR ONE OUT OF TWO CARS

SEA GULL

ELLIOTT'S NEW LOWER PRICED, QUALITY GASOLINE

You may be driving one of the many cars that can save money by using *Sea Gull* gasoline—an entirely new brand of gasoline from Elliott. About half the cars on the road don't need—in fact, can't make use of—extra octanes. They include cars that are several years old as well as many of the newer economy cars.

All that extra octanes can do for them is raise the cost of driving.

Sea Gull was designed specifically to meet the needs of such cars, without the added cost of extra octanes.

Yet, *Sea Gull* is a quality gasoline. It lubricates intake valves and upper parts of the piston. It is especially for easy starting in all seasons.

Can your car use *Sea Gull?* The one best way to find out is to try a few tankful and see. Octane appetites vary. Even cars of the same age, make, and model can have different octane requirements.

If your car is the one out of two that does not require extra octanes, you'll get all the performance that was built into your engine—and lower your cost of driving.

Your Elliott dealer has always offered you superior products and values. Now, once again, he is able to do just that by bringing you, in addition to *Good Ogg* and *New Premium Ogg*, Elliott's newest gasoline . . . *Sea Gull—to lower your cost of driving.*

There will also be a two-page ad on all three gasolines.

ELLIOTT DELIVERS THREE NEW GASOLINES TO LOWER YOUR COST OF DRIVING

New Premium Ogg—the finest premium gasoline ever made
Super-premium gasoline qualities at usual premium price.

Good Ogg—improved performance
More value than ever, but no increase in price.

And now, Sea Gull—lower-priced quality gasoline for one out of two cars
Provides full power for older cars and many economy cars that don't need extra octanes.

To make the advertising campaign completely effective, point-of-sale material will also be used. There will be identification emblems on the island pumps, and a large light pole with a metal sign, visible for several blocks, will be positioned in front of the station.

You finally finish the long task you set out to accomplish early in the morning. You have studied the five reports thoroughly. Now questions are running through your mind.

   a.   How am I going to inform the 251, widely located dealer stations of the new program?
   b.   How am I going to introduce the program and still maintain the elements of impact and surprise to the public?
   c.   What am I going to communicate in various media to the dealers?

Write a report on what is to be done. Include copies of any communications you plan to use.

11.   *The listener.*[2]   Bob Blakeley was on his first full-time job. He had just completed his degree in petroleum engineering at the State University and was prepared to set the world on fire with his knowledge, vigor, and personality. He knew from his courses at the university that the job of roustabout required a lot of stamina, a good strong back, and "staying on the ball."

Bob had been interviewed by many companies during his last semester at school for he had made a good record in his engineering courses. Of the several rather attractive offers he had for jobs, he had

<hr>

   [2] This case has been prepared by Dr. Ike H. Harrison, formerly Dean of the Business School, Texas Christian University, and member of the Southern Case Writers Association, as a basis for class discussion. Southern Case Writers' cases are not intended as examples of correct or incorrect administrative or technical practices. Names of company and persons have been disguised.

selected Acme as the company he would like to work for. As is the practice, petroleum companies assign new employees to field duty initially. And here he was on his first assignment.

Bob was in a work crew on a lease in a newly developed section of the East Texas field. His supervisor, Bill Paxton, was the Farm Boss. Bill had worked for the company for over ten years and had spent some twenty-five years in the oil fields. He was well thought of by the company and was frequently given new men soon after they came with the company, because he had the reputation of being a good person to "break in new men."

The third day Bob was on the job he was minding his own business—doing his assigned duties. He noticed that Bill Paxton and some of the other crew members seemed worried. One of the wells was not making its production. After working over the well, it had been necessary to use some artificial lift, and flow valves were selected. In spite of this, the pressure was not building up and it looked as if some adjustments would have to be made. Bob remembered that this was a problem he had studied at the university and he watched the changes with interest. He remembered that the placement of the valves and the number of valves required to properly control the pressure was a matter of judgment. He had noted the spacing of the valves when they were being installed. He thought about this as he moved over to the tool house.

Although Bob Blakeley was new on the job, he understood some of the theoretical problems involved in production. So, after he had rechecked the log which indicated the placement of the valves, he approached Bill Paxton, his supervisor, and said, "I think I know what your trouble is. The flow valves that belong in the pump are too far apart."

Bill Paxton had been working in the oil fields for over twenty-five years and knew the business. He had seen many of the pieces of equipment which were now in use developed through the years, although he had used flow valves very seldom. When Bob made his comment, Bill looked at him knowingly, somewhat annoyed at being interrupted, and said, "Kid, what in the hell do you know about this business? Scram!"

With this brush-off, Bob went back to his job and thought to himself that he had better mind his own business and do as he was told. This, he remembered, had been a bit of advice his Dad had given him many years ago. It was about quitting time for the day, anyway, so he relaxed.

Several days later the trouble still had not been found. Bob could tell that Bill Paxton was worried, and he thought, "I had better stay out of his way."

About this time, Ashley Adams, the District Superintendent, drove up. Bill had called Ashley and told him about the trouble they were having and asked him to come over and talk about it. Adams was a younger man than Bill Paxton, but he, too, had served his appentice-ship in the oil business for many years. He was well liked by the men who worked for him and by his bosses. Ashley and Bill talked for a few minutes and then looked over the installation. Bob Blakeley saw them shaking their heads and decided that he would try again to tell them what he thought was wrong. As he walked up to his boss and the District Superintendent, he gulped and said, "I still think I know why the pressure is not building up. The flow valves are too far apart."

Bill Paxton, his supervisor, looked at him as if to say why are you bothering me again, and started to say something when Ashley interrupted, "And what in the hell makes you think that?"

This was the encouragement Bob had been waiting for and he said, "Sir, I believe in order to have better pressure, it will be necessary to add the top valve. When I said the valves are too far apart, I meant that the top valve was not installed—it is hanging there in the tool house."

Ashley looked at Bill Paxton, who by this time had moved over to the tool house.

Discuss the following questions applicable to this case:

a. How could this problem have been prevented?
b. What should have happened? Why didn't it?
c. What should be done now?
d. What principles are applicable?

CREATING PUBLIC RELATIONS
THROUGH
ANNUAL REPORTS

11

IT IS ESSENTIAL that a corporation consistently grow better, and its image must grow and change with it. Just as important as interpreting management and the company to employees through informational reports and publications is building an image of the company to the public, for in either situation good relationships are at stake. Thus this chapter should instill in you an awareness of the public relations process and how annual reports help create favorable images and relations with various publics.

THE PUBLIC RELATIONS PROCESS

Customer and public communication includes all sales promotional and advertising materials that advertise and sell the company name and products, that create goodwill, and that build favorable relations. The public relations process is the continuing effort to bring about harmonious adjustment between a firm and its publics. Take a look at the advertisement from Westinghouse on page 376. It not only calls attention to the home services the company performs for the customer but also the effort being made to build a better world in which to live—this at a time also in which large segments of the public are deeply concerned with the ecology effort. How can one keep from feeling goodwill and having a favorable image of such a company?

The public relations process parallels the communication process and has four basic stages:

1. *Research.* Getting public opinions, attitudes, and reactions. Listening to people, customers and potential customers. Conducting interviews and surveys. Then coming up with our problem, with what is needed now, and with how we can meet this need. What image do we have, what image do we want to have, and how can we change to build a goodwill image?

2. *Planning.* Making decisions relative to questions raised from the research stage. Bringing action, opinions, and so forth to bear on policies and procedures of the firm. Then considering alternatives and deciding "Here's what we should and can do." Planning the message, media, channel, and time for communicating the results of careful planning based on research. Planning is in line with purposes and publics to be reached.

3. *Communication.* Explaining and dramatizing courses of action to those persons affected. Telling what we did and why. Using various media and

The Westinghouse Story in LIFE--

We're building a plant to help clean up water pollution

while we heat, cool and clean your environment at home.

Westinghouse has developed the capabilities necessary to help clean up water pollution.
For example, we're building the world's first plant for converting stream-polluting acid mine drainage into pure water. The plant will treat 5,000,000 gallons of polluted water now flowing daily into Pennsylvania's Susquehanna River.
The pure water produced will be added to the drinking water supply and will also serve new industrial needs in the area.

At the same time, Westinghouse assures you of year-round comfort with a central heating and air-conditioning system for any kind of home, with any kind of fuel, wherever you live.
Westinghouse is also active in health services, nuclear power, better and safer lighting, urban redevelopment and transportation.
These are a few of the many ways Westinghouse serves you in your community and in your home.
You can be sure . . . if it's Westinghouse.

Westinghouse...we serve people

Appearing in LIFE, October 30, 1970

EQUAL SPACE AND EMPHASIS—Society's needs and consumer needs again get equal space in the seventh ad of the "Westinghouse . . . we serve people" series appearing in LIFE. To help solve one of society's major environmental problems, the Company is building—on the Susquehanna River in Pennsylvania-the world's first plant for converting stream-polluting acid mine drainage into potable water. And, to serve you in your home, Westinghouse supplies heating and cooling systems to fit any need. Eight ads in all show what the Company is doing to improve the quality of life.

Courtesy Westinghouse News, October 16, 1970

carrying out plans made in the preceding stage, plans based on analysis and prediction of reaction and the desired image.

4. *Evaluation.* Testing the results. Assessing what was done and how good was the communication. Determining the effectiveness of the communication through feedback, listening, surveys, and so forth—all of which may show a need for another attempt or approach and thus start the whole process over again with research.

CONCEPT OF THE ANNUAL REPORT

Annual reports have always been a direct and vital communication tool with which a company can tell its story. True, in the beginning of annual reports in the late nineteenth century, information provided was largely financial in nature but discussed briefly what operations the firm was involved in, and the report was intended primarily for stockholders. Today a few annual reports are mere compilations of figures that only an accountant can readily understand, but most of the reports are highly informative and analytical, telling of the status and progress of the company in terms readily comprehensible to all its readers and creating favorable public relations.

Early annual reports were black and white, were less than ten pages in length, had no charts and illustrations, and were stilted and formal in language, style, and tone. Today they are very attractive and colorful, generally twenty to forty pages in length, filled with easy-to-read charts, tables, and other visual aids that not only support the analysis and statements made but that get the attention and interest of the reader—enticing him to read the narrative portions. Many companies view the annual report as the most important publication they issue, one to be prepared with thought and care. Thus reports tend to provide one of the most sensitive of indicators of the spirit and outlook of corporate business enterprises. Alert management recognizes the annual report as a dynamic force in constructive public relations that foster a wholesome understanding of industry among stockholders, employees, dealers, customers, and members of communities in which their products are manufactured or distributed. Annual reports are an integral part of a company's public relations program.

The modern philosophy of annual reporting would

1. Make the report of company operations and finances as nearly complete as possible.

2. Interpret company operations in terms of human experience so as to make the report understandable to the average reader.

3. Use illustrations, color, visual aids, good paper, and legible printing to make the report interesting.

4. Give the report wide distribution among all groups whose approval of the company will create a healthy atmosphere for U.S. free enterprise, for industry, and for the company.

An up-to-date annual report can be a strong, interesting, and convincing review of the company, welding together, for the general good of the corporation, all the elements on which it depends.

PURPOSES AND READERS

The annual report accomplishes specific purposes with each group of readers to whom it communicates its message.

To the stockholder the report gives an account of stewardship. By explaining the financial and business operations of the company, the report keeps him interested and satisfied that things are going well. By making the business live, the report sells the company to the stockholder. As a result favorable attitudes and good relations have been maintained. The stockholder is satisfied; he will retain his holdings and may even invest further in the company.

To the employee the report gives specific facts and general information about his company that he can get in no other way. As employees are oriented to the inner workings of the firm, misconceptions are corrected and misunderstandings avoided; the worker develops a sense of identity and pride with his company. High company morale, intelligent understanding, and a cooperative approach to problems pave the way for greater productivity. A well-informed worker is usually receptive to his responsibilities and does his job willingly. He also represents the company to others, and in his contacts in his community he will sell the company to others, recommend its products, and further favorable public opinion.

Aiming the annual report toward public relations involves considering the interests of credit men, banks, security analysts, and financial officers of corporations. In many instances, the annual report is the most important means of contact with hundreds of analysts all over the country in brokerage offices and investment advisory concerns, which hold stock of record for thousands of beneficial owners. Furthermore, many individual stockholders of record depend primarily on their bank or on their brokerage or investment advisory concern for advice about the companies in which they hold stock and for interpretation of the financial statements, even though they themselves may receive copies directly from the company. By providing financial data and focusing attention on company earning power, stability, and future outlook—all centered around financial analysis, ratios, and trends—the annual report places the analyst in a position to give advice to clients.

Among other readers of the annual report are the government, customers, and the general public. For the government the report establishes the proper basis for taxes and regulations. The customer who is sold on the company and its products will buy more, will be willing to pay the price, and will be satisfied.

More and more companies are accepting the social obligation of explaining to the general public their contribution to U. S. industry. There is a recognition of and concern for the company's part and place in the free enterprise system, ecology, and general economic order. Each report is a part of the story of the achievements of that order and seeks to win favorable opinion and attitude to its side.

In utilizing the annual report to foster constructive public relations, managements must distribute the report to as many thinking people as possible. The corporation that wishes to expand the readership of its annual report must reach audiences on both the "national level" and the "community level." By making the information in the report available to more and more people, the company broadens the understanding of its activities for all those to whom the report is aimed.

Representative of readers on the national level are associated groups, such as suppliers of raw materials, dealers and jobbers, retailers, trade associations, and professional societies; press and radio, such as big city newspapers, journals of commerce and finance, selected business and trade papers, feature writers and columnists, news syndicates, radio newsrooms, and selected radio commentators; financial institutions, such as big city banks and trust companies, stock exchange members, investment counselors, financial services, insurance companies, trustees of estates, and credit agencies; government departments and officials, such as SEC, ICC, FTC, FCC, departments of commerce and labor, selected senators and representatives, and state officials; and other groups, such as big city libraries, leading universities and colleges, selected magazines and journals, and philanthropic institutions.

Representative of readers on the community level are associated groups, such as labor unions, employment agencies, Rotary, Kiwanis, Lions, and Chambers of Commerce; press and radio, such as local news editors and local broadcasting stations; financial institutions, such as local banks, loan associations, and brokerage office managers; opinion leaders, such as heads of local firms, clergy, city officials, professional association members, and officers of clubs; and other groups, such as local libraries, movie theaters, small business owners, and church and fraternal groups.

Classified on the basis of the main group of readers aimed at and the major purposes, there are joint stockholder-employee reports, separate stockholder and employee reports, combined stockholder-employee-public reports, and reports prepared for many groups. There is a marked trend away from separate reports toward the joint or combined report. Because there is sufficient overlapping of interests among the different groups, the report to one group can be adapted at the same time to other groups for readability and understanding. In appealing to several groups in the same report, firms may speak to each group in separate paragraphs or sections. This is the natural result of thinking about each group's characteristics and interests and adapting to them. A merging, however, if it is to be successful, should bind all groups together. Because the groups have mutual interests, those interests should be welded together with group lines broken down in the final report.

Annual reports may be printed, mimeographed, lithographed, or reproduced by some other method. The larger the company, the greater the need for a printed report. In some very small firms a typewritten report may serve the purpose. In this chapter, however, emphasis is on the printed corporation report aimed at reaching as many readers as possible and toward accomplishing as many purposes as possible. Here there may be a choice between the conservative, conventional report and the humanized, popularized report. Impressions gleaned from examining hundreds of annual reports of the last two decades have indicated definite trends toward the humanized report, through which the corporation can reach a vast, varied audience and make fullest use of the annual report.

CONTENT AND ORGANIZATION

What To Include

What does a company talk about in its annual report? Details of financial condition and operational activities are of paramount interest to all readers of annual reports. Some readers are more interested in details than others. Not all parts of an annual report will be read by all, nor will those that are generally read receive the same amount of interest from everyone. The reader will read what he needs to and what appeals to him. Therefore, in determining the contents of an annual report, the writer should consider two main questions: What does the reader want and need for his purposes, and what must I tell him to accomplish my purposes? In many cases the information the reader wants is also necessary for accomplishing the company's purposes.

The following checklist of information for stockholders, although not all-inclusive, suggests what is necessary for the stockholder's information and for the company in maintaining appropriate relations with the stockholder. Probably no annual report would include all the items listed, but the company would select and use those items that apply to its particular situation.

The stockholder chiefly interested in the financial condition and operational activities of the company wants to know how the business is being run and its prospects for the future. Details that will show him the stability of the firm and its successful operation will encourage him to keep his holdings and invest further.

The report should contain all information necessary to meet the needs of those audiences which the firm considers to be the most important. It should answer all the questions that a stockholder, employee, or the general public might ask.

The topics in the checklist of information for employees that follows overlap somewhat with those in the list for the stockholders. They do, however, indicate what the employee is interested in knowing and what he may have questions about. Like the stockholder list, this one is suggestive and can serve as a reminder. Employees are principally interested in operational facts affecting their jobs, which are their first concern. What makes the job? What keeps it? How does it fit into the work of the company? How secure is the employee in the job? What are his promotional

Checklist of Information for Stockholders

Financial Statistics and Data

Financial highlights and summary

Balance sheet

Income statement, operating statement

Explanatory notes and auditor's
certificate

Earned and capital surplus statements

Financial position

Sales, earnings, dividends

Taxes and reserves

Income other than operations

Income distribution

Capital expenditures

Working capital

Payroll and investments

Depreciation and depletion

Value of plants and net worth

Financial Narrative

Sales, earnings, dividends

Taxes, reserves, and net worth

Exports and imports

Inventories and capital inventories

Unfilled orders

Fixed assets

Intangible assets

Investment per employee

Capital requirements

Supplies

New policies

Research

Employee and community relations

Dealer and consumer

Future outlook

Nonfinancial Narrative

Facts about the company:
Brief history of company
Summary of growth of industry
Contributions to growth
Production process
Distribution facilities
Plant size, location, etc.
Advertising and sales promotion
Departmental operations
Company publications

Employee benefits:
Pension plan
Insurance
Health and safety practice
Vacation
Work productivity
Employee training
Personnel development

Other Information

Number of employees

Average age

Length of service

Thumbnail biographies

Organization chart

Management as a trusteeship

Employment and sales volume

Price and wage increase

Lower or higher costs

Issues

Number

Sex

General distribution

List of officers

Stock transfer agents

Registrars, attorneys, & auditors

Proxy notices

Date of annual meeting

Year-to-Year Comparisons

Sales

Earnings

Dividends

Market value of stock

Reserves

Taxes

Financial progress

Treatment of Social and Economic Aspects of the Business

Business partnership

Employee relations

Research development

Industry education

Taxation

Legislation

Labor

Wages and selling price

Economic conditions

Company contributions

Capital assets

Sales dollar breakdown

Income dollar breakdown

Earnings, dividends, taxes and payroll
compared

Ecology

opportunities? These are questions an employee wants answered. A stable firm means security to him, and he is interested in the financial condition from that standpoint. He wants to know how the running of the business affects him, who the real boss is, who the owners are. If the company report gives him facts that he wants, he is likely to read it, and as a result, he will be a better-informed and more productive worker.

Checklist of Information for Employees

General Information

The company's position in the business world	Discussion of capitalistic system of free enterprise
The worker, stockholder, and consumer in U.S. industry	Basic economics of U.S. business growth

Employee Benefits

Employee training program	Bonus plan
Opportunities for advancement	Incentive plan
Job evaluation	Credit union
Safety practices	Company loan plan
Health practices	Paid vacation
Insurance	Social security
Pension plan	Suggestion system
Medical plan	Recreational facilities
Wage plan	Activities program

Facts About the Company

History and development:	Business operations:
Personnel	Raw materials used
Executives	Supply and supplies
Products	Sales and advertising
Sales record	Employment statistics
Production record	Stockholder statistics
Expansion of facilities	Distribution
Research	Inventories
Company competition	Plant maintenance
Community relations	Company awards
Stock issues	Prices
Owners of the business	Government regulations
Manner of growth	Income and disbursements
	Assets and liabilities
	Future prospects

The contents of an annual report that are of interest to the employee and the stockholder also interest the general public. By informing the public and encouraging them to think favorably about the company, the firm can go a long way toward creating good public relations. A policy of frankness and sincerity in reporting facts helps. Emphasizing how the company serves human needs and contributes to the general well-being of the community also furthers favorable public reaction.

Deciding what to include in the annual report merely involves selecting items based on the interests of the audiences and the purposes of the report. Two other aspects of annual report preparation loom as greater problems: arrangement of facts in the various parts of the report and the style of presentation and writing.

Arrangement of Parts

Annual reports differ in makeup and arrangement, but there are some similarities among them. Most begin with a summary or highlights-of-the-year section and then a letter to the stockholders from the president of the company. A financial and operational review of the year is presented next. It is followed by the financial statements and notes and the auditor's certificate or sections on employee activities, the advertising of products, and the future outlook of the firm. The balance sheet and income statement generally are placed in the middle or appear last in the annual report. The order and the treatment of specific details in each part vary from report to report.

Cover. In recent years the trend has been to attract the reader by making covers as attention-getting as possible, or making them simple and dignified. This is in line with the tendency to popularize annual reports. Thus color and illustration are widely used to obtain a favorable first impression. Many covers highlight the chief feature of the report, present a new product or old products in use, show product benefits, or depict the character and activities of the company and its peoples.

Other successful covers might show a manufacturing operation, an aerial view of a plant or factory, an entrance, sources of raw materials, new additions, or future plans. Pictures of employees at work, at home, or engaged in some recreational activity add human interest too. More and more corporations are using the back cover and the inside of the front and back covers. Favorite items used inside the front cover are a list of officers and directors of the company, the table of contents, highlights of the year, or some point of major importance. The back cover is used mostly for advertising and selling the company's products.

Highlights. The most important parts of the annual report are selected and highlighted by brief statements with supporting figures. When a summary statistical table is used, it is made up of items extracted from the financial statements included in the report. Sometimes outstanding developments of the year are listed with no figures. Facts and figures are selected to reflect the progress during the year and are sometimes presented entirely in graphic form. Comparisons with the previous year or several years make the figures significant and point up the progress of the company. The summary may cover such items as sales figures, earnings before and after income taxes, income per share of common stock, dividends per share of common stock, net working capital, capital expenditures, long-term debt, number of employees, number of stockholders, investments, book value per common share, and any special features of the particular company.

President's Letter. The chairman of the board or the president of the company usually writes a letter, and it has generally become known as the president's letter. Specific items usually fall into categories, such as finance, accounting, production, employee relations, marketing, research development, relation of the company to the industry, and the economic and political condition of the country. They are frequently presented under main headings and in summary form or in the light of current conditions or future plans. The president's message should be brief and should deal with important points only. A few letters are long; in some instances, the entire report is written in letter form. The letter is an opportunity for the president to merge his group of readers into one. He should recognize that business is a human affair and thus present points of human interest—not mere, cold facts. He should be sincere, clear, and informal. The letter should reflect a certain amount of human warmth toward the readers. A personal conversational style is good.

In essence the letter is a letter of transmittal and a summary of the report. It should attract the reader and interest him in reading the report. Synchronized with the report, it sets the tone for what follows.

Table of Contents. The contents page shows what is in the report and serves as a page reference for items of special interest to the reader. Generally the table of contents is either on the inside front cover or the first page of the report. Sometimes placed in a similar position is a list of officers and directors of the company. This list may also be on the inside back cover or at the end of the report.

Narratives. The operational and financial narratives make up the bulk of the report. No one plan or order of subjects is followed. Often a central theme is selected and the topics are organized with it in mind. For example, on the company's twenty-fifth or fiftieth anniversary, emphasis would be on the historical development and progress made during the period of operation, and topics would be related to the anniversary theme.

The narratives in the annual report are financial and nonfinancial, depending on the basic subject matter. Nonfinancial narrative takes up such subjects as history of the company, what the company does, its products and sales methods, production, sales, advertising, employee relations and benefits, public relations, and research. The financial narra-

GENERAL MOTORS CORPORATION SIXTY-THIRD ANNUAL REPORT 1971
YEAR ENDED DECEMBER 31,

PRINCIPAL OFFICES
3044 W. Grand Boulevard, Detroit, Michigan 48202
767 Fifth Avenue, New York, New York 10022

Stock Transfer Offices
767 Fifth Avenue, New York, New York 10022
100 W. Tenth Street, Wilmington, Delaware 19899
55 Hawthorne Street, San Francisco, California 94120
231 S. La Salle Street, Chicago, Illinois 60690
220 W. Congress Street, Detroit, Michigan 48226
21 King Street, E., Toronto 1, Ontario
1350 Sherbrooke Street, W., Montreal 25, Quebec

The Annual Stockholders' Meeting
will be held on May 19, 1972, in Detroit,
Michigan. It is expected that proxy material
will be sent to stockholders beginning about
April 13, 1972, at which time proxies for use
at this meeting will be requested.

Table of contents indicates subject matter and organization
of what's in the annual report.

Courtesy General Motors Corporation

tive discusses such subjects as dividends, earnings, sales, cost, taxes,. and income.

Financial Statements. The majority of the companies include a consolidated balance sheet and income statement. The balance sheet is the hub around which the rest of the report, especially the financial data, revolves. This may be the reason some firms place it in the center of the report. The center position also has a mechanical advantage—allowing the double-page spread when putting the report together. Another favorite position for financial statements is at the end of the report. The statements are followed by explanatory notes and the auditor's certificate. Because some readers are not familiar with accounting practices, explanatory notes are necessary. They may be in the form of footnotes to the statements or on separate pages succeeding the statements. The auditor's certificate is customary practice and reflects a standard pattern.

Statements are further clarified by the use of simplified terminology and form. They must, however, conform to accepted accounting practice and are thus standardized by accountants. To be of value, statements should be for two years or more, showing changes. For one year they are somewhat meaningless. Care should also be taken to avoid incompleteness for simplification. The statements should contain figures which will enable readers to compute such ratios as that of expenses to net earnings and that of total sales to total money employed in the business. Of course, figures for this purpose may be given in comparative statistical tables. At any rate, adequate financial information must be in the report.

When the financial statements are in the middle of the report, the narrative sections are divided, and part of the narrative follows the financial section. Usually the emphasis in the narrative sections is on such items as stockholder data, employee information, sales, and advertising. The end of the report, particularly the inside back cover, lends itself to product advertising and activities surrounding the product or services offered for sale. If the statements are at the end of the report, the center spread may be devoted to advertising copy and a layout of the products.

Presentation of Data

Use of Visual Aids. In recent years there has been a tremendous increase in the number of tables, charts, graphs, and pictures used in annual reports. They not only add interest to the report but also increase understanding. Figures presented in the balance sheet and other financial statements mean more to the general reader of the annual report if they are displayed in appropriate charts. Figures on sales, earnings, taxes, reserves, and dividends lend themselves to visual treatment in chart or graph form. Frequently used is a pie chart, which shows the breakdown of the income dollar and can be conveniently and quickly understood.

The following pages, reproduced from the General Electric 1970 Annual Report, illustrate the increasing emphasis on the consumer plus the growing use of pictures replacing charts, tables, and graphs which repeat and highlight figures from the financial statements.

When each page is illustrated with some form of visual aid, attention is attracted to that page, and the interested reader will be encouraged to start reading the accompanying text material. Probably as much as 50 percent of the space could be filled with interpretative charts, pictorial graphs, maps, photographs, and other appealing illustrations. The remaining space should be devoted to explanatory text material and the financial statements. The visual aids help the reader grasp the facts presented in the textual message and create attention and interest. The explanatory material presents facts and indicates their significance and relationship. Thus the reader's understanding and favorable opinion and action are obtained.

Many visual aids used as examples in Chapter 4 were taken from annual reports. They indicate the wide variety of aids that may be used and the variety of information they can display in annual reports. Pies, bars, columns, flow diagrams, and all their variations are easily comprehended and are interesting to look at. Photographs of the company president, major officers, and board of directors show the stockholders and employees what the officers look like. Pictures of employees at work on the production line or participating in recreational or operational activity and of plant facilities and equipment add interest. A map may be used to show the distribution of the stockholders or of the product. An organizational chart may also be useful. In general, the more visual aids used, the more likely the report is to be looked at and read by the layman. The specialist will read the financial statements and more serious text material because he must use the data, and his position and background qualify him to comprehend all parts of the report.

Humanized Style. Much human interest can be achieved in the annual report just by a careful selection of visual aids. Illustrations help dramatize the important points. For the report to be highly humanized, however, the style of writing in the textual parts must also create human interest. This is achieved largely through the use of the "you" attitude in writing. Material is presented on the basis of what the reader wants, needs, and is interested in reading.

Very much in contrast to the objective, impersonal, and impartial tone used in problem-solution reports, the humanized, "you" style in annual reports is personal and subjective and reflects the human warmth

Consumer

Consumer		*(In millions)*
	1970	1969
Sales	$1,969	$2,155
Net Earnings	77	122

Growth plans maintained despite strike's effects on 1970 results.
Taking shape on an 1100-acre site near the new town of Columbia, Md., are three huge buildings, the first to be constructed at General Electric's Appliance Park-East. The buildings—a range plant, air conditioning plant and regional warehouse expected to be in operation during 1971—together with others to be added in the '70's, represent a substantial commitment by General Electric to the belief that appliance markets will grow strongly during the decade. Growth will result from population increases—particularly in young adults who, by sharply accelerating new family formations, will open up new demands. But growth will also come as new life styles call for greater use of more productive electrical servants to free families for more leisure time and an enhanced personal environment.

By the end of the decade the new Park is expected to comprise nine major facilities, with over six million square feet of floor space, employment of some 12,000 and output approaching the capacity of the present Appliance Park in Louisville, Ky.

During this decade the two GE Appliance Parks and other consumer goods facilities will be kept busy, in part, as the U.S. begins to catch up on its needs for new housing. Addition of appliances to existing homes will offer a still larger market, while replacement sales should generate more volume than either.

The strike had a more severe impact on '70 operations than on those for 1969, largely because customer shipments continued to be made in 1969 from inventory stocks. The result was that 1970 consumer sales were off 9% from '69 levels. The sharp earnings decline resulted from sales lost because of depleted inventories and the added costs of production startup and of rebuilding stocks throughout the distribution system. Weak consumer markets, particularly in consumer electronics, also dampened results during the year, as did costs associated with new facilities.

A new GE entry into services businesses, Command Performance® Network is a custom video-network service providing closed-circuit large-screen TV in 25 cities for business, industry and professional use.

The number of young adults reaching their 22nd birthday has recently surged upward and will continue in the '70's at levels 50% greater than in the sixties. Forming new families, these young adults provide a principal source of new demand for the array of GE appliances, consumer electronics and housewares pictured in the kitchen at left.

General Electric and Hotpoint appliance operations recovered strongly after the strike period. Preparations for further growth were maintained. In addition to the expansion at Appliance Park-East, a new Applied Research and Design Center at Louisville's Appliance Park was completed early in 1971. Expansion will almost double manufacturing capacity both at the central air conditioning plant in Tyler, Texas, and the Bloomington, Ind., plant producing side-by-side refrigerator-freezers.

Sales of General Electric color television sets held up well in a year when industry sales generally were off. Customers responded to greatly improved quality throughout the line and to significant consumer-oriented features such as One Touch® tuning.

The Company is strengthening its leadership in appliance service by instituting a new Customer Care-Everywhere system. All elements of the service network—servicing dealers, independent servicing agencies and the 87 factory-service branches—are being tied more closely together with the

Pictures highlight financial statements

GE products change to meet consumers' changing needs and tastes, as photographed at the GE Residential Lighting Center in Cleveland, Ohio. **1** High-quality, reliable color TV performance comes with One Touch® tuning in GE 25-inch set. **2** Versatronic® microwave oven cooks food in a fraction of the time required by conventional ovens. Innovative electronics include **3** youth-styled stereo phonograph and **4** miniature use-anywhere tape recorder. Personal care products: **5** hair setter with tangle-free rollers and make-up mirror with four light settings. Housewares that ease home chores: **6** lightweight but powerful vacuum cleaner and **7** Dutch skillet, Toast-R-Oven®, can opener-ice crusher, Rapid-Brew coffee maker and eight-pushbutton blender. And for photographers: **8** the FlashPack® electronic flash unit.

urtesy of General Electric

389

felt by the company toward the reader. In a sincere, friendly, cordial manner the facts are presented. All three persons of personal pronouns are used with emphasis on you. "Your company," "your dividends," "improvements that will help you," and "your benefits" are expressions indicating the unlimited possibilities in the use of the second-person pronoun. The style is conversational. The report, which represents the company, is talking with the readers. Both are put on the same level. In this way the annual report may become humanized, because to become so it must take on the characteristics or personality of a warm, friendly individual.

Also in line with humanizing the style of writing, one must consider adapting the terminology to the reader's understanding. To reach the various publics, the annual report must be written simply. In this way it can be understood by all, and, as long as he is not talked down to, the educated reader will appreciate the simplicity because it saves him time and energy. The trend toward simplified terminology in financial statements is not altogether a new one nor one that is followed by all companies. For convenient and easy comprehension, firms are using "Statement of Financial Position" or "Financial Condition" instead of "Balance Sheet," replacing "company owns" for "assets," "company owes" for "liabilities," and using other phrases such as "allowance for" instead of "reserves."

Making the narrative readable by presenting it interestingly, clearly, and convincingly, by keeping to short sentences, by using the "you" attitude, by writing as you talk and adding personal touches, and by letting the text reflect characteristics of human personality will go a long way toward obtaining readership of the report and favorable reaction. Enlivening the annual report by attractive appearance and use of visual aids, and making the statistics, financial statements, and text comprehensive and clear, will also help tremendously in making it a public relations document. Business is a service to the public and needs all the goodwill and public confidence that it can get. A humanized style of writing is one means to accomplish this function of the annual report.

Design Factors. Typographical appeal is vitally important. Advertising art and book design are used to influence opinion in favor of the company. Expert printer's advice on paper, printing processes, illustrative techniques, printing colors, typefaces, and type sizes should be secured and followed.

The 8½- by 11-inch page is the size of the majority of annual reports. The wide pages allow for the balance sheets, other financial statements, and statistical tabulations. With this wide a page the text should be broken into two or three columns for readability. The type should lend dignity and clarity. It is an aid to the accomplishment of the total communication process. Appropriate good taste should be followed in selecting colors in the report. Reports with a four-color cover may use only two or three colors throughout the text material or even be done entirely in black and white.

The usual report varies from sixteen to thirty-two pages in length. A report that is less than sixteen pages usually will lack visual aids and will be too brief to be interesting. Likewise, one longer than thirty-two pages will tend to be wordy and drawn out, may have too many visual aids, and therefore may lose its readers.

INNOVATIONS AND TRENDS

What is innovation for one company or year may not be for another company, and when several companies pick up the innovative feature or technique then it may become a trend. Then after a trend has been set, it becomes common practice. Much of what was done in annual reports as trends five or ten years ago has become practice now.

In 1965 Litton Industries were very innovative in the theme used in their annual report—Leadership in the Market Place. In the introduction to their report that year they stated

> Throughout history the market place has traditionally been the arena of resolve for the economic needs of man. Here the resourceful innovator brought his creations and produce before a critical and potentially receptive public. Here, man's awareness was kindled by an increasing array of goods and services which enhance his welfare, and here he sought the satisfaction of his desires.
>
> . . . .
>
> Attesting to its importance throughout history are the paintings of great artists who down through years felt the impact of the market place and were moved to record it for posterity. The brushes of the masters portray eloquently the development of man's society and the commerce which made it possible. What better way to relate the story of the market place than through the art which it motivated?
>
> Beyond the beauty of form and the exquisiteness of color, this great art discloses a message—that the market place, like life itself, is everchanging. It is this change that has brought man's progress, and with it the hope that the future will hold even greater promise.
>
> . . . .
>
> The people of Litton cherish their leadership in the market area and chart their course to assure its continuation in the service of mankind.

Interspersed on almost every other page throughout the narrative story and financial data of the company were art reproductions in full color by the masters depicting the historical development of the market place.

Each art reproduction was accompanied by a description of the painting relating it to a business concept, such as foresight, quality in quantity, and expediting the economy, and a note about the artist and the present location of the painting.

It was no surprise that the Litton report that year became a collector's item. Since 1965, Litton has been an innovator every year in the use of theme. In 1966 the focus was on ideas. Interspersed through the report on facing pages were photographs and ideas, appropriately related. The note about the cover stated

> The history of progress is a history of evolution of men's ideas. As the sun quickens seed and pollen, the cover pictured the sun and wheat so the ideas we cultivate are part of that limitless realm man can never cease exploring. Man best attains the reward of a bountiful harvest by managing to productive fruition those ideas written by and about him.

As an example, on one page was the photograph of a beautiful child's face with an expression of pleasantness and faith. On the page facing it (white print on black paper) was this idea:

> "As faith in progress grows, we should bear in mind certain truths about ideas . . . some concepts are good, some bad, but in the end the best will win the race." As Free men, we dedicate ourselves to the task of managing ideas to gain a secure world where our children and their children after them may pursue responsible, fruitful lives.

The last idea-concept was opposite a lighted candle and the face of a boy:

> "The search for ideas is a never-ending adventure." For the light of ideas sets fires to the inquiring mind, "touching the world's imagination and giving perceptive men and women a broader, brighter view of the future of existence."

In 1970, the Litton report focused on people, but focusing on people has been predominate in enough annual reports in the last two or three years to designate it as a trend rather than an innovation. People are shown either as customers using the various products of a corporation or as workers manufacturing the products. Harris-Intertype Corporation did a very effective presentation (of people) in their 1971 report, as did the American Can Company (1971, product emphasis) and the Chase Manhattan Corporation (1971, customer emphasis).

The most innovative report following the trend of focusing on people was the one put out by General Motors, 1971. Representative pictures on page 393 indicate added human interest in their employees ac-

Jose Mora, employed by Central Foundry Division, organized and conducts a weekly program instructing young people in baseball and basketball. He was appointed to his local YMCA's Board of Directors in 1971, and is also captain of the Defiance, Ohio, Auxiliary Police Department.

Rodger H. Rewitzer, machine operator with Hydra-Matic Division, is one of 31 GM employes honored in 1971 as a winner of the GM Award for Excellence in Community Activities. Active in work with young people, he participates in community and youth activities and teaches baseball and fishing five nights a week. Other winners are pictured on the pages that follow.

Mrs. Evelyn Sutton is an assembly line operator, Delco Products Division, Rochester, N.Y. The mother of seven children, she was president of the Rochester Federation of Negro Women's Clubs and a member of Mothers Who Care club, which sends servicemen gifts. In 1971, she hosted ten young ladies attending the State Convention of Negro Youth Federation.

Focusing on people creates good public relations.

Courtesy General Motors Corporation

tive in community service. Photographs such as these were interspersed through the narrative on operations, creating a very favorable public image of General Motors.

The trends of the 1950s and 1960s have now become common practice:

1. Clarity of presentation and exposition.
2. Simplified, nontechnical statements and terminology.
3. Data in comparable form and covering several years for comparison.
4. Appearance and form attractive, pleasing, and attention-getting.
5. Visual aids such as charts and tables supplementing and supporting the financial statements.
6. Natural color used in photographs.

American Can Company focused on the American Family, which they serve in many ways. The family photographs in their 1970 report illustrate the company's role in today's living. They show many of the products and services the company supplies, but at the same time they include other less obvious company products used in cosmetics, pharmaceuticals, and industry.

A few companies are experimenting with a size of report other than 8½ by 11 or 9 by 12 inches. In 1971 Amstar Corporation did sections alternately on white and gray paper and used side (index file) headings for each section, which made for ready reference.

Eastern Airlines received the gold "Oscar-of-Industry" award for their 1971 report, largely because they abandoned some of the traditions of presentation and emphasized their poor financial condition, did the whole report as a letter from the president, used no photography, and had an enlarged financial review, wide lines of text, and extensive use of charts and graphs. This, although effective once, may not be so again.

One prominent trend emerging in the last few years is the creativity in the use of colored photographs throughout the reports. Another one is the focusing on the consumer and services to the public. Along with the trend of emphasizing services is the emphasis on what the company is doing with the environment—ecology. Annual reports are definitely increasing their readership and accomplishing the public relations function.

FOR DISCUSSION AND WRITING

1. Discuss how an annual report accomplishes various purposes with different readers.
2. Bring to class a recent annual report and show how it is or is not

following the trends in annual reporting in its makeup and presentation.

3. How does style of writing in an annual report differ from that in other types of reports? Why?

4. Write a summary, suitable for mailing to stockholders, of a company annual report.

5. Making use of pertinent summary information in an annual report, prepare a full-page newspaper advertisement aimed at obtaining public interest and goodwill for your company.

6. Write a summary of an annual report for publication as a feature article in the January issue of your employee magazine.

7. Select one of the following features of an annual report and suggest ways for improving a particular report:

   a. Presentation of financial statements.
   b. Use of visual aids.
   c. Design factors.
   d. Style of writing.

8. The American Management Association has set up three criteria for evaluating the effectiveness of an annual report—interest, clearness, and completeness. Select an annual report and criticize it on this basis.

9. Make a study of selected annual reports of one company over a period of years to find out changes, progress, trends, and the like. Your results are to be presented to top management as a basis for recommending improvements.

10. As director of industrial relations in your company you have been asked to prepare an article for publication in your company magazine, *Company Life*. The editor plans to devote most of this issue to telling employees the company story that stockholders received in the annual report. Your article will be the main feature article.

    a. What will be your purpose and objectives?
    b. What will you plan to tell the employees? Why?
    c. How will your style of writing differ from the style used in most annual reports?
    d. How will your presentation differ from that commonly found in problem-solution reports?

11. There are five areas in which business can meet its community-living responsibilities—serving, sharing, knowing, organizing, and informing. Serving is doing the company's job to the best of its ability in an atmosphere of friendliness. People want more than just good products or services—they like to see that the firm has a heart as well as technical competence. Sharing means participation in worthwhile activities, both as a company and as individuals, to help solve community problems. Knowing is being aware of how the community feels about the business—what it thinks and expects. Organizing means making it possible for employees at all levels to have the information, responsibility, and opportunity to help build better relations between com-

pany and community. Informing encompasses all those activities whereby the company lets people know what it is doing and why.

a. Discuss how the annual report can help in each of these five areas.

b. Select a company annual report and analyze its contents, style, and format to see to what extent it meets community-living responsibilities. You might present suggestions to the firm on what it could do.

c. Analyze five to twenty-five annual reports to determine what trends, if any, companies are following in each of these five areas through their annual reports.

SOURCES OF
BUSINESS INFORMATION

Facts, ideas, and data necessary for making sound decisions, solving problems, and presenting them in oral, written, and visual reports may be found in company records, reports, bulletins, and pamphlets and in periodicals, books, and newspapers. It behooves every businessman to keep abreast of current information and activity in his field and to know what sources to go to for various kinds of data.

PERIODICALS

General News Magazines

Business Week	*Nation's Business*
Newsweek	*U.S. News and World Report*
Time	

General Business Magazines

Fortune	*Forbes*
Harvard Business Review	*Survey of Current Business*
Changing Times	*Dun's Review and Modern Industry*
Journal of Business	

Accounting Magazines

The Accountant's Digest (quarterly) for digests of articles currently appearing in the accounting magazines.

The Accounting Review (monthly) for articles covering principles, theory, and applications. Issued by American Accounting Association.

Business Budgeting (bimonthly) for articles on budgeting, decision making, and forecasting. Issued by National Society for Business Budgeting.

The Journal of Accountancy (monthly) for practical articles largely of a "how to" nature.

The NAA Bulletin (monthly) for articles reporting current company practices. Issued by National Association of Accountants; material is provided by members and associate members.

The Taxes, Journal of Taxation, and *Tax Digest* for tax data, provisions of tax laws, and the way they affect the businessman.

Advertising Magazines

The Advertiser (monthly) for articles on agencies, media, promotions, and general news.

Advertising Age (weekly) for coverage of current information and developments.

Editor and Publisher (weekly) for current proceedings and events in brief.

Markets of America (annually) for articles and reports on media, agencies, promotions, and general advertising news.

The Reporter of Direct Mail Advertising (monthly) for all aspects of direct mail. Includes case histories.

Economics Magazines

The American Economic Review (quarterly) for scholarly discussions of current economic problems.

Economic Indicators (monthly) for charts showing data ranging from expenditures for new plants to corporate profits for various years. Information on economic growth.

The Engineering Economist (quarterly) for articles devoted to problems of capital investment. Contains some case studies and book reviews. Published by the Engineering Economy Division of American Society for Engineering Education.

The Journal of Political Economy (bimonthly) for a wide variety of articles on economic areas, theoretical and practical problems.

The Quarterly Journal of Economics (quarterly) for articles on theory and practice in current economics.

The Southern Economic Journal (quarterly) for articles on many phases of economics. Not limited to southern region.

Finance Magazines

Barron's (weekly) for current data on government and specific companies, for statistics on bond quotations, stock markets, indexes, Dow-Jones averages, financial indicators. Devoted primarily to investments.

The Commercial and Financial Chronicle (semiweekly) for general corporation and financial news, investments, bonds, rates, and quotations.

Federal Reserve Bulletin (monthly) for articles on national and international trade and finance, and for statistics and tables on finance, industry, and commerce.

Financial World (quarterly) for analyses of investment opportunities and earnings and dividend data.

Journal of Finance (quarterly) for authoritative articles and scholarly reviews on finance, government, and money and banking.

The Wall Street Journal (daily except Saturday and Sunday) for current events in financial circles, stock market quotations and news, Dow-Jones averages, and corporation reports.

Labor and Industrial Relations Magazines

AFL and CIO News (weekly) for union's point of view on national politics, unemployment, acts of Congress, and the like.

The American Federationist (monthly) for news of labor, conventions, industry, and government.

Industrial and Labor Relations Review (quarterly) for articles, reports, and news items dealing with labor and management topics and problems.

Industrial Management Review (biannually) for authoritative articles on industrial management, most of which are the result of research.

Industrial Relations (three times a year) for articles on all aspects of the employment relationship; pertinent developments in labor economics, sociology, psychology, political science, and law emphasized.

Industrial Relations Magazine (monthly) for all aspects of employer-employee relations.

International Labour Review (monthly) for subjects and problems related to world labor.

Monthly Labor Review (monthly) for reports on trends in employment, payrolls, hourly and weekly earnings, agreements, accidents, disputes.

Management Magazines

Administrative Management (monthly) for new developments, equipment, and office procedures. News and activities of the Administrative Management Association.

Administrative Science Quarterly for articles written to advance the understanding of administration through empirical investigation and theoretical analysis. Contains book reviews and abstracts.

Advanced Management—Office Executive (monthly) for articles on all phases of management, office problems, equipment, and personnel.

Automatic Data Processing (monthly) for scientific and practical articles on data processing and management information systems.

Factory and Industrial Management (monthly) for articles dealing with production, industrial relations, maintenance, and equipment.

Journal of the Academy of Management (three times a year) for results of significant research and scholarly analysis of questions dealing with all aspects of management thought, philosophy, theory, applicable techniques, curriculum, and teaching. Published by the Academy of Management.

Management International (semimonthly) for articles on management and managerial sciences. Articles published in English, French, German, and Italian for promoting comparative studies on an international scale.

Management Review (monthly) for general aspects of industrial relations, office management, production, finance, and marketing.

Management Science (quarterly) for authoritative research articles for viewpoint of top management and scientific management. Scholarly and theoretical; published by the Institute of Management Sciences.

Modern Management (monthly) for articles on factory operations and labor relations.

Operations Research (bimonthly) for research articles dealing with the science of management. Issued by the Operations Research Society of America.

Marketing Magazines

Credit and Financial Management (monthly) for data on laws, court decisions, and problems of interest to credit men.

The Credit World (monthly) for articles on problems in retail credit.

Industrial Marketing (monthly) for problems and solutions in advertising and selling industrial products. Sales promotion ideas, facts, and case histories.

Journal of Marketing (quarterly) for articles resulting from marketing research presented from scientific viewpoint. Issued by the American Marketing Association.

Journal of Retailing (quarterly) for analysis of retailing problems.

Purchasing (monthly) for variety of topics of interest to purchasing agents. New product emphasis.

Sales Management (semimonthly) for sales methods, programs, and media.

Personnel Magazines

Personnel (bimonthly) for all aspects of personnel management, hiring, training, paying, and others.

Personnel Administration (bimonthly) for personnel practices in government agencies.

Personnel Journal (monthly) for reports on research and conferences. Articles on personnel practices and labor relations.

Supervision (monthly) for industrial relations and operating management.

REFERENCE BOOKS

Numerous books provide information and data helpful in keeping abreast of developments in related areas and in providing specific facts and ideas needed for decisions, solutions, and reports. Statistical compilations, trends and developments, guides to markets, changing methods, administrative practices—all are part of the factual data businessmen need and use. Much of this type of information is contained in handbooks, yearbooks, encyclopedias, dictionaries, almanacs, directories, and publications of various subscribed-for services. Some of these are general references; others are specialized according to the fields they cover.

Handbooks and Yearbooks

Business handbooks present within a single volume the condensed picture of an entire field of business. Highly factual, they assume some familiarity with the subject on the part of the reader. A few are revised annually, keeping information up-to-date. They provide a "refresher" of the field. Some handbooks catalog organizations, trade names, and so forth similarly to directories.

Most libraries will have the following handbooks for reference. The titles indicate the area covered.

Accountants' Handbook
Handbook of Auditing Methods
Industrial Accountant's Handbook
Handbook of Business Administration
Corporate Secretaries' Manual and Guide
Handbook of Insurance
Handbook of International Organizations in the Americas
Financial Handbook
An Estate Planner's Handbook
Handbook of Labor Unions
Management's Handbook
Marketing Handbook
Production Handbook
Sales Executives' Handbook
Printing and Promotion Handbook
Sales Manager's Handbook
The Real Estate Handbook
Current Abbreviations
The United States Government Organization Manual
United States Postal Manual
Public Relations Handbook
Guide to Women's Organizations
Corporate Treasurer's and Controller's Handbook
Coffin's Interest Tables
Handbook of Foreign Currencies

Yearbooks are published annually and give the year's summary of facts and data of a particular nature.

The Statistical Abstract of the United States presents summary statistics in industrial, social, political, and economic fields and covers statistics on such topics as population, education, employment, military affairs, social security, manufacturing, commerce, and vital statistics.

The Commerce Yearbook provides information on commerce, trade, and industry.

The Shipping World Yearbook gives shipping data for the year.

The Spectator Insurance Yearbook presents pertinent facts on insurance companies such as history, administration, policy types, officers, and firms.

The Pan American Yearbook provides a ready reference to direction of the western hemisphere. New developments and changes in law are covered.

Encyclopedias, Dictionaries, and Almanacs

Encyclopaedia Britannica
Encyclopedia Americana
New International Encyclopedia
The Accountant's Encyclopedia
The Encyclopedia of Banking and Finance

The Encyclopedia of the Social Sciences
The Exporters' Encyclopedia
Prentice-Hall's *Encyclopedic Dictionary of Business*
Crowell's *Dictionary of Business and Finance*
The Government Printing Office's *Dictionary of Occupational Titles*
E. L. Kohler's *Dictionary for Accountants*
Frank Henius' *Dictionary of Foreign Trade*
Marquis' *Who's Who in America*
Marquis' *Who's Who in Commerce and Industry*
Marquis' *Who's Who in the Midwest, In the Southwest,* etc.
M. G. Kendall and W. R. Buckland's *Dictionary of Statistical Terms*
World Almanac and Book of Facts
The Economic Almanac
The Management Almanac
Information Please Almanac
International Television Almanac

Directories

A directory provides a ready reference for those seeking specific facts about or listings of a particular subject or field. These consist of alphabetized names and addresses, geographic locations, product listings, professional organizations, and the like. Varying in size and length, some directories give general information, and others details. City and telephone directories are the most common general directories.

Thomas' Register of American Manufacturers (annually). A complete and informative buying guide for people in purchasing activities. It is divided into alphabetically arranged lists of manufacturers, trade names, international trade sections, commercial organizations, and trade papers.

Mac Rae's Blue Book. Not as voluminous as *Thomas' Register* but a good purchasing guide. Its information is arranged under product headings.

Directory of House Organs (annually). It lists both internal and external publications as well as employee and sales magazines and gives the name, editor, and company.

Ayer's Directory of Newspapers and Periodicals (annually). It gives name of newspaper, editor, publisher, and circulation.

Moody's Manual of Industrials (annually). Separate volumes deal with public utilities, railroads, government and municipals, together with banks, insurance, real estate, and investment firms. The volume on corporations includes U.S., Canadian, and foreign corporations. It gives information on company history, organization, operation, and financial condition. It includes financial statements from reports submitted to the Securities and Exchange Commission. It is indispensable to sellers of securities and to the banking community generally, and is useful in market research, sales, credit reference, production, planning, financing, and investment analysis work. The material is cumulated and issued in annual volumes.

Standard's Corporation Manual (monthly). Similar to Moody's except for corporations only. It is also issued cumulatively so that current information is always available.

Poor's Register of Directors and Executives (annually). About 90,000 names of executives and directors of manufacturing and mining concerns, utilities, railroads, banks, and insurance companies, as well as partners of financial and investment institutions and of law firms are listed. It is divided into six main sections, each alphabetically arranged: product index, classified index, corporation directory, register of directors, obituary, and new names. Cumulative supplements are issued in May, August, and November.

The Congressional Directory. Published annually by the U.S. Government Printing Office; gives alphabetical lists and short sketches of United States senators and representatives; lists committees and outlines special agencies and commissions and main departments of government.

National Organizations of the U.S. Lists associations, societies, federations, chambers of commerce, unions, etc. Gives name, headquarters, number of members, staff, chapters, committees, publications, dates and places of conventions. Associations classified as business, education, and agriculture.

Trade Names Index. Lists trade names, definitions and uses, name and address of firms, etc.

Guide to American Directories. Published by B. Klein and Company, New York. Lists alphabetically United States and foreign directories.

In addition to the commonly referred to directories listed here, most trade and professional associations have directories of their members. In the communication area, for instance, the American Business Communication Association and the International Communication Association have directories listing their officers, members, and committees each year. There is also the *Directory of Communication Organizations* compiled and published by the Council of Communication Societies. It lists approximately 85 associations and 40 communication centers in the United States. Information on officers, background, purposes, activities, membership, publications, dues, benefits, and meetings given.

Government Publications

The Monthly Catalog of U.S. Government Publications lists publications issued by the various government agencies and departments. Includes prices, catalog numbers, and annotations.

The Congressional Record gives the proceedings and debates of Congress.

The Congressional Digest contains digests and summaries of the bills in Congress.

The Congressional Directory gives names and sketches of Senators and Representatives. Lists committees, agencies, commissions, and their memberships.

The Occupational Outlook Handbook gives salary scales, opportunities, and trends pertaining to all occupations.

The World Trade Information Series is useful in studying the economy and development of any country.

The Small Business Management Series is helpful to anyone owning or managing a small business.

Survey of Current Business presents data on industrial and business activity in the United States. Issued monthly with weekly supplements. Contains charts, maps, statistics, and articles.

Services

Dun and Bradstreet Credit Service.   Listings and financial ratings of manufacturers, wholesalers, and retailers in a large *Reference Book* published annually. Information is collected and analyzed on operations, management progress, financial statements, and payment records of each concern.

Rand McNally Services.   The *Commercial Atlas and Marketing Guide* contains monthly maps of the current business conditions in the United States, maps of U.S. government bureaus and agencies, time-zone maps, retail sales and trading area maps of the United States, reference maps for the world, and the like.

Real Estate Analyst Reports.   Monthly, in loose-leaf form, dealing with agriculture, appraisal, construction, mortgages, real estate taxes, and trends.

Bureau of National Affairs Service.   Reports on government's actions affecting business and the legal profession. Information useful to business and industry, labor organizations, government, and management.

Commerce Clearing House Services.   Over 100 loose-leaf reports, each on a specific subject dealing with tax and business regulatory law.

Prentice-Hall Services.   Loose-leaf, current publications on laws, rules, and regulations. Includes interpretations and comments. Covers federal tax services, state tax services, and other tax services, such as Social Security, insurance, and stock transfers.

RESEARCH ORGANIZATIONS

Several major business research organizations, national in scope, carry on a tremendous amount of research each year and make available in printed form a wealth of material which businessmen need and use daily. They may be written to for specific material and help. Part of their output is listed in the *Vertical File Service* catalog, obtained on a subscription basis by libraries from the H. W. Wilson Company. *The Vertical File* indexes pamphlets, brochures, leaflets, and other material falling outside the classification of periodicals and books. The researcher will check with his librarian for material of this nature available in the library files. Most associations publish lists of their own materials, and these are available to members and others upon request.

The American Management Association (1515 Broadway, New York) works closely with business firms, reprints articles, publishes several monthly magazines for members, conducts research, and puts on special training conferences. All phases of management receive special emphasis, for the purpose of the association is to advance understanding of management, commerce, and industry.

The National Industrial Conference Board (247 Park Avenue, New

York) is an impartial and nonprofit institution for research and education in economics, business, and management techniques. Its chief purpose is to promote development of private productive enterprise. It assembles, analyzes, interprets, and disseminates information regarding economic conditions and policies in the United States and in other countries. It also holds conferences and serves as a public information bureau.

The Chamber of Commerce of the United States (Washington, D.C.) is a federation of over 3,000 local chambers of commerce and trade associations throughout the United States. Its prime purpose is to obtain the mature judgment of businessmen on national questions and to present and interpret these views to the public and to government agencies. It makes available to the public and members a large number of bulletins, reports, and surveys—the results of research and study. Local chambers also act as a clearing house for industrial problems and constantly work to improve their communities for their people and for business.

The National Bureau of Economic Research (261 Madison Avenue, New York) conducts impartial studies dealing with questions of national significance such as income, capital formation, business cycles, prices, and wages. It provides detailed knowledge of quantitative measures of activity and objectively derived data for policy makers to use in making sound decisions. Conferences are held, issues discussed, and an exchange of ideas made. Results are published in a general or a special series, a pamphlet, or a report.

The National Association of Manufacturers (2 East 48th Street, New York) provides industrial information and strives to protect domestic industrial interests, to improve foreign commerce, and to support legislation for furthering association aims. It plans programs for studying economic trends and assembles views of industry for making the U.S. competitive enterprise system work more efficiently.

SUGGESTIONS FOR REFERENCE

B

ABBREVIATIONS

Acceptable standard abbreviations may be used in some personal, informal short reports—if used consistently. In general, however, abbreviations should be avoided, especially in formal reports.

It is good business to use the following abbreviations when the company uses them as part of its firm name:

> *Co.—Company*   *Inc.—Incorporated*
> *Bros.—Brothers*   *Ltd.—Limited*

Standard abbreviations used in footnote and bibliographical references are indicated in the suggestions presented under those headings.

BIBLIOGRAPHY

A bibliography lists sources of information used in gathering data and writing a report. It must include all those mentioned in footnotes and may include any other references which would be helpful to others in pursuing further the subject of the report. Although not actually bibliographical materials, personal interviews, lectures, TV and radio talks, and the like are included for convenience, reference, and for authenticating data.

Placement. The bibliography is always at the end of the report. It is part of the supplemental material included for reference purposes. It may be a separate section appearing before the appendix, although it usually follows it. Sometimes it is a part of the appendix, in which case it may be either first or last.

Organization. The entries in a bibliography are classified either according to subject matter or according to types of publications and sources of information. Thus there would be sections of the bibliography corresponding to the main subject divisions of the report, or there would be one section listing books, one listing articles, and so forth. Within each classified section of the bibliography, individual entries are alphabetized by authors' last names, or by titles when the authors are not known.

When subject divisions are used to classify items of the bibliography, it may be necessary to have one section called "General References" for listing those pertaining to several subject divisions of the report or to the report's subject as a whole. When the items are classified according to sources, it may be necessary to have a section called "Miscellaneous" for entries that do not warrant a separate section.

Arrangement of Elements.   The arrangement of elements in both foot-notes and bibliographical references follows the same general pattern. The major difference is that the bibliographical items list the last name of the author first, because they are arranged alphabetically.

Example bibliographical entries follow:

For a Book:

LESIKAR, RAYMOND V., *Business Communication Theory and Application,* 2nd ed., Richard D. Irwin, Inc., Homewood, Ill., 1972.

[Note that simplified punctuation is used. Each item is separated from the other by a comma. The period ending the entry may or may not be used as long as consistency is maintained. This is an informal style, and the publisher's name precedes the place of publication.]

SIGBAND, NORMAN B. *Communication for Management.* Glenview, Ill.: Scott, Foresman and Company, 1969.

[Note that series of items are separated by a period: author, title, and publication facts. This is a formal style, and the place of publication precedes the name of the publisher. This is used for formal reports, theses, and dissertations. It is more scholarly and academic than the informal entry.]

MENNING, J. H., and C. W. WILKINSON. *Communicating Through Letters and Reports.* 5th ed. Homewood, Ill.: Richard D. Irwin, Inc., 1972.

[Note that when there are two authors, the second one's first name precedes his last name, and a comma precedes the *and.* Two initials may replace the person's first name. In typing, underlining is used to indicate italics for the book title. When more than two authors, the first one may be used and *et al.* indicates *and others.*]

AMERICAN MANAGEMENT ASSOCIATION. *Institutional Investors: An Appraisal of Policies and Practices.* New York: American Management Association, 1967.

[Note that when there is no author given but an association is responsible for the work, the name of the association is used in place of the author's name. It is also used as the publisher. For a city such as New York or Chicago, the state is not given.]

CAMPBELL, JAMES H., and HAL W. HEPLER (editors). *Dimensions in Communication: Readings,* 2nd edition. Belmont, Calif.: Wadsworth Publishing Company, Inc., 1970.

[Note that editors are so indicated after their names.]

For a Newspaper Item:

The New York Times, November 10, 1972, p. 10.
The Times (London), March 19, 1973, p. 8.
MAYER, ALLAN J., "Beautiful Old Siwash: Schools Wax Eloquent in Vying for Students," *The Wall Street Journal* (New York) July 6, 1972, p. 1.

[Note the difference when there is a title, in quotation marks, and an author as reporter.]

For a Report:

Eastern Michigan University. *Annual Report of the President.* 1973.
Atlanta: *Division of Housing Report,* 1973.

For an Interview:

Personal interview, Henry J. Minks, President, First National Bank,
Fayetteville, Arkansas, April 2, 1973.
Personal interview with Henry George Bronson, Personnel Director, XYZ
Corporation, New Brunswick, Maine, October 15, 1973.

[Note that simplified punctuation, a comma, separates the items and that
essential identification items are called for, such as name, position, company, place, and date.]

For an Article:

Bruno, Sam J., "Effects of Personality on Perception of Written Mass
Communication," *The Journal of Business Communication,* Winter 1972, pp.
25–38.

[Note the use of quotation marks for the article title, italics (in typing,
underscoring) for the periodical, and the comma separating each item. This
is an informal style for informal reports. For formal reports, scholarly
and academic style would follow the more formal examples that follow.]

Douglas, George H. "Doldrums of the Advanced Writing Course," *The
Journal of Business Communication,* 9 (Winter, 1972), 25–38.

[Note that this is more formal by citing the volume number and placing
the date within parentheses. Roman numerals and *Vol.* for the abbreviation of volume may be used, such as Vol. IX.]

Almaney, Adnan. "Government's Resistance to International Communication: Report on a Unesco Study," *The Journal of Communication,* 22:1, 77–88,
March 1972.

[Note another way of indicating volume, number, and pages—volume 22,
number 1, pages 77–88 inclusive.]

Westley, Bruce A., and Malcolm S. MacLean, Jr., "A Conceptual Model
for Communications Research," *Dimensions in Communications: Readings,* 2d
edition, ed., J. H. Campbell and H. W. Hepler. Belmont, Calif.: Wadsworth
Publishing Company, Inc., 1970. 61–70.

[Note that when an article is referred to from a book, the publication facts
of the book are given following the author and article title. The example
entries here also follow the current trend of omitting *p.* and *pp.* for *page*
and *pages* preceding page numbers.]

It is important that consistency in form be observed throughout a bibliography.
A good reference manual such as the Chicago *A Manual of Style* should
always be consulted for forms less commonly used than those which have been
presented in this section.

Bibliographical references are single-spaced, with a double space between entries. Items are unnumbered. Indentation of five to ten spaces may be used at the beginning of each entry. Each entry, however, may be blocked with no indentation, or hanging indentation may be followed.

The total number of pages may be given for each book when the whole book has been used. Of course, if only part of the book or reference has been consulted, inclusive pages are indicated for the chapter or section used.

Abbreviations. The following abbreviations are used as necessary within the bibliographical entries:

anon.	No author known
2d or 2nd ed.	Second edition
et al.	And others (when more than three authors, first author's name is used and *et al.*)
n.d.	No date known
p., pp.	Page, pages
pp. 50–60	Pages 50 to 60, inclusive
Vol., Vols.	Volume, volumes

Annotation. Annotation indicates the significance of the reference and summarizes in a sentence or two the contents of the reference. Annotations are single-spaced and typed on the line following the bibliographical entry.

BINDING

Typed reports are usually bound on the left-hand side. Sometimes they are bound at the top. Adjustments in the margins are made on the side or top and according to the binding used.

The report may be bound

1. With staples or wire stitching.
2. With paper fasteners, in which case holes must be spaced and punched to match the spacing of the fasteners.
3. With spiral bindings.
4. In a two- or three-ring note book.
5. By the use of gummed-tape covering on the stapled side.
6. In a semirigid or rigid leatherlike cover.

Not all reports are bound. Often they are merely stapled at the top left-hand corner and enclosed in a self-cover or manila folder. If the report is to be used permanently or handled a great deal, it should be bound. The binding keeps the pages intact and provides a protective cover for the report. Information usually consisting of title, author, and date of completion should be placed on the cover to identify the report.

BOXING AND RULING MATERIAL

Material to be set off for emphasis in a report—both figures and facts—may be surrounded by lines or a decorative border. The advertising principle of always leaving white space around the material may also be followed.

It is easier to read tables when lines are drawn between groups of items and between columns.

Tables of more than three columns are generally boxed at the top and bottom. They may also be enclosed in a complete box by ruling the sides, or the sides may be left open. Consistency should be followed throughout any one report.

CAPITALIZATION

The following uses of capital letters are standard:

1. All proper names, derivatives, and abbreviations of them, such as specific persons or places, organizations of all kinds, races, citizens, languages, days of the week, months, special days, historical periods or events, words pertaining to deity and personifications, and sections of the country when used as nouns.

2. Titles preceding names or any words used as parts of a proper name.

3. Words in titles of books, magazines, articles, and newspapers except *a, an, the,* and internal prepositions and conjunctions.

4. Main words in names of schools, colleges, associations, and business firms.

5. The first word of every sentence or line of poetry, including quoted sentences, questions, and complete statements inserted in sentences.

6. The pronoun *I* and the interjection *O*.

7. Specific course titles.

FOOTNOTE DOCUMENTATION

Footnotes should be used to give credit for the source of quoted material and statistical data in the text, to lend authority to a statement not generally accepted, to explain or give additional information, to give an appraisal of the source, or to provide a cross reference to material presented in some other part of the report.

Placement. They should be placed at the bottom of the page and may be separated from the report text by a solid line partly or all the way across the page. After typing the last line of the text, one should single-space, type the solid line, double-space, then indent about five to ten spaces from the left margin, and begin the first line of the footnote entry. Succeeding lines of the footnote should be spaced even with the margin. The footnote entry should be single-spaced. A space should be left between entries. Double space the entry when the material is to be printed (for the convenience of the editor).

Sometimes for the convenience of the typist and printers, footnotes are arranged and numbered in consecutive order and placed on a *Footnote* page at the end of the report. This practice is followed in some periodicals. A few publications advocate that the footnote be placed in the body of the text to forewarn the editor and printer to allow space for it at the bottom of the page:

---------------------------------- .2

²Norman B. Sigband, *Communication for Management* (Glenview, Ill.: Scott, Foresman and Company, 1969), p. 267.

Numbering.   Footnotes are numbered consecutively by Arabic numerals in unbroken series throughout the report. The reference figure in the text should always follow the passage to which it refers and should be placed after the punctuation marks (except for semicolons and colons) and slightly above the line.

The reference figure in the footnote should be typed one-half space above the line, without punctuation, and at the beginning of the footnote entry. Sometimes asterisks (*, **, ***) are used in the place of numbers, and on each page numbering starts over with a single asterisk.

Arrangement of Elements.   For a *book,* footnote *items* should be arranged as follows:

> Author's name with given name or initials first, title of the book, place of publication, publisher's name, date of publication, and page reference.

A sample footnote following this arrangement could be punctuated as follows:

> ¹Lee Thayer, *Communication and Communication Systems* (Homewood, Ill.: Richard D. Irwin, Inc., 1968), p. 51.

Or simplified punctuation may be used (the comma separating each item) and the publisher's name preceding the place of publication:

> ¹Lee Thayer, *Communication and Communication Systems,* Richard D. Irwin, Inc., Homewood, Ill., 1968, p. 51.

When a bibliography accompanies the report, a short form of footnote may be used:

> ¹Thayer, *Communication and Communication Systems,* p. 51.

There are several manuals of style that sanction giving only the publisher or the place and not both items in a footnote.

For a book with two or more authors and in another edition, these items are designated as in the sample bibliographical entries, page 412.

For an *article* or component of a larger work, *items* should be arranged as follows:

> Author's name with given name or initial first, title of the article, or section or chapter, title of the magazine or work, volume number, date, and page reference.

Following this arrangement, a sample footnote would be arranged and punctuated as follows:

     [3]John B. Colby and Joseph A. Rice, "Team Instruction—A Relevant Teaching Method," *ABCA Bulletin,* Vol. XXXV, No. 2 (June 1972), pp. 5–12.

or

     [3]John B. Colby and Joseph A. Rice, "Team Instruction—A Relevant Teaching Method," *ABCA Bulletin,* June 1972, p. 7.

Note that the essential differences are the omission of volume and number and the use of parentheses. Volume and pages can also be indicated as *35:5–12.*

For a *newspaper item,* the name of the paper, the date, and the page reference are usually given:

     [4]*Chicago Tribune,* May 16, 1973, p. 10.

For a reference to *letters, interviews,* and so forth, the items given depend on the significance for the particular report. There may be

     [5]Statement by Mr. Henry Jonson, personal interview.

     [5]Personal interview, Mr. Henry Jonson, Personnel Director, Union Oil Company, Houston, Texas, May 10, 1973.

     [6]Letter from Mr. Henry Jonson, Personnel Director, Union Oil Company, Houston, Texas, May 12, 1973.

     [6]Statement by Mr. Henry Jonson, letter, May 12, 1973.

Short Footnote Forms. After the first full citation of a particular work has been given, the full form need not be repeated in a footnote entry. The last name of the author, appropriate Latin abbreviation, and specific page reference are given.

Where references to the same work follow without intervening footnotes, *ibid.* (for the Latin *ibidem,* meaning *in the same place*) should be used. If the reference is to the same page, merely *ibid.* is sufficient; for a different page, cite the page, as: *Ibid.,* p. 10.

When there are intervening footnotes and it is necessary to refer to a previous entry for a reference, *op. cit.,* meaning *work cited,* should be used for reference to a different page of the book cited, as:

     [7]Jones, *op. cit.,* p. 150.

If reference is to the same page in the book, *loc. cit.,* meaning *the place cited,* is used. *Loc. cit.* is also used for repeated reference to an article or part of a work:

     [8]Zirkle, *loc. cit.,* p. 121.

There is a trend today to ignore *ibid., op. cit.,* and *loc. cit.* by using an abbreviated title or simply the last name and page reference:

     [9]Zirkle, *Management Styles,* p. 150.

or

⁹Zirkle, p. 150.

Abbreviations. In footnote and bibliographical entries abbreviations are used for words designating parts when followed by numbers:

> *Bk. 1* (plural, *Bks.*)—Book I
> *chap. 2* (plural, *chaps.*)—Chapter 2
> *col. 2* (plural, *cols.*)—Column 2
> *2nd ed.* (plural, *eds.*)—Second edition
> *fig. 2* (plural, *figs.*)—Figure 2
> *No. 7* (plural, *Nos.*)—Number 7
> *l. 9* (plural, *ll.*)—Line 9
> *p. 7* (plural, *pp.*)—Page 7
> *pp. 7f.*—Page 7 and page following
> *pp. 7ff.*—Page 7 and pages following
> *pp. 5–7*—Pages 5 to 7 inclusive
> *sec. 9* (plural, *secs.*)—Section 9
> *Vol. III* (plural, *Vols.*)—Volume III

Other abbreviations commonly used are *cf.* for compare and *ed.* for editor.

Numerals. Roman numerals (capitals) should be used for designating volume, book, part, or division:

> *Volume I*   *Book II*   *Part III*

Roman numerals (lower case—i, ii, iii, iv, and so forth) should be used for designating introductory or prefatory pages in a book.

Arabic numbers are used for designating pages, lines, and references to chapters:

> *pp. 10–15*   *p. 5, l. 3*   *chap. 2*

Continuation of Long Footnotes. When it is necessary to continue a long footnote from one page to the next, it should begin on the page where reference to it is made in the text and break in the middle of a sentence, ending on the next page, to indicate that it is continued.

MARGINS

Throughout the report, uniform standard margins should be maintained on each page. The same width of margin, varying from 1 to 1½ inches, should be followed on each of the four sides of the typewritten page. Or the top and bottom margins may be the same, preferably 1¼ inches, with the left margin wider than the right, preferably 1¼ inches on the left and ¾ inch on the right.

If the manuscript is bound at the top, an additional ¾ inch is allowed for the top margin. If the manuscript is bound on the left side, an additional ½ to 1 inch is allowed as needed for the left margin.

An overragged margin on the right should be avoided. An even margin should be maintained without dividing many words.

NUMERALS

Most businessmen agree that the number *ten* and all numbers below should be written out because they are simple and easy to remember and that most other numbers should be expressed in figures.

Numbers. Many numbers are used in business writing. Although they present no trouble on invoices, orders, and statements, recording them in letters and reports does pose a problem. For quick readability and clarity the following modifications are recommended *:

1. *If a sentence begins with a number, the number should be expressed in words:* This rule is used when the sentence cannot be effectively revised.

Correct: Fifty applicants were interviewed for the position.

2. *When a number standing first in the sentence is followed by another number to form an approximation, both should be in words:*

Correct: Fifty or sixty will be enough.

NOTE: *Try not to begin a sentence with a number:* Rewrite the sentence to place the number within or at the end of the sentence.

Correct: The confirmation request was answered by 559 businesses.

3. *When a sentence contains one series of numbers, all members of the series should be expressed in figures:*

Correct: There were 25 applicants from Arkansas, 15 applicants from Texas, and 10 applicants from Oklahoma.

4. *When a sentence contains two series of numbers, the members of one series should be expressed in words while those of the other series should be expressed in figures.* If this rule is not followed, confusion results because of too many groups of numbers.

Correct: Five students scored 95 points, seventeen students scored 80 points, and eleven scored 75 points.

Correct: Three senior accountants made $50 a day, two semiseniors made $40 a day, and five junior accountants made $35 a day.

NOTE: More than two series of numbers should be tabulated for clarity.

Name of Accountant	Daily Rate	Estimated Working Days	Total Estimated Earnings
Barlow, Helen	$50	3	$150
Dickinson, Al	35	2	70
Oman, Charles	40	1	40

* Material presented here concerning numerals is modified from a Committee Report (Robert D. Hay, chairman), *American Business Writing Association Bulletin,* April 1953, pp. 6–11.

5. *When an isolated number is ten or below, it should be expressed in words:* This rule does not apply to exact dimensions.

Correct: He hired 56 women employees.
Correct: The new salesman sold eight refrigerators last month.

6. *When numbers are expressed in words, as at the beginning of a sentence, a hyphen should be used to join the compound numbers, twenty-one through ninety-nine:* A compound number usually acts as a compound adjective. Compound adjectives are usually hyphenated.

Correct: Fifty-six; twenty-one; ninety-three

7. *When one number immediately precedes another number of different context, one number should be expressed in words, and the other, in figures:*

Correct: The specifications call for twenty-five 2 × 4's.
Correct: The deposit slip listed four 5's as the only currency.
Correct: You ordered 275 three-inch bolts.

8. *When a numerical quantity contains more than four digits, each group of three digits (starting at the right) should be set off by a comma:* Obviously, this rule does not apply to dates, street numbers, serial numbers, and page numbers.

Correct: 1000; 1021; 5280
Also correct: 1,000; 1,021; 5,280
Correct: 1,000,000; 1,253,878; 35,000; 43,120

9. *When large numbers (more than three digits) are to be tabulated, special care should be taken to align them properly:* When tabulating, the right or last digit of the longest number should be used as the main guide. Consequently, the longest number is found and the plan made accordingly.

Correct:

	1,150
	1,000
	25,150
	500
	325,200
	25
	1,250,000
	5
Total	1,603,030

Money. Amounts of money, generally speaking, should be expressed in figures. This is particularly true when a sentence, a paragraph, a letter, or a report mentions several different amounts of money. However, some questions invariably arise on how to use numbers in money amounts. The following practices are recommended:

1. *When several amounts are written close together, all should be expressed in figures:*

Correct: The assets were $17,000, the liabilities were $3,000, and the net worth was $14,000.

2. *When an amount of money consists of dollars and cents, the amount should always be expressed in figures:* The dollar sign should precede the amount (unless in a tabulated column).

Correct: The invoice total was $50.51.
Correct: The bonds were sold at $999.50 each.

3. *When an amount of money consists only of dollars, it should not be followed by a decimal point and a double zero:* The double zero is not necessary, unless the amount is tabulated in a column which includes both dollars and cents.

Correct: The invoice total was $150.
Correct: $ 250.80
                     200.00
                     312.70
                     286.50
                   ─────────
                   $1,050.00

When a series of money amounts contains mixed figures, all even figures should include the double zero for consistency.

Correct: The committee raised amounts of $15.00, $33.75, and $75.00 in the three rummage sales.

4. *An amount should not be written in both figures and words:* This procedure is acceptable only in legal documents and financial documents.

Correct: The check was for $57.
Correct: The total assets are $23,000.

5. *An isolated amount of money of more than ten cents but less than one dollar should be expressed in figures:*

Correct: The piggy bank yielded $.57.
Correct: The piggy bank yielded 57¢.
Correct: 'The piggy bank yielded 57 cents.
Correct: The piggy bank yielded nine cents.

6. *An isolated amount of money in even dollars should be written in figures. When the even amount is ten dollars or less it should be written in words:*

Correct: The check was for $57.
Correct: The other check was for five dollars. (Assuming an isolated amount.)

7. *When amounts of money are to be tabulated, care should be taken to align the numbers correctly:* The right-hand digit of the largest amount governs the tabulation. All decimals, commas, and dollar signs should be aligned properly. A dollar sign should be used both at the beginning of a column and at the end of a column after the underline. It should be set far enough to the left to take care of the longest amount.

Correct:	$ 50.00	Correct:	$1,000.50
	100.90		$5,000.00
	1,100.10		475.00
	10,133.10		5,475.00
	$11,384.10		$6,475.50
			1.00
			35.00
			$6,511.50

Miscellaneous. The following numbers should be expressed in figures:

1. *Dates*
2. *Street numbers*
3. *Numerical names of streets*
4. *Decimals*
5. *Dimensions*
6. *Time*
7. *Percentages*
8. *Fractions*
9. *Numbered items such as page numbers, chapter numbers, figure numbers, table numbers, chart numbers, serial numbers, and telephone numbers*

PAGINATION

All pages of a report should be numbered except the fly leaf, if used, and the title page. The plan followed for numbering pages differs according to the type of report. The following practices are generally observed:

For Letter Reports. The first page of a letter is counted as page 1, but no number appears on the page. Additional pages are numbered in the same manner as a business letter:

Either

Mrs. S. J. Brounson   2   January 10, 1973

Or

Mrs. S. J. Brounson
January 10, 1973
Page 2

Often the subject of the report is used instead of the name of the person for whom the report is written.

For Memorandum Reports. The first page of a memorandum report, although it is counted as page 1, contains no number. Successive pages are numbered:

Either

The Loading of Trucks   2   January 10, 1973

Or

The Loading of Trucks
January 10, 1973
Page 2

The numbering of the pages also includes identification of the report by subject and date. Sometimes a memorandum number is also used:

Memorandum #56
The Loading of Trucks   2   January 10, 1973

For Short and Long, Formal Reports. The elements are broken down and arranged according to prefatory material, report, and supplemental or reference material.

Pages of prefatory sections are numbered with small Roman numerals (ii, iii, iv, and so forth) centered at the bottom of the page. Pages of the report text sections are numbered with Arabic numbers (2, 3, 4, and so forth to the end of the report) placed at the top right-hand corner of the page, serving as a right marginal guide. Pages of the supplemental material are numbered with Arabic numerals, a continuation of the numbering of the report text. If the report text ends on page 21, for example, the first page of the supplemental material is page 22.

On special layout pages, such as title fly, title page, division title pages, and first page of the report text, or on any special page carrying extra white space at the top for display, the page number is centered at the bottom of the page or omitted. It is *always* omitted, however, on the title page and on blank pages used for part divisions.

The page number may stand alone—no period after it, no dashes or parentheses around it—or may be followed by a period or surrounded by parentheses or dashes.

For Other Report Types. Bulletins, since they generally follow a similar format, are numbered in the same way as the memorandum report. Pamphlets, booklets, and other similar reports follow the numbering plan of short, formal reports, except that they often do not contain prefatory material and therefore only Arabic numbers are used.

PAPER

Standard-size typing paper, 8½ by 11 inches, is used for most reports. Some business files are designed, however, for the 8½ by 13-inch size, and accordingly companies sometimes have their reports done on the legal-size paper.

A good-quality white bond paper that will stand handling and neat erasures should be used. Onionskin or lighter-weight paper may be used for carbon copies, but when the copies are to be circulated and used, it is better for them to be on the same quality of paper as the original. The thin paper is better used for only routine filing record purposes.

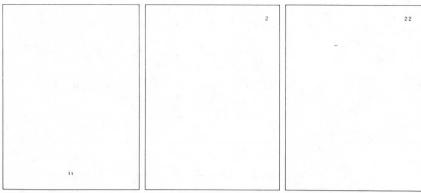

PREFATORY PAGES   REPORT TEXT PAGES   SUPPLEMENTAL PAGES

Numbering the pages of a business report.

PUNCTUATION

The following rules for punctuation reflect custom and the usual practice and should serve as a reference guide for those who want to check a particular question:

Apostrophe. The apostrophe shows possession:

1. To indicate the possessive case of singular nouns, plural nouns which do not end in *s*, and indefinite pronouns, the apostrophe is added before *s*.

2. When the plural ends in *s*, only the apostrophe is added.

3. When the singular ends in *s*, the apostrophe and *s* are added unless the second *s* makes pronunciation difficult.

The apostrophe is also used to indicate omissions in contracted words or numerals as in *can't, o'clock,* and *class of '63*. It also helps to form the plurals of letters, figures, and words referred to as words: three *A's, 2's, if's*. Used with *s* it forms the possessive of a noun preceding a gerund such as in the sentence

The secretary's typing the report well made a good impression on her boss.

Colon. The colon is used after an introductory word, phrase, or statement calling attention to what follows. The colon also separates two main clauses when the second explains or amplifies the first:

The teacher serves as a guide: he shows the student how to acquire knowledge and helps him over the rough places.

Comma. Major uses of the comma are

1. To separate main clauses connected by a coordinating conjunction *(and, but, or, nor, for)*, as:

You have maintained an average checking account balance of over $250 during the past year, but you did not add to your savings account.

The comma may be omitted when clauses are short.

2. To set off introductory phrases or clauses, as:
Although the chairman refrained from expressing an opposing point of view, he did not agree with the committee's recommendation.

Here again the comma may be omitted when the introductory phrase is short and there is no danger of confusion.

3. To set off items in a series, as:
Delivery dates for the office furniture, rugs, and draperies were postponed.

The comma is omitted by some writers before the last item joined by the conjunction unless required for clarity.

4. To separate coordinate adjectives (equal in value) that modify the same noun, as:
The unbalanced, ambitious leader in time is overthrown by his people.

5. To set off nonrestrictive clauses and other parenthetical elements, as:
Mr. Korachie, who read his report very enthusiastically, stirred up a lot of challenging ideas in the group.

Restrictive clauses are not set off.

6. To set off appositives, geographical names, items in dates and addresses, and parenthetical expressions, as:
Mr. Henri Beauregard, director of public relations at La Touriste Travel Agency, is a personal friend of mine. The tours he plans, moreover, are usually inexpensive yet inclusive.

7. To set off words of direct address, as:
It is your recommendation, John, and you must decide how forcefully you want to support it.

Dash. A dash (formed by typing two hyphens in succession) is used to mark a sudden break in thought, to give emphasis in setting off parenthetical elements, and to set off a summary. In some instances the dash is beginning to supplant the colon, but it is in danger of being too broadly used.

For the advertising campaign we shall have to consider all mass media—newspaper, radio, and TV.

End Punctuation. After every complete declarative sentence and after an abbreviation, a period is used. After every complete sentence that asks a question, a question mark is used. For a demand or request expressed in question form, a period is used for sake of courtesy instead of a question mark. To express strong feeling or emphasis, whether at the end of a complete sentence or a fragmentary thought, the exclamation point is used.

Hyphen. A hyphen is used in compound words, and the dictionary should be consulted whenever the writer is in doubt. A hyphen may join two or more words to form a compound adjective before a noun:

> These are up-to-the-minute figures.
> They lived in a well-kept suburban area.
> She wore a greenish-blue dress.

Hyphens are also used with compound numbers from twenty-one to ninety-nine and with the prefixes *ex-, self-, all-,* and the suffix adjective *-elect:*

ex-mayor	self-educated
all-American	governor-elect

Quotation Marks. Quotation marks are used to set off direct quotations and to set off titles of articles from magazines and of subdivisions and chapters of books. When punctuating the close of quotations, the comma and period are placed within the quotation marks, and the colon and semicolon outside. Other punctuation marks, the question mark and the exclamation point, may be either inside or outside, depending on their application to the quoted material.

Semicolon. The semicolon separates two main clauses not connected by *and, but, or, nor,* or *for* (the coordinating conjunctions) and separates two main clauses connected by a conjunctive adverb, such as:

however	in fact
nevertheless	thus
therefore	yet
accordingly	so

The semicolon also separates coordinate elements which themselves contain commas:

> The business conference was to include the public relations director, advertising manager, personnel director, and the sales manager; but the executive secretary was finding it difficult to arrange a suitable time.

QUOTATIONS

Quotations of fewer than four lines are incorporated in the report text and enclosed in double quotation marks. When they consist of four or more lines, they are indented from both margins and single-spaced; no quotation marks are used. When several paragraphs are quoted, double spacing is used between paragraphs.

Quotations used in footnotes are likewise set off from the text of the note, but they are enclosed in quotation marks.

When portions of a quotation are omitted, ellipses (. . .) should be used to designate the omission. If a complete paragraph of prose or a full line of poetry is omitted a row of dots (. . . . .) is typed all the way across the quotation.

Direct quotations should always be reproduced exactly—content, capitalization, spelling, and punctuation the same as in the original material. The Latin *sic*, enclosed in brackets, may be interpolated within the body of the direct quotation to indicate that the error quoted is a part of the quoted material, not the author's own. The report writer's remarks may also be interpolated within the body of the direct quotation and set off by brackets. Parentheses are not used in either case.

To set off a quotation within a quotation, single quotation marks should be used.

In most cases frequent and long quotations are not justified in reports. In some instances they may be placed in a footnote or in the appendix. Many times it is preferable to summarize or paraphrase instead of quoting directly. Quoting should be done with discretion—where the statement is relatively concise and particularly apt, or where the idea is not a generally accepted fact.

REPRODUCTION

Except for certain confidential reports, it is advisable always to make a minimum of three to five copies of a report. The number of copies necessary for adequate use of the report and the cost of reproduction determine the method of duplication to be followed.

When ten or fewer copies are desired, carbon copies are typed. Making ten copies will necessitate the use of onionskin paper for the copies and bond paper for the original. Even then two typings may be needed for clear results. Of course, for only two or three copies bond paper may be used entirely. A black ribbon and black carbon are usually used for the clearest possible type.

For 10 to 100 copies, a ditto or mimeograph machine is used. The kind of paper most appropriate to the method of duplication must be selected. A master copy is typed for the ditto machine and a stencil for the mimeograph.

When 100 or more copies are desirable the multilith is often used. Multilith plates (duplimats) are typed and copies run off on the multilith machine. The plates are more expensive than the stencils used in mimeographing.

If several hundred copies are to be distributed, the report would warrant printing. Typed carbon copies on bond paper are prepared for the printer and instructions set up for printing.

SENTENCE STRUCTURE

1. Write each sentence so it will present a complete thought.
   a. Avoid putting two or more unrelated thoughts in the same sentence.
   b. Avoid breaking ideas into short, choppy sentences.
   c. Keep related parts of the sentence together, and avoid dangling modifiers.
2. Construct sentences with proper attention to unity, subordination, coherence, and emphasis.

    a. Put the main idea of a sentence in an independent clause and less important ideas in subordinate clauses.

    b. Combine short sentences into longer ones by subordinating the less important ideas.

    c. Arrange a sentence to give emphasis to the important ideas at the beginning or end or by placing a word or phrase out of its natural order.

    d. Make sure conjunctions and prepositions express the exact relationships among clauses, phrases, and words.

    e. Avoid long, rambling sentences with too many qualifying clauses and phrases.

    f. Avoid putting words between *to* and the verb form of an infinitive unless a natural expression cannot be achieved any other way.

    g. Place adverbs such as *only, almost,* and *merely* close to the words they modify.

    h. Place modifiers so they will be logically and naturally connected with the words they modify.

3. Vary sentences to avoid monotony for the reader.

    a. Change the basic pattern by placing a clause or phrase ahead of the main subject and verb.

    b. Vary length of sentences.

    c. Vary kinds of sentences by using simple, compound, and complex sentences.

    d. Use your own words instead of worn-out expressions that have lost cleverness and force through overuse.

SPACING

Reports may be single- or double-spaced, depending on the length and type of report and its purpose or use.

1. Reports that consist of fewer than three pages are usually single-spaced; those longer are double-spaced.

2. Letter reports, memoranda, and bulletins are generally single-spaced.

3. Routine, intraoffice reports are usually single-spaced.

4. Complete, formal reports are double-spaced.

Since double spacing is easier to read, the longer the report, the more necessary it is to consider the reader's time and effort in reading the report.

In single-spaced reports double spacing is used between paragraphs. In double-spaced reports the beginning of each paragraph is indented five to ten spaces, and double spacing is used between paragraphs. Occasionally the paragraphs are blocked and triple spacing used between paragraphs.

SPELLING

The dictionary should be consulted constantly to find the correct spelling of words. Keeping a list of words one commonly misspells and concentrating on learning, through practice, to spell them correctly help reduce spelling errors.

Being aware of one's pronunciation as it compares with the correct pronunciation and learning to pronounce a word correctly frequently help one to spell correctly. Of course, all written and typed work should be carefully proofread, and the rules of spelling as given in any good handbook of English should be reviewed and applied. Some standard rules for spelling difficult words are as follows:

1. In combinations of *i* and *e*, the *i* precedes *e* except after *c:*

believe	*exceptions:*
deceive	either
perceive	leisure
piece	neither
receive	seize
	weird
	their

2. Words ending in *l* do not drop the *l* before *ly:*

especially	generally
finally	practically

3. Words ending in a consonant and *y* change the *y* to *i* and add *es* to form the plural:

   ability—abilities   city—cities

4. For words ending in *s, sh, ch, z,* or *x,* the plural is usually formed by adding *es:*

   couches   kisses   paradoxes

5. For singular nouns ending in *o* preceded by a consonant, the plural is generally formed by adding *es:*

echoes	*exceptions:*
potatoes	banjos
tomatoes	solos
	pianos

6. A few nouns ending in *f* or *fe* change the *f* to *v* and add *s* or *es* to form the plural:

calves	selves
knives	scarves
leaves	wives

7. Compounds usually add the plural to the most important word:

   brothers-in-law   lieutenant-colonels

8. Verbs ending in *ie* change to *y* before adding *ing:*

   dying   lying   tying

9. A monosyllable or a word accented on the last syllable, when ending in a consonant preceded by a single vowel, doubles the consonant before a suffix beginning with a vowel:

allotted	controlled
beginner	occurred
committal	omitting
committed	stopped
compelling	transferred

10. Words ending in a silent *e* usually drop the *e* before a suffix beginning with a vowel:

arising	noticing
choosing	preceding
having	using
hoping	writing

11. Words ending in *y* preceded by a consonant change *y* to *i* before suffixes which do not begin with *i:*

certified	flies	spies
cried	justified	tried
defiance	replies	varies
denied	replied	varied

12. A prefix or a suffix and a main word are generally written as one word:

      antedate   postgraduate   slothfulness

13. Some compound words vary their spelling according to their use in the sentence:

Altogether unwilling to study, he wasted time.
He gathered his artist supplies *all together.*
Already the papers had been collected.
The children were *all ready* to go home.

SUBJECT HEADINGS

The text material of a report is divided into sections and subsections.

Subject headings are used to indicate the content of the material of each section and the degree of relationship between the different sections. Headings should be descriptive in content and parallel in construction. A detailed table of contents is composed of the subject headings throughout the report. A general table of contents lists only the major headings. The instructions on typing and spacing different degrees of subject headings as given on pages 83 and 84 are often followed.

When only one degree of subordination is needed, a center heading and a heading beginning flush with the margin—or a center heading and a heading beginning at the margin indentation—are commonly used. The subject headings may be numbered and lettered as in outlining, or the numbers and letters may be omitted. Subject headings may be underscored or left free of underscoring, or a combination of the two may be worked out if consistency is observed throughout the report.

A great deal of flexibility in the selection and use of subject headings is often desirable. Check Chapter 3, pages 83 and 84, for suggestions on typing and spacing subject headings.

SYLLABICATION

To divide words at the ends of lines, to keep the right margin as even as possible, and thus to produce a neatly typed page, the following suggestions should be helpful:

1. Divide words only according to their syllabic division.
2. Divide hyphenated words at the hyphen and nowhere else.
3. Do not divide words of one syllable.
4. Do not divide words of only four or five letters, e.g., *many.*
5. Keep prefixes and suffixes intact, e.g., *pre-, ex-, -cial, -sion,* and *-tion.*
6. Avoid divisions leaving one letter of the word to a line, e.g., *o-ver, a-mong.*
7. Avoid divisions leaving syllables of two letters, such as *-ed, -en, -ly,* and the like.
8. Do not divide the last word in a paragraph or on a page.
9. Do not divide initials, names of persons, numbers, abbreviations, and titles.
10. When in doubt, always consult the dictionary.

TABULATION

1. Present systematized material or figures in tables.
2. Display a short and simple group of figures as a paragraph inset.
3. Place tables either in the text material or in the appendix, depending on the purpose and use of the table.
   a. For reference, place them in the appendix.
   b. For analysis, place them in the text.
4. Place tables as close as possible to the discussion point with which they are used.
5. Number tables consecutively.
   a. Use either Roman or Arabic numerals. Be consistent.
   b. Use a separate numbering system for tables and charts or other types of visual aids.
   c. Usually center the table number above the title at the top of the table.
6. Construct tables so the contents are easy to follow and readily understood.
   a. Place the title above the table.
   b. Use captions as column headings, making them concise and descriptive.
   c. Let each column heading apply only to material in that particular column by naming the item and unit in which it is expressed.

    d. Use footnotes for supplemental information, placing them at the bottom of table.

    e. Cite the source(s) of data at the bottom of table. (Sometimes this may be done beneath the title caption.)

    f. Avoid a crowded effect in typing and spacing tables. Use plenty of white space for display purposes.

    g. Rule tables of over three columns.

TENSE

1. Use the correct tense form of the verb to show the time relationship.
   a. To express present time, use the present tense.
   b. To express actions which take place habitually or ideas which are true, use the present tense.
   c. To express action completed in the past, use the past tense.
   d. To express action or condition that will take place in the future, use the future tense.
2. Make verbs in subordinate clauses, infinitives, and participles agree in tense with the verb in the main clause.
3. Use *shall* and *will* interchangeably except for the more formal types of writing.
   a. To express simple futurity, use *shall* in the first person and *will* in the second and third persons.
   b. To express determination, willingness, desire, or promise use *will* in the first person and *shall* in the second and third persons.
4. To express obligation, use *should* in all three persons.
5. To express habitual action, use *would* in all three persons.
6. Put infinitives in the present tense unless they represent action prior to that of the governing verb.

UNDERLINING

There are two major uses of underlining in reports.

1. Titles and words that are usually printed in italics are underlined in typed reports:

   Titles of books, works of art, music
   Titles of periodicals
   Footnote reference abbreviations
   Foreign words and phrases

2. Material may be underlined for emphasis in the text of the report:

   Subject headings and subheads
   Words and phrases containing important facts or figures

A single, solid line may be used in underlining or a broken line under each individual word:

Kate L. Turabian, A Manual for Writers of Term Papers, Theses, and Dissertations

or

Kate L. Turabian, A Manual for Writers of Term Papers, Theses, and Dissertations

VOICE

1. Use the active voice of verbs (somebody or something does something) when a direct, personalized style is appropriate for the purpose and reader.
2. Use the active voice of verbs to gain emphasis.
3. Use the passive voice of verbs (subject is acted upon) when an impersonal, indirect style suits the subject matter and reader.
4. Use the passive voice for suggestions, instructions, and recommendations when an impersonal style is appropriate.
5. Avoid shifting from the active to passive or from the passive to active voice.

C

The following references were selected and listed for their pertinence to the study of business report writing specifically and in general to the study of business communication. They should prove helpful for further reading and investigation by the student, businessman, and instructor.

BUSINESS REPORT WRITING

DAWE, JESSAMON, and WILLIAM JACKSON LORD, JR., *Functional Business Communication*, 2/E. Englewood Cliffs, N.J.: Prentice-Hall, Inc., 1974.
Behavior approach to business letters and management approach to decision-making reports. Treatment is comprehensive.

KEITHLEY, ERWIN M., and PHILIP J. SCHREINER, *A Manual of Style for the Preparation of Papers and Reports*, 2nd ed. Cincinnati: South-Western Publishing Company, 1971.
Designed as a reference on how to present papers and reports. Contains many illustrations. Includes *what* and *why* of the *how*.

LESIKAR, RAYMOND V., *Report Writing for Business*, 4th ed. Homewood, Ill.: Richard D. Irwin, Inc., 1973.
Emphasis on the process and stages of researching and developing the long, formal report for business use.

MENNING, J. H., and C. W. WILKINSON, *Communication Through Letters and Reports*, 5th ed. Homewood, Ill.: Richard D. Irwin, Inc., 1972.
Largely a business-letter-writing text, the part of the text on business reports is as comprehensive on essential basics as most report-writing texts. A good overall view of the stages necessary for reports. Emphasis on analytical reports.

ROBINSON, DAVID M., *Writing Reports for Management Decisions*. Columbus, Ohio: Charles E. Merrill Publishers, 1969.
A logical sequence of report-preparation events ranging from problem analysis through research and writing activities. Considers the relation of the decision-making process to the kinds of information presented in written reports.

SIGBAND, NORMAN B., *Communication for Management*. Glenview, Ill.: Scott, Foresman and Company, 1969.
Design of text divided into three areas: theories and processes of communication, business reports, and business letters. A fourth part, selected readings, supplements the text portions.

TECHNICAL WRITING AND REPORTS

DAMERST, WILLIAM A., *Clear Technical Reports*. New York: Harcourt Brace Jovanovich, Inc., 1972.

In paperback. Divided into five major parts: understanding clear communication, mastering the skills of technical writing, presenting common finished products, presenting special finished products, and a technical writer's handbook. Covers all aspects and kinds of technical writing from internal memos, letters, short reports, to research proposals, formal reports and articles in professional journals.

PEIRCE, J. F., *Organization & Outlining: How to Develop & Prepare Papers, Reports & Speeches*. New York: Arco Publishing Co., Inc., 1971.

Stresses the prewriting steps in the writing process.

RATHBONE, ROBERT R., *Communicating Technical Information*. Reading, Mass.: Addison-Wesley Publishing Company, Inc., 1966.

Self-improvement guide for engineers and scientists on writing reports. Includes writing the technical article and the abstract.

WEISMAN, HERMAN M., *Basic Technical Writing*. Columbus, Ohio: Charles E. Merrill Publishers, 1964.

Includes the semantic approach to communication, the scientific method for investigation, technical correspondence, and technical reports.

GENERAL AREA OF BUSINESS COMMUNICATION

AURNER, ROBERT R., and MORRIS PHILIP WOLF, *Effective Communication in Business*, 5th ed. Cincinnati: South-Western Publishing Company, 1967.

Management approach and emphasis. Comprehensive study of business letter writing. Includes oral and written reports.

BROWN, LELAND, *Communicating Facts and Ideas in Business*, 2nd ed. Englewood Cliffs, N.J.: Prentice-Hall, Inc., 1970.

Building on a communication theory base, covers principles, illustrations, and applications to letter writing, oral communication, and business reports.

DAMERST, WILLIAM A., *Resourceful Business Communication*. New York: Harcourt Brace Jovanovich, Inc., 1966.

Attention to writing letters and reports.

DUGAN, J. M., et al., *Guide to Audio-Visual Presentations*. New York: Wolf Business Publications, 1963.

Handbook on audiovisual methods used in presenting all kinds of data.

GORDON, JOHN, *Stuff, Etc. A Collection*. Philadelphia: J. B. Lippincott Company, 1970.

Unusual book about language, semantics, advertising, and mass communications. A collection of pictures, advertisements, news stories, letters, and all kinds of communication with comments, philosophical points, and practical suggestions.

LESIKAR, RAYMOND V., *Business Communication: Theory and Application*. Homewood, Ill.: Richard D. Irwin, Inc., 1968.

Semantic approach to communication theory. Emphasis on writing letters and reports.

WILEY, BARRON J., *Communication for Management*. Elmhurst, Ill.: The Business Press, 1966.
A guide for improving the efficiency of industrial communication in all media. Good treatment of symbols, channels, and media. Emphasis on selection of best medium for specific problems.

ORAL COMMUNICATION, REPORTS, AND CONFERENCES

BORMANN, ERNEST G., *Discussion and Group Methods: Theory and Practice*. New York: Harper & Row, Publishers, 1969.
Behavioral science theory integrated with group methods.

BRETH, ROBERT D., *Dynamic Management Communications*. Reading, Mass.: Addison-Wesley Publishing Company, Inc., 1961.
Impressive chapters on conferences and direct personal relations.

HOWELL, WILLIAM, and ERNEST G. BORMANN, *Presentational Speaking for Business and Professions*. New York: Harper & Row, Publishers, 1971.
Useful how-to guidance. All factors considered in developing the presentation as well as the mechanics of graphs, slides, tables, etc.

KELTNER, JOHN W., *Interpersonal Speech-Communication: Elements and Structures*. Belmont, Calif.: Wadsworth Publishing Company, Inc., 1970.
Interdisciplinary approach. Interaction emphasized. Each chapter discusses some specific aspect of the process and structure.

LONEY, GLENN M., *Briefing and Conference Techniques*. New York: McGraw-Hill Book Company, 1959.
Presents problem-solution approach to conferences. Good sections on written and oral "briefings."

MAIER, NORMAN R. F., *Problem-Solving Discussions and Conferences: Leadership Methods and Skills*. New York: McGraw-Hill Book Company, 1963.
Seeks to improve leadership and decisions growing out of discussion and conferences.

SATTLER, WILLIAM M., and N. EDD MILLER, *Discussion and Conference*, 2nd ed. Englewood Cliffs, N.J.: Prentice-Hall, Inc., 1968.
Treats problem solving, leadership, participation, language, and public meetings. Contains industrial case problems.

TACEY, WILLIAM S., *Business and Professional Speaking*. Dubuque, Iowa: William C. Brown Company, Publishers, 1970.
Communication theory and dyadic relationships explained. Listening and interview preparation and presentation included.

WEISS, HAROLD, and J. B. MCGRATH, JR., *Technically Speaking*. New York: McGraw-Hill Book Company, 1963.
Geared for scientists, engineers, and technicians. Oral communication principles applied to various situations. Includes interview, discussion meeting, and conversation.

WIKSELL, WESLEY, *Do They Understand You?* New York: The Macmillan Company, 1960.

Discusses boss-subordinate relationships and handles specific situations.

WILCOX, ROGER P., *Oral Reporting in Business and Industry.* Englewood Cliffs, N.J.: Prentice-Hall, Inc., 1967.

Details on how to prepare and present oral reports within organizations. Excellent treatment of how and why to use visual aids.

ZALEZNIK, ABRAHAM, and DAVID MOMENT, *The Dynamics of Interpersonal Behavior.* New York: John Wiley & Sons, Inc., 1964.

Group processes and interpersonal interaction. Emphasis on work groups and analysis of problems in face-to-face group encounters.

ZELKO, HAROLD P., *The Business Conference: Leadership and Participation.* New York: McGraw-Hill Book Company, 1969.

Five parts deal with the *why, what,* and *how* of conferences, conference results, and other conference-discussion applications.

ZELKO, HAROLD P., and FRANK E. X. DANCE, *Business and Professional Speech Communication.* New York: Holt, Rinehart and Winston, Inc., 1965.

Covers communication process, speaking and listening, interviewing, conferring, persuading and speaking via TV, radio, telephone.

OTHER AREAS OF BUSINESS COMMUNICATION

CAMPBELL, JAMES H., and HAL W. HEPLER, eds., *Dimensions in Communication,* 2nd ed. Belmont, Calif.: Wadsworth Publishing Company, Inc., 1970.

Book of readings covering concepts, persuasion, message systems, and sub-systems.

DALE, EDGAR, *Audio-Visual Methods in Teaching,* rev. ed. New York: McGraw-Hill Book Company, 1969.

Theory, materials, and methods dealt with relating to learning and instruction.

GRIFFIN, KIM, and BOBBY R. PATTON, *Fundamentals of Interpersonal Communication.* New York: Harper & Row, Publishers, 1971.

Much of the material will give reader insights about himself and relationships with other people.

HANEY, WILLIAM V., *Communication and Organizational Behavior: Text and Cases,* 3rd ed. Homewood, Ill.: Richard D. Irwin, Inc., 1973.

Focuses on the organizational climate and behavior. Chapters on patterns of mis-communication and techniques for correcting them or preventing their recurrence.

JOHNSON, H. WEBSTER, *How to Use the Business Library,* 3rd ed. Cincinnati: South-Western Publishing Company, 1964.

Includes all sources of information plus how to use the library efficiently.

McCROSKEY, JAMES C., CARL E. LARSON, and MARK L. KNAPP, *An Introduction to Interpersonal Communications.* Englewood Cliffs, N.J.: Prentice-Hall, Inc., 1971.

Defines and describes the communication process; focuses on primary outcomes of interpersonal communication; concentrates on the source, receiver, and messages; and considers interpersonal communication in relation to marriage, on the job, and mass communication.

MURDICK, ROBERT G., and JOEL E. ROSS, *Information Management Systems*. Englewood Cliffs, N.J.: Prentice-Hall, Inc., 1971.

Information distinguished from data. Systems approach in the larger perspective of organization and management theory and behavioral insights.

MURGIO, MATTHEW P., *Communications Graphics*. New York: Van Nostrand Reinhold Company, 1970.

Treats audio-visual aids in communication and the techniques of graphic art.

RICHARDSON, STEPHEN A., BARBARA S. DOHRENWEND, and DAVID KLEIN, *Interviewing: Its Form and Functions*. New York: Basic Books, Inc., 1965.

Methods and principles of interviewing in behavioral-science investigations. Emphasis on interview as a research tool, question-and-answer process, and the roles and relation of the interviewer and respondent.

THAYER, LEE, *Communication and Communication Systems*. Homewood, Ill.: Richard D. Irwin, Inc., 1968.

Contains five major parts: nature and dynamics of human communication; communication, messages, and communication systems; functions of communication; technology and techniques; and theory and research.

TOWL, ANDREW R., *To Study Administration by Cases*. Boston: Harvard University, Graduate School of Business Administration, 1969.

Covers the case method of teaching, developing a case, developing a case course, and uses of cases.

INDEX